The Norman Conquest

Marc Morris is an historian and broadcaster. He studied and taught history at the universities of London and Oxford, and his doctorate on the thirteenth-century earls of Norfolk was published in 2005. In 2003 he presented the highly acclaimed television series *Castle*, and wrote its accompanying book. His bestselling biography of Edward I, *A Great and Terrible King*, was published in 2008.

D1342629

ALSO BY MARC MORRIS

Castle: A History of the Buildings that
Shaped Medieval Britain

The Bigod Earls of Norfolk in the
Thirteenth Century

A Great and Terrible King:
Edward I and the Forging of Britain

Praise for *The Norman Conquest*

'I loved it – a suitably epic account of one of the most seismic and far-reaching events in British history.'

Dan Snow

'This is a wonderfully shrewd, engaging and readable account of the most pivotal event in English history.'

Tom Holland

'*The Norman Conquest* is a scrupulously researched and well-written book. But it is also that rare thing: a work undertaken with enormous integrity. Dr Morris questions the received wisdom from past scholars, considers the Conquest and its aftermath anew, and expresses his findings with great conscientiousness.'

Ian Mortimer

'A muscular, vivid narrative full of compelling historical insight – not just a brilliantly told story, but required reading for anyone interested in the real 1066 and all that.'

Helen Castor, author of *She Wolves*

'As every schoolboy knows, or used to, 1066 is the most important date in English history. But as Marc Morris points out in this enormously enjoyable book, the Norman Conquest was much more violent, complicated and ambiguous than we usually think. Carefully steering the reader through the partisan and often contradictory sources, he paints a vivid picture of the collapse of the sophisticated Anglo-Saxon realm, and shows how William the Conqueror relied on sheer terror to establish his reign.'

Dominic Sandbrook, *Sunday Times*, Books of the Year

'Almost everything you know about 1066 is wrong. And there's no better historian to put you right than the wonderful Marc Morris. His new book grips not only as a work of narrative history but also as a sleuthing exercise . . . Morris has captured the triumph and the tragedy of this tumultuous era with verve, insight and a rollicking narrative.'

Mail on Sunday

'Marc Morris is one of a new breed of young historians who take a narrative-based attitude to history. Both in historical biography and in period chronicle, they are driven by the storytelling impulse. Their books are the equivalent of the swagger portrait – a lively subject, depicted with dash and colour, brought to bright life with telling detail. Morris gives a compelling account of the invasion by William the Conqueror in 1066 and the violent struggle thereafter to maintain the occupation against Anglo-Saxon resistance, Viking invasions and the power struggle among the Norman lords themselves . . . Morris sorts embroidery from evidence and provides a much-needed, modern account of the Normans in England and that respects past events more than present ideologies.'

The Times

'Marc Morris's lively new book retells the story of the Norman invasion with vim, vigour and narrative urgency. He shows pre-Conquest England for what it was – a sophisticated but turbulent realm, which had been susceptible to invasion for centuries . . . He gives a stirring account of 1066 itself . . . Throughout this tale, the politics are complex, and the evidence patchy. Rather than gloss over this, Morris invites the reader to consider it all with him . . . To do all this while keeping a firm grip on the thrust and style of a popular history demonstrates the sure hand that the author demonstrated in his previous book, a very good modern biography of Edward I.'

Evening Standard

'Marc Morris's new book is an exciting arrival . . . a strong and often gripping story, developed with enormous verve, a clear sense of direction and considerable confidence . . . carries the reader on a spirited ride across the subject . . . A stimulating history which has both some new dimensions and internal coherence . . . Morris is committed to teasing out what he thinks the evidence is saying and he writes well.'

BBC History Magazine

The Norman Conquest

MARC MORRIS

 WINDMILL BOOKS

Published by Windmill Books 2013

15 17 19 20 18 16

Copyright © Marc Morris 2012

Marc Morris has asserted his right under the Copyright, Designs and
Patents Act, 1988, to be identified as the author of this work.

This book is a work of non-fiction.

First published in Great Britain in 2012 by Hutchinson

Windmill Books
The Random House Group Limited
20 Vauxhall Bridge Road, London SW1V 2SA

Addresses for companies within The Random House Group Limited
can be found at: www.randomhouse.co.uk/offices

The Random House Group Limited Reg. No. 954009

www.randomhouse.co.uk

A CIP catalogue record for this book
is available from the British Library

ISBN 9780099537441

Typeset in Bembo by Palimpsest Book Production Ltd, Falkirk, Stirlingshire
Printed and bound in Great Britain by Clays Ltd, Elcograf S.p.A.

Penguin Random House is committed to a sustainable
future for our business, our readers and our planet.
This book is made from Forest Stewardship
Council® certified paper.

To Peter
my prince

Contents

Acknowledgements   xiii

England Map   xiv

Normandy Map   xv

England Family Tree   xvi

Europe Family Tree   xvii

A Note on Names   xviii

Illustrations   xix–xxi

Introduction   I

1 The Man Who Would Be King   II

2 A Wave of Danes   23

3 The Bastard   43

4 Best Laid Plans   59

5 Holy Warriors   80

6 The Godwinesons   95

7 Hostages to Fortune   110

8 Northern Uproar   120

 9 The Gathering Storm   132
10 The Thunderbolt   155
11 Invasion   166
12 The Spoils of Victory   189
13 Insurrection   205
14 Aftershocks   232
15 Aliens and Natives   251
16 Ravening Wolves   272
17 The Edges of Empire   288
18 Domesday   300
19 Death and Judgement   327
20 The Green Tree   343

Abbreviations   354
Notes   357
Bibliography   395
Index   415

Acknowledgements

My thanks to all the academics and experts who patiently responded to emails or otherwise lent advice and support: Martin Allen, Jeremy Ashbee, Laura Ashe, David Bates, John Blair, David Carpenter, David Crouch, Richard Eales, Robin Fleming, Mark Hagger, Richard Huscroft, Charles Insley, Robert Liddiard, John Maddicott, Melanie Marshall, Richard Mortimer, Mark Philpott, Andrew Spencer, Matthew Strickland, Henry Summerson and Elizabeth Tyler. I am especially grateful to Stephen Baxter for taking the time to answer my questions about Domesday, and to John Gillingham, who very kindly read the entire book in draft and saved me from many errors. At Hutchinson, my thanks to Phil Brown, Caroline Gascoigne, Paulette Hearn and Tony Whittome, as well as to Cecilia Mackay for her painstaking picture research, David Milner for his conscientious copy-edit and Lynn Curtis for her careful proof-reading. Thanks as always to Julian Alexander, my agent at LAW, and to friends and family for their support. Most of all, thanks, love and gratitude to Catherine, Peter and William.

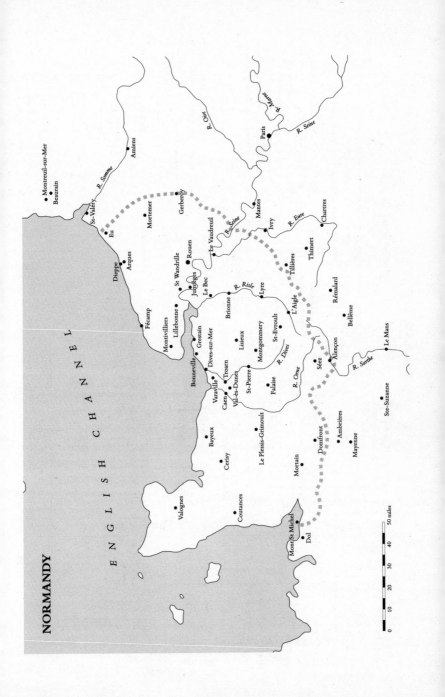

NORMANDY

ENGLISH CHANNEL

Montreuil-sur-Mer
Beaurain
Amiens
R. Somme
St-Valéry
Eu
Arques
Dieppe
Fécamp
Montivilliers
Lillebonne
Bonneville
Gerberoy
Mortemer
St Wandrille
Jumièges
Rouen
Le Bec
Grestain
Dives-sur-Mer
Varaville
Caen
Troarn
Val-ès-Dunes
St-Pierre
Bayeux
Cerisy
Le Plessis-Grimoult
Mortain
Valognes
Coutances
Mont St Michel
Dol
Brionne
R. Risle
Lisieux
Montgommery
St-Evroult
Falaise
R. Dives
R. Orne
Domfront
Ambrières
Mayenne
Le Vaudreuil
R. Seine
Mantes
Ivry
R. Eure
Chartres
Lyre
L'Aigle
R. Aigle
Thimert
Tillières
Rémalard
Bellême
Séez
Alençon
R. Sarthe
Le Mans
Ste-Suzanne
Paris
R. Marne
R. Seine
R. Oise

0   10   20   30   40   50 miles

ENGLAND

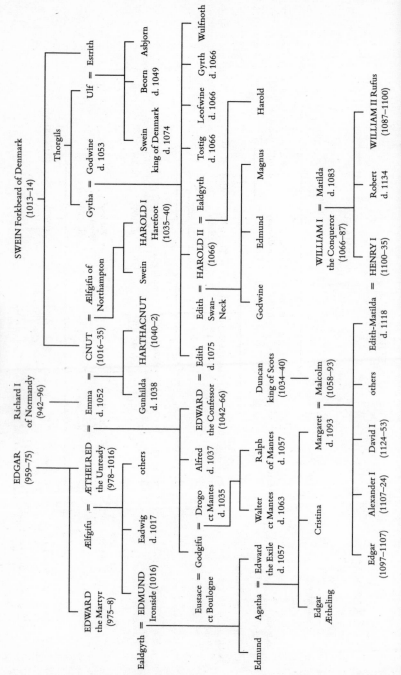

EUROPE

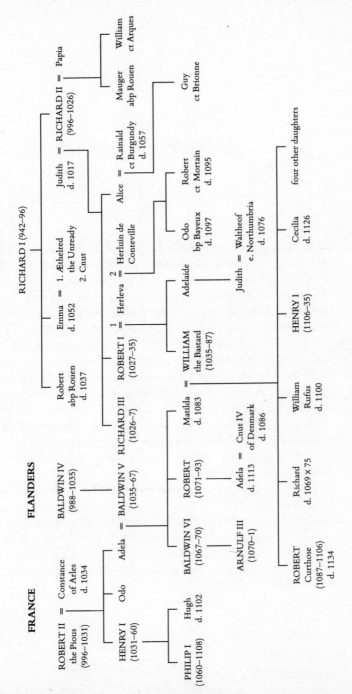

FRANCE

FLANDERS

NORMANDY

RICHARD I (942–96)

A Note on Names

Many of the characters in this book have names that can be spelt in a variety of different ways. Swein Estrithson, for example, appears elsewhere as Svein, Sven, Swegn and Swegen, with his surname spelt Estrithson or Estrithsson. There was, of course, no such thing as standard spelling in the eleventh century, so to some extent the modern historian can pick and choose. I have, however, tried to be consistent in my choices and have not attempted to alter them according to nationality: there seemed little sense in having a Gunhilda in England and a Gunnhildr in Denmark. For this reason, I've chosen to refer to the celebrated king of Norway as *Harold* Hardrada rather than the more commonplace Harald, so his first name is the same as that of his English opponent, Harold Godwineson. Contemporaries, after all, considered them to have the same name: the author of the *Life of King Edward*, writing very soon after 1066, calls them 'namesake kings'.

When it comes to toponymic surnames I have been rather less consistent. Most of the time I have used 'of', as in Roger of Montgomery and William of Jumièges, but occasionally I have felt bound by convention to stick with the French 'de'. Try as I might, I could not happily write about William of Warenne in this book, any more than I could have referred to Simon of Montfort in its predecessor.

Illustrations

ENDPAPERS

The Temple Pyx, c.1140–50 (*Burrell Collection, Glasgow, Scotland*). Photo: © Culture and Sport Glasgow (Museums) / The Bridgeman Art Library

FIRST PLATES SECTION

Edward the Confessor: detail from the Bayeux Tapestry (*Musée de la Tapisserie, Bayeux*). Photo: The Bridgeman Art Library

William of Jumièges presents his history to William the Conqueror (*Bibliothèque municipale de Rouen, MS Y. 14 (CGM 1174), fol. 116*). Photo: Thierry Ascencio-Parvy

Cnut and Emma present a cross to the New Minster, Winchester (*British Library, Stowe MS. 944, fol. 6*). Photo: akg-images / British Library

Harold rides to Bosham Church: detail from the Bayeux Tapestry (*Musée de la Tapisserie, Bayeux*). Photo: The Bridgeman Art Library

The tower of All Saint's Church, Earls Barton, Northamptonshire. Photo: © Laurence Burridge

Arques-la-Bataille. Photo: © Vincent Tournaire

Jumièges Abbey. Photo: Robert Harding

St Stephen's, Caen. Photo: © Achim Bednorz

The Normans cross the Channel: detail from the Bayeux Tapestry (*Musée de la Tapisserie, Bayeux*). Photo: The Bridgeman Art Library

Skuldelev 3 (*Viking Ship Museum, Roskilde, Denmark*). Photo: Robert Harding

Normans burning a house: detail from the Bayeux Tapestry (*Musée de la Tapisserie, Bayeux*). Photo: The Bridgeman Art Library

The Normans charge the English shield-wall at Hastings: detail from the Bayeux Tapestry (*Musée de la Tapisserie, Bayeux*). Photo: The Bridgeman Art Library

Odo of Bayeux at Hastings: detail from the Bayeux Tapestry. Musée de la Tapisserie, Bayeux. Photo: The Bridgeman Art Library

SECOND PLATES SECTION

The field of Hastings and Battle Abbey. Photo: © English Heritage Photo Library

Berkhamsted Castle. Photo: © Skyscan Balloon Photography

Pickering Castle. Photo: © English Heritage Photo Library

Winchester Cathedral. Photo: © Skyscan.co.uk

A penny of William I (*by permission of the Syndics of The Fitzwilliam Museum, Cambridge*). Photo: The Bridgeman Art Library

Chepstow Castle, the Great Tower. Photo: © Cadw, Welsh Assembly Government (Crown Copyright)

Colchester Castle. Photo: Shutterstock

The White Tower, Tower of London. Photo: Historic Royal Palaces

Old Sarum. Photo: © English Heritage Photo Library

Great and Little Domesday. Photo: © The National Archives, London

The Domesday Book, page showing Bedfordshire (*The National Archives, London*). Photo: Mary Evans Picture Library

Durham Cathedral (*Collection du Musée historique de Lausanne*). Photo: © Claude Huber

TEXT ILLUSTRATIONS

p. 114. Harold swears his oath to William: detail from the Bayeux Tapestry (*Musée de la Tapisserie, Bayeux*). Photo: The Bridgeman Art Library

p. 119. Harold returns to Edward the Confessor: detail from the Bayeux Tapestry (*Musée de la Tapisserie, Bayeux*). Photo: The Bridgeman Art Library

p. 134. Edward on his deathbed: detail from the Bayeux Tapestry (*Musée de la Tapisserie, Bayeux*). Photo: The Bridgeman Art Library

p. 139. The coronation of Harold: detail from the Bayeux Tapestry

(*Musée de la Tapisserie, Bayeux*). Photo: The Bridgeman Art Library

p 147. Halley's Comet: detail from the Bayeux Tapestry (*Musée de la Tapisserie, Bayeux*). Photo: The Bridgeman Art Library

p. 184. The death of Harold: detail from the Bayeux Tapestry (*Musée de la Tapisserie, Bayeux*). Photo: The Bridgeman Art Library

p. 185. An unarmed man is decapitated: detail from the Bayeux Tapestry (*Musée de la Tapisserie, Bayeux*). Photo: The Bridgeman Art Library

p. 185. A son of Zedekiah is decapitated (*Los Comentarios al Apocalípsis de San Juan de Beato de Liébana, fol. 194v, Santa Cruz Library, Biblioteca Universitaria, Valladolid, Spain*)

All images of the Bayeux Tapestry are reproduced with special authorisation of the city of Bayeux.

Introduction

There have been many attempts to tell the story of the Norman Conquest during the past millennium, but none of them as successful as the contemporary version that told it in pictures.

We are talking, of course, about the Bayeux Tapestry, perhaps the most famous and familiar of all medieval sources, at least in England, where we are introduced to it as schoolchildren, and where we encounter it everywhere as adults: in books and on bookmarks, postcards and calendars, cushions and tea towels, key rings, mousemats and mugs. It is pastiched in films and on television; it is parodied in newspapers and magazines. No other document in English history enjoys anything like as much commercial exploitation, exposure and affection.[1]

The Tapestry is a frieze or cartoon, only fifty centimetres wide but nearly seventy metres long, that depicts the key events leading up to and including the Norman invasion of England in 1066. Properly speaking it is not a tapestry at all, because tapestries are woven; technically it is an embroidery, since its designs are sewn on to its plain linen background. Made very soon after the Conquest, it has been kept since the late fifteenth century (and probably a lot longer) in the Norman city of Bayeux, where it can still be seen today.

And there they are: the Normans! Hurling themselves fearlessly into battle, looting the homes of their enemies, building castles, burning castles, feasting, fighting, arguing, killing and conquering. Clad in mail shirts, carrying kite-shaped shields, they brandish swords, but more often spears, and wear their distinctive pointed helmets with fixed, flat nasals. Everywhere we look we see horses – more than

200 in total – being trotted, galloped and charged. We also see ships (forty-one of them) being built, boarded and sailed across the Channel. There is Duke William of Normandy, later to be known as William the Conqueror, his face clean-shaven and his hair cropped close up the back, after the fashion favoured by his fellow Norman knights. There is his famous half-brother, Odo of Bayeux, riding into the thick of the fray even though he was a bishop.

And there, too, are their opponents, the English. Similarly brave and warlike, they are at the same time visibly different. Sporting longer hair and even longer moustaches, they also ride horses but not into battle, where instead they stand to fight, wielding fearsome, long-handled axes. There is Harold Godwineson, soon to be King Harold, riding with his hawk and hounds, sitting crowned and enthroned, commanding the English army at Hastings and – as everybody remembers – being felled by an arrow that strikes him in the eye.

When you see the Tapestry in all its extensive, multicoloured glory, you can appreciate in an instant why it is so important. This is not only an account of the Norman invasion of 1066; it is a window on to the world of the eleventh century. No other source takes us so immediately and so vividly back to that lost time. The scenes of battle are justly famous, and can tell us much about arms, armour and military tactics. But look elsewhere and you discover a wealth of arresting detail about many other aspects of eleventh-century life: ships and shipbuilding, civilian dress for both men and women, architecture and agriculture. It is thanks to the Tapestry that we have some of the earliest images of Romanesque churches and earth-and-timber castles. Quite incidentally, in one of its border scenes, it includes the first portrayal in European art of a plough being drawn by a horse.[2]

Precise information about the Tapestry's creation is entirely lacking, but it is as good as certain that it was made within a decade or so of the events it depicts, and that its place of manufacture was Canterbury (many of its scenes and motifs are based on illustrations in surviving Canterbury manuscripts). We can be almost as certain – despite a host of other far less convincing candidates having been proposed over the years – that its patron was the aforementioned Bishop Odo, who is self-importantly portrayed throughout as being the driving force behind the planning and execution of the invasion.

Odo's patronage, of course, would explain how the Tapestry came to reside in Bayeux, his episcopal city, and also fits well with its creation in Canterbury, since he was made earl of Kent immediately after the Conquest.[3]

By any law of averages, the Tapestry ought not to exist. We know that such elaborate wall-hangings, while hardly commonplace in the eleventh century, were popular enough with the elite that could afford them, because we have descriptions in contemporary documents. What we *don't* have are other surviving examples: all that comes down to us in other cases are a few sorry-looking scraps. That the Tapestry is still with us almost 1,000 years after it was sewn is astonishing, especially when one considers its later history. It first appears in the written record four centuries after its creation, in 1476, when it is described in an inventory of the treasury at Bayeux Cathedral, from which we learn that the clergy were in the habit of hanging it around the nave every year during the first week of July (an annual airing that would have aided its conservation). Its survival through those four medieval centuries, escaping the major hazards of war, fire and flood, as well as the more mundane menaces of rodents, insects and damp, is wondrous enough; that it successfully avoided destruction during the modern era is nothing short of miraculous. When the cathedral's treasury was looted during the French Revolution, the Tapestry came within a hair's breadth of being cut up and used to cover military wagons. Carted to Paris for exhibition by Napoleon, it was eventually returned to Bayeux, where for several years during the early nineteenth century it was indifferently stored in the town hall on a giant spindle, so that curious visitors could unroll it (and occasionally cut bits off). During the Second World War it had yet more adventures: taken again to Paris by the Nazis, it narrowly escaped being sent to Berlin, and somehow managed to emerge unscathed from the flames and the bombs. The Tapestry's post-medieval history is a book in itself – one which, happily, has already been written.[4]

And yet, wonderful as it is in its own right, the Tapestry is not without its limitations as a historical source. In the first place, despite its remarkable condition, it is sadly incomplete, breaking off abruptly after the death of King Harold. Secondly, as we have already noted, some of its scenes are drawn not from observation but copied from illustrations in older manuscripts, which obviously greatly reduces their value if we are concerned about recovering historical reality. Thirdly, despite the fact it seems to have been made for a Norman patron, the Tapestry is curiously (and probably deliberately) non-committal in its portrayal of events; although most of its scenes have captions, these too are for the most part wilfully obscure or ambiguous. Take, for example, the question of when it begins: most historians believe that the story starts in 1064, but the fact that they cannot say for certain is indicative of the wider problem. Lastly, the story that the Tapestry tells is inevitably selective and in places demonstrably inaccurate; some events are left out and others are deliberately distorted. No other source, for example, suggests that Harold swore his famous oath to William at Bayeux, or that it was Odo who heroically turned the tide for the Normans during the Battle of Hastings. The Tapestry, it bears repeating, is really an embroidery.[5]

We are able to expose such distortions in the Tapestry's story because, fortunately, we have other sources to help us work out what happened: documentary ones such as chronicles, charters and letters, as well as non-documentary ones in the form of art, architecture and archaeology. Scholars who study the Early Middle Ages (the half-millennium, say, before 1066) will tell you that collectively these sources constitute an immensely rich corpus – and this is true, at least in comparison with other regions of Europe in the eleventh century, and with earlier centuries in England. But then scholars who work in these fields can usually get all their primary source material on a single shelf and still have room for ornaments. To scholars who cut their teeth studying later medieval centuries (or to this one at least) the sources for the Norman Conquest can sometimes seem woefully impoverished.

As an example – one I've used in tones of increasing despair while writing this book – consider the evidence base for eleventh-century English kings compared with their thirteenth-century successors. My previous book was about Edward I, who ruled England from 1272 to 1307, a period of thirty-five years. Thanks to a massive number of surviving government documents from that time – literally thousands of closely written parchment rolls – we can say where Edward was for almost every day of his reign: his itinerary, compiled and published in the 1970s, runs to three large volumes of print. Now compare and contrast the itinerary of William the Conqueror, king of England from 1066 to 1087: expressed in terms of precise dates and places, it runs to a grand total of three printed pages. Most of the time, we simply have no idea where William was; sometimes we cannot even say for certain whether he was in England or Normandy at any given point. This is because, apart from the Domesday Book (the other miraculous survival in this story), government archive from the Conqueror's reign is non-existent. Where we have official documents it is because they have been kept or copied by other institutions – chiefly by monasteries that received charters from the king commemorating and confirming grants of land or other privileges. Naturally, at a distance of over 900 years, the survival rate for such documents is not good. And even where such documents have survived, they are rarely dated more precisely than the particular year they were issued, and often not dated at all. The upshot is that, in the case of William the Conqueror – one of the most famous figures in English history, and obviously a major character in this book – we are barely able to say where he was from one year to the next.[6]

Fortunately, given this dearth of administrative documents, we also have chronicles – again, mostly thanks to the diligence of monks. These contemporary histories can help put considerable amounts of flesh on what would otherwise be very bare bones, providing us with facts, dates, anecdotes and opinions. The Anglo-Saxon Chronicle, our most important source for the history of England during this period, has much to say about events before and after the Conquest, and without it our understanding would be infinitely poorer. At the same time, the Chronicle can on occasion remain infuriatingly tight-lipped. Its entry for the year 1084, for instance, reproduced in full, reads: 'In this year passed away Wulfwold, abbot of Chertsey, on 19 April.' For other years – crucial years – it has no entries at all.[7]

Another major problem with contemporary accounts is their bias. All of the writers in this period are churchmen, and as such are prone to interpreting the turn of events as the unfolding of God's will. More insuperably, some of these accounts are extremely partisan. The story of the Conquest is full of dramatic reversals of fortune and often quite despicable deeds; in several instances, the key players in the drama sought to justify their actions by commissioning what are essentially propaganda pieces. Some of our most important sources, including the Bayeux Tapestry, fall into this category and have to be handled with extreme caution.

Because of the shortcomings of the source material, it is often difficult, and sometimes impossible, to say exactly what happened – which, of course, makes it tough if you are trying to construct a narrative history. For this reason, many books about the Conquest concentrate on a discussion of the sources themselves, examining them from every angle, and explaining how different historians have arrived at different interpretations. Some of these books are excellent, but others are a bewildering mix of analysis and opinion, some strictly contemporary, some slightly later, some drawn from earlier scholarship and some the author's own, the overall effect of which is to leave the reader confused and exhausted, unsure about who or what to believe. The alternative approach is to tell the story in an entirely straightforward fashion, banishing all debate and controversy to the back of the book. Such was the method of Edward Augustus Freeman, who wrote a giant history of the Norman Conquest in the late nineteenth century. As he explained in a letter to a friend, serious academic discussion was strictly for the appendices: 'I have to make my text a narrative which I hope may be intelligible to girls and curates.'[8]

Not wanting to baffle the uninitiated, but equally anxious not to offend female readers or members of the lower clergy, I have tried to steer a middle course between these two extremes, and create what might be called a justified narrative. Rather than discuss all the source material separately at the end of the book, I have introduced each source as the story progresses – without, I hope, sacrificing too much forward momentum.

Readers can rest assured I haven't left out the juicy bits. I say this because there are some who assume that historians seek to keep these bits to themselves, like the best silver, to be brought out only in academic seminars. If I had a pound for every time I've heard a comment along the lines of 'I would have liked to know more about his wife/children/private life/emotional state', I might not be a rich man, but I would probably be able to go out for a nice meal. We would *all* like to know more about these topics, but for the most part they remain closed to us. One of the frustrations of travelling back almost a millennium into the past is precisely that many of the characters we encounter are two-dimensional. Often they are no more than names on a page – shadows cast by a single, flickering flame. There are *kings* in this story for whom we do not possess a reliable contemporary description – not even so much as an adjective. Any attempt to discuss their personalities would be idle speculation. As William of Poitiers, our most important Norman source, explains at one point, poets are allowed to amplify their knowledge in any way they like by roaming through the fields of fiction. So too are the historical novelists of our own day, and goodness knows there are enough of them if such invented detail is desired. In this respect alone I sympathize with Professor Freeman (an otherwise deeply unsympathetic character) who, having completed his massive six-volume history of the Conquest, received an enquiry from a painter, wanting to know what the weather had been like on the day of the Battle of Hastings. 'What odd things people do ask!' he exclaimed in a letter to a friend. 'As if I should not have put it into my story if I had known.'⁹

So I've put in the good stuff where it is known. I have also tried to be as fair and balanced as possible. There is still a widespread assumption with the Norman Conquest that the Normans are 'them' and the English are 'us'. The Normans, it goes without saying, are the villains of the piece, responsible for introducing into England bad things like feudalism and the class system. The notion persists that pre-Conquest England had been a much nicer place – freer, more liberal, with representative institutions and better rights for women. Thus the Conquest is still regarded in many quarters a national tragedy.¹⁰

But almost all of this is myth. It arises not from contemporary evidence, but from opinions passed on the Conquest in later centuries. In the case of the status of women, it arose as recently as the nineteenth and early twentieth centuries, when it was argued that before the coming of the Normans women had better legal rights, allowing them to control their own property and to have a say in whom they married. The period before 1066 was imagined as a golden age, when women and men rubbed shoulders in rough and ready equality, only to be ended by the coming of the nasty Normans. Latterly, however, these arguments have been comprehensively discredited. The reality is that women were no worse off under the Normans than they had been under the Anglo-Saxons; they simply had a bad time both before and after 1066.¹¹

Certainly, Englishmen at the time were extremely sore about being conquered by the Normans. 'They built castles far and wide throughout the land, oppressing the unhappy people, and things went ever from bad to worse,' wept the Anglo-Saxon Chronicle in 1067. 'When God wills may the end be good!' But, as we shall see, the English had largely overcome these feelings by the end of the twelfth century. The notion that the Conquest ushered in new and enduring forms of oppression for Englishmen is the work of writers and propagandists working in later periods. It began to develop as early as the thirteenth century, when Normandy and England were once again ruled by different dynasties, after which time the English began to develop a hatred of France that lasted for the rest of the Middle Ages and beyond. It was given a further twist in the seventeenth century, in the struggle between Parliament and Crown, when Parliamentarians went looking for a golden age of English liberties, found it in the Anglo-Saxon era, and declared the absolutism of the Crown to be a Norman creation. Although this view was challenged at the time, Parliament's triumph ensured that it remained the dominant one for the next two centuries. It was championed by Freeman who, like many men of his day and age, despised everything French and Norman and considered all things German and Anglo-Saxon to be pure and virtuous. Freeman's *History of the Norman Conquest* was, indeed, so obviously biased in favour of the English that it provoked instant reaction from other academics, most notably John Horace Round, who spoke up in defence of the Normans.[12] Since then scholars have tended to support one side or the other, Saxon or Norman, even to the extent of declaring which side they would have fought on had they been present at Hastings.[13]

Some readers may come away with the impression that, in the unlikely event of having to choose, I would line up with the Normans; if so it would only be because I know that they are going to win. I have no particular fondness for William and his followers. Like all conquerors, they come across as arrogant, warlike and inordinately pleased with themselves, as well as (in this particular case) holier than thou. But, at the same time, I don't much care for the English either, as they were in the eleventh century, with their binge drinking, slavery and political murders. Whoever these people were, they are not 'us'. They are our forebears from 1,000 years ago – as are the Normans. At the risk of sounding more pious than the most reformed Norman churchman, it is high time that we stopped taking sides.

Needless to say, however, I still think the Conquest is hugely important; indeed, I would agree with those historians who continue to regard it as the single most important event in English history.[14] Many of the traditional claims made for the Normans, it is true, have been overturned in recent decades. Some of the things we once thought had been changed by their coming have been shown to have changed at other times and for other reasons, or simply not to have changed at all. Nobody now thinks that the Conquest introduced the nucleated village or much affected the development of the parish system; it is generally thought to have had little long-term effect on existing political structures, the economy or the arts.

But even as these questions have been settled on the side of continuity, other areas have been shown to have experienced dramatic change. Not only did the Normans bring with them new forms of architecture and fortification, new military techniques, a new ruling elite and a new language of government; they also imported a new set of attitudes and morals, which impinged on everything from warfare to politics to religion to law, and even the status of the peasantry. Many of these changes could be grouped under the heading 'national identity'. The Conquest matters, in short, because it altered what it meant to be English.[15]

One last thing: this book is about the impact of the Normans on England, not about their impact in general. The Normans had all sorts of other exciting adventures in the course of the eleventh century, invading both Italy and Sicily and, eventually, as participants in the First Crusade, the Holy Land. These adventures are not part of this story, which is focused on the Conquest of 1066. This means we will look at events in Normandy and France up to that point, but not have much room for events in these regions thereafter. Also, because the book concentrates on England, we will not have much to say about the other countries and peoples in the British Isles. In recent decades there have been many brilliant books and articles reminding us always to consider the British Isles as a whole, and not just as England and its 'Celtic Fringe'. The Normans did have an enormous impact on the peoples of Wales and Scotland – eventually. In the first generation after 1066, however, that impact was minimal. Some contemporary Celtic chroniclers failed even to register the Conquest, or noted it only in passing as something that was happening elsewhere that would not affect them. Events would soon prove them wrong, but they are events that fall outside the time span of this story.[16]

Stories have to stop somewhere. The Bayeux Tapestry stops with the death of Harold, but only because the original ending is lost. Most scholars assume that in its complete state the Tapestry stretched a little further, and probably concluded with the coronation of William the Conqueror at Christmas 1066. This story also stops with William, but it stretches a good deal further, ending with the king's death in 1087.

Similarly, stories have to have a beginning. The Tapestry begins not long before the Norman invasion, with events that probably took place in 1064. To tell our story properly, we must necessarily go back much further. But, again, we do start with the same person.

1

The Man Who Would Be King

T he Bayeux Tapestry begins with three men in conversation, two standing and one seated. The standing men are not identified, but the seated figure carries a sceptre and wears a crown, while above his head the caption reads '*Edward Rex*' – King Edward. Today he is known, more conveniently, as Edward the Confessor. His memorable byname arose in 1161, almost a hundred years after his death, when he was recognized as a saint by the pope. The pope was satisfied that Edward had performed miracles while alive, and that miracles had continued to occur after his death.[1]

From the record of events in his own day, Edward does not appear to have been particularly saintly. There are suggestions in contemporary sources that he may have been more pious than most, but otherwise he seems to have cut a typical, indeed unexceptional, figure. He lived a fairly long life by medieval standards, dying in his early sixties. On the Tapestry he is shown as an old man with a long white beard, and his death forms one of the most important scenes. The date of his death – 5 January 1066 – is enough to indicate that he is crucial to our story. But in order to understand that story properly, we need to travel back to his youth, and explore how he came to be king of England in the first place. It is a remarkable tale – the one aspect of his career that is indubitably miraculous.

England at the start of the eleventh century was a country both old and new. Old, because its roots stretched back into a distant past, when tribes of Germanic peoples, now collectively known as the Anglo-Saxons, had begun migrating to the island of Britain in the

fifth century. Fierce warriors, these newcomers eventually made themselves masters of southern and eastern Britain, defeating the native
Celtic peoples, subjugating them and driving them into the upland
regions to the north and west. In the areas where the Anglo-Saxons
settled, new kingdoms had arisen, the names of which are still familiar
as the counties and regions of today: Kent, Sussex and Essex; East
Anglia, Mercia and Northumbria. Pagan at first, the rulers of these
kingdoms began to convert to Christianity from the end of the sixth
century, and so in time did their peoples.[2]

But in the ninth century, this galaxy of competing kingdoms was
destroyed by new invaders – the Vikings. Despite attempts to reha-
bilitate them in recent times, the Vikings, with their lust for blood
and glory and their gruesome human sacrifices, were not surprisingly regarded with horror by the settled Anglo-Saxons, who
witnessed their monasteries being torched, their gold and silver
treasures being looted, their precious illuminated manuscripts being
destroyed, their young men and women being led away as slaves,
and anyone else who stood in the way being mercilessly put to the
sword. One by one the several kingdoms of the Anglo-Saxons fell:
first Northumbria, then East Anglia, and finally even Mercia, the
mightiest kingdom of all, collapsed in the face of the Viking
onslaught.[3]

But the kingdom of Wessex endured. Led first by the celebrated
King Alfred the Great, and afterwards by his sons and grandsons, the
people of the most southerly Anglo-Saxon kingdom at first doggedly
defended themselves, and then successfully fought back. And not
just in Wessex. During the first half of the tenth century, the West
Saxon kings became the conquerors, pushing their frontier northwards, driving the Vikings into retreat, and bringing the neighbouring
peoples of Mercia and East Anglia under their dominion. In 954,
the Viking capital of York finally fell, and the lands north of the
Humber were also annexed by the heirs of Alfred.

In driving the Vikings out, the kings of Wessex had forged a
powerful new state. As their armies had advanced, their conquests
had been cemented by the foundation of fortified towns, known as
burhs (boroughs), around which they had established new administrative districts, or shires. Where there had once been several, competing
kingdoms there was now a single source of authority. Henceforth
the various Anglo-Saxon peoples would swear an oath to one king,

and live under one law; they would use a single silver coinage and worship a single Christian God.

But, having conquered, the kings of Wessex took care not to be seen as conquerors. Anxious not to alienate his new Anglian subjects, Alfred had urged them to forget their former differences, and emphasized the common Christian culture that united them against the pagan hordes they were fighting. Diplomatically he was not a *rex saxonum* in his charters but a *rex angul-saxonum*, and his people were collectively described as the *angelcynn*. In a further effort to promote unity, he also stressed their common history, commissioning a chronicle that would circulate around the kingdom's major monasteries. Remarkably, this Anglo-Saxon Chronicle (as it was later known) was written not in Latin, as was the practice in virtually every other literate corner of Europe, but in the everyday language that people spoke. By the end of the tenth century, this language had a name for the new state: it was 'the land of the Angles', *Engla lond*.[4]

Such was the kingdom, at once ancient and modern, that Edward the Confessor would eventually inherit. Dynastically speaking, his credentials for doing so were impeccable, for he had been born into the royal family at some point between 1002 and 1005, a direct descendant of King Alfred (his great-great-great-grandfather). Statistically speaking, however, Edward's chances must have seemed vanishingly slim, for he was the product of a second marriage: six older half-brothers were already waiting in line ahead of him in the queue for the succession. And yet, at the time of Edward's arrival, it would have been rash to have placed a bet on any particular candidate, because the world was once again being turned upside down. A decade or so earlier, the Vikings had come back.

They came at first in small parties, as they had done in the past, testing the waters, raiding and then retreating with their loot. But in 991 a large Viking horde had landed at Maldon in Essex and defeated the overconfident English army that had set out to meet them, and from then on the Vikings had returned to burn, pillage and plunder on a more or less annual basis; by the time of Edward's birth, the violence had become almost a matter of routine. Under the year 1006, the Anglo-Saxon Chronicle records that the Vikings 'did as they had been wont to do: they harried, burned and slew as they went'. The citizens of Winchester, Wessex's ancient capital, 'could watch an arrogant and confident host passing their gates on its way to the coast, bringing provisions and treasures from a distance of more than fifty miles inland'.[5]

Why did the powerful kingdom of England, so good at expelling the Vikings in the tenth century, fail to repel them in the eleventh? In part it was because the Vikings who came in the second wave did so as part of bigger, better equipped and better organized armies: the giant circular fortresses they built around this time in their homelands at Trelleborg and elsewhere give some indication of their power. But Viking success was also caused by an abject failure of leadership in English society, beginning at the very top, with Edward's father, Æthelred.

Just as Edward has his famous cognomen 'the Confessor', so too his father will forever be remembered as Æthelred 'the Unready'. As it stands, 'unready' is a pretty fair description of Æthelred's level of preparedness for Viking attack and kingship in general. In actual fact, however, 'unready' is a modern misreading of his original nickname, which was the Old English word *unraed*, meaning 'ill-counselled' or 'ill-advised'. (It was a pun on the king's Christian name, which meant 'noble counsel'.)[6]

That Æthelred was ill-advised is not open to doubt: the king himself admitted as much in a charter of 993, in which he blamed the mistakes of his youth on the greed of men who had led him astray. From that point on he put more faith in peaceable churchmen, but they regarded the Viking attacks as divine punishment, and thus saw the solution as spiritual reform: more prayers, more gifts to the Church, and, in the meantime, large payments of tribute to persuade the invaders to go away. Naturally, this last policy only encouraged the Vikings to come back for more. At length – by the time his son Edward was a small boy – Æthelred embarked on a more confrontational policy. In 1008, says the Chronicle, 'the king gave orders that ships should be speedily built throughout the whole kingdom'. But this shift coincided with Æthelred placing his trust in his most discreditable counsellor of all, the contemptible Eadric 'the Grabber' (Streona), who had risen to power at court by having his rivals variously dispossessed, mutilated and murdered. The result was that the English aristocracy was riven by feud and rivalry, with disastrous consequences. When the newly constructed fleet, for instance, eventually put to sea, arguments broke out between the two factions; twenty ships deserted, then attacked and destroyed the others.

And so the Viking attacks continued. Large areas of the country were ravaged in both 1009 and 1010. In 1011, the invaders besieged Canterbury and carried off the archbishop; when he refused to be ransomed the following year they killed him, drunkenly pelting him with ox heads and bones. 'All these disasters befell us', says the Chronicle, 'through bad counsel [that word *unraedas* again], in that they were never offered tribute in time, nor fought against, but when they had done most to our injury, peace and truce were made with them; and for all this they journeyed anyway in war bands everywhere, and harried our wretched people, and plundered and killed them.'

The end came in 1013, when the Vikings came led by the king of Denmark himself. Swein Forkbeard, as he was known, had raided several times in the past, but this time his ambition was outright conquest. Landing in Lincolnshire, he quickly took the north of England, then the Midlands, and finally Wessex. Æthelred, holed up in London as his kingdom collapsed, had just enough presence of mind to get his two youngest sons, Edward and his brother Alfred, out of the country. A few weeks later, having spent what must have been a miserable Christmas on the Isle of Wight, the king himself followed them overseas. England had been conquered by the Vikings, and its ancient royal family were in exile – in Normandy.

On the face of it, Normandy might seem a strange place for anyone to go in order to escape the Vikings, because it had begun life as a Viking colony. At the start of the tenth century, having been dissuaded from attacking England by the kings of Wessex, a group of Norsemen had crossed to France and concentrated on ravaging the area around Rouen. Like the Vikings who had visited England a generation earlier, these invaders arrived intending to stay; they differed from their cousins in England in that they were successful. Try as they might, the kings, dukes and counts of France could not dislodge their new Scandinavian neighbours; by the end of the tenth century, the Viking rulers of Rouen controlled an area equivalent to the former French province of Neustria. But by then it had acquired a new name. It was now Normannia, 'the land of the Norseman'.[7]

For Æthelred and his sons, however, it was not a case of 'out of the frying pan, into the fire', because in the century since their first arrival, the Norsemen of Normandy had been evolving rapidly. It was obvious from their names. Their first leader bore the suitably-Viking name of Rollo, or Hrolfr. His son and grandson, by contrast, had been given the French names William and Richard. They had also (as their new names imply) converted from paganism to Christianity. Gradually their followers did the same, shedding their Viking ways and adopting Continental ones. They learned to speak French, increasingly using it instead of their original Norse tongue, and their leaders began to style themselves with French titles: 'count' at first, and then, when they were feeling even grander, 'duke'. Eventually, they ceased fighting to expand Normandy's borders and entered into more settled relations with their neighbours. Counts William and Richard, for example, were both married to French princesses.

The extent to which Normandy had cast off its connections to the Viking north, a vexed question for modern historians, was also a matter of great moment to King Æthelred.[8] When, at the start of his reign, the Vikings had returned to England after their long absence, they naturally looked upon Rouen as a friendly port of call. It was a handy place to put in for repairs during the winter, and plunder from England – gold, silver and slaves – could be conveniently unloaded there for profit rather than sailed all the way back to Scandinavia. Æthelred was understandably keen to dissuade the Normans from engaging in this trade; he tried both force (an unsuccessful attack on Normandy) and diplomacy (a treaty in 991), but neither had much long-term success in reducing the number of Viking fleets that put into Rouen laden with English loot. The king's diplomatic initiative did, however, have one result with far-reaching consequences. In the spring of 1002, Æthelred agreed to marry the sister of the new Norman duke, Richard II. Her name was Emma.

It is difficult, of course, to assess people's personalities, never mind their personal relationships, at a distance of 1,000 years, but it is probably fair to say that, despite the participation of papal legates, the marriage of Æthelred and Emma was not a match made in heaven. The couple, it is true, got on well enough to produce three children: Edward, the future Confessor, his brother Alfred, and their sister, Godgifu. But since Æthelred had six sons by a previous marriage, the production of more male heirs was hardly a top priority. The match with Emma was intended to stop Vikings seeking shelter in Normandy, and this it signally failed to do. Only when the Vikings decided to conquer England in 1013 did Æthelred belatedly reap some benefit from having taken a Continental bride, which was, of course, a convenient cross-Channel bolt-hole. Whether Emma had any part in suggesting or arranging his reception is unclear. Tellingly, perhaps, the Chronicle records that she made her own way to Normandy, travelling separately from both her children and her husband.

In the event, Æthelred's exile was remarkably short. Just a few weeks after his arrival in Normandy, his supplanter, King Swein, died suddenly, leaving the question of who would succeed him in suspense. The Viking army, camped in Lincolnshire, immediately declared in favour of Swein's teenage son, but the English magnates decided to give Æthelred a second chance, and sent messengers inviting him to come home – but on conditional terms. According to the Anglo-Saxon Chronicle, they declared (in a phrase that provides one of the most damning indictments of Æthelred's rule) that 'no lord was dearer to them than their rightful lord, if only he would govern his kingdom more justly than he had done in the past'.

Æthelred, being in no real position to negotiate, naturally accepted. If his subjects took him back, he promised, 'he would be a gracious lord to them, and would remedy each one of the things which they all abhorred, and everything should be forgiven'. As a mark of his sincerity, the messengers who conveyed the king's acceptance back to England were accompanied by his son, the youthful Edward the Confessor. 'A complete and friendly agreement was reached and ratified with word and pledge on every side', said the Chronicle, adding that shortly afterwards Æthelred himself crossed the Channel and was joyfully received by his subjects. In this new-found mood of national unity, the king achieved the one notable military success of his career, leading an army into Lincolnshire and driving the Danes out.[9]

Once they were gone, however, the mood of English co-operation quickly evaporated; very soon Æthelred was back to his old ways. The year after his return saw a fresh round of killings at court, orchestrated, as before, by his henchman, Eadric the Grabber. But the king's attempt to neutralize his enemies served only to increase divisions: his eldest son by his first marriage, Edmund, now emerged as the champion of a party of opposition. By September 1015, England was once again in total disarray; Æthelred was ill, and his heir apparent was in rebellion. It was at this moment that the Vikings returned, led by their new king, Cnut.

Today Cnut is generally remembered only for the story, first told in the twelfth century, that he once sat on the shore and ordered the waves not to wet him. This has the unfortunate effect of making him appear a comical character, which was anything but the case. 'In your rage, Cnut, you mustered the red shields at sea', sang a contemporary Norse poet, describing the invasion of 1015. 'Dwellings and houses you burned, Prince, as you advanced, young though you were.' When he had been forced to flee England the previous year and return to Scandinavia, Cnut had signalled his disappointment at English disloyalty by stopping off en route at Sandwich to unload the hostages taken by his father, minus their hands, ears and noses.[10]

With his return in 1015, a long-drawn-out and bloody struggle for England's throne ensued. The English remained paralysed by their own rivalries until the following April, at which point Æthelred made an invaluable contribution to the war effort by dropping dead, clearing the way for Edmund to succeed him. For six months the new king led a spirited resistance – not for nothing was he later dubbed Edmund Ironside. Battle followed battle, and the Danes mostly had the worst of the fighting. In the end, however, the English cause was again fatally compromised by treachery. Eadric the Grabber, having gone over to Cnut at the first opportunity, had rejoined Edmund's army in 1016 when the tide seemed to be turning. But when the two armies engaged in Essex in October that year, Eadric deserted again, ensuring a decisive Viking victory. Edmund's death the following month, perhaps from wounds sustained in battle, ended all talk of truce and any hope of an English recovery. The crown passed to Cnut, and England once again had a Danish king.

In these dramatic, fast-moving events, the young Edward the Confessor finds no place. We can assume, from his role in the negotiations for his father's return, that he was in England during these years, though we can safely dismiss the later Scandinavian legend that imagined him fighting alongside his half-brother Edmund, and at one point almost carving Cnut in two (at this time Edward was still no more than thirteen years old).[11] With Cnut's victory it became imperative for Edward and the rest of his family to flee the country again. As the mutilated hostages of 1014 would no doubt have attested, the new king was not a man from whom to expect much mercy. Edward was lucky: before Christmas 1016 he managed to cross the Channel and return to Normandy, probably taking with him his younger brother Alfred and his sister Godgifu. The wisdom of their hasty exit quickly became apparent, as Cnut began his reign by ruthlessly eliminating potential rivals. Battles and natural causes had already reduced the number of Edward's older half-brothers from six to one: the Danish king reduced it to zero by killing the sole survivor, Eadwig, at the same time dispatching any members of the English nobility whose loyalty seemed suspect. With grim satisfaction, the Anglo-Saxon Chronicle notes that Eadric the Grabber was among those executed.[12]

Amidst all the carnage there was one notable survivor: Edward's mother, Emma, who contributed to the stability of the new regime in England in a wholly different way. As the Anglo-Saxon Chronicle explains, Cnut 'ordered the widow of the late King Æthelred to be fetched as his wife'. This makes it sound as if Emma had little personal choice in the matter, which is probably the case; a Norman chronicler, writing not long afterwards, casually reports that she was captured in London by Cnut in the course of his conquest. Emma herself would later tell a different story: one which implied she had returned to Normandy after Æthelred's death, and was wooed back by Cnut with promises and presents. As we will see in due course, Emma's own testimony is riddled with half-truths and outright lies, so there is good reason to discount her version. Whichever way it happened, though, willingly or no, Emma became queen of England for a second time, providing a sense of continuity at Cnut's court, but in the process abandoning her children to a life of cross-Channel exile.[13]

At this point, it becomes hard to follow the story of our protagonist, Edward the Confessor, for obvious reasons: few people at the time were interested in the affairs of a boy barely into his teens whose prospects must have seemed exceedingly dim. Later, once Edward had surprisingly become king of England, some Norman writers showed a retrospective interest in his youth. At the monastery of St Wandrille, for example, it was remembered around 1050 that Edward and his brother Alfred had been warmly welcomed by Normandy's then duke, Richard II, 'generously nurtured as if they were his own sons, and as long as he lived they were kept in Normandy with the greatest honour'.[14]

While this may well be true, it is also fair to point out that there is no evidence that Richard did anything in particular to promote the interests of his English nephews (they apparently received no lands from him, for example). Some historians would argue that this was deliberate, supposing that the duke must have been involved in the remarriage of his sister Emma to Cnut, which actually represented a new alliance between England and Normandy. One of the conditions of such an alliance would obviously have been not to furnish the exiles with material aid, or to foster their hopes of reclaiming the English crown.[15]

Even if this was the case, however, it ceased to apply after Richard's death. In 1026 the old duke, after a long rule of thirty years, was succeeded by his namesake eldest son – but only for a short time. Barely a year later Duke Richard III was also dead – poisoned, some people whispered, by his rebellious younger brother, Robert. At this distance it is impossible to say whether there was any truth in this allegation, but Robert had certainly resented his brother's pre-eminence, and swiftly stepped into his shoes as Normandy's new ruler.[16]

Robert, it soon became clear, had not signed up to his father's policy of quiet neutrality with regard to the English exiles. According to the most important Norman chronicler for this period, William of Jumièges, Edward and Alfred 'were treated with so much honour by the duke that, bound to them by great love, he adopted them as brothers'. One historian has recently suggested that this meant the three young men had sworn oaths to each other, and become, in effect, blood brothers. That might seem to be stretching the evidence rather further than is strictly necessary: Robert, Edward and Alfred were already, of course, cousins by birth; they had all been born within a few years of each other, and had been raised together in the ducal household. It would be perfectly understandable if Robert felt compelled to champion his cousins' cause.[17]

According to William of Jumièges, this is exactly what happened. The duke, we are told, sent envoys to Cnut, demanding the restoration of Edward and Alfred. Cnut, unsurprisingly, sent them back empty-handed, at which point Robert decided to mount an invasion on his cousins' behalf. He commanded a great fleet to be constructed 'from all the maritime regions of Normandy' and assembled on the coast.

For a long time this was regarded as a cock-and-bull story by historians; apart from anything else, it seems suspiciously similar to the events of 1066. The most frustrating thing about William of Jumièges is that, although he first wrote his chronicle in the 1050s, we know that he subsequently revised it after the Norman Conquest; what we don't know is which sections are original and which ones might have been improved with the benefit of hindsight. In this instance, however, the chronicler's story finds considerable support in the dry administrative record. Jumièges tells us that the Norman fleet was assembled at the coastal town of Fécamp, and a charter issued by Duke Robert in 1033 shows he was indeed at Fécamp that year, probably at Easter, accompanied by both Edward and Alfred, who appear among the list of witnesses. If this provides a plausible date for the expedition, two other charters issued around the same time substantiate the notion that Edward in particular was entertaining hopes of reclaiming his birthright, for in each of them he is styled 'king'. One is particularly interesting, as it is a charter issued by Edward himself in favour of the monks of Mont St Michel, another location mentioned in William of Jumièges' account.[18]

Jumièges continues his story by telling us that the ships at Fécamp were 'carefully supplied with anchors, arms and hand-picked men', but explains that these preparations were soon undone. 'Having got underway at the given signal, they were driven by a gale until, after great peril, they were at length brought to the island which is called Jersey.' There, says the chronicler, 'the fleet was long held up as the contrary winds continued to blow, so that the duke was in despair and overwhelmed by bitter frustration. At length, seeing that he could in no way cross, he sailed his ships in another direction and landed as soon as possible at Mont St Michel.'[19]

Because he was writing after Edward's succession, Jumièges was able to interpret this disaster in terms of divine providence: God clearly had plans for the future king and wished his reign to come about without the shedding of blood. But Edward himself, in the immediate wake of the disaster, is unlikely to have been so philosophical. His grant of land to Mont St Michel might plausibly be read as a pious vote of thanks for his safe deliverance from the storm, but the same storm appeared to have wrecked his chances of ever wearing the English crown. At this point Robert decided that the fleet assembled for England could be usefully redeployed closer to home, and proceeded to mount an attack on neighbouring Brittany.[20]

Moreover, it soon became clear that there was little hope of another expedition to England in the future. At Christmas 1034 Robert summoned all the great men of Normandy and astounded them by announcing that he was going on pilgrimage to Jerusalem (guilty conscience, said some, for the death of his brother). In the short term this meant all the duke's wealth and resources would be devoted to funding this highly costly adventure. In the longer term it meant that Normandy might well lose yet another ruler, for a round trip to the Middle East in the Middle Ages was a hazardous undertaking, fraught with all manner of perils. And so it proved when Robert set out early the following year. The duke succeeded in reaching Jerusalem, where he reportedly wept for a week at Christ's tomb and showered it with costly gifts. On the return journey, however, he grew sick, and on 2 July 1035 he died in the city of Nicaea, where he was buried by his own men.[21]

News would not have reached Normandy until the autumn, at which point Edward the Confessor must have abandoned all hope. Robert had died leaving only one son, a seven-year-old bastard called William.

But then, a few weeks later, fresh news arrived, this time from England. Cnut was dead and the succession to the English throne was undecided.

Perhaps God had plans for Edward after all.

2

A Wave of Danes

Whatever Cnut died of, it wasn't old age. Contemporaries were agreed that he had been very young at the time of his conquest of England in 1016, which has led modern historians to place his date of birth at some point in the last decade of the first millennium. Thus when the king died in the autumn of 1035, he was probably around forty years old (a thirteenth-century Scandinavian source says he was thirty-seven). According to William of Jumièges, he had been seriously ill for some time, and this statement finds some support in a charter that Cnut gave to the monks of Sherborne Abbey in Dorset in 1035, asking for their daily prayers to help him gain the heavenly kingdom. It was at Shaftesbury, just fifteen miles from Sherborne, that the king had died on 12 November.[1]

Given his Viking ancestry, and the bloodshed that had accompanied his conquest, Cnut's anxiety to enter heaven rather than Valhalla may strike some as surprising. But in fact the Danish royal house had been converted two generations earlier, and Cnut himself had been baptized as a child (his baptismal name was Lambert). Indeed, the point of the famous story about the king and the waves, as originally told, was not to illustrate his stupidity, but rather to prove what a good Christian he had been. 'Let all the world know', says a damp Cnut, having conspicuously failed to stop the tide from rising, 'that the power of kings is empty and worthless, and there is no king worthy of the name save Him by whose will heaven, earth and sea obey eternal laws.'[2]

Cnut had in fact been famous for such acts of ostentatious piety.

Having conquered England and dispatched his opponents in the traditional Viking manner, the king had sought to convince his remaining subjects that his rule was legitimate, and this meant, above all, demonstrating that it was approved by God. In 1027, for example, Cnut had gone on pilgrimage to Rome. He had also attempted to salve the wounds inflicted in the course of the Danish takeover – for example, by having the bones of Ælfheah, the murdered archbishop of Canterbury, moved from St Paul's Cathedral in London to a new shrine at Canterbury; by causing a church to be built on the site of the battlefield where his opponent, Edmund Ironside, had been defeated; and by visiting Edmund's tomb at Glastonbury, where he honoured the late king's memory by presenting a cloak embroidered with pictures of peacocks. The giving of such valuable objects was also typical, and helped Cnut secure a good reputation at home and abroad. 'When we saw the present you sent us,' wrote the bishop of Chartres, responding to the king's gift of some beautifully decorated books, 'we were amazed at your knowledge as well as your faith . . . you, whom we had heard to be a pagan prince, we now know to be not only a Christian, but also a most generous donor to God's servants.'[3]

There was nothing incongruous, therefore, when Cnut was eventually laid to rest in Winchester, in the cathedral known as the Old Minster, alongside the bones of St Swithin and several earlier kings of England and Wessex. His reign – almost twenty years long, as the Anglo-Saxon Chronicle noted at the time – had been a success, largely because he had striven to observe and maintain English traditions. Even the few novelties that were once ascribed to Cnut are now reckoned not to have been novel at all. Once, for example, he was thought to have introduced a new breed of warriors from Scandinavia, his 'housecarls', to serve as a separate standing army. But closer examination suggests that the housecarls were no different from the household warriors maintained by his English predecessors. Cnut *did* have a standing army of sorts, since he maintained a permanent fleet of ships with paid Danish crews. But here he was simply following the example of Æthelred the Unready, who had maintained just such a fleet from 1012, and had introduced a new national tax to pay for it. The only difference was that Æthelred's fleet had been bigger.[4]

Nevertheless, for all Cnut's determination to portray himself as a traditional Old English king, his reign had altered English society dramatically. Or rather, that society had been altered in the tumultuous period up to and including his conquest.

English society in the eleventh century was highly stratified. We know that there were approximately two million people living in England at the end of the century, and that the population was rising all the time, so there must have been rather fewer than that number at the century's start.[5] At a fundamental level, these people were divided into two categories: the free and the unfree.

Although many books on the Anglo-Saxons do not say much about it, more than ten per cent of England's population were slaves.[6] Slavery was a widespread institution in early medieval Europe, and the sale and export of slaves was one of the main motors of the economy. Since the ninth century the trade's most outstanding exponents had been the Vikings, whose warfare was predicated for the most part on seizing young men and women as merchandise, to be sold either at home in Scandinavia or – very commonly – to Arab merchants in the Middle East. England was one of their principal hunting grounds, so individuals abducted from the coasts of Devon, Wales or Northumbria might eventually find themselves labouring under a desert sun to construct a caliph's palace, or members of a sultan's harem.[7]

Slaves were similarly used in England for hard labour and sexual gratification, to judge from contemporary comments. Male slaves were generally used as agricultural workers, and something of the nature of their condition is captured in a celebrated passage written by Ælfric, a late tenth-century abbot of Eynsham, which imagines the speech of an unfree ploughman:

> I go out at daybreak, goading the oxen to the field, and I join them to the plough; there is not a winter so harsh that I dare lurk at home for fear of my master. But after yoking the oxen and securing the ploughshare and coulter to the plough, throughout the whole day I must plough a full acre or more . . . I must fill the stall of the oxen with hay and supply them with water and carry their dung outside. Oh! Oh! The work is hard. Yes, the work is hard, because I am not free.[8]

The ploughman had good reason to fear his master. Slaves were regarded not as people but as chattels, and as such could be punished like animals, by branding or castration. They could even be killed – stoned to death by other slaves if they were male, burnt to death if they were female.[9] The purposes for which female slaves were kept are not entirely certain. Many of them were no doubt used as domestics or dairymaids, but several sources suggest that women were also purchased for sexual purposes. In the early eleventh century, shortly before Cnut's conquest, Bishop Wulfstan of Worcester delivered a famous sermon to the English people, lambasting them for their manifold sins. Certain Englishmen, he said,

> club together to buy a woman between them as a joint purchase, and practise foul sin with that one woman, one after another, just like dogs, who do not care about filth; and then sell God's creature for a price out of the country into the power of strangers.[10]

Above the slaves were the remaining ninety or so per cent of the population who were free. The vast majority of the people in this category were classed as ceorls (or churls), a term we might translate as peasants. They too in most instances worked the land, and most of the time the land they worked was their own. In some areas of England they were less free than in others, because lords had started to insist that they were tenants who ought to perform labour services. But ceorls, unlike slaves, were no one's property.

Above the ceorls were the nobility, a class that included approximately 4,000 to 5,000 people, or just 0.25 per cent of the total population. The nobility were distinguished from the people below them chiefly by virtue of owning a lot more land. An anonymous tract on status, written in the first quarter of the eleventh century, explains that it was possible for a ceorl to prosper and become a thegn (or thane). But he needed to have a suitably noble residence, with a gatehouse and bell-tower, and at least five hides of land – a hide being roughly 120 acres. This was crucial – it was insufficient simply to strut about in fancy armour. 'Even if he prospers so that he possesses a helmet and a coat of mail and gold-plated sword,' the tract continues, 'if he has not the land, he is still a ceorl.'

To be a noble it was also deemed necessary to have a connection of some kind with the king. For the great majority of thegns this may simply have entailed fulfilling some minor role in royal government – administering a local court or assisting in the collection of national taxes. But for a select few it meant serving the king personally – riding in his household, as the tract explains, or going on special missions. According to a twelfth-century source, the minimum property requirement for entry into this charmed circle of 'king's thegns' was forty hides of land, and based on this figure it has been calculated that there were only around ninety such men in England.[11]

Lastly, at the very apex of aristocratic society, there were the ealdormen. These were the individuals who ran entire regions in the name of the king – East Anglia, for example, or Northumbria. As the king's immediate deputies in these regions, they presided, twice a year, over the shire courts, handing down judgements of life and death, while in times of war they led royal armies. Because their commands had been created by the kings of Wessex as they had extended their power across England in the course of the tenth century, most ealdormen were themselves descended from the ancient royal line, and related to each other by ties of kinship and marriage.

This society – slaves, ceorls, thegns and ealdormen – had been severely shaken by the Danish invasions in the decades prior to Cnut's conquest. Naturally the population as a whole had suffered as Viking armies hacked their way across the landscape. 'There has been devastation and famine, burning and bloodshed in every district again and again', lamented Bishop Wulfstan in his sermon of 1014. Some slaves, he complained, had run away, abandoning Christianity to become Vikings (and who, wonders the modern reader, can blame them?). Some thegns, who had once fancied themselves brave and strong, had been forced to watch while Vikings had gang-raped their wives and daughters. And all the while the invaders had been doing as they had always done and seizing people to sell overseas. 'Often two or three seamen drive the droves of Christian men from sea to sea, out through this people, huddled together, as a public shame to us all . . . We pay them continually and they rob us daily; they ravage and they burn, plunder and rob and carry on board.'[12]

But while everyone suffered from the invasions, no section of society suffered more than the upper ranks of the English aristocracy. Consider, in the first instance, the fate of the ealdormen. The elderly Birhtnoth had been the first of them to fall, dying during the Battle of Maldon in 991; four of his fellow ealdormen had perished during the struggle against Cnut in 1016, and almost all the remainder had been killed the following year as part of the new king's notorious purge. Then there were the high-ranking thegns, many of whom appear to have met similarly bloody ends: the Anglo-Saxon Chronicle contains frequent references to the large numbers of nobles slain, and this testimony is confirmed by the lack of continuity between the thegns who witness Cnut's charters and those who attest the acts of his predecessors. Two and a half decades of fighting, in other words, had all but wiped out the highest echelons of the English nobility.[13]

Unsurprisingly, Cnut chose in the first instance to fill England's depleted aristocratic ranks with Scandinavians. The rank and file of his army had gone home soon after the conquest, satisfied with their share of the great tribute that the new king had exacted at the start of his reign (and, in some cases, raising runestones back home in Scandinavia to celebrate their winnings).[14] But at the highest level, in place of the fallen ealdormen, Cnut appointed a new set of Nordic provincial governors. The greatest of all his supporters, Thorkell the Tall, he placed in charge of East Anglia, while his brother-in-law, Erik, was given the responsibility of ruling Northumbria. Smaller commands were created elsewhere in England for the king's other captains and kinsmen: a trio of shires in the west Midlands, for example, went to Hakon, Hrani and Eilífr. In their own Norse tongue men of such exalted rank were known as *jarls*, and the new term was swiftly adopted in the conquered country. England, latterly governed by ealdormen, was henceforth governed by earls.[15]

There was, however, a striking exception to Cnut's general policy of promoting his Scandinavian friends and family. From the very start of his reign, one of the king's foremost advisers was Godwine, an Englishman of obscure origins. Probably he was the son of a Sussex thegn named Wulfnoth, an opponent of King Æthelred's regime who had commandeered part of the royal fleet and terrorized England's south coast. Was there, perhaps, a connection between this piracy on his father's part and Godwine's subsequent rise under Cnut? All we know is what we are told by a tract written in Godwine's praise half a century later: he 'was judged by the king himself the most cautious in counsel and the most active in war'. Soon into his reign, having succeeded to the Danish throne after the death of his brother, Harold, Cnut took his new favourite to Denmark, and there too the Englishman apparently demonstrated his indispensable wisdom and courage. The king responded by showering Godwine with honours: as early as 1018 he had been raised to the rank of earl, and not long afterwards he was drawn into the royal family by his marriage to Cnut's sister-in-law, Gytha.[16]

Such, indeed, was the king's reliance on Godwine that the Englishman was soon pre-eminent even among England's new Danish ruling class. By the early 1020s his command had been extended across the whole of southern England, and included the entirety of the ancient kingdom of Wessex. At the same time, the number of Danish earls was steadily declining. Thorkell the Tall was exiled in 1021, Erik of Northumbria died in 1023, and the following year Eilífr disappears from the record. As the decade wore on, other Scandinavians in England were redeployed to fill positions in Cnut's expanding northern empire. Earl Ulf, for example, was sent at some point to serve as the king's deputy in Denmark, while Earl Hakon was dispatched to govern Norway after the latter kingdom was conquered in 1028.[17]

During this period, however, Godwine's supremacy did not pass entirely unchallenged, for into the vacuum created by the disappearing Danes stepped another favoured Englishman. Leofric, son of Leofwine, came from an existing aristocratic family: his father had been the only ealdorman to survive Cnut's house-clearing, albeit in reduced circumstances, his authority in the Midlands being subordinated to the region's new Danish earls. But after his father's death in 1023, and the eclipse of his Danish rivals, Leofric's own star began steadily to rise. By the late 1020s he too had acquired the rank of earl, and thereafter seems to have become the principal power in the Midlands – what had once been the kingdom of Mercia. The witness-lists to royal charters show that, in the final years of Cnut's reign, Leofric was second only to Godwine in the king's counsels.[18]

Thus, by the time of his death in 1035, Cnut had transformed the English aristocracy. The old guard of ealdormen – descended from royalty, close-knit and long-established – were gone, killed off in the course of the bloody Danish takeover. But gone too, for the most part, were the Danes who had initially replaced them. By the end of the reign, most of England was back under the command of Englishmen, with Earl Godwine governing Wessex and Earl Leofric in charge of Mercia; only in distant Northumbria, where Earl Siward had succeeded Earl Erik, did a Dane control an earldom of any consequence. These three earls, however, shared the common quality of being new men. Godwine's family can be traced back only a single generation, Leofric's no more than two, while nothing certain at all can be said about the parentage of Siward. Their rapid rise under Cnut had made them immensely powerful – probably more powerful than any English noblemen up to this point. But they lacked the ancient roots of the aristocracy that they had replaced. England's three new earls were not linked by ties of blood or marriage. As subsequent events would show, they were not partners, but rivals.[19]

The death of Cnut triggered a protracted and extremely bitter struggle. On the most fundamental level, the late king had provided for the succession by fathering no fewer than three healthy sons. The problem was he had fathered them by two different women.

As we've already seen, in the year after his conquest Cnut had married Emma – sister of Duke Richard II of Normandy, widow of King Æthelred, and mother of the future Edward the Confessor. Emma was Cnut's official partner – his anointed queen – and she figures frequently as such in royal documents and devotional artwork. Together they had two children: a son called Harthacnut, said to have been born soon after their wedding, and a daughter, Gunhilda, who had latterly been married to the German emperor.

But some time earlier, perhaps in the course of his father's short-lived conquest of 1013, Cnut had married another woman called Ælfgifu of Northampton. As her surname suggests, Ælfgifu came from an English family based in the Midlands. An important family: her father had for a time been the ealdorman of southern Northumbria, until he was murdered on the orders of King Æthelred. This raises the strong possibility that Cnut's marriage to Ælfgifu had been arranged to cement an alliance with a disgruntled faction of Englishmen who had wanted to see Æthelred replaced.

Whether it was to preserve such an alliance, or simply because he enjoyed having his cake and eating it, Cnut apparently took no steps to dissolve his marriage to Ælfgifu before or after his subsequent marriage to Emma. He may have felt there was no need, for it is clear that the first match, unlike the second, had not been blessed by the Church. Whether or not this distinction mattered much to society as a whole, however, is debatable. At this date the laity regarded the Church's involvement in marriage as an option, not a requirement. The unconsecrated match between Cnut and Ælfgifu was clearly considered as sufficiently legitimate by both parties at the time it was arranged. This in turn meant that the children it produced could be regarded as legitimate as well.

Ælfgifu had given Cnut two children, both boys, called Swein and Harold. They were probably born before the king's second marriage in 1017 (that, at least, was Emma's later assertion) and so were probably in their late teens or early twenties at the time of his death in 1035. We hear next to nothing about them or their mother before this date, but one fact alone indicates the high esteem in which they continued to be held. In 1030, after the death of Earl Hakon, Cnut sent Ælfgifu and Swein to Norway in order to rule there as his regents.

Did this indicate some plan for the succession? At some point before 1035 the king had similarly dispatched Harthacnut, his son by Emma, to rule on his behalf in Denmark; indeed, surviving coins show that Harthacnut had begun styling himself as king of Denmark even before his father's death. Some later chroniclers imagined that Cnut's intention had been to divide his empire in just such a way, with Norway going to Swein, Denmark going to Harthacnut and England passing to Ælfgifu's other son, Harold. This, however, is probably no more than historical hindsight, for at the time of Cnut's death there was no agreement at all.[20]

Soon after Cnut's death, says the Anglo-Saxon Chronicle, there was a meeting of all his counsellors in Oxford. England already had a long tradition of such assemblies: it is a mark of the kingdom's political maturity that in times of crisis its leading men would generally come together to debate their differences rather than immediately reaching for their swords. But the decision to meet in Oxford that autumn shows how serious the situation had already become, for the town lay on the River Thames, which in turn marked the boundary between Wessex and Mercia. And, sure enough, when the meeting took place, the two earldoms were divided over the succession. 'Earl Leofric and almost all the thegns north of the Thames', to quote the Chronicle, wanted their next king to be Harold. But

'Earl Godwine and all the most prominent men in Wessex' declared in favour of Harthacnut.[21]

Godwine was almost certainly the single most powerful man in England, but on this occasion he found the odds stacked against him. We are not told anything about the sympathies or whereabouts of Earl Siward at this crucial moment, though it is hard to imagine he was not present; possibly the Chronicle's comment about 'all the thegns north of the Thames' implies that he also supported Harold. But the Chronicle does tell us that Harold's candidacy was backed by Cnut's mercenary fleet in London, a formidable force of several thousand men, and more than a match for the late king's housecarls, who had apparently declared for Harthacnut. The greatest problem for Harthacnut's supporters, however, was that their candidate was still in Denmark; Harold, by contrast, was resident in England, probably present at the Oxford meeting, and therefore in a much better position to push his claim.

At length a compromise was reached which recognized the regional split. Wessex, it was agreed, would be held in trust for Harthacnut by his mother, Emma, who was to reside at Winchester with the housecarls. The rest of England, by implication, would be held by Harold, who would also act as regent of the whole kingdom on behalf of himself and his brother. Godwine and his supporters evidently opposed this arrangement but, as the Chronicle says, 'they could put no obstacle in the way'. Their only consolation was that no firm decision had been taken on who should be the next king: as the Chronicle's talk of trust and regents implies, the succession was to hang fire until Harthacnut's return.[22]

But Harthacnut, who had his hands full in Denmark, failed to appear, and the competition between the two rival camps intensified. Each side worked to undermine the support of the other, and no one worked harder than Queen Emma. A few years later, she commissioned a highly tendentious political tract, known today as the *Encomium Emmae Reginae* ('In Praise of Queen Emma'), which above all else sought to justify her behaviour during this period. It is the source of the notion, noted in the previous chapter, that her marriage to Cnut had been a consensual affair rather than a fait accompli. The *Encomium* also claimed, conveniently, that there had been a prenuptial agreement: Cnut had apparently sworn an oath to Emma 'that he would never set up the son of any wife other than herself to rule after him'. Harthacnut, in other words, was the only true heir; Harold, son of Ælfgifu of Northampton, could have no legitimate claim. Emma also set out to discredit her rivals in less subtle ways. The author of the *Encomium* assures us that Harold was not actually a son of Cnut at all, but a changeling, taken by Ælfgifu from the bed of a servant. It was crude propaganda, but clearly believed in some quarters: the Anglo-Saxon Chronicle reports the same slur.[23]

Not that Ælfgifu was above playing the same game. It is not entirely certain at what point she returned to England, but her regency in Norway had ended in disaster around 1034 – she and her other son, Swein, had been driven out of the country, and Swein had died not long afterwards. Ælfgifu may therefore have already been in England at the time of Cnut's death; she was certainly back before June 1036, for at that point we catch wind of her struggle against Emma in a letter written at the imperial court in Germany. Emma had sent messengers to her daughter, Gunhilda, complaining about Ælfgifu's activities. 'Your wretched and wicked stepmother, wishing to deprive your brother Harthacnut of the kingdom by fraud, organized a great party for all our leading men, and, eager to corrupt them at times with entreaty and at times with money, tried to bind them with oaths to herself and her son.' According to Emma's messengers, Ælfgifu's wining and dining was unsuccessful. 'Not only did the men not give their consent to her in any such way; but of one accord they dispatched messengers to your aforesaid brother, so that he might soon return to them.'

But this seems to have been wishful thinking on Emma's part. There was still no sign of Harthacnut, and meanwhile Harold's power was clearly growing. We can see as much by looking at the coinage that was in circulation. The English coinage system at this time was highly sophisticated; each coin, as well as bearing the name of the king, also carried the name of the place it had been minted. This means we can not only see at a glance which coins were struck for Harold and which for Harthacnut; we can also, with more considered analysis, see how much of the country each had under his control. What we see at first is power split along the line of the Thames, as had been agreed in the meeting at Oxford. But, as time goes on, the geographical spread of Harthacnut's coinage contracts, while that of his rival expands. Throughout 1036, it seems, support for Harold was growing stronger. At some point, he sent men to Winchester, and deprived Emma of what the Anglo-Saxon Chronicle calls 'all King Cnut's best valuables' – including, perhaps, the regalia necessary for a coronation. It looked as if the queen's grip on power, assiduously maintained through her marriage to two English kings, was about to end because of her son's continued absence. It must have been around this point that she recalled that she had two other sons living in exile across the Channel.[24]

The future Edward the Confessor and his brother, Alfred, of course, remained in Normandy. As far as we can tell, nobody in England – least of all their mother – had considered either of them as potential candidates for the throne in the immediate wake of Cnut's death. The Norman chronicler William of Jumièges tells us that, upon hearing the news of that 'long-desired death', Edward had set out for England 'immediately', but Jumièges was writing about twenty years later, and in any case careful chronology was never his major concern. It is more likely that his story belongs to the autumn of 1036, when Emma appears to have turned to the sons of her first marriage in a desperate attempt to improve her diminishing political fortunes.

Edward, said William of Jumièges, set sail for England with a fleet of forty ships, full of soldiers. This suggests that he intended to make a forceful bid for the throne, and, despite Jumièges' best efforts to pretend otherwise, it clearly ended in failure. Edward landed safely at Southampton, but was immediately confronted by a large army of Englishmen. Battle was joined and Edward, we are assured, was the victor, but he concluded that the prospect of further success was slight. 'Seeing that he could not possibly obtain the kingdom of the English without a larger army, he turned the fleet about and, richly laden with booty, sailed back to Normandy.'[25]

There are two reasons for supposing that Edward's botched bid for power had taken place at his mother's behest. First, William of Jumièges has his English hero landing at Southampton, which would be the most obvious port of entry for a rendezvous with Emma at nearby Winchester. Secondly, and more compellingly, Emma herself, in the pages of her *Encomium*, goes to elaborate lengths to deny having ever encouraged her sons in Normandy to return to England. A letter *was* sent to them in her name, says the anonymous author, but it was a forgery, devised by her enemy Harold. As ever, the *Encomium*'s very insistence on this point suggests that what it is attempting to deny is the truth. Emma clearly had a hand in persuading her sons to come back, however much she may have subsequently wished to pretend otherwise.[26]

For at some point in the same autumn of 1036, Alfred also decided to cross the Channel to England. Precisely how, why and when he went is unclear. The *Encomium*, for instance, says that he went with only a few men, and the Anglo-Saxon Chronicle insists that his aim was simply to visit his mother. William of Jumièges, by contrast, says that Alfred crossed with a considerable force, which would seem to imply a more ambitious objective.[27] Later English chroniclers believed that Alfred, who sailed from Wissant to Dover, set out at the same time that Edward sailed for Southampton; most modern historians think it more likely that Alfred set out later, after his brother's expedition had failed. Accounts of Alfred's adventure differ in their detail largely because no one writing in England wished to be associated with its outcome. All versions of the story, however, agree that soon after arriving in England, Alfred and his men were met by Earl Godwine.

Godwine, as we have seen, had been the principal ally of Queen Emma in the aftermath of Cnut's death – 'her most devoted supporter', in the words of the Anglo-Saxon Chronicle. But that had been when he, like she, had been confident of Harthacnut's imminent return. Once that return started to look increasingly unlikely, Godwine's support must have begun to waver. At some stage he decided to switch his allegiance to Harold, and the trigger for his desertion may well have been Emma's attempt to promote Edward and Alfred. Godwine had been the principal beneficiary of the Danish conquest; the last person he wanted to see on the throne was one of that conquest's principal victims, seeking to settle old scores. A creature of Cnut, he could only hope to prosper under one of Cnut's sons; if not Harthacnut, then Harold. His only problem was how to make up for his late conversion to Harold's cause; the arrival of Alfred in the autumn of 1036 presented him with the perfect opportunity.[28]

Despite the equivocation of some modern commentators, there is considerable agreement in our sources about what happened next. Both the *Encomium* and William of Jumièges agree that when

Godwine met Alfred he took him under his protection; according to the *Encomium* this entailed diverting him from his intended destination of London and leading him instead to Guildford, where he and his followers were feasted with plenty of food and drink, and shown to beds in separate lodgings. Then, during the night they were seized and attacked. According to the Anglo-Saxon Chronicle, which breaks into mournful verse, 'some of them were sold for money, some cruelly murdered; some of them were put in chains, some of them were blinded; some were mutilated, and some were scalped'. It was, the Chronicle laments, the single worst atrocity in England since the Danish conquest. Alfred himself was spared, but cast in chains and taken to Ely in Cambridgeshire, where he was blinded and left in the care of the local monks. A short while later, in February 1037, he died from his wounds and was buried in the town's abbey.[29]

There can be little doubt that Godwine was responsible for this massacre. One version of the Anglo-Saxon Chronicle discreetly excises his name from its account, but another accuses him directly ('Godwine prevented him [Alfred], and placed him in captivity / Dispersing his followers besides, slaying some in various ways').★ William of Jumièges, who offers what is arguably the most neutral version of events, says that Godwine imprisoned and slew some of his guests, but sent Alfred and certain others to Harold in London; it was Harold who was responsible for ordering his rival's subsequent blinding. Emma, in her *Encomium*, endeavoured to shift all the blame on to Harold, claiming it was *his* men, not Godwine's, who appeared in the night at Guildford and carried out the atrocities – a suggestion so implausible that even her hired author seems to have found it difficult to swallow.[30]

All these accounts, however, were written with the benefit of hindsight. At the time the killing of Alfred achieved its objective for those involved. Godwine had successfully ingratiated himself with Harold by removing a potential rival for the throne; Harold, with Godwine by his side, enjoyed universal political support. 'In this

---

★ Because the Chronicle was copied at different monasteries, it exists in different versions, which historians have labelled alphabetically, A–I. The ones that cover the period for this book are C, D and E. Often, as here, these three versions have a different take on events.

year', says the Anglo-Saxon Chronicle in its entry for 1037, 'Harold was everywhere chosen as king, and Harthacnut repudiated because he remained too long in Denmark.'

'His mother', the Chronicle adds, 'was driven from the country without any mercy to face the raging winter.'[31]

It might be supposed that Emma, on being forced into exile, would cross to Normandy. But the queen had long ago severed any vestigial links, political or emotional, which might have pulled her towards the land of her birth. She chose instead to settle in Flanders, an independent county to the north of France. It is possible that she had been there once before, for Cnut had passed through the same region during his celebrated visit to Rome (the author of Emma's *Encomium*, a Fleming himself, recalled how the king had characteristically showered the churches of St Omer with valuable gifts). Whatever the case, Emma, as Cnut's widow, was well received by the count of Flanders, Baldwin V, and furnished with a suitably luxurious residence in the town of Bruges.[32]

As soon as she and her supporters were comfortably ensconced, the exiled queen began to plot her next move. If the *Encomium* is to be believed, her first thought was to send messengers to Edward in Normandy, asking him to visit her without delay. He, we are told, duly rode to Flanders, but explained that he could offer no help. It is easy enough to believe that Edward, having already made two unsuccessful bids for the English throne, and having seen his brother brutally murdered in an apparently similar attempt, would want no further part in any of his mother's schemes. According to the *Encomium*, however, he declined to assist her on more technical grounds, explaining that 'the English nobles had sworn no oaths to him'. This sounds altogether more suspicious: Edward is being wheeled on only to renounce his claim, thereby legitimizing Emma's next move, which, as the *Encomium* makes clear, was to send messengers to Harthacnut. As the queen must have appreciated, Edward, a long-term exile, was in no real position to offer her any serious help. Only Harthacnut, in his capacity as king of Denmark, could command the resources necessary for a new invasion of England.

He kept everyone waiting for a further two years, but at length the young Danish king showed his hand. According to the *Encomium*, he assembled a great fleet in anticipation of an armed struggle, but in the first instance set out with only ten ships to meet his mother in Bruges. This, says the *Encomium*, was nearly a disaster, because they sailed into a storm and were forced to drop anchor while at sea. During the night that followed, however, Harthacnut received divine encouragement, dreaming that Harold, 'the unjust usurper of his kingdom', would die in just a few days' time. And so it came to pass. The storm subsided, Harthacnut completed his voyage to Bruges, and was at last reunited with his mother. A short while later, messengers arrived from England, informing them that Harold was dead, and begging Harthacnut to take the crown.[33]

As the dream sequence makes clear, the *Encomium*'s account is informed by its knowledge of future events. Unfortunately, we have few other sources against which to check its version of events. The Anglo-Saxon Chronicle, having dealt with the murder of Alfred, thereafter maintains a studious silence on political matters for the rest of Harold's reign, commenting only on ecclesiastical affairs and the state of the weather. Had Harold lived longer, we might know more about these missing years; as it is, he remains one of the most anonymous kings ever to have sat on England's throne. Even his colourful cognomen, Harefoot, tells us nothing, for it was not recorded until the twelfth century (as Harefah) and probably arose from confusion with the Norwegian king Harold Fairhair. Nor do we know anything about the circumstances of his death. The Chronicle notes only that he died at Oxford on 17 March 1040 and was buried at Westminster.[34]

In lieu of other evidence, the most reasonable assumption must be that Harold's death was unsuspicious and unexpected; it certainly seems to have caught the great men of England unprepared. The substance of the *Encomium*'s story, that Harthacnut received a peaceful offer of the crown after Harold's death, is confirmed by the Chronicle. 'They sent to Bruges for Harthacnut', it says in one version, 'with the best intentions.' The Danish king duly arrived a week later and was accepted as England's new ruler. But, as the comment about best intentions suggests, the various versions of the Chronicle for these years were also written retrospectively, and the brief rule of Harthacnut was a disaster from the first. In the words of the Chronicle, 'he never did anything worthy of a king while he reigned'.[35]

To be fair to Harthacnut, the political situation he inherited was ghastly. The great men of England – in particular, its three principal earls – had previously rejected him in favour of his half-brother. But with Harold now dead the tables had been unexpectedly turned; everyone must have felt acutely anxious about the recent past and how it might affect their future prospects. Harthacnut himself did nothing to calm matters when he ordered his predecessor's body to be dug up from Westminster Abbey and, in the words of the Anglo-Saxon Chronicle, 'flung into a fen'. Clearly the new king was not about to let bygones be bygones; one imagines that he received plenty of encouragement from his mother. According to a later chronicler called John of Worcester, Harold's corpse was subsequently thrown into the Thames, before being recovered by a sympathetic fisherman and taken for reburial in London's Danish cemetery.[36]

John of Worcester (until recently known to historians as Florence of Worcester) is, in fact, our best source for the reign of Harthacnut (and also one of our best informants for the Norman Conquest); although he lived and wrote in the early twelfth century, he used the earlier Anglo-Saxon Chronicle as a model, and added many credible details.[37] As his account makes clear, it proved impossible to blame all the mistakes of Harold's reign on the dead king himself. The murder of Alfred, about which men had remained silent for so long, now became the subject of recrimination, and the archbishop of York openly blamed Earl Godwine and the bishop of Worcester (which would explain John of Worcester's inside knowledge). The bishop was for a while deprived of his office, while the earl was obliged to make public amends for his crime, albeit using the oldest excuse in the book. 'He swore to the king', explains John of Worcester, 'that it had not been by his advice or at his wish that his brother was blinded, but that his lord, King Harold, had ordered him to do what he did.'[38]

What ultimately seems to have compromised Harthacnut's kingship, however, was his attempt to raise extortionate sums of money. Although in the event his accession had occurred by peaceful invitation, he had come to England accompanied by his pre-prepared invasion fleet, manned by mercenaries who still expected to be paid. Thanks to the initiative of King Æthelred, the country had a tax system specifically designed for such purposes, but Harthacnut seems to have pushed it much harder than any of his predecessors. As one version of the Anglo-Saxon Chronicle explains (in astonishing detail), the new king paid his troops at the customary rate, established in the days of Cnut and continued during the reign of Harold. But whereas these earlier rulers had each maintained a permanent fleet of sixteen ships, Harthacnut had arrived in England with sixty-two. Thus the sum he raised in taxation during his first year – a credible-sounding but nevertheless gargantuan £21,000 – represented something like a four-fold hike; another version of the Chronicle described it as 'a severe tax which was borne with difficulty'. Perhaps worse still, the punishment looked set to continue indefinitely. The following year the new king dismissed thirty of his ships, but exacted a tax of £11,000 to pay the thirty-two that remained. Even his reduced fleet meant a tax demand double the size of the old days.[39]

Such a rapacious level of taxation seems to have had disastrous effects on the kingdom's economy. 'Wheat rose in price to fifty-five pence a sester, and even higher', says the Anglo-Saxon Chronicle, expecting us to share its outrage, and unwittingly giving us the first recorded instance of price inflation in English history. In order to compel payment Harthacnut sent his housecarls out into the provinces to act as collectors. The two that went to Worcester were chased into the cathedral and killed by an angry mob, leading to royal retribution that was still vividly recalled some eighty years later. So enraged was the king, says John of Worcester, that he dispatched a great army of earls and housecarls, 'ordering them to slay all the men if they could, to plunder and burn the city, and to lay waste the entire region'. Luckily, the people of Worcester received advanced warning of the army's coming, allowing most of them to withdraw to Bevere, an island in the middle of the River Severn, which they fortified and successfully defended. Nevertheless, the king's forces spent four days looting and burning the city before his anger was slaked.[40]

Needless to say, none of this did much good for what we might call Harthacnut's public relations. 'All who had been zealous on his behalf', says the Chronicle, 'now became disloyal to him.' And that was merely in response to his initial demand of tax in 1040; the following year the Chronicle also complained that the new king had betrayed one of his earls, Eadwulf, having guaranteed his safety, 'and thereby became a breaker of his pledge'. Tax-raiser, pledge-breaker, harrier of his own people: small wonder some powerful people started to look at Harthacnut and wonder if they might have made a mistake.[41]

The king's rapidly diminishing popularity is that background against which we have to try to make sense of the extraordinary events that followed. At some point in the year 1041, Harthacnut apparently invited his half-brother Edward to come over from Normandy, in the words of the *Encomium*, 'to hold the kingdom with him'. Something like this certainly happened: Edward in due course crossed the Channel and was, according to the Anglo-Saxon Chronicle, 'sworn in as king'.

There is no wholly satisfying explanation as to why Harthacnut should have wished to act in this way. The *Encomium* says it was because he was 'gripped by brotherly love'. It also calls Harthacnut, Edward and Emma herself 'sharers of rule', comparing them to the Holy Trinity that rules in heaven, and seeks to reassure its readers that there is 'no disagreement between them'. As usual, this is almost as good as having a statement from an independent witness that there *was* disagreement of some sort between Emma and her two sons, and this in turn raises the possibility that Harthacnut may have had little choice but to recall Edward, the half-brother he had almost certainly never met before.[42]

This impression is reinforced by a short description of Edward's return to England in 1041 that occurs in a twelfth-century legal text known as the *Quadripartitus*. When Edward arrived, says the anonymous author, 'the thegns of all England gathered together at Hursteshevet, and there it was heard that he would be received as king only if he guarantee to them upon oath the laws of Cnut and his sons'. 'Hursteshevet', it has been persuasively argued, should be read as 'Hurst Head', and identified with the spit of land near Southampton, at the western end of the Solent, where Hurst Castle now stands. Edward, in other words, seems to have been met at a point of disembarkation, almost before he had set foot in England itself, and obliged to make a promise of good governance. Moreover, it was a promise made to what sounds like a large, representative body – 'the thegns of all England' – which raises intriguing possibilities. Edward's return and Harthacnut's increasing unpopularity are usually seen as connected, but it is generally assumed that it was the king's own decision to share power. Yet we only have the *Encomium*'s word for this. The author of the *Quadripartitus* attributes no initiative at all in the business of Edward's return to Harthacnut; rather, the matter is said to be the work of Earl Godwine and the bishop of Winchester. Plausibly, therefore, this may have been a decision that was forced upon Harthacnut by his disgruntled subjects, with Godwine figuring as a key player.[43]

There is a third and arguably simpler explanation, which is that Harthacnut may have been mortally ill in 1041. A later Norman writer, William of Poitiers, implies as much in his account of affairs leading up to the Norman Conquest. If this was indeed the case, it is conceivable that Harthacnut may have needed Edward to act as a regent in the first instance and to succeed him in the event of his death. There are, however, difficulties in accepting this tidy solution. The first is that William of Poitiers, as well as being late, is far from being an entirely reliable witness; it seems quite likely, though by no means absolutely certain, that he imagined that Harthacnut suffered from 'frequent diseases' simply because he knew how the king's story ended. The second difficulty is that William's picture of an ailing Harthacnut is contradicted by that of John of Worcester, who says that the king was 'merry, in good health and great heart' up to the very end. This turned out to be a wedding feast held at Lambeth near London in the summer of 1042. Harthacnut, says John, was standing with the bride and a group of other men when 'he suddenly crashed to the ground in a wretched fall while drinking'. 'Those who were nearby took hold of him', says the Anglo-Saxon Chronicle, 'but he never spoke again, and passed away on 8 June.' A good Viking way to go, to be sure, but also one with more than a hint of suspicion about it, given his massive unpopularity, and the cup that had been in his hand. Sinister or not, Harthacnut's death resolved the anomaly of the recent experiment in joint rulership. In due course the dead Dane was lowered into the ground in Winchester's Old Minster, alongside the bones of his father. 'Before he was buried', says the Chronicle, 'the whole nation chose Edward to be king.' As a hurriedly revised version of the *Encomium* observed, the wheel had turned full circle.[44] Against all odds, England's ancient royal house had been miraculously restored.

3

The Bastard

Bad as things had been in England in the wake of Cnut's death, they had been worse in Normandy after the death of Duke Robert.

The duke had set out for the Holy Land in 1035 knowing full well that he might not return, and so had taken steps to safeguard Normandy's succession. Although he had never succeeded in finding a suitable duchess, he had once enjoyed a liaison with a girl from the town of Falaise called Herleva.[1] Later chroniclers romanticized this relationship, reporting that Robert had been smitten as he watched Herleva from a distance (dancing in one version, washing her clothes in another), but the truth was probably more prosaic. The most reliable account states that she was the daughter of Fulbert, described on different occasions as an undertaker and a ducal chamberlain. Robert probably began their affair before his accession in 1027, for in that year, or possibly the next, Herleva bore him a son. The new duke chose to honour the memory of his great-grandfather, and called the boy William.[2]

Little William, of course, had a glorious future ahead of him. After his death he was commonly called 'the Great', though posterity would eventually settle on 'the Conqueror'. Contemporaries, however, preferred to describe him with reference to the circumstances of his birth: as a young man he was reportedly taunted on account of his mother's humble origins, and chronicles composed towards the end of his life – non-Norman ones, at least – routinely call him 'the Bastard'.[3] Whether his parentage was a problem at the start of his career is a more open question. A strictly contemporary French writer, Ralph Glaber, seems to have been in two minds about it, one minute assuring us that Duke Robert's lack of a legitimate child was 'a cause of great distress to his people', but then explaining in the same breath that the Normans had always accepted rulers who were the products of unions with concubines (which was quite true). Probably by the time William was born opinion was becoming divided: Glaber's further comment that the custom might be thought an abomination suggests that some sections of society considered it so, and William of Jumièges was clearly embarrassed by the practice, for he refers to earlier Norman dukes taking wives 'in the Danish manner' (*more Danico*) and makes no mention at all of Robert's liaison with Herleva.[4]

But if monks were bothered by bastardy, secular society seems to have regarded it with equanimity. The English, as we have seen, originally preferred Harold Harefoot, son of Cnut's concubine, over Harthacnut, the son of his anointed queen. Similarly, although Robert ended his relationship with Herleva soon after his accession as duke, he promoted her male kinsfolk to honourable positions at his court, and found Herleva herself a respectable husband called Herluin de Conteville, by whom she had at least two more sons. Most tellingly of all, Robert made it known that his own son by Herleva was to be his heir, and seems to have had no difficulty in persuading the rest of society to accept this decision; before the duke left for the Holy Land the Norman magnates swore an oath recognizing William as their future ruler.[5]

According to Ralph Glaber, William's status as Robert's heir was also officially sanctioned by the king of France, Henry I, who had recently been restored to power thanks to Norman assistance.[6] Such was the kind of co-dependent relationship that the two powers had developed in recent decades: the kings of France had frequently looked to the dukes of Normandy for military support, and the dukes had always looked to the kings for legitimization. Strictly speaking, though, 'France' did not exist in the eleventh century: the earliest reference to the 'kingdom of France' does not occur until over a hundred years later, and the kings of France did not style themselves as such until the thirteenth century. Prior to that point, the title they used was *Rex Francorum* – king of the Franks.[7]

The Franks, originally, were one of the barbarian tribes who had dwelt beyond the fringes of the Roman Empire. After that empire crumbled in the middle of the first millennium, it was the Franks who eventually made themselves Europe's new masters. Under the leadership of a succession of warrior rulers, they expanded from their homelands in what is now north-eastern France and conquered more or less everything in their path, from the North Sea to the Mediterranean and from the Atlantic to the Elbe. This expansion reached its zenith during the reign of the celebrated Frankish king Charles the Great, or Charlemagne as he is better known. Charlemagne's power was such that in AD 800 the then pope crowned him as a new emperor, and by the time of his death fourteen years later, his empire stretched 1,500 miles from north to south and a similar distance from east to west. Historians call it the Carolingian Empire, from Carolus, the Latin for Charles.

But very soon after Charlemagne's death his empire began to collapse. For all its imperial pretensions, it was a dominion founded on predatory warfare: plunder, booty and tribute. While the treasure and the slaves kept pouring in, the Franks willingly turned out to swell their emperor's armies. Once there was nothing left to conquer, and only a hostile frontier to defend, they tended to stay at home. Added to this was the problem of dynastic rivalry. Rather like we do today, the families of early medieval Europe expected inheritances to be shared, at least among the male descendants of the deceased. In 843, barely a quarter of a century after Charlemagne's death, his feuding grandsons agreed to split the empire into three. A few decades later, having been briefly reunited (by Charles the Fat), it was divided again, this time into two, and this time for good. The eastern part would eventually become Germany, the western half France.[8]

But in the meantime West Francia (as historians call it) continued to disintegrate. Denied the ability to plunder their neighbours, the Franks took to fighting against each other. They also found themselves in the uncomfortable situation of being attacked, by Vikings from the north, Saracens from the south, and even Magyars (Hungarians) from the east. There was no sense in summoning great imperial armies against such fast-moving, hit-and-run raiders, so Frankish kings delegated the responsibility for defence to their great men in the localities – their counts and dukes. But, of course, such power and authority, once relinquished, is hard to claw back. The great counts and dukes of France still governed in the king's name, but increasingly without reference to him. They began building their own fortifications, holding their own courts, even minting their own coins. Royal authority was also eroded by further dynastic division. For much of the tenth century, the throne of West Francia passed between the direct Carolingian line and a rival branch called the Capetians. Eventually, in 987, the Capetians established themselves decisively as the new royal family, but by then the kingdom they ruled was only a shadow of its former self, and their authority was confined to a small area of northern France. 'Although first among the Franks', a sympathetic bishop told King Robert II (996–1031), 'you are but a serf in the order of kings.'

But it was not just the king who witnessed his authority ebbing away. In a society that had been militarized by the raids, the dukes and counts of West Francia soon found themselves in exactly the same predicament of being challenged from below. Power ultimately devolved to those who could marshal the resources to resist their supposed superiors, while at the same time repressing those beneath them. The clearest manifestation of this trend was fortification. During the time of the Viking raids, the dukes and counts had built large fortresses, generally called *castella*, in order to protect whole communities. In the second half of the tenth century, however, a new breed of *castella* emerged, built not so much to protect communities as to dominate them. What we, in short, would regard as castles.[9]

Some of these new castles are easily identified as such today: along the valley of the River Loire stand several giant stone towers built around the turn of the first millennium by the buccaneering Fulk Nerra, count of Anjou, whose grasp of the potential of this new weapon transformed him from a comparatively minor figure into one of West Francia's greatest regional rulers. The wonderful thing about castles, however, from the point of view of the ambitious potentate, was that they did not have to be fashioned in stone, laboriously and expensively, in order to be effective. It was equally possible to dominate a particular area on a fraction of the budget by raising earthworks to form protective enclosures, and topping them with wooden palisades. Instead of a stone donjon, castle-builders could opt for a single large mound of earth, known as a motte, topped with a simple wooden tower. Such innovation (both the great stone tower and the motte have no precedents) enabled men of comparatively modest means – cadets of established noble families, or ambitious men of non-noble rank – to resist their overlords, assert themselves against their neighbours, and to impose their own lordship – however debatable or unwelcome – on their localities.[10]

Provided, that is, they had the men with which to garrison them. If the appearance of a new species of fortification was one indication of the changes occurring in Frankish society around the turn of the millennium, the other was the appearance of a new breed of warrior. Again, change occurred initially as a consequence of the Viking raids. The switch from offensive to defensive warfare meant that it was no use relying on a system where armies had to be called up from among the local aristocracy; effective defence required men who were armed and ready all year round, and accordingly dukes and counts began to recruit such full-time professionals into their entourages. Of course, great men had always retained warriors; what seems to have happened as the millennium approached, and traditional structures of authority in West Francia continued to crumble, is that they began to increase the size of their retinues. As society became ever more dog eat dog, the top dogs were those who could maintain the biggest military followings. In search of extra muscle, lords reached out beyond the ranks of the nobility, recruiting the landless and sometimes even the unfree, and issuing them with swords, mail shirts and horses. Because they were mounted, such men were sometimes referred to in French as chevaliers. In England, they would be known as knights.[11]

Around the turn of the millennium then, power and authority in West Francia (which from now on we shall call France) was increasingly about the control of castles and the recruitment of knights. In each case, it is important to emphasize not only their novelty, but also their crudeness. Great and noble stone castles were very rare – the vast majority were rough and ready constructions of earth and timber. Great and noble knights were rarer still. Most were little better than peasants in terms of their social origins. Not only were they a long way from donning shining armour; chevaliers were also a long way from embracing a code of chivalry, with high ideals of justice and honour. These early knights did not see it as their responsibility to protect the poor and the weak. On the contrary, a large part of their job was to terrorize the lower orders, persuading them to accept the authority and the material demands of the new castellan lords. No sooner do we encounter castles and knights than we start to hear about 'bad customs' – new tolls, new taxes, restrictions on movement and behaviour. To be a knight originally was to help discipline a peasantry that had hitherto enjoyed considerably greater freedom, coercing them into accepting the new order that was starting to emerge.[12]

If we had to sum this new society up in a single word, we might describe it as feudal – but only if we were prepared for an outbreak of fainting fits among medieval historians. The problem with the word feudal, they will tell you, is that it is not actually a medieval word at all, but a coinage of sixteenth-century lawyers, while the abstraction 'feudalism' does not occur until as late as the nineteenth century. This is undeniably true, as is the more reasonable objection that both 'feudal' and 'feudalism' have been employed so loosely and so variously by historians in the past as to be all but meaningless to scholars working in the present. It is worth pointing out, however, that the term 'feudal' does derive from the medieval Latin word *feodum*, meaning fief, which was a parcel of land given to some knights in reward for their service. Since we first start to hear of fiefs in significant numbers from the start of the eleventh century, there are still good reasons for using the words 'feudal' and 'feudalism' to describe a society that was everywhere affected, if not yet entirely dominated, by the arrival of knights and castles.[13]

How, then, does this generalized picture of society in France compare with what was happening in Normandy? Obviously, Normandy was very different in having been a Viking colony. The Norsemen had not merely raided here; they had settled and stayed to rule. We might expect, therefore, that the duchy would be different by virtue of its Norseness. It seems, however, that this was not the case. As we have already seen, the Normans had been quite quick to abandon much of their Scandinavian heritage, dropping Norse in favour of French, and converting – at least at the higher levels of society – from paganism to Christianity. More surprising still, they appear to have successfully maintained (or resurrected) many of the governmental structures of their Carolingian predecessors. They ruled, for example, from centres associated with the old Carolingian counts, and issued a Carolingian-style silver coinage. Normandy's borders remained more or less where they had lain in earlier centuries. Far from demonstrating the kind of comprehensive disruption that one might expect from a violent takeover, the duchy exhibited notable administrative continuity. It *was* an exceptional region, but paradoxically this was because the Normans had preserved the public authority of the Carolingians that elsewhere had collapsed.[14]

Consequently, if we look at Normandy around the turn of the millennium, we find that the rule of Duke Richard II (996–1026) was comparatively strong. If his predecessors had struggled to assert their authority over other Viking chieftains who had settled in Normandy, by Richard's day that authority was uncontested. It is at this time, for instance, that we have the first evidence of a titled aristocracy beneath the duke himself. Richard conferred the title 'count' on his brothers and half-brothers, as well as on his uncle Rodulf (the earliest individual to use the title, in a charter of 1011). Around the same time, Richard appointed a number of 'viscounts', administrative officials for his own demesne. The significant point is that in each case the duke was in charge of appointments, and these titles remained revocable. They were not simply assumed by their holders, as was the case in other regions.[15]

Nor is there any evidence in Normandy of the kind of fragmentation we see elsewhere in France. Take castles, for instance. We *do* see castles in the duchy by this date, but they are few in number, and either in the hands of the duke or his deputies. At Rouen, for example, we know that the dukes had a great stone tower from the time of Richard's namesake father (now sadly vanished, but possibly depicted on the Bayeux Tapestry). Those castles entrusted to counts were seemingly to help them to defend difficult border regions. Count Rodulf, for example, had a mighty donjon at Ivry (substantial ruins of which still survive) on Normandy's eastern frontier.[16] We also see knights in Normandy, at least to the extent that we see men in mail shirts fighting on horseback. The Normans had long since abandoned the Viking practice of fighting on foot, and had quickly become adept at the Frankish art of mounted warfare. But the fighting they engaged in during the early years of the eleventh century was external; within the duchy itself there is no evidence of the proliferation of unlicensed castles, or the endemic violence associated with independent castellans and lawless gangs of knights.[17]

One fact illustrates this better than any other. In southern France the collapse of public authority in the years immediately before the millennium had provoked a remarkable reaction. At the instigation of local religious leaders, but driven too by a groundswell of popular enthusiasm and indignation, large crowds had gathered in great open-air assemblies to decry the violence, and to call upon the power of the Almighty to bring it to an end. Armed with relics, penances and the power of excommunication, the Church aimed to impose a 'Peace of God' to protect the most vulnerable members of society. A little later, when lay rulers responded to the same imperative, they would declare a 'Truce of God', restricting feuds and fighting to certain days of the week.[18]

In 1023, a council was convened at Compiègne, a town in the territory of the king of France, to discuss the introduction of the Peace of God, or the Truce, into northern France. Duke Richard attended the meeting, accompanied by his leading churchmen, as did the king of France and the count of Flanders. But while in other areas the Peace was proclaimed as a result of the meeting, in the end it was agreed that it would not be introduced into Normandy. Richard's duchy had no need of such drastic measures. In Normandy, the duke's own peace was enough.[19]

This situation changed, however, after the old duke died in 1026, and the duchy was divided in the rancorous dispute between his two sons, Richard and Robert. While it remains unclear whether Robert had any direct hand in Richard's death the following year, the fact that he had encouraged rebellion against ducal authority did him no favours when he himself took over as duke. The fallout from the feud between the two brothers may in itself explain why Robert soon clashed with two senior members of his own family. Hugh, bishop of Bayeux and son of the late Count Rodulf, was besieged in his father's castle at Ivry and fled into exile. More serious still, Robert fell out with his namesake uncle, the archbishop of Rouen, who similarly fled after a siege and promptly laid Normandy under interdict. Since both of Robert's opponents were leading churchmen, it is equally possible that they objected as much to his methods as to the man himself. In his bid for power, the new duke had built up a substantial military following on the promise of future reward, and once in power he made good that promise by plundering the lands of the Church. Estates that his predecessors had granted to monasteries for the good of their eternal souls Robert seized and turned into fiefs for his knights.

Feudalism, it seems, was arriving in Normandy with a vengeance.

And yet in the event the threat to ducal authority was arrested. Robert made peace with the Church, restoring the confiscated lands, and candidly admitting in his charters that he had been led astray by 'the counsel of evil men'. He recalled the exiled archbishop, who not only lifted the interdict but became his most trusted counsellor, lending the administration a valuable air of continuity and stability. It was therefore obvious that the archbishop should be the principal prop of government when his nephew decided to head off to the Holy Land in 1035, and even more so when the duke failed to return, leaving the seven-year-old William as his heir. That there was some measure of stability in Normandy after William's accession is suggested by the ongoing support that his government afforded to the English exiles, Edward and Alfred, in their bids to return home, and that stability doubtless owed much to the archbishop's steady hand on the tiller. The problem was that by this time Archbishop Robert was already an elderly man. Not long afterwards, in March 1037, he died, and with him all sense of order in Normandy.[20]

The clearest manifestation of the chaos that followed was the sudden emergence of unlicensed castles. 'Lots of Normans, forgetful of their loyalties, built earthworks in many places', explains William of Jumièges, 'and erected fortified strongholds for their own purposes. Having dared to establish themselves securely in their own fortifications they immediately hatched plots and rebellions, and fierce fires were lit all over the country.' The duchy rapidly descended into violence as magnates struggled to gain the upper hand against their rivals. A well-informed twelfth-century writer called Orderic Vitalis tells the story of the unfortunate William Giroie, who was seized by his enemies at a wedding feast, taken outside and horribly muti-lated – his nose and ears cut off, his eyes gouged out. Normandy seems to have experienced a rash of mafioso-style killings, as powerful families used any methods against each other, knowing that the government of the young Duke William was powerless to protect or punish them.[21]

During this dangerous time William was not without guardians. Besides the late archbishop, Duke Robert had arranged for a number of leading laymen to aid and protect his son. Alan, count of Brittany, and Gilbert, count of Brionne, both cousins to the late duke, were supposed to be William's principal protectors. It soon became apparent, however, that these men could offer their young charge very little protection at all. Count Alan was the first to fall, killed in a siege at the start of October 1040; Count Gilbert followed soon afterwards, assassinated by his rivals while out riding one morning. With his most powerful guardians gone, the violence moved even closer to William. In 1041 his tutor, Turold, was murdered, and then Osbern, his household steward – the latter had his throat cut while he slept at the castle of Le Vaudreuil in the same chamber as the duke himself. Such well-attested atrocities later inspired Orderic Vitalis to put words into William's own mouth. 'Many times', the future Conqueror says on his deathbed, 'I was smuggled secretly out of the castle at night by my Uncle Walter and taken to the cottages and hiding places of the poor, to save me from discovery by traitors who sought my death.'[22]

Despite the attention to detail – William *did* have an Uncle Walter on his mother's side – this wonderfully evocative passage falls some way short of total conviction. Had the men who murdered his guardians really intended William's death they could clearly have achieved it. Their intention was almost certainly not to do away with the duke but to control him, and by extension control Normandy's government. What we appear to be witnessing, in other words, is not simply random acts of violence arising from private feuds, but a carefully orchestrated coup. William of Jumièges, writing shortly after these events took place, refused to name the murderers, for the good reason that 'they are the very men who now surround the duke'. Orderic Vitalis, writing several generations later, could afford to be less cautious, and named one of them as Rodulf of Gacé – a man who, when we next encounter him, is described as William's guardian and 'the leader of the Norman army'.[23]

It is also apparent from the chroniclers' accounts that this coup was supported by the king of France. As we have already noted, Henry I had regained the French throne in 1033 thanks in part to the help of Duke Robert, and soon afterwards had returned the favour by formally recognizing William as Robert's heir. But support for William, it seems, did not necessarily translate into support for the guardians chosen by his father. 'They scattered the firebrands of Henry, king of the French,' says William of Jumièges of the plotters, 'shamelessly inciting him to bring ruin on the country.'

The problem was that, having involved Henry in their successful bid for power, Normandy's new regents subsequently found it difficult to persuade him to bow out. Not long afterwards, the king demanded the surrender of Tillières, a Norman castle close to the French border – possibly because rebels from his own realm were sheltering inside. The regents agreed, and helped the king besiege the castle until its garrison surrendered. A year or so later, however, for reasons that are altogether unclear, Henry sponsored a rebellion right in the heart of Normandy, supplying soldiers to a viscount who had seized William's birthplace of Falaise and invading the south of the duchy in support of the rebels. In the event this revolt was defeated; the viscount fled into exile and the king eventually withdrew. Even so, it illustrates how lightly some Norman lords wore their loyalty, and how vulnerable to invaders the duchy had become as a result.

Significantly, these two episodes involving the king of France – tentatively dated by historians to the period 1041–3 – seem also to locate an important milestone in the life of the young Duke William. In his account of the siege of Tillières, William of Jumièges describes the duke as a boy and attributes all the decision-making to his regents. By contrast, when Jumièges describes the decision to deal with the viscount who seized Falaise it is presented as William's own. ('As soon as the duke heard the plans of this spiteful character, he summoned troops and swiftly laid siege to him.') William, in other words, seems to have come of age at some point between the two sieges. At this stage, of course, he would still have been quite young, probably no more than fifteen years old; but an early assumption of authority accords well with other evidence. To come of age in the warrior society of eleventh-century Francia meant, above all, to be invested with arms, and the chroniclers agree that in William's case this happened when he was very young – 'at the earliest possible age,' according to the later writer William of Malmesbury, 'in the hope of restoring peace in the provinces'. Malmesbury also tells us that the duke was invested with arms by the king of France, which would fit well with the collaboration of William's guardians and Henry I in taking Tillières.[24]

One writer who made much of the young duke's assumption of arms was William of Poitiers, whose *Gesta Guillelmi* ('Deeds of William') is without doubt our most important source for the

Conqueror's career. Although he did not start writing it until the 1070s, Poitiers had lived through the earlier events he describes and had served since the 1050s as a chaplain in the duke's own household. As such he is not only a contemporary witness but also the chronicler who stood closest to the man himself (as a household chaplain he would have heard William's confession). Like all our sources, Poitiers is not without his problems. The fact that he was writing a history for consumption at the Conqueror's own court means that we have to allow for a cloying degree of obsequiousness, and take much of what he says about William's motives with a large pinch of salt. Despite this, however, he remains a uniquely valuable voice, not least because his own career had been so varied. Poitiers took his surname from the place he had studied; but by birth he was a Norman. Moreover, according to Orderic Vitalis, 'he had been a brave soldier before entering the church, and had fought with warlike weapons for his earthly prince'. Unlike most learned men, therefore, Poitiers knew much of the practicalities of warfare and could empathize with warriors like William in a way that most cloistered monks could not.[25]

Both his bias and his military experience are apparent when Poitiers describes William's coming of age:

> At last a most joyful day dawned splendidly for all who desired and eagerly awaited peace and justice. Our duke, adult more in his understanding of honourable things and in the strength of his body than in his age, was armed as a knight. The news of this spread fear throughout Francia; Gaul had not another man who was reputed to be such a knight in arms. It was a sight both delightful and terrible to see him hold the reins, girded honourably with his sword, his shield shining, formidable with his helmet and javelin.[26]

Despite his insistence on the delight and terror that the newly armed adolescent inspired, even Poitiers admits that William faced an uphill struggle trying to govern Normandy, adding 'there was too much licence everywhere for unlawful deeds'. Years of anarchy had led not only to the unauthorized construction of castles and the proliferation of murderous feuds; it had also led to the duke's own officials – his counts and viscounts – going their own way. If such men did not openly rebel, as had been the case at Falaise, nor did they pay much heed to the authority of the young duke and his advisers. Around the time of William's knighting, the situation was still sufficiently desperate that his government made a belated attempt to introduce the Peace of God into Normandy, effectively admitting that the duke's own authority was inadequate. The move, however, proved a failure. The bishops of Normandy, who would have been expected to enforce a ban on violence, belonged to the same feuding aristocratic families.[27]

Nevertheless, there is reason to think that William must have made some progress in combating disorder in the years that followed. According to William of Poitiers, the young duke 'began to remove completely from his entourage those whom he knew to be incompetent or wicked, and to draw on the counsels of the wisest and best'. By the mid-1040s, the two new names which stand out in particular among the witness-lists to his charters are William fitz Osbern and Roger of Montgomery. On the face of it they were an unlikely pair, one being the son of Osbern, the murdered ducal steward, the other the son of the man who had arranged the murder. In all other respects, however, they were men of a similar stamp to the duke himself – young, ambitious and warlike – and together they would serve him faithfully for the rest of their lives.

This rise to prominence of his friends suggests that William's personal authority was beginning to grow; that he was, as Poitiers says, selecting his own associates and dismissing those who had appointed themselves during his minority. At the same time, the ducal chaplain tells us, his young master began 'forcefully demanding the services owed by his own men'. William, in other words, once surrounded by a team he could trust, set about reining in the counts and viscounts who had grown accustomed to ignoring his authority. Inevitably, such behaviour provoked a reaction.[28]

Towards the end of the year 1046, a new rebellion raised its head. Unlike the successful coup of five years earlier, it was directed squarely at the duke himself with the aim of killing and replacing him. According to the chroniclers, the leader was one of William's cousins, Guy, who had been raised alongside him in the ducal household, and rewarded with the castle and county of Brionne. The suspicion remains, however, that Guy was little more than a figurehead; as a legitimate grandson of Duke Richard II, he could be talked up to justify opposition to the bastard William. The real ringleaders, one suspects, were Guy's known associates, a group of viscounts and nobles based in western Normandy, displeased by the duke's efforts to curtail their independence.[29]

Sadly, no contemporary writers go into any great detail about this most dangerous challenge to William's rule. Over a century later, however, a Norman historian called Wace wrote a dramatic account that fits well with the other known facts and is therefore likely to be true in its essentials. According to Wace, William was staying at Valognes in the far west of Normandy when he was woken one night and warned that his life was in immediate danger. At once the duke leapt on his horse and rode hard across the country, fearfully fording rivers in the dark and taking care to avoid major towns in case he was recognized and captured. Near Bayeux he met a loyal lord whose sons helped him to reach Falaise, over sixty miles from the start of his frantic dash.

But Falaise, as Wace explains, offered only a temporary respite. Realizing that he was powerless against the combined might of the western viscounts, William left Normandy and sought the assistance of the king of France – a fact confirmed by both William of Jumièges and William of Poitiers. Given the events of a few years earlier, this action might seem surprising; it was certainly desperate. William probably appealed to Henry as a vassal to his superior lord; very likely the duke had sworn allegiance to the king, either on the occasion of his knighting, or perhaps at the time of his accession. If so, William was now calling in his side of the bargain, demanding his sovereign's assistance.[30]

Henry agreed. Early in 1047, the French king summoned his army and rode to William's aid. The duke assembled such forces as he could from eastern Normandy, and together they set out into the west to confront the rebels. The rebels, for their part, rose to the challenge, summoning their kinsmen and vassals to create a formidable army of their own, and thus setting the scene for that rarest of medieval military events: a set-piece battle.

The rebels had marched east, crossing the River Orne at various points, and congregated about nine miles south-east of the town of Caen, at a place called Val-ès-Dunes. This topographical detail is provided by Wace, who as a sometime resident of Caen clearly knew the area well, and who once again compensates for the brevity of more strictly contemporary chroniclers. As Wace explains, it is wide-open country: 'the plains are long and broad, without great hills or valleys . . . there are no wooded areas or rocks, but the land slopes down towards the rising sun'.

It was out of the rising sun that the young duke of Normandy and the king of France emerged to meet their enemies. Wace's blow-by-blow description of the battle itself is the least credible part of his account; his casual mention of 'common' troops might be taken to indicate that infantry as well as cavalry were involved, but apart from that we have no idea of the size or composition of the two armies. William of Poitiers, naturally, assures us that the crucial factor in deciding the outcome was the prowess of the duke himself. 'Rushing in, he spread such terror by his slaughter that his adversaries lost heart and their arms weakened.' Wace, while allowing that William 'fought nobly and well', believed that the result was determined by the defection of one of the leading rebels, Ralph Taisson, on the eve of battle. Whatever the true cause, all writers agree that the combined French and Norman forces eventually gained the upper hand, and the remaining rebels turned and fled. At that point the battle became a rout, and those fugitives that were not cut down by their pursuers drowned as they tried to re-cross the Orne. (According to Wace, the mills downriver came to a standstill, so great was the number of bodies.)[31]

Count Guy, the revolt's nominal leader, managed to escape the battlefield and shut himself up in his castle at Brionne. Of his few known accomplices, some were killed in the battle, while others fled to exile in Brittany. The fate of Grimoald of St Plessis, whom Wace names as the lord responsible for the attempt on William's life at Valognes, provides a particularly good illustration of the importance of the victory, since he had built an unlicensed castle at Le Plessis-Grimoult, the remains of which can still be seen today. Grimoald was captured during the battle and cast into prison, so the assumption is that his castle was destroyed as part of the general pattern described by the chroniclers. 'Happy battle', exclaimed William of Jumièges, 'that in one day ruined so many castles of criminals and houses of evildoers.' Val-ès-Dunes, said William of Poitiers, was momentous, and deserved to be remembered by future ages, because it 'threw down many castles with the impelling hand of victory'.[32]

It was indeed a great victory. William, nineteen years old, had vindicated his right in the face of those who had tried to overthrow and destroy him. There remained much to do in restoring the authority of the duke of Normandy to what it had been in the time of his illustrious ancestors, but the threat to the duchy's integrity had been banished. That Val-ès-Dunes had shifted the balance of power decisively was made plain for all to see the following autumn, when the duke convened a great council outside of Caen, close to the site of his triumph. Relics were brought especially from Rouen, the great magnates and the bishops of Normandy dutifully assembled, and, at last, the Truce of God was proclaimed.[33]

4

Best Laid Plans

In the autumn of 1047 Edward the Confessor was also breathing a huge sigh of relief, a major threat to his rule having providentially passed.

Five years earlier, the new king's reign appears to have begun well enough – unsurprisingly, since his candidacy for the throne had been accepted by all parties before his accession. It was surely a mark of confidence on the part of Edward and his counsellors, rather than any lingering sense of uncertainty, that caused them to wait almost ten months before staging a coronation. English kingship was elective – a reign began when the new ruler was recognized by his leading subjects, just as Edward had been recognized in June 1042, within days of Harthacnut's death. Coronation, by contrast, was simply confirmation – a ritual designed to secure God's blessing. Edward, being both devout and unhurried, probably decided to delay his own coronation so it could be held on the holiest day of the year. The new king was eventually crowned in Winchester on Easter Sunday 1043 – 'with great ceremony', says the Anglo-Saxon Chronicle, 'before all the people'.[1]

Before the same year was out, however, Edward discovered that certain people had already failed him. In mid-November 1043, continues the Chronicle, the king went to Winchester and deprived his mother, Emma, of all her possessions, both lands and treasure – 'all that she owned in gold and silver and things beyond description'. Given her treatment of him since his childhood, Edward might be thought to have acted simply out of long-standing resentment, and indeed one version of the Chronicle explains the king's actions by saying that his mother had been very hard on him in the past. But it also goes on to imply that Emma had offended her son far more recently, saying 'she did less for him than he wished, both before he became king *and afterwards as well* [my italics]'.²

The real reason Edward had taken offence in 1043 is illuminated incidentally in a saint's life written later in the century. While the king was reigning in peace like Solomon, it says,

> his own mother was accused of having incited the king of the Norwegians, who was called Magnus, to invade England, and of having given countless of her treasures to him, as well as her support. Wherefore this traitor to the kingdom, enemy of the country, betrayer of her son, was judged, and all of her property was forfeited to the king.³

Some modern historians have dismissed this story as nothing more than rumour, pointing out that within a year Emma had apparently been pardoned and at least partially rehabilitated.⁴ But whether the former queen was guilty or not, the notion that Edward *suspected* her of treason accords perfectly with his actions as described by the Chronicle, where the king is seen to act as a result of information he has only just received, racing to Winchester from Gloucester and catching his mother unawares. He also reportedly confronted her in considerable force, taking with him all three of his major earls and their military followers. This was clearly not a cold dish of revenge, but a heated response to a breaking crisis.

Moreover, the notion that Emma might have made overtures to Magnus of Norway was far from being an absurd conspiracy.⁵ She was a serial hatcher of plots and his designs on England were becoming alarmingly real. Elected around ten years earlier by Norwegian nobles opposed to the imperial rule of Cnut, Magnus had gone on to vie for power with Harthacnut, keeping the latter pinned down in Denmark from 1035 while the English succession crisis had unfolded. At length the two rivals had come to terms, agreeing that, in the event of one of them dying, the survivor should be the other's heir – or such at least was the tradition by the mid-twelfth century.⁶ True or not, when Harthacnut died in 1042 Magnus had moved swiftly to make himself Denmark's new master, and it soon became clear that England was to be his next target.

The seriousness with which Edward and his counsellors regarded the threat from Norway is evident from their actions during the years that followed. In 1044, says the Anglo-Saxon Chronicle, 'the king went out to Sandwich with thirty-five ships'. Sandwich, now a landlocked little town close to the east Kent coast, was then one of England's principal seaports – 'the most famous of all the ports of the English', as the author of the *Encomium* calls it – and the place where royal fleets would assemble to protect the country against invasion.[7] The summer of 1045 saw Edward again at Sandwich, this time with men and ships in even greater numbers. 'No one had ever seen so large a naval force in this country', says the C Chronicle, while the D version tells us explicitly that this force had been assembled 'because of the threat of Magnus of Norway'.

In the event Magnus did not sail for England in 1045, a fact which the D Chronicle attributes to his struggle against Swein Estrithson. Swein, the son of Cnut's sister, Estrith, had acted as regent in Denmark for his cousin, Harthacnut, during the latter's reign in England. After Harthacnut's death he had advanced his own claim to the Danish throne, though apparently without much initial success. In 1045 he seems to have done rather better, and his progress clearly frustrated Magnus' plan to invade England.

But, as subsequent reports in the Chronicle make equally clear, Swein's luck failed to hold: 'Magnus conquered Denmark', says the D version for 1046. The following year, we are told, Swein sent messengers to England, hoping to enlist the support of fifty ships, but his request was turned down 'because Magnus had a great naval force'. 'And then Magnus drove out Swein and seized the country with great slaughter, and the Danes paid him a large amount of money and accepted him as king.'

With Swein defeated and Magnus established as master of both Norway and Denmark, it was surely only a matter of time before the plan to conquer England was revived, and the Anglo-Scandinavian empire of Cnut was restored. But, providentially, in October 1047 – even as the Truce of God was being proclaimed in Normandy – Magnus suddenly died. Accounts of his death differ, but all are late and none is very exciting. According to one thirteenth-century writer, the king was riding a horse which was startled by a hare and dashed him into a tree. Another thirteenth-century source says Magnus simply fell sick and died in bed.[8]

But, boring or not, Magnus' death meant that England was

suddenly released from the threat of invasion. Swein was able to assert his right to Denmark, while in Norway power passed to Magnus' paternal uncle. As his earlier request for help shows, Swein was already on good terms with the English, and the new Norwegian king began his reign by sending ambassadors to England in order to make peace.[9] Once again, Edward had triumphed over a younger rival by the simple expedient of living longer.

During these anxious years of invasion fear, Edward had clearly been worried about the possibility of Scandinavian sympathizers lurking in England. First there had been the rumour in 1043 that his mother was plotting to replace him with Magnus; then the following year the king had banished a niece of Cnut named Gunhilda, along with her two children, while in 1046 he had similarly sent into exile one of Cnut's supporters called Osgod Clapa. As in his mother's case, Edward was probably responding to a mix of present fears and past grievances. These people may have constituted a genuine Scandinavian fifth column, or simply have been the victims of what the king regarded as a long-overdue house-cleaning exercise by which the effects of the earlier Danish conquest were gradually undone.[10]

So where did that leave Earl Godwine, by far the greatest beneficiary of Cnut's takeover? Despite his efforts to exculpate himself, Godwine had clearly been deeply implicated in the murder of Edward's brother, Alfred. Yet by all accounts the earl had also been the key figure in helping Edward ascend to the throne.[11] Did this indicate that at some point between the two events the pair had agreed to sink their differences? Had Edward forgiven his brother's murder in exchange for Godwine's support in recovering his birthright?

A case can certainly be made for their reconciliation. At the very start of the reign, the earl sought to appease the new king by presenting him with a magnificent warship, ornamented with gold, and manned by eighty soldiers, their helmets, armbands and armour all similarly gilded. It was the subject of a lengthy contemporary poem, and the poet explicitly links the gift with Godwine's new-found loyalty:

This he gave to the newly enthroned king, begging that it be received and found acceptable, promising that he will often and with pleasure add to it. Wherefore he holds out his hands, takes oaths of loyalty, swearing to protect Edward as his king and lord with faithful vow and service.[12]

In the early years of his reign the Confessor had also agreed to raise three of Godwine's kinsmen to the highest rank. In 1043 the earl's eldest son, Swein, had been given an earldom in the south-west Midlands, and two years later his second son, Harold, had been handed control of East Anglia: both were in their early twenties. Another of Godwine's young male relatives, his nephew Beorn, was similarly promoted to an earldom in the south-east Midlands at some point in 1045.[13]

More significant still was the fact that, at the start of the same year, Edward married Godwine's daughter, Edith. We know a reasonable amount about Edith because several decades later she commissioned one of the most important sources for her husband's reign, a text known as the *Life of King Edward*. Unsurprisingly the anonymous author is fulsome in praise of his patron's appearance, character and accomplishments. Edith, we are assured, was 'inferior to none, superior to all . . . recommended by the distinction of her family and the ineffable beauty of her surpassing youth'. Educated by the nuns of Wilton in Wiltshire, she was also apparently quite the bluestocking, fluent in four languages, and so learned and talented that she was famous for her own poems, prose, needlework and painting. Dignified and reserved, serious and modest, affectionate, generous and honest: Edith was clearly 'a wife worthy of so great a husband'. She and Edward were married at an unknown location on 23 January 1045.[14]

But did Edward really have an alternative? Any assessment of his relationship with Godwine has to take into account the fundamental weakness of the king's position at the start of his reign. Although he was fast approaching forty, he had not lived in England since his childhood; for a quarter of a century he had been living the life of an exile in Normandy. This meant that on his arrival in 1041 Edward had exceedingly few friends and allies – his only real confidants were the handful of Continental supporters who accompanied him from Normandy, many of whom were clerics. Godwine, by contrast, had been the principal force in English politics for almost all of the same twenty-five-year period. His lands and wealth, great as they were, could not quite rival those of the king; but in terms of lordship, the earl greatly outclassed Edward, with scores of followers in almost every shire in southern England, all ready to do his bidding. Events suggest that his will was all but irresistible. In 1040 he had supported Harthacnut, but the following year he had changed his mind and given his backing to Edward. What if he changed his mind again, and switched his support to another candidate – Magnus, for example, or perhaps Swein Estrithson? The reality was that, if Edward wanted to survive, he had little choice other than to do what Godwine suggested – and probably no say at all in choosing his own bride. As the author of the *Life of King Edward* explains with surprising candour, 'Edward agreed all the more readily to contract this marriage because he knew that, with the advice and help of Godwine, he would have a firmer hold on his hereditary rights in England.'[15]

The corollary of this statement is pretty clear: had Edward refused, he would probably have found himself out of a job.

The suspicion, borne out by later events, is that Edward never forgave Godwine for Alfred's murder, and merely went through the motions in marrying Edith. It is a suspicion reinforced by the fact that the match never produced any children. Later chroniclers insisted that this was because it was never consummated; most modern commentators, by contrast, ascribe it to sheer bad luck, and point to infertility as the more likely cause. Yet according to Edith's own testimony (i.e. the *Life of King Edward*), the reason there were no children was because Edward had lived 'a celibate life'; indeed, 'he preserved with holy chastity the dignity of his consecration, and lived his whole life dedicated in true innocence'. This testimony deserves to be taken seriously; after all (as one modern historian has observed), had the reality been different, the *Life* would have been a laughing stock. More importantly, subsequent events do not support the idea that Edward was anxious to beget an heir. The reasonable conclusion remains that Edward agreed to marry Edith for purely political reasons and resisted her extensively chronicled charms.[16]

This may not have been an obvious problem for the first few years of the couple's marriage. We know that Edward was at least forty in January 1045, but we have no clear idea of the age of his bride. If Edith was the eldest of Godwine's many children, she could have been as old as twenty-five, but equally she could have been the minimum age for marriage as set by the Church, which was twelve. If the latter was the case, then the initial absence of children might not have been too surprising. As time wore on, however, public anxiety about the lack of a successor must have grown, and with it the tension between Edward and Godwine.[17]

There are signs of this happening in the chronicle accounts. At first we see the two men collaborating. When, for example, the archbishop of Canterbury resigned due to ill health in 1044, the shady deal by which he appointed his own replacement proceeded, says the Anglo-Saxon Chronicle, 'by permission of the king and Earl Godwine'. But later in the decade the pair are seen to part company over England's foreign policy. When Swein Estrithson sought English help against Magnus of Norway, Godwine was all in favour (his own marriage to Cnut's sister-in-law meant that he was Swein's uncle); according to John of Worcester, the earl 'advised the king that he might safely send at least fifty ships' – but Edward refused. 'It seemed a foolish plan to everybody', explains the Anglo-Saxon Chronicle, while John of Worcester adds that the opposition was led by Earl Leofric of Mercia. Whether or not Edward was actively cultivating Leofric as an ally, the episode shows that there were clearly others willing to help him stand up to Godwine.[18]

Nor was this Godwine's only embarrassment at the time. That same year his eldest son, Swein, fled into exile, having caused a scandal the previous year by abducting the abbess of Leominster. This was bad enough, but two years later Swein returned to England in search of a pardon, only to compound his crime by betraying and murdering his cousin, Beorn Estrithson, the brother of the Danish king. This was regarded as a truly heinous offence. Swein was declared to be a 'nithing', says the Chronicle – a man without any honour – and once again fled overseas.[19]

And yet, if the case of Swein shows anything, it is that the power of Earl Godwine, despite the setbacks and embarrassments, remained as firm as ever. In 1050, just months after his second banishment, the earl's good-for-nothing son received a royal pardon and was allowed to re-enter the country. Edward was evidently still obliged to accommodate his father-in-law's every wish. The Godwines, it seems, could quite literally get away with murder.[20]

To add to the king's woes at the end of the 1040s, the threat from Scandinavia persisted; the death of King Magnus, it seems, had provided only a temporary respite. Norway and Denmark were once again at war, and such instability must have caused great anxiety for both the English king and his peaceable subjects. In 1048 the coasts of Kent and Essex were attacked by a pair of old-school Vikings, named by the Chronicle as Lothen and Yrling, who 'seized indescribable booty, both in captives, gold and silver'. The following year Essex was raided again by an ever larger fleet, led this time by the exiled Osgod Clapa.[21]

By the end of the year 1050, however, Edward had come up with a plan – a plan which, if it worked, would rid him of the over-mighty Godwine, safeguard England from Viking attack, and simultaneously solve the pressing problem of the English succession. It was, in short, ambitious, and it required the participation of his kinsman, the duke of Normandy.

In the months and years after the battle of Val-ès-Dunes, William had been busy consolidating his victory, destroying castles and capturing rebels. Count Guy, the leader of the failed revolt, proved a particularly stubborn problem, having fled to his castle at Brionne which, according to William of Poitiers, was virtually impregnable, its stone keep surrounded on all sides by the unfordable waters of the River Risle. As William of Jumièges explains, the duke was forced to surround Brionne with siege castles in order to strangle it into submission. At length (after three years in one account) the starving count surrendered and was sent into exile.[22]

As William ousted the man who had tried to topple him, his loyal subjects worried about the security of his dynasty. 'Now that the duke, flourishing in the strength of his youth, was passed the age of adolescence', says William of Jumièges, 'his magnates urgently drew attention to the problem of his offspring and succession.' Like Edward the Confessor, William needed to get married and busy in his bed so that others could sleep easy in theirs. William of Poitiers indicates that there was discussion and disagreement amongst the duke's advisers about where he ought to go looking for a wife. In the Middle Ages, matrimony among the great was often an extension of diplomacy; historically, the dukes of Normandy had sought brides beyond their borders. In the end it was decided that William should marry Matilda, a daughter of Baldwin, count of Flanders.[23]

We don't know much about the young Matilda – her date of birth, like Edith's, is unknown.[24] So too, for that matter, is her height: the popular notion that she was only four feet two inches is a modern myth.[25] William of Jumièges tells us that she was 'a very beautiful and noble girl of royal stock'. The 'beautiful' part sounds conventional, but given that the principal concern was to produce children, Matilda's attractiveness must have mattered. 'Royal stock' refers to the fact that Matilda's mother, Adela, was a daughter of the late French king, Robert the Pious, who had died in 1031. This, of course, meant that Matilda herself was a niece of Robert's son and successor, Henry I, and indeed it seems quite possible that the king, William's ally in 1047, may have suggested the marriage alliance with Flanders. Certainly in May the following year both William and Count Baldwin appear together as witnesses on a charter drawn up at Henry's court.[26]

What William of Jumièges fails to mention (unsurprisingly) is that before the marriage could be celebrated it was forbidden by the pope. Indeed, the first certain information we have about the match comes in October 1049, when Pope Leo IX, then holding a celebrated council in the French city of Rheims, intervened to ban it. Chroniclers writing in the early twelfth century believed that he did so because William and Matilda were too closely related, but the fact that no modern historian has been able to discover a credible genealogical link between the couple suggests that the real reason for the ban lay elsewhere.[27]

The true explanation was probably political. In 1049 Leo had only been pope for a few months, and had been appointed by his relative, the emperor Henry III, who – it just so happened – was on extremely bad terms with Baldwin of Flanders. Earlier in the year, as the Anglo-Saxon Chronicle explains, Baldwin had attacked the imperial palace at Nijmegen, and the emperor, in revenge, had assembled a great army against him, made up of famous men from all regions – including Pope Leo. By the time the Council of Rheims met in October Baldwin had submitted, but neither Henry III nor Leo IX would have been happy at the thought of their former enemy strengthening his position in any way – say, for example, by entering a marriage alliance with the duke of Normandy.[28]

So the pope's objections were probably political rather than canonical; but being political meant they could be speedily overcome.

Within months of the Council of Rheims senior Norman churchmen were visiting Leo in Rome, and by 1051 we find Matilda witnessing charters as William's countess. Most likely, therefore, the marriage was celebrated at some point in 1050, when William was in his early twenties and Matilda in her mid-to-late teens. The wedding took place in the small town of Eu on Normandy's north-eastern border. The bride arrived escorted by her father, who also brought many gifts, and the groom came accompanied by his mother and stepfather, as well as many knights. 'He married her legally as his wife,' says William of Jumièges, 'and led her with the greatest ceremony and honour into the walls of Rouen.' The ducal capital, adds William of Poitiers, gave itself over to rejoicing.[29]

In England, however, there may have been rather less jubilation. Edward the Confessor, of course, had an extremely long and close relationship with Normandy and its rulers, and there is no reason to suppose that this had in any way suffered since he had left to reclaim his father's crown. But his relationship with Flanders was, by contrast, terrible. Possibly this was due to the malign influence of his mother, who may have poisoned the mind of Count Baldwin during her long sojourn in Bruges. Whatever the cause, throughout the 1040s the count had repeatedly given refuge to the king's enemies. Gunhilda and her children; Osgod Clapa; the incorrigible Swein Godwineson – all had fled to Flanders after Edward had sent them into exile. So too had Lothen and Yrling, the two pirates who raided Kent and Essex in 1048, in order to sell their plunder. Flanders, in short, had become for Edward what Normandy had been for his father – a harbour for his enemies and place to unload English riches. Small wonder that when the German emperor had asked Edward to mount a naval blockade of Baldwin's ports in 1049, the English king had readily obliged.[30]

The marriage of William and Matilda must therefore have filled Edward with considerable foreboding: an alliance between Normandy and Flanders raised the alarming prospect of a Channel coast hostile from one end to the other. Clearly, the king had to do something to counteract this latent threat to English interests. It was yet another reason why the young Norman duke was an essential part of his plan.

At the start of the year 1051 a storm was already brewing between Edward and Earl Godwine. For some time, it seems, the two men had not seen eye to eye over the government of the English Church. The king may not have had much power in secular politics, but he did have the final say in the appointment of abbots and bishops, and, unsurprisingly, he preferred to advance his own associates – the clerks of his chapel who had crossed with him from Normandy – rather than those put forward by his father-in-law. As the *Life of King Edward* explains, 'when the holders of dignities died, one set of men wanted vacant sees for their own friends, and others were alienating them to strangers'.

This argument reached its highest pitch following the death, in October 1050, of Eadsige, the archbishop of Canterbury. The monks of Canterbury, who had the first say in choosing a replacement, elected one of their own, a certain Æthelric, and asked Godwine to seek the king's approval. The earl readily agreed – Æthelric was one of his kinsmen – but his request was refused. Edward already had a candidate in mind in the shape of his long-time friend and mentor, Robert of Jumièges, who, as his surname suggests, was a Norman. The former abbot of Jumièges, Robert had crossed with Edward in 1041 and thereafter remained his most intimate counsellor – 'the most powerful confidential adviser of the king', as the *Life of King Edward* puts it. Towards the start of the reign Edward had elevated him to be bishop of London, possibly in the teeth of native opposition (unusually, there is no mention of the appointment in the Anglo-Saxon Chronicle). The prospect of his promotion to Canterbury certainly caused consternation in Godwine circles. 'All the clergy protested with all their might against the wrong', says the author of the *Life*. But they protested in vain, because ultimately the will of the king prevailed. In March 1051, Edward held a meeting of his council in London and Robert's appointment was confirmed.[31]

At the same time, the king almost certainly dropped another, even bigger bombshell. Six years into their marriage, he and Edith still had no children, despite the prayers we know that certain churchmen had been offering up for their fertility. Of course, this fact is not surprising if we believe Edith's later claim that Edward had never slept with her, and our grounds for believing as much are greatly reinforced by the king's actions during this crucial year. It was probably in the same council of March that year that Edward announced that he wanted the English succession to go to his kinsman, William of Normandy.

'Almost certainly'; 'probably': the announcement of William's candidature for the throne has to be hedged around in this way because no English source written at the time admits that it happened. The suggestion that Edward promised William the succession occurs only in Norman sources written, or at least revised, after the Norman Conquest itself. This has led some historians to doubt that the promise was ever made at all, and to argue that it was a simply a story dreamt up after the event to justify William's accession.[32]

Taken together, however, the English and Norman sources strongly suggest that the promise was made. Both William of Poitiers and William of Jumièges, for example, aver that the offer was carried to William in the first instance by Robert of Jumièges, and English sources confirm that the new archbishop of Canterbury did indeed leave England in the spring of 1051 (like all newly appointed arch-bishops, he had to travel to Rome to collect his pallium, or scarf of office, from the pope in person).[33]

Given the silence of our English sources, the reaction of Earl Godwine can only be guessed at, but we may suppose that it was not favourable. Defeated in recent years on the issue of foreign policy; frustrated in recent months in his scheme for a new arch-bishop, the earl was now, it seems, expected to abandon the hope of one day seeing a grandson on the English throne, and to accept instead that the position would be filled by yet another foreigner. The prospect can hardly have pleased him. William, if he came to England, would not be like Edward, a powerless exile with a small entourage. He would be an independent power, a duke of one of France's most formidable provinces, with a reputation already estab-lished for prowess in arms. As such, he would be unlikely to tolerate the over-mighty earl, and well placed to destroy him.

What *is* clear from the English sources is the mounting tension between Godwine and the king in the months that followed the March council. Towards the end of June Robert of Jumièges returned from the Continent and immediately caused fresh controversy by refusing to consecrate the Godwinist candidate who had been elected to succeed him as bishop of London. He also clashed with Godwine himself, claiming that the earl had invaded certain lands belonging to Canterbury ('a cause in which right was on the bishop's side', says the author of the *Life of King Edward*, with remarkable candour). In general the *Life* identifies the new archbishop as the source of all the trouble, accusing him of poisoning Edward's mind against the blameless Godwine, and causing the king to believe that the earl was planning to attack him, 'just as he had once attacked his brother'.[34]

At the end of the summer the situation exploded. The last days of August saw the arrival in England of Eustace, count of Boulogne, Edward's brother-in-law (at some point after 1035, Eustace had married Edward's sister, Godgifu). The reason for his visit is unknown. Some historians have suggested, on fairly flimsy evidence, that he and Godgifu might have had a daughter, and have inferred from the timing of the visit that its purpose was to discuss her right to the English throne. Less speculatively, as count of Boulogne, sandwiched between Normandy and Flanders, Eustace may well have wished to discuss with Edward the implications of the recent Norman-Flemish alliance. All we can say for certain is what the E Chronicle tells us: that the count came to see the king, 'talked over with him what he wished', and on his return journey got into a fight with the citizens of Dover. The D Chronicle presents it as an accident: Eustace's men 'behaved foolishly when looking for lodgings' and an argument ensued. The E version says that before they entered Dover Eustace's men donned their mail shirts, which makes it sound as if they came with hostile intent, and raises the possibility that they may have been put up to it. Whatever the case, by all accounts a large number of men on both sides ended up wounded or dead, and Eustace returned to the king, by then in Gloucester, to give a one-sided account of what had happened. Edward, incensed on his brother-in-law's behalf, determined to punish the people of Dover, and gave orders that the town be harried, much as his predecessor, Harthacnut, had done in the case of Worcester a decade earlier. The orders, however, were given to the earl responsible for Dover – Godwine – who refused to carry them out. 'It was abhorrent to him to injure the people of his own province', says the E Chronicle.[35]

And so, at last, the argument between the two men burst into the open. At the start of September the defiant earl raised the men of Wessex, while his sons rallied their men from the shires of East Anglia and the south-west Midlands. At Beverstone, fifteen miles south of Gloucester, they assembled what the D Chronicle calls 'a great army, without number, all ready for war against the king'. But Edward was finally ready to confront his father-in-law, and responded in kind, summoning England's other great earls – Leofric of Mercia and Siward of Northumbria – who in turn raised the men of their earldoms and rode to his aid, 'ready to attack Godwine's levies if the king had wished it'.

On the very brink of civil war, England's great men hesitated. 'Some of them considered that it would be great folly if they joined battle', explains the D Chronicle, 'because almost all the noblest in England were present in those two companies, and they were convinced they would be leaving the country open to the invasion of her enemies, and be bringing utter ruin upon ourselves.' Clearly, the lessons of Æthelred's reign had been well learned. Both sides agreed to stand down, and it was also agreed that Godwine would come to London in two weeks' time in order to stand trial. Unfortunately for the earl, during that fortnight the balance of power shifted; his host, says the D Chronicle, 'decreased in number more and more as time went on', while the E Chronicle admits that the king's own army seemed 'quite the best force there ever was'. By the time the two sides reached London – their camps separated by the River Thames – it must have been obvious that Godwine was going to have to accept fairly humiliating terms.

Only when these terms were delivered, however, was the full extent of Edward's wrath revealed. According to the author of the *Life* – a seemingly well-informed source at this point – the earl was told he could have the king's peace 'when he gave him back his brother alive'. On hearing these words, the same text continues, Godwine pushed away the table in front of him, mounted his horse and rode hard for his manor of Bosham on the Sussex coast. From there he took ship for Flanders (where else?), taking with him his wife, and his sons Swein and Tostig. Two other sons, Harold and Leofwine, had already fled west and sailed to exile in Ireland. That left the earl's daughter, Queen Edith, as the only Godwine remaining in England, and Edward immediately banished her to a nunnery.

'If any Englishman had been told that these events would take this turn he would have been amazed', said the author of the D Chronicle. 'Godwine had risen to such great eminence as if he ruled the king and all England.' And now he was gone.[36]

It is worth pausing at the point of Edward's triumph to consider some of its implications. In the first place, there can be little doubt that this episode reveals the full extent of his hatred for Godwine. The *Life of King Edward* strives throughout to make Robert of

Jumièges the villain of the piece, but it is clear even from this partisan account that it was the king himself who was for once making the running. The author's decision to include (and, more-over, not to deny) the damaging accusation about Alfred's murder suggests that this really did lie at the heart of the matter, and rein-forces the belief that Edward had never truly forgiven the earl for his part in that terrible crime.

Equally revealing is Edward's treatment of his queen. The decision to send Edith to a nunnery suggests that there was little in the way of genuine affection in their marriage, at least on Edward's part. When she later commissioned the *Life*, Edith tried to put the best possible gloss on these events, suggesting that she was sent her to childhood home at Wilton, merely to wait until the storm had passed. But the Anglo-Saxon Chronicle, far more credibly, says that the queen was taken to the nunnery at Wherwell in Hampshire, where one of Edward's elder half-sisters was the abbess. Edith, through the *Life*, also reveals in passing that there was a plan to divorce her, though she insists that it was Archbishop Robert's idea and says that Edward himself suspended the proceedings.[37]

Some modern historians have seized on the mention of a divorce as proof that the marriage itself was not celibate, arguing that it shows a king preparing to remarry in the hope of siring children.[38] The problem with this, of course, is that it requires us to discount the Norman sources which assure us that Edward had promised the throne to William earlier in the same year. And the suggestion that the king did make this promise is reinforced at precisely this moment, in one of our English sources. Having described Edith's banishment, the D Chronicle immediately adds:

> then soon came Duke William from beyond the sea with a great retinue of Frenchmen, and the king received him and as many of his companions as it pleased him, and let him go again.

This single sentence has caused a great deal of controversy: it occurs only in the D version of the Chronicle, and in the 1950s one eminent scholar suggested that it was not part of the original text at all but a later interpolation. Aside from the obvious objection (why would a later copyist bother to introduce such a short and ambiguous state-ment?), there are good grounds for rejecting this conspiracy theory and accepting the testimony of this evidence at face value. The D Chronicle, once dismissed as a late source written in the faraway north of England, is now considered to have been compiled at the instance of Ealdred, bishop of Worcester, a figure often present at Edward's court and, indeed, a player in the dramatic events of 1051. As such we can be fully confident that what it says is true: soon after the banishment of the Godwines, William of Normandy crossed the Channel to visit the king of England.[39]

The reasonable supposition is that this visit was in some way connected with the claim to the throne: with Godwine gone, Edward would have finally been in a position to welcome William and perhaps to confirm in person the offer made by proxy earlier in the year. Of course, the D Chronicle says nothing about the business of the succession; all it tells us, apparently, is that the king received his kinsman and let him go again. The problem is that the meaning of the word 'received' has been lost in translation. The original Old English word used by the chronicler is *underfeng*, and a comparison of its use in other texts shows that it clearly means 'received *as a vassal*'. Thus, when the Chronicle says that Edward received William 'and as many of his companions as it pleased him', it does not mean that certain unlucky members of the duke's entourage were left standing outside in the autumn cold. Rather, it means that William and some of those with him did homage to the English king, swearing to serve him faithfully and acknowledging him as their lord.

This brief statement in the D Chronicle is therefore doubly valuable. Not only does it tell us that the duke of Normandy crossed to England in the immediate aftermath of the crisis, thus reinforcing the belief that Edward had promised him the throne, it also reveals the king's side of the bargain. Grateful as he may have been for the support of William's family during his long years of exile, and affectionate as he clearly was towards his Norman friends and advisers, Edward is unlikely to have dropped so substantial a cherry into his kinsman's lap without demanding something in return. What the king wanted, we may surmise, was a guarantee of the duke's loyalty – a guarantee all the more urgent given William's recent marriage to the daughter of England's long-standing enemy, the count of Flanders. Edward can never have liked the idea of such an alliance, and he must have liked it even less after Godwine had fled to

Flanders that autumn. Now, more than ever, it was imperative to bind William and Normandy to England. And so the duke was invited to visit the king in person, not merely to become his heir, but to kneel before him, and become his man.[40]

By the end of the momentous year 1051, therefore, Edward's plan had succeeded brilliantly. His friend Robert of Jumièges was in place as archbishop of Canterbury, his kinsman William of Normandy had been bound firmly to an alliance with England and, most importantly and dramatically, his hated father-in-law, Earl Godwine, was gone. The king was not so foolish as to suppose that the earl, whose rise had been in large part predicated on his skill in war, would take his losses lying down. Sooner or later the exile would try to fight his way back. For this reason Edward took immediate steps to safeguard his victory, rewarding others with the Godwine family's confiscated lands and titles. It seems likely, for example, that his two principal allies, Leofric of Mercia and Siward of Northumbria, saw the extent of their domains expanded with portions of the earldoms of Godwine's sons. Certainly Leofric's eldest son, Ælfgar, was given the earldom of East Anglia vacated by Godwine's son Harold. At the same time, the western half of Godwine's own earldom of Wessex, along with the title of earl, were given to Odda, one of the king's greatest thegns and probably also a kinsman. ('A good man, pure and very noble', says the D Chronicle, providing a rare character note.) In addition, Edward could count on the support of his nephew, Ralph (the son of his sister, Godgifu), who had been given the earldom left empty by the murder of Godwine's nephew, Beorn Estrithson, in 1049. All these men had a vested interest in keeping the Godwines out.[41]

But, in spite of his careful preparations against a counter-revolution, the king had made one major miscalculation. In March 1051, during the same council in which he had appointed the new archbishop of Canterbury and almost certainly announced his plan for the succession, Edward had also instituted a tax break. As the D Chronicle explains, it was at this moment that the king had done away with the geld – the tax his father, Æthelred, had introduced thirty-nine years earlier in order to pay for England's mercenary fleet. If the move was calculated to increase the king's popularity, it was seemingly effective. 'This tax vexed the English nation for all the aforesaid time', continues the D Chronicle. 'It always had priority over other taxes that were paid in various ways, and was the most generally oppressive.' This, of course, had been especially true in the time of Edward's immediate predecessor, Harthacnut, whose demand for a geld of almost four times the usual size appears to have cost him his kingship. It is, indeed, entirely likely that the pledge of good governance extracted from Edward on his return in 1041 could have contained a specific promise to reduce the level or incidence of geld in the future.[42]

Of course, abolishing the geld also meant abolishing the mercenary fleet, but this too may have been considered a desirable outcome. Edward and others around him probably disliked the ongoing presence of a mercenary force in their midst. Historically, at least, the fleet had been crewed by men of Scandinavian extraction, and if that remained the case in 1051 they would have been viewed warily by a king who had spent the past decade banishing Scandinavian sympathizers. Moreover, there is a possible connection between the fleet and Earl Godwine, in that the earl's nephew, Beorn Estrithson, may have been its captain. Certainly, soon after Beorn's murder in 1049, the king paid off nine of the fleet's fourteen ships, and gave the five remaining crews a year's notice. By the time he abolished the geld in 1051, the entire force had been disbanded.[43]

Edward and his advisers must have believed that they could manage perfectly well by relying on the established royal right to raise an army (or a navy – the sources make little distinction) on demand as the need arose. According to the Anglo-Saxon Chronicle, in 1008 Æthelred the Unready had demanded a helmet and coat of mail from every eight hides of land in England – a demand which, given that the kingdom contained some 80,000 hides, suggests an army of around 10,000 men. Similarly, we know from the Domesday Book that in Edward's own day the rule in Berkshire was for every five hides of land to supply and subsidize one soldier for a two-month period – a system which, if applied across the whole kingdom, would have produced a 16,000-man host.[44] Thus when in the spring of 1052 the king and his counsellors got wind that Godwine was preparing to invade, a fleet was raised by just such conventional means and assembled at Sandwich. The C Chronicle tells us that it was formed of forty small vessels, and the E Chronicle adds that it was captained by two of Edward's new earls, Ralph and Odda.

When, after a lengthy wait, Godwine sailed at midsummer, it seemed as if the king's ships might be a sufficient deterrent. Although the earl slipped past Sandwich and made a landing further along the Kent coast, he was pursued by Ralph and Odda and forced to keep moving. A storm in the Channel subsequently caused Godwine to sail back to Flanders and the king's fleet to return to Sandwich.

Not long afterwards, however, the disadvantages of relying on a non-professional navy became apparent. As the E Chronicle explains, the king's ships were ordered back to London to receive new crews and captains, but long delays meant that 'the fleet did not move, and they all went home'.

This dispersal of the royal forces gave Godwine his chance. Again he set sail for England, this time harrying the Isle of Wight and linking arms with his sons Harold and Leofwine, who had raised a fleet of their own from Ireland. Probably towards the end of August, their combined armada sailed east along the coasts of Sussex and Kent, seizing provisions, ships and hostages, and recruiting more and more men to their banner. By the time they reached Sandwich, they had, according to the C Chronicler, 'an overwhelming host'. 'The sea was covered with ships', says the *Life of King Edward*. 'The sky glittered with the press of weapons.'

Had there still been a royal navy stationed in Sandwich, the Godwines could hardly have achieved such success. But Edward, although aware of his enemies' return, was struggling to assemble a force with which to oppose them. 'He sent up country for reinforcements', says the C Chronicle, 'but they were very slow in coming.'

And so Godwine and his sons were able to sail their fleet unopposed along the north Kent coast and up the River Thames. On Monday 14 September they reached London and stationed themselves at Southwark on the river's southern bank. By this time the king had succeeded in assembling a fleet of fifty ships and also a large army. The Godwines sent a message to him, demanding the restoration of their lands and titles. Edward sent back an angry refusal. It was, in short, an almost exact replay of the previous autumn, with the two sides once again separated by the River Thames, each waiting for the other to blink.

But this time round the advantage clearly lay with Godwine. During his absence public opinion seems to have swung behind him, possibly because Englishmen were against the idea of a Norman succession; certainly all versions of the Anglo-Saxon Chronicle are at this point laced with ill-disguised hostility towards the king's Norman advisers. The *Life of King Edward* says that reinforcements were swelling the earl's ranks from all directions, while the Chronicle informs us that the citizens of London were also quick to fall in with his wishes. It seems obvious that, as the *Life* claims, the military superiority lay with Godwine, and that no one was prepared to risk a civil war by fighting for Edward. The earl had stopped at Southwark that Monday morning at low tide, but all day long the tide had been rising in his favour. When it reached its peak his fleet raised anchor and swung across the river to encircle the king's ships on the opposite bank. Godwine's supporters reportedly had to be restrained from attacking the royal forces. Negotiations followed, and an exchange of hostages, but everyone realized that this was now checkmate.

The king's Norman friends certainly realized it, and responded by mounting their horses and fleeing. Some went north, says the Chronicle, and others rode west. Robert of Jumièges and his companions forced their way out of London's east gate, slaying those who tried to stop them, and hastening all the way to the headland in Essex known as the Naze. There the archbishop committed himself to a boat that was barely seaworthy and risked a dangerous voyage across the Channel to Normandy. The E version of the Chronicle, pro-Godwine in its sympathies, was pleased to note that in his haste Robert left behind his pallium, and opined that this proved that God had not wanted him to be archbishop in the first place.

The next morning a council met outside of London, and the revolution of the previous year was formally reversed. Godwine ostentatiously begged Edward's forgiveness, claiming he and his family were innocent of all the charges brought against them. The king, barely able to contain his fury, had no option but to grant his pardon and restore to the earl and his sons their confiscated estates. The council ratified the complete friendship between them, says the C Chronicle, and made a promise of good laws to the whole nation. Archbishop Robert was declared an outlaw, adds the E Chronicle, together with all the Frenchmen, 'for they had mainly been responsible for the discord that had arisen between Godwine and the king'. A short time later, concludes the *Life of King Edward*, now that the storm had finally subsided, 'the queen, the earl's daughter, was brought back to the king's bedchamber'.[45]

It was now abundantly clear that there was not going to be a Norman succession. Robert of Jumièges, once he recovered from his perilous crossing of the Channel, was probably the first to relate to the duke of Normandy the terrible turn that events in England had taken.

But by the time the archbishop arrived in Normandy that autumn, events in England were the least of William's worries.

5

Holy Warriors

L ike Edward the Confessor, William of Normandy had begun
the year 1052 with a sense of triumph, having successfully
bested a fearsome opponent.

The man in question was Geoffrey Martel, count of Anjou. Son
of the notorious Fulk Nerra, whose skills as a warlord and castle-
builder had transformed Anjou into one of France's great principalities,
Geoffrey was a figure cast very much in his father's mould. His
surname, which translates as 'the Hammer', was later said to be self-
awarded, and signified his belief that he could beat anyone into
submission. 'A man of overweening pride', confirmed the contemporary William of Poitiers, but also a man 'remarkably skilled and
experienced in the art of war'.[1]

Even before he succeeded his father in 1040, Geoffrey had been
pursuing the same policy of ruthless expansion, capturing his
neighbours in battle and detaining them until they agreed to
his extortionate demands: both the count of Poitou to the south
and the count of Blois–Chartres to the east had suffered in this
way and been forced to cede territory. But when in 1047 Geoffrey
moved northwards into Maine and seized and imprisoned the
bishop of Le Mans, his other neighbours eventually decided that
something had to be done. Two years later, the king of France
summoned a coalition army of other French rulers and led a punitive invasion of Anjou. The duke of Normandy, being heavily in
the king's debt since the battle of Val-ès-Dunes, naturally rode by
his sovereign's side.[2]

But despite the invasion, and excommunication by the pope,

Geoffrey continued to grow stronger. He refused to relinquish his grip on the bishop of Le Mans in the hope of extending his power northwards, and in 1051 that ambition was realized. In March that year the young count of Maine died, and the citizens of Le Mans invited Geoffrey to come and take over the whole county.[3]

This was ominous news for Normandy, for Maine had been a buffer with Anjou. From March 1051 the expansion of Anjou menaced Normandy directly, and indeed it was probably soon after that date that Geoffrey invaded the duchy, seizing the town of Alençon.[4] No doubt he considered this justifiable revenge for William's participation in the earlier invasion of Anjou, but the doubly distressing fact for the duke was that here too the invader had come by invitation. The lords of Alençon, who took their name from nearby Bellême, held lands that straddled the border between Maine and Normandy, and, like border families everywhere, they tended to wear their loyalties lightly as a result. After Geoffrey had advanced into Maine they evidently decided that he, not William, was their preferred overlord, and threw open the gates of Alençon in welcome.

William responded forcefully, but indirectly, laying siege to the Bellême stronghold of Domfront, a fortified town some thirty-five miles to the west of Alençon but on the Maine side of the border. A short while later Count Geoffrey advanced with an army towards Domfront, intending to raise the siege, but withdrew on hearing that William was advancing to meet him with an army of his own (a fact that William of Poitiers naturally made much of). With his men up in arms and the way ahead suddenly clear, the duke proceeded towards his own town of Alençon, which fell very quickly: 'almost without a battle', says William of Poitiers.

Poitiers is in fact being rather coy. A fuller version of the encounter given by William of Jumièges reveals that the duke rode through the night to reach Alençon, but on his arrival was confronted by the defenders of a fortress, set apart from the town itself, who mocked him with insults. Orderic Vitalis, adding to Jumièges' account, explains that the men inside the fortress beat animal skins and shouted 'pelterer' at William – the joke apparently being that his mother's family, as undertakers, had also worked with skins. Suffice to say, the duke was unamused. In short order the fort was attacked and its defenders captured. Then, 'under the eyes of all the inhabitants of

Alençon', William ordered his mockers maimed. Thirty-two men, says Orderic, had their hands and feet cut off. It was a spectacle sufficiently horrifying that the citizens of Alençon immediately surrendered, fearing that they would receive similar treatment if they held out any longer. Nor was it just Alençon. When news of the duke's actions reached Domfront, the defenders there also decided that submission would be the wisest course of action.

Thus, by a calculated act of brutality which provides us with an early character note, William swiftly regained one town and acquired another into the bargain. 'The victor returned home and made his whole native land famous by his recent glory and triumph,' says William of Poitiers, resuming his airbrushed panegyric, 'at the same time inspiring even great love and terror everywhere.'[5]

It is likely that the siege of Alençon was over before the end of 1051, leaving William free to cross the Channel and visit Edward the Confessor before the year was out. But, like Edward, William soon discovered how quickly fortune's wheel could turn. A few months after his victory, the duke made the alarming discovery that the king of France and Geoffrey Martel had sunk their differences and forged a new alliance. The first we hear of it – and perhaps the first William knew of it – is a charter of August 1052, which shows Geoffrey keeping company with the king at Orleans.

What had driven the former enemies into each other's arms, it is clear, was their shared anxiety about Normandy. No longer was William a desperate teenager who needed to be saved from his own subjects. On the contrary, he was a rising star, with a burgeoning reputation in arms and a marriage that allied him to the count of Flanders. But, most of all, he was now the recognized heir to the kingdom of England. If he succeeded to the English throne, he would become the most powerful figure in France, able to deploy England's vast wealth and resources in any future Continental struggles. This, one suspects, was the development that drew Anjou and France together.

William, for his part, immediately realized the implications of the rapprochement. The friendship between France and Normandy, assiduously cultivated by his ancestors and maintained in his own time, was over. In September 1052, just weeks after the visit of Count Geoffrey, we find William himself at Henry I's court. Doubtless he tried hard to dissuade his overlord from this change of heart, but evidently without success, for this is the last occasion we find the two men in each other's company. 'King Henry conceived a cruel enmity towards him,' says William of Poitiers, 'persuaded by the eloquence of evil men.'[6]

It was not long before enmity became open hostility. Henry's first move was to sponsor a rebellion within Normandy itself, led by a senior member of William's own family. The count of Arques – yet another William, unhelpfully – was the duke's half-uncle, a son of Richard II by a second marriage. During the minority he had been pre-eminent among ducal counsellors, and had been rewarded with vast estates in Upper Normandy. But thereafter, for reasons unknown, he had become disaffected: William of Poitiers reports that he deserted from the siege of Domfront, and that as a result the castle he had built at Arques (near Dieppe) had been confiscated.[7]

It was by retaking Arques that the count signalled the start of his rebellion. At some point, probably in the first half of 1053, he bribed the ducal garrison, re-entered the castle and began plundering the surrounding countryside to stock it for war. William, warned that almost the whole of Upper Normandy was in revolt against him, responded swiftly and succeeded in forcing the count to retreat inside the castle walls. The fortress itself, however, could not be easily recaptured. 'A rampart of pride and folly', as William of Poitiers described it, Arques was probably the mightiest castle in all of Normandy. The duke's only option was to build a siege castle to confine the rebels, with the hope of eventually starving them into submission.[8]

King Henry entered the fray in the autumn of 1053, leading an army into Normandy with the intention of raising the siege. Norman chroniclers report with satisfaction how some of his forces were lured into a trap by the garrison of the siege castle, with the result that many French knights were killed or captured, a disaster that apparently decided the king to retreat. Nevertheless, the same chroniclers admit that in spite of their losses the French succeeded in getting additional men and supplies into Arques. Not until William returned to prosecute the siege in person did the castle finally surrender, probably towards the end of the year.[9]

There was little time, however, to celebrate its fall, because soon into the new year (1054) the king of France returned. Anxious to avenge his earlier humiliation, Henry had assembled a great army, a coalition of the kind he had earlier directed against the count of Anjou. Except now, of course, it was Count Geoffrey who rode at the king's side, along with the counts of Aquitaine and Blois, while the duke of Normandy had become the target. Julius Caesar himself, says William of Poitiers, who loved a classical reference, would have been terrified of such a mighty host.[10]

Sadly, our accounts of the action that followed are extremely scant. From what little the chroniclers do tell us, we can see that the French had decided on a two-pronged invasion: one army, led by Henry's brother, Odo, was to advance into north-eastern Normandy, while another, led by the king himself, would enter from the south-east. The intention may have been for the two forces to converge on the Norman capital at Rouen.[11]

We can also see that the tactics that Henry employed were entirely typical. Medieval commanders, contrary to popular belief, rarely went in search of battle. Only when their very survival was at stake (as William's had been in 1047) would they take such a colossal risk. Normally (as William's more usual resort to siege-craft suggests) they relied on attrition. Invading armies did not have supply lines stretching back to base; they lived off the land, seizing supplies from the inhabitants as they advanced. Inevitably this meant that many of those inhabitants were killed, but there was no law against that. On the contrary, harming non-combatants was an integral part of warfare, for it exposed the weakness of the enemy's lordship, and showed that his protection was not worth having. Thus William of Poitiers, commenting on the French strategy in 1054, said that the people of Normandy 'feared for themselves, their wives, their children and their goods'. The French intention, he added, was to reduce the duchy to a desert.

Faced with such a prospect, yet anxious to avoid battle, what could a conscientious defender do? Poitiers, predictably, gives the impression that William set out in 1054 to confront his enemies head-on, but the reality was probably different. According to William of Jumièges, the duke, 'accompanied by some of his men, shadowed the king, and inflicted punishment on any member of the royal army whom he was able to catch'. By staying close to Henry's army, William could prevent it from spreading out, limiting the amount of damage it could do and – crucially – the amount of food it could collect. Denied the opportunity to ravage and forage, the invaders would soon be forced to retreat.[12]

It was the need to keep themselves fed, and the failure to realize that they were being followed, that cost the invaders the campaign. While William shadowed Henry's own forces through south-eastern Normandy, another group of Normans had been dispatched to meet the king's northern army. According to Jumièges, they found their opponents near the town of Mortemer, just across the border, 'engaged in arson and the shameful sport of women' – in other words, exactly the kind of ravaging operation that would have left them dangerously exposed. Seizing the opportunity, the Normans surprised their enemies by attacking at dawn. The battle that followed was clearly hard-fought – the bloodshed reportedly lasted until noon – but the attackers' advantage proved decisive. 'At length', says Jumièges, 'the defeated French took to flight, including their standard-bearer, Odo, the king's brother.' William of Poitiers adds that a great many were captured as they fled.

Defeat at Mortemer spelt the end of the French invasion. When news of the Norman victory reached Duke William later that night, he immediately dispatched a herald to Henry's camp, who shouted the details into the darkness from the top of a nearby tree. 'Stunned by the unexpected news,' says William of Poitiers, 'the king put aside all thought of delay and roused his men to flight before dawn, convinced of the need to escape Norman territory with the utmost speed.'[13]

And so the invasion crisis of 1053–4 drew to a close. Not long afterwards William and Henry formally made peace: in return for the release of the prisoners taken at Mortemer, explains William of Poitiers, the king recognized the duke's right to retain any territory he had taken from Geoffrey Martel, and any further lands he might wrest from him in the future. In other words, William had effectively compelled Henry to abandon his alliance with Anjou, and ensured that any future fighting would be concentrated on a single, southern frontier.[14]

It remained for William to deal with those Normans who had supported the French invasion. The chief rebel, of course, was the count of Arques, who surrendered his giant castle and went into exile, where he would remain for the rest of his life. His fall, and the similar fate of those who had supported him, handed William a welcome opportunity to impose his authority more firmly on Upper Normandy, awarding lands confiscated from rebels to those who had proved their loyalty, and almost certainly obtaining in return more precise professions of dependency and service.[15]

The other outstanding casualty of the failed revolt was the count's brother, Mauger. Precisely how involved he had been is impossible to say: later chroniclers took his complicity for granted, but contemporaries were altogether less committal.[16] The reason for their caginess probably owed much to the fact that Mauger, as well as being the duke's half-uncle, also happened to be the archbishop of Rouen (he had succeeded William's great-uncle, Robert, after the latter's death in 1037). As the most senior churchman in Normandy, Mauger could not be dismissed in the same summary manner as his brother; in order to secure his removal in the spring of 1054 William had to go to the trouble of convening a special Church council. From William of Poitiers' account, the case against the archbishop was constructed entirely on the grounds of his unfitness for office, and the charges were fairly obviously trumped-up. Nevertheless, Mauger was in due course deposed and sent to live out his remaining days on the island of Guernsey. In truth he was probably no worse a churchman than any of his episcopal colleagues. It was simply his misfortune to have been implicated in his brother's rebellion, and to have been the head of a Church which in his lifetime had experienced revolutionary change.[17]

The Normans had arrived in Normandy as destroyers of churches – marauding Vikings, pirates in search of treasure, they had fallen like wolves upon the province's undefended cathedrals and monasteries, massacring their occupants and making off with their sacred objects of silver and gold. Very little in the way of institutional Christianity can have survived this initial onslaught. In the case of the monasteries it seems likely that none survived at all, except in a few instances where the monks stole a march on the invaders, fleeing into neighbouring regions to preserve their communal existence in exile.

Quite soon, of course, the Normans had settled down to a more peaceful way of life, and their leaders, anxious to adapt to the norms of the host society, had converted. Within a few decades of their arrival, the dukes of Normandy had re-established some of the monasteries their ancestors had ruined, tempting back their former residents with promises of protection and restituted riches. But progress during these early generations was painfully slow. By the turn of the first millennium, only four monastic houses had been re-founded, while as late as 1025 the bishop of Coutances was still living as an exile in Rouen, he and his predecessors having all but abandoned their diocese in western Normandy to the rule of the heathen.[18]

Matters began to improve soon after the millennium when Duke Richard II, having re-founded the monastery in the coastal town of Fécamp, invited the celebrated monastic reformer William of Volpiano to act as its new abbot. Father William had established a reputation as the man to whom the powerful turned when they were serious about their pious investments. Born in northern Italy, he had trained at the abbey of Cluny in Burgundy, itself the birth-place in the early tenth century of a movement that aspired to reform not just monasticism but Christian society as a whole. At first he reportedly rejected Duke Richard's offer, declaring that Normandy was too barbarous even for his considerable talents. But at length he was persuaded, and under his direction Fécamp became the model for all other Norman monasteries, as well as a training ground for priests who would reintroduce Christianity to the world beyond the cloister.[19]

During the rule of Richard's son, Robert, reform initially stalled and went into reverse, as the new duke and his aristocracy preyed upon the Church for land with which to reward their knights. Robert in due course repented, restoring his usurpations and founding two new monasteries of his own at Cerisy and Montivilliers. Moreover, for the first time, the duke's example was followed by certain Norman aristocrats, a handful of whom also established new religious houses during the final years of his rule. But this nascent trend was arrested after Robert's death in 1035 and the accession of his underage son. William's troubled minority saw no new founda-tions, ducal or private, and the fortunes of existing houses threatened by the eruption of violent aristocratic feuds.[20]

It was in the worst throes of this convulsion, however, against all odds and expectations, that the most influential of all new Norman monasteries was nurtured into existence. Its story began in the early

1030s when Herluin, a knight in the service of Count Gilbert of Brionne, grew tired of the pursuit of arms and fixed his mind on higher matters. Much to the amusement and derision of his military companions, the thirtysomething nobleman prayed and fasted, dressed in cheap clothes, let his hair and beard grow long and gave up his horse for an ass. At length his lord gave him leave to follow his new vocation, but Herluin failed to find solace in any of Normandy's existing religious houses. And so, in 1034, he established a community of his own on his estate at Bonneville-Aptot. Around five years later, it migrated a few miles to a more suitable site beside the River Risle called Le Bec. Today, appropriately, it is known as Le Bec-Hellouin.[21]

Herluin's humble establishment would have doubtless remained just that, had it not been for the unexpected arrival of Lanfranc. A scholar of international distinction, Italian by birth, Lanfranc had come to Normandy several years earlier to teach the liberal arts, but he too had grown disenchanted with his lot and increasingly religious. In or around 1042 he entered Bec as a monk in search of a simpler existence. It was not long, however, before the great scholar began once again to take on students, who began to arrive in droves from every corner of France and eventually beyond. By the end of the 1040s, with Herluin as abbot and Lanfranc as prior, Bec had become the most celebrated centre of learning not just in Normandy but across the whole of Europe.[22]

It was also by the end of the same decade, if not before, that Lanfranc had become spiritual mentor to the young Duke William. The first evidence of their friendship concerns its temporary breakdown around this time, when William, for reasons that remain obscure, destroyed one of Bec's estates and ordered Lanfranc into exile. As the latter was leaving, however, he chanced to encounter the duke on the road, and (thanks to an icebreaker occasioned by Lanfranc's amusingly useless horse) all was forgiven. Thereafter the most famous scholar in Europe became the most trusted of all William's advisers. 'He venerated him as a father, revered him as a master, and loved him as a brother or a son', says William of Poitiers. 'He entrusted to him the direction of his soul, and placed him on a lofty eminence from which he could watch over the clergy throughout the whole of Normandy.'[23]

And, indeed, throughout the whole of Normandy there are clear signs that the end of the duke's minority marked the start of a remarkable religious revival. In terms of the establishment of monasteries, for instance, it was a veritable golden age. William contented himself for the time being with the completion of his father's house at Cerisy, but elsewhere in the duchy his closest followers were establishing brand-new communities. William fitz Osbern, for example, founded one at Lyre, Roger of Montgomery another at Troarn, while the duke's stepfather, Herluin de Conteville, established a new monastery at Grestain. 'At that time the people of Normandy rejoiced in the profound tranquillity of peace and the servants of God were held in high esteem by all', wrote Orderic Vitalis, whose own monastery at St Evroult was established by the Grandmesnil family in October 1050. 'Each of the magnates strove to build churches in their land at their own expense to enrich the monks.' In the period between the battles of Val-ès-Dunes (1047) and Mortemer (1054), the Norman aristocracy founded no fewer than seven new houses, and would create as many again during the decade that followed.[24]

Their actions were not without self-interest. Some of these new aristocratic benefactors had previously been among the worst despoilers of monastic property, and the houses they founded might still be expected to provide benefices for their knights or to assist in the organization of military service. An abbey or a nunnery also advertised its owner's status, and proclaimed his lordship over a particular locality almost as effectively as his castle. As the number of monasteries multiplied, so too did the competition between magnates to be seen as the most magnanimous. Nevertheless, even when all these considerations are taken into account, there can be little doubt that piety was the major factor behind most if not all new foundations. It was, after all, in his own monastery that a lord would eventually be buried, and here that the monks, in gratitude for his munificence, would say prayers for his soul in perpetuity.[25]

These monasteries were also new in another sense, in that they were built in a wholly novel architectural style. Prior to this point, the churches of Normandy had been constructed in the fashion that had prevailed across Europe since the fall of Rome, their walls simply flat expanses, devoid of decoration unless it was added in the form of paintings or tapestries. But in the second quarter of the eleventh century, thanks to the bigger budgets of patrons and the superior skills of masons, the surfaces of such buildings suddenly burst into three dimensions, their designers alternately adding and subtracting depth with shafts, arches, niches and galleries. It was a revival of the kind of sophisticated, monumental and above all orderly architecture that had ended with Rome, a fact which led historians of the early twentieth century to dub it 'Romanesque'. Having first appeared in neighbouring Anjou in the 1020s, it was adopted with enthusiasm by the Normans in the decades that followed. One of its earliest and best-surviving examples is the abbey church at Jumièges, rebuilt from 1040 on the orders of Abbot Robert, shortly before he embarked for his tumultuous career in England at the side of Edward the Confessor.[26]

Quite how much the wider Church was affected by these developments in the monastic world is difficult to say. Normandy's bishops, for instance, certainly liked the new Romanesque style, and were quick to begin rebuilding their cathedrals on a lavish scale.[27] When it came to some of the other ideas espoused by their cloistered colleagues, however, the secular clergy were less enthusiastic. To be a bishop in the Middle Ages was essentially to be a great administrator, wielding considerable power over people, cities and provinces here on earth. For this reason, kings and princes liked to ensure that the men who filled such positions were reliable, and this usually meant they appointed their closest relatives. As we have seen, the archbishopric of Rouen was held during William's minority successively by Robert and Mauger, both of whom were the sons of earlier dukes. Similarly, when it fell to William himself to make new appointments, he too kept it in the family, appointing his cousin Hugh as the new bishop of Lisieux in 1049, and a short time later awarding the bishopric of Bayeux to his half-brother, Odo.[28]

Being drawn from the highest level of society meant that medieval bishops were generally loath to forsake the luxurious lifestyle in which they had been raised – even if it occasionally meant selling a Church appointment to the highest bidder, or divesting their cathedral of some of its excess property. They were also usually unwilling to give up other pleasures enjoyed by their non-clerical relatives: like the majority of the parish priests under their jurisdiction, many bishops had wives or mistresses, which naturally meant that many of them also had children.[29] To monastic reformers, these were matters of the highest concern. The selling of ecclesiastical offices (simony) obviously meant that Church positions frequently went to unsuitable candidates, as did the existence of married clergy if they insisted on promoting their offspring. But while the selection of senior churchmen remained in the hands of kings, dukes and princes, there was little hope that the reformers' denunciation of such practices would have any real effect.

It came as a shock to everyone, therefore, when the reformers suddenly took over the Church at the very top. For centuries the papacy had been a distant irrelevance to all but the ruling dynasties of Rome itself, who preferred to have one of their own on the throne of St Peter. But the picture changed dramatically in 1048 when the German emperor, Henry III, appointed his kinsman Leo IX as the new supreme pontiff. Both men were champions of reform, and Leo immediately set about enforcing its ideals, demanding that the clergy should be celibate and dismissing any bishops who had bought their offices. In 1049, only ten months into his pontificate, he visited France – the first pope to do so in 171 years – and held his celebrated council at Rheims, denouncing any attendees who failed to meet his exacting standards and excommunicating those who stayed away.[30]

Those members of the Norman episcopate who obeyed the papal summons, like their colleagues from other parts of France, were tested and found wanting. The bishop of Séez was condemned for having accidentally burnt down his cathedral during a military operation; the bishop of Coutances, who had obtained his position earlier in the year by purchase (presumably from Duke William), escaped dismissal only by swearing that his family had forced him into accepting the job. As for the duke himself, this was of course the occasion when the pope forbade his planned marriage to Matilda of Flanders. One can only imagine what Leo would have made of William's decision to fill the bishopric of Bayeux with his half-brother, Odo, barely out of his teens and allegedly 'devoted to the delights of the flesh'. As it was, Odo appears to have been appointed shortly after the council had ended.[31]

Even a firebrand like Leo, however, could be persuaded to change his mind, provided the sinful showed themselves to be truly repentant. The bishop of Séez accepted his error and promised to build a new cathedral church, to which end he set off across Europe on a fund-raising tour, returning with riches from his relatives in Italy as well as a relic of the Holy Cross from Byzantium. One suspects that the bishop of Coutances, who also immediately embarked on the rebuilding of his cathedral, again after a successful Italian tour, may have done so for similar penitential reasons. Moreover, as we have already seen, the papal prohibition of William's marriage to Matilda was lifted within a matter of months, a reversal that was almost certainly due to the advocacy of Lanfranc. The duke's chief spiritual adviser was probably also present at Rheims, and during most of the year that followed he remained in Leo's entourage, earning the new pope's praise and admiration. During these months Lanfranc must have convinced Leo that great things were afoot in Normandy; that new monasteries were being founded, new priests were being trained, and that its new young duke, despite his regrettable choice of bride, would be a sincere and valuable ally in advancing the work of reform. The pope was duly convinced, and the ban was lifted – probably on condition that the newlyweds should each found a monastery by way of atonement.[32]

Thanks to Lanfranc's efforts, then, and the dynamic response of the duchy's bishops, what could have been a crisis in Normandy's relationship with Rome proved to be a crucial turning point. During the decade that followed the Council of Rheims the signs are that William actively promoted the cause of reform – for example, by convening regular councils of the Church over which he personally presided – and that as a result he came to be regarded as one of the papacy's favourite sons.[33]

Hence, when the duke wanted to remove his half-uncle, the archbishop of Rouen, following the great rebellion that had threatened to end his rule, Leo IX was happy to oblige. Chief among those who heard the case against Mauger in May 1054 was Ermenfrid of Sion, a papal legate dispatched especially for the occasion. As we have noted, the archbishop's record, while hardly outstanding, was not all that bad. He had, for example, convened at least one Church council of his own, the statutes of which had condemned the prevalence of simony in Normandy several years before Leo had done so at the Council of Rheims. Judged by the standards now being demanded by Rome, however, Mauger was inevitably deemed inadequate and deposed. The only problem with removing him in this way was that no Norman nobleman could possibly meet such standards, and so the solution had to be a break with tradition. In place of Mauger, and no doubt at Lanfranc's suggestion, William appointed a monk named Maurilius. A scholar of distinction, a former abbot and sometime recluse, Maurilius was in many respects the reformers' dream candidate – a man so committed to rigorous discipline that monks had previously rebelled against his rule. 'The worthiest of all men for the archbishopric by merit of his birth, person, virtue, and learning', said William of Poitiers, Maurilius effectively placed the Church in Normandy above all criticism, and showed how far the Normans had travelled since the days of their Viking ancestors.[34]

Having sent both rebels and suspected sympathizers into exile, and settled matters with the king of France, William immediately resumed the struggle on his southern border against Geoffrey of Anjou. His aim was now to carry war back into enemy territory, weakening Geoffrey's recently established hold on the intermediate county of Maine. Six weeks after sealing the French peace, William led an army into Maine and began constructing a new castle at Ambrières, some thirteen miles south of Domfront. Geoffrey did all he could to resist this advance, raising a large army of his own and laying siege to the fortress, but ultimately to no avail: the garrison held out, and the count's forces withdrew on learning of William's approach. In the end the local lord of Ambrières decided that the wisest course of action would be to accept the duke of Normandy as his overlord.[35]

Geoffrey, however, was not about to take such losses lying down. Nor, it soon transpired, was the French king prepared to forget his humiliation at the duke of Normandy's hands. By the start of 1057, as a surviving charter shows, the two former allies were once again in each other's company. William must have known about this and probably feared the worst. Possibly it was at this point that he took action against another of his paternal relatives, the count of Mortain, on suspicion of disloyalty. The count's crime was apparently to have advised one of his knights not to leave Normandy, on the grounds that a time of plunder was imminent; when this news reached the duke he packed the count off into exile and handed the lordship of Mortain to his other half-brother, Robert. Orderic Vitalis, our only source for the undated story, clearly thought that the charges against the count were flimsy, but William would have had good reason to be suspicious if these rumours reached his ears in the spring of 1057. Mortain lies just fourteen miles from Domfront, close to the area that he and Geoffrey Martel were contesting. Perhaps the count of Mortain really had known what was coming.[36]

For in August 1057 Normandy was again invaded by Count Geoffrey in alliance with King Henry of France. William of Poitiers' comment that their combined army was not quite as large as before has led some modern historians to downplay this invasion; but the rest of the chronicler's description suggests that the result was, if anything, more serious. Previously they had barely crossed the border before being defeated, but now, having entered Normandy from the south, they burned their way far into the interior – ravaging William's land, as Poitiers puts it, 'as far as the seashore by fire and sword'. Moreover, on this occasion, the skill in reconnaissance that had served William so well in the past seems temporarily to have failed him, to judge from Poitiers' remark that the invaders kept their movements as secret as possible.[37]

At last, however, William caught up with his enemies on the north coast of Normandy, at the mouth of the River Dives. Poitiers says that the duke had only a small number of men with him, which suggests that once again he was shadowing his opponents, hoping for an opportunity of some kind. And, at that very moment, an opportunity presented itself. Henry and Geoffrey had forded the Dives at a place called Varaville, presumably intending to continue their path of destruction towards Caen and Bayeux. But while their troops were crossing the river the tide had begun to rise, leaving their army divided, and thus handing William an unmissable advantage. The duke and his small force, says Poitiers, fell upon the stranded rearguard, cutting them down under the eyes of the king and the count who could only watch, powerless, from the opposite bank. Some were captured, says William of Jumièges, but the impression is that many more were killed. 'Fearful and distressed at the death of his men' says Poitiers, 'the king, with the Angevin tyrant, left the bounds of Normandy with all possible speed.' As both chroniclers noted, it was a signal victory, for the king of France never again dared to invade William's duchy.[38]

The king of England, meanwhile, had discovered he had a long-lost nephew.

6

The Godwinesons

'There was deep joy both at court and in the whole country', says the *Life of King Edward*, describing England in 1052 after the forceful return of Earl Godwine. But despite – or perhaps because of – such assurances, we may suspect that the lot of Edward the Confessor in the autumn of that year was not a happy one. His enemies had been restored to all their former possessions and power – Godwine and his sons to their earldoms, Edith to her estates and her place in the royal bedchamber. His friends, meanwhile, had fled into exile, some returning to Normandy with Archbishop Robert, others riding to Scotland, where they had taken service with a certain Macbeth. By Christmas (at which point England was visited by a particularly devastating storm) the king had some small causes for cheer. Late in the year came the news that Godwine's eldest son, the murderous Earl Swein, had died in Constantinople while returning from a pilgrimage to Jerusalem; his death meant that Edward's kinsman, Odda, who had briefly held Godwine's own earldom of Wessex, could be compensated with a small command in the west Midlands. Similarly Edward's Norman friend, Bishop William of London, who had fled abroad in September, was permitted to return at some point thereafter 'on account of his goodness'.[1] But these concessions serve only to emphasize the essential point that, when it came to control of appointments, and even his choice of friends, the king no longer had the final say. That much is made clear, above all, by the man he was obliged to accept as his new archbishop of Canterbury.

★ ★ ★

According to the *Life of King Edward*, the Confessor was an exceptionally pious individual. 'He lived in the squalor of the world like an angel,' it says at one point, 'and zealously showed how assiduous he was in practising the Christian religion.' Throughout his whole reign, we are told, Edward was wont to converse humbly with monks and abbots; he would meekly and attentively listen to Mass and was generous in his almsgiving, every day feeding the poor and infirm at his court. Elsewhere we are assured that the king had religious visions and performed miraculous cures, touching people to rid them of scrofula, or tuberculosis of the neck ('the King's Evil'). As we have already seen, the *Life* also claims that the Confessor showed his dedication to God by living a life of chastity.[2]

The *Life* further illustrates its subject's deep devotion by describing how he re-founded Westminster Abbey. Prior to this point, as the author explains, Westminster had been an insignificant and impoverished community, capable of supporting only a small number of monks. Thanks to Edward's patronage, however, all that changed. The church he built was pulled down and replaced in the mid-thirteenth century, but excavation has shown that following its first rebuilding Westminster was the largest church in the British Isles, and the third largest in Europe. It was built, naturally, in the new Romanesque style that had recently come into fashion in Normandy, with strong similarities in layout and design to the new church at Jumièges. The common link between the two buildings is, of course, Robert of Jumièges, which suggests that construction at Westminster commenced during the first decade of Edward's rule (i.e. before Robert's flight), and probably sooner rather than later: despite its exceptional size, the new abbey was all but complete by the time of the king's death in 1066.[3]

Edward's reasons for building Westminster were probably as mixed as those of any Norman duke or magnate. Piety doubtless played a major part: the *Life* explains that the king was drawn to the abbey because of his particular devotion to St Peter. But at the same time even the *Life* admits that there were other attractions. Westminster is described as a delightful spot, surrounded by green and fertile fields, conveniently close to London and easily accessible by boat, where merchants from all over the world would come to unload their goods. Such considerations were important not just to the monks but to Edward personally, for he also seems to have established a palace at

Westminster, on the site of the present Houses of Parliament. What the king created, in other words, was a royal complex of abbey and palace, much like similar ducal complexes in Normandy, and – crucially – far removed from the existing English equivalent at Winchester. Once the heart of the West Saxon monarchy, Winchester had latterly been claimed by the Danes. It was there that Cnut and Harthacnut were buried, and there that Edward's mother Emma had continued to dwell up to her death in 1052, after which she too was interred in the Old Minster. The Confessor, we may reasonably suppose, did not want to be associated with any of these people, either in this life or the next. As the *Life* explains, the king intended from the first that he would be buried at Westminster.[4]

As for the rest of the *Life*'s evidence for Edward's piety, historians have been understandably sceptical. The *Life* is, after all, the basis for the later legends about the king that ultimately led to his canonization. The same historians will also point out, quite reasonably, that in other places – particularly in the context of Edward's clash with Earl Godwine – it suits the *Life* to describe him in less than saintly terms, depicting him as angry and vengeful. The chief reason for modern scepticism, however, is that the *Life* was commissioned by his queen, Edith, who had her own reasons for wishing to stress her husband's religiosity and in particular his alleged chastity. Although the date that the *Life* was composed continues to be a matter of debate, it was clearly completed after the Norman Conquest. This is significant because had Edith borne Edward an heir, the Conquest itself would not have taken place. If, on the other hand, he had elected never to sleep with her on account of his religious scruples, then Edith herself could scarcely be blamed for the cataclysm that followed.[5]

Against this, however, one may make two related observations. First, if Edward's piety is a construct, it is a massively sustained and elaborate one. Second, although the precise date of the *Life*'s composition is debated, all historians agree that it was written in the period 1065 to 1070 – i.e. when Edward was either still alive or the memory of him still very fresh. As with the claim about his chastity, therefore, so too with his piety in general. Had the *Life*'s picture of a religious king – a saint in all but name – been significantly at odds with reality, it would have been laughed out of court, or perhaps taken to be a mischievous piece of satire.[6]

There is, in fact, other contemporary evidence to support the *Life*'s picture of a genuinely pious Confessor. William of Jumièges, as we've seen, believed the king's peaceful accession in 1042 was divinely ordained, while the Anglo-Saxon Chronicle later imagined his soul being guided to heaven by angels. Less than a decade after Edward's death, William of Normandy (by then the Conqueror) described him in a letter to the abbot of Fécamp as 'the man of blessed memory, my lord and relative King Edward', and had a reliquary of gold and silver made for his remains. Similarly, while we may reasonably doubt whether Edward actually cured anyone simply by touching them, the *Life*'s comment that he began the practice during his youth in Normandy is lent credibility by the fact that the kings of France, supported by monks and abbots, had begun to do so at exactly this time. Lastly, the *Life*'s claim that Edward loved to associate with monks and abbots, particularly foreign ones, is well supported by the evidence. Of the four individuals who are known to have crossed to England with him in 1041, three are churchmen.[7]

From the identities and careers of these individuals we can see that Edward was an active supporter of church reform. Robert of Jumièges had been abbot of a monastery reformed by William of Volpiano.[8] The remaining two, Hermann and Leofric, had both received their training in Lotharingia (Lorraine), a region which, like Burgundy, was a byword for reform.[9] Edward made both of them bishops in the mid-1040s, and they both distinguished themselves by reforming and reorganizing their dioceses (Leofric, for example, moved the seat of his bishopric from Crediton to Exeter). Edward's support for reform is also apparent from his enthusiastic response to the papacy of Leo IX. English representatives were sent to the Council of Rheims in 1049, according to the Anglo-Saxon Chronicle, 'so that they might inform the king of whatever was there decided in the interests of Christendom'. The following year Edward sent two further delegations of bishops to attend Leo's Easter and September councils, and in 1051 Robert of Jumièges set out for Rome to collect his pallium.[10]

But these links with reform and the reform papacy were severed with the return of the Godwines in 1052. It would be going too far to suppose that the earl and his sons were opposed to reform per se. The quarrel between Godwine and Robert of Jumièges, for example, seems to have been primarily political and personal, concerned with Church property rather than Church practice. At the same time, we have clear testimony from the *Life of King Edward* that the Godwines believed that too many bishoprics were going to foreigners, and we also know that when Bishop Hermann sought to transfer his episcopal seat to Malmesbury Abbey, the earl and his sons backed the monks of Malmesbury in resisting the move.[11] Most of all, when Edward's revolution was reversed and Robert of Jumièges had fled, the Godwines ensured that the archbishopric of Canterbury went to Stigand.

Stigand, like Godwine, was a creature of Cnut. Although he was apparently a native of East Anglia, his name is Norse, which suggests that he may have been of mixed Anglo-Danish parentage. He first appears as early as 1020, when Cnut appointed him as minister of his new church at Assandun,★ built to atone for and commemorate the most decisive battle of the Danish conquest. In 1043 Stigand became bishop of East Anglia, a position awarded to him by the newly crowned Confessor, but clearly arranged at the behest of Cnut's widow, Emma, to whom he had evidently remained attached. When Emma fell later that same year, Stigand fell too, but unlike her he quickly recovered his position, and in 1047 he was promoted again, this time to Winchester, the very heart of the Anglo-Danish connection, where Emma continued to dwell. Although there is no direct evidence to connect his rise in this period to the patronage of the Godwines, Stigand acted as go-between during their confrontation with the king in 1051, and reportedly wept when Godwine went into exile.[12]

As his background as a secular priest suggests, Stigand was not a reformer. In September 1052 he became the first non-monk to be made archbishop of Canterbury for almost a century. He was, in addition, guilty of committing what supporters of reform regarded as the most serious of abuses. According to twelfth-century sources, Stigand was notorious for his simony, openly buying and selling bishoprics and abbacies. Certainly he had no problem with pluralism – holding more than one Church appointment at the same time, a practice which was another of the reformers' principal concerns.

★ Either Ashdon or Ashingdon in Essex. Most historians now seem to favour the former.

Having been promoted to Canterbury, Stigand saw no reason to relinquish his grip on Winchester, and continued to hold the two bishoprics in tandem. Naturally, given the circumstances of his promotion in 1052, the new archbishop chose not to follow in the footsteps of his immediate predecessors and travel to Rome to collect his pallium. Instead, he used the one that Robert of Jumièges had left behind.[13]

There can be no doubt, given the past histories and attitudes of all involved, that Stigand was Godwine's appointment in 1052, and no clearer demonstration of the extent to which the counter-revolution had restored the earl to all his former power. If Edward was gloomy that Christmas it was with good reason, for he had been returned to a state of political tutelage of the sort he had experienced at the start of his reign. By the same token, if the king's mood seemed to brighten the following spring, the cause was almost certainly Godwine's sudden death.

As the Anglo-Saxon Chronicle explains, Edward was at Winchester to celebrate Easter, as was Godwine. But as they sat down to dinner on Easter Monday, the earl suddenly collapsed, 'bereft of speech and deprived of all his strength'. Hopes that it was a passing fit proved false; Godwine lingered for three more days in the same enfeebled state before dying on 15 April. This makes it sound as if he suffered a fatal stroke, but according to William of Malmesbury (who loved a good story), the earl choked to death, having first said to Edward: 'May God not permit me to swallow if I have done anything to endanger Alfred or to hurt you.' He was buried in the Old Minster, taking his accustomed place beside Cnut, Harthacnut and Emma.[14]

His father-in-law's death did not make Edward any stronger; the funeral was not followed by the return of any of the king's exiled friends, nor the removal of Stigand, for Godwine was immediately succeeded as earl of Wessex by his eldest surviving son, Harold. Probably around thirty years old in 1053, Harold was apparently everything his father had been and more. 'A true friend of his race and country,' says the *Life of King Edward*, 'he wielded his father's powers even more actively, and walked in his ways of patience and mercy.' Strong in mind and body, kind to men of goodwill but ferocious when dealing with felons, Harold ensured that the Godwine grip on what had once been the royal heartland was sustained. At his appointment to Wessex, says the *Life*, 'the whole English host breathed again and was consoled for its loss'.[15]

But if the king was no stronger, the Godwines as a family were weaker. Prior to his father's death, Harold had been earl of East Anglia, and before taking up the reins in Wessex he was required to surrender his former command. Pluralism might be tolerated in the case of England's most senior churchman but evidently not in the case of its greatest earl. Whether Edward was in any position to insist upon this point is doubtful; one suspects that the law was laid down in council by the kingdom's other leading families. For into the earldom of East Anglia vacated by Harold stepped Ælfgar, son of Earl Leofric of Mercia. Ælfgar, sadly, is one of the many ghosts in this story, whose character passes entirely without comment in contemporary annals. Even his age is unknown: the best we can say is that he was of approximately the same generation as Harold. What we *can* say with some certainty, however, is that he and Harold were rivals. Ælfgar, you may recall, had been earl of East Anglia once before, during the Godwines' short-lived exile, only to be demoted without compensation after their triumphant return. His reappointment in 1053 must therefore have seemed to Ælfgar and his supporters nothing less than his due. Whether Harold and his family saw it in this light is another matter.[16]

The effect of Ælfgar's promotion was to recalibrate English politics. In September 1052 Godwine and his sons seemed set to enjoy a monopoly of power but, barely seven months on, the deaths of Swein and Godwine himself had reduced the number of earldoms under their control from three to one. As the new earl of Wessex, Harold was now the kingdom's most powerful magnate, but his power was checked by the combined weight of Leofric in Mercia and Ælfgar in East Anglia, as well as Earl Siward, who remained in charge in Northumbria. For the first time in a generation, barring the brief exception of 1051–2, there was something approaching a balance of power between England's earls.

Whether this balance handed any initiative back to the king is a moot point.[17] If we consider the most pressing and controversial of all political questions – the succession – then the answer seems to be: probably not. The return of the Godwine family clearly meant that there was little or no chance that the crown would pass peacefully to William of Normandy. Yet even the Godwines, determined as they had been to see Edith honourably restored to her position as queen, must have realized that there was even less likelihood that Edward was going to beget an heir of his own body. An alternative plan therefore had to be found. One option might have been to consider the candidacy of Earl Ralph, the king's nephew, son of his sister Godgifu, but there is no sign that this was ever discussed, or that Ralph ever entertained any hopes in this direction.

Edward, however, had another nephew, descended in the male line, and the son of a former king. The king in question was Edward's elder half-brother, Edmund, by this date if not before remembered as 'Ironside' for his heroic but ultimately unsuccessful struggle against his supplanter, Cnut. Shortly before his death in 1016 Edmund had fathered two sons who had subsequently fallen into Cnut's clutches. According to John of Worcester, the Dane wanted them dead, but to avoid scandal in England sent them to be killed in Sweden. The Swedish king, however, refused to comply, and sent the infants on to Hungary, where they were protected and raised. One of them, named after his father, died in Hungary at an unknown date. But the other, whose name was Edward, survived and prospered. For obvious reasons, historians have dubbed him Edward the Exile.[18]

In 1054 it was decided to find Edward the Exile and bring him to England, evidently to become the kingdom's heir: in the first half of the year Bishop Ealdred of Worcester set out across the Channel to put the plan into action. Precisely whose plan it was, however, is difficult to say. The D version of the Anglo-Saxon Chronicle says that the bishop went overseas 'on the king's business', a statement which carries some weight since the D version was compiled in Ealdred's own circle. At the same time, Ealdred is known to have been a Godwine sympathizer: he had secured Swein's pardon in 1050 and aided Harold's escape in 1051. It is hard to believe that the embassy could have left in the teeth of opposition from either Edward or the Godwines, though fair to point out that raising a powerless exile to the throne had worked very well for the Godwines in the past. Given the balance of power in England, perhaps the most plausible scenario is that both the king and his in-laws agreed to drop their most cherished schemes for the succession in favour of a compromise candidate who enjoyed something like cross-party support.

As it turned out, however, the mission was unsuccessful. Ealdred travelled as far as the imperial city of Cologne, where he was received by the local bishop and the emperor Henry III himself, but that appears to have been the furthest extent of his itinerary. No doubt he looked to Henry's influence to get his message to Hungary, but either the distances were too great or the politics too complicated (Hungary had frequently been in rebellion against imperial rule). Or perhaps Ealdred's offer did reach its intended recipient, only to be greeted with an indifferent response. Edward the Exile, having left England as an infant, can have had little or no memory of his native country, and almost certainly spoke no English. He had grown to manhood in Hungary and married a Hungarian lady named Agatha. To all intents and purposes he was simply an eastern European aristocrat with a curious family history. Whatever the reason, after almost a year abroad, Ealdred returned to England empty-handed.[19]

By the time of his return the country was embroiled in a fresh crisis. The early months of 1055 had brought the death of Siward, the long-serving earl of Northumbria. A warlike man, appointed by Cnut and nicknamed Digri ('the Strong') in Danish, Siward had remained usefully strenuous to the end. One of his chief responsibilities had been to check the ambitions of the kings of Scotland, who had been steadily advancing southwards from their heartlands around the River Tay for over a century. The summer before his death, apparently at Edward's behest, the earl had led a campaign across the border to depose Macbeth (and thereby earned lasting fame: he is Old Siward in Shakespeare's play). The operation was successful but, as in literature, so in life: Siward's eldest son was killed in the fighting, and thus when the earl himself died a few months later there was debate about who should succeed him. Siward had another son, Waltheof, but he was evidently too young – or at least, *deemed* to be too young – to assume such an important strategic command. Instead, the royal council that met in March 1055 decided that the earldom of Northumbria should pass to Tostig, the second surviving son of Earl Godwine.[20]

The *Life of King Edward* is naturally in no doubt about the merits of this appointment. Tostig, it claims, was 'a man of courage, endowed with great wisdom and shrewdness of mind'. Although shorter than Harold, he was in every other respect his older brother's equal: handsome, graceful, brave and strong. 'No age or province', the *Life* concludes, 'has reared two mortals of such worth at the same time.'[21]

But clearly not everyone agreed. The *Life* also explains that Tostig had obtained his new title with the help of his friends, especially Harold and Queen Edith, 'and with no opposition from the king' – an assertion that would seem rather redundant unless the truth lay some way in the opposite direction. At the very least, the *Life* seems to be answering other voices which claimed that Edward had been against promoting yet another Godwineson to high office.

One of those voices almost certainly belonged to Earl Ælfgar, whose recent reappointment to East Anglia had served to restore some equilibrium to English politics. The promotion of Tostig to Northumbria now threatened to upset that equilibrium, and left Ælfgar and his father, Leofric of Mercia, sandwiched between the Godwines to the north and south. It seems very likely that Ælfgar angrily opposed Tostig and his family in the king's council that March, for in the course of the same meeting he was declared an outlaw. The three different versions of the Anglo-Saxon Chronicle offer sharply contrasting (though typically brief) accounts of this incident, reflecting the sympathies of their compilers and the tensions that were threatening to destabilize the kingdom. According to the E Chronicle, written at Canterbury and broadly pro-Godwine, Ælfgar was exiled 'on the charge of being a traitor to the king and the whole country', having accidentally admitted his guilt. But the C Chronicle, written at a monastery in Mercia, insists that the earl 'was outlawed without having done anything to deserve his fate'. Significantly, the D Chronicle, compiled in the circle of Bishop Ealdred and usually careful not to take sides, echoes the sentiment that Ælfgar was essentially innocent.[22]

If the events of the Confessor's reign had proved anything, however, it was that exiles rarely accepted their punishment. Like Harold before him, Ælfgar fled in the first instance to Ireland, where he bolstered his own military household by hiring a fleet of eighteen mercenary ships. From there he sailed back across the Irish Sea in order to seek the assistance of Gruffudd ap Llywelyn, king of the whole of Wales since a bloody victory over his southern rival earlier in the year. Gruffudd had no particular love for the English, nor indeed the family of his visitor: as recently as 1052 he had led a devastating raid across the English border, and at the start of his career in 1039 he had been responsible for the death of Ælfgar's uncle, Eadwine. But like all successful participants in the bear pit that was Welsh politics, Gruffudd knew a golden opportunity when he saw one. He and Ælfgar evidently agreed to sink their differences and join together for an attack on England. In late October 1055, their combined forces crossed the border into Herefordshire, where they defeated the local levies led by Earl Ralph and sacked the city of Hereford. When a larger English army was subsequently assembled against them, the invaders wisely withdrew, leaving its commander, Earl Harold, with nothing to do apart from ringing Hereford's charred remains with an improved set of defences. At length Harold took it upon himself to negotiate and terms were agreed. 'The sentence against Ælfgar was revoked,' says the C Chronicle, 'and he was restored to all his possessions.'[23]

Signs are that this reconciliation was genuine: the following year, when further Welsh victories meant that similarly favourable terms had to be granted to Gruffudd ap Llywelyn, negotiations were led on the English side by Harold and Earl Leofric, Ælfgar's father, working in partnership. Certainly by the summer of 1056 Harold must have felt that affairs in England had been satisfactorily settled, for at some point during the autumn he left for the Continent: a charter drawn up on 13 November shows he was present at the court of the count of Flanders.

Historians have for some time now speculated on the purpose of this trip. One possibility is that we are catching Harold on the outward or return leg of a journey to Rome, for the *Life of King Edward* assures us that at some point the earl made a pilgrimage to the Holy City. Equally he could have been in Flanders simply to visit Count Baldwin – 'that old friend of the English people', as the *Life* calls him on two separate occasions – to whom the Godwines obviously felt a great debt of gratitude for his former hospitality. Any number of scenarios is theoretically possible, so it is not surprising to find that Harold's trip of 1056 has been interpreted in some quarters as a second attempt to secure the return of Edward the Exile. This is really nothing more than an enticing theory, based on join-the-dots reasoning rather than actual evidence. The only certainties are that Harold was on the Continent in the autumn of 1056, and the following spring Edward the Exile arrived in England.[24]

And as soon as he arrived in England he dropped dead. From a variety of sources we can surmise that he died on 17 April 1057, probably in London, and was buried in St Paul's, but no source reveals the manner of his passing. The fact that he died so soon after his return looks suspicious, as does the revelation that he did not even get to meet his namesake uncle. 'We do not know', says the D Chronicle, enigmatically, 'for what reason it was brought about that he was not allowed to visit his kinsman King Edward.' Unsurprisingly this comment has provoked modern writers to reach a variety of opposing conspiracy theories: the Exile was murdered on the orders of Harold, or by agents working for William of Normandy, are among the most popular and least likely scenarios. One author has even suggested that the reason that the two Edwards did not meet was down to the Confessor himself, who still clung to the hope of a Norman succession and therefore refused to meet his prospective replacement. Suffice to say, whether the D Chronicler knew the truth or not, his coyness means that we can never know.[25]

The problem with the conspiracy theories is that, as much as this latest tragedy upset the author of the D Chronicle, it did not end the hope of an English succession, for Edward the Exile and his wife Agatha had produced three children, one of whom was a boy. We do not know whether any of them accompanied their father across the Channel in 1057, but they and their mother had all certainly arrived in England before 1066. The boy, named Edgar, cannot have been more than five years old in 1057, but his credentials for kingship were obviously impeccable. In a book written at Winchester around the year 1060, Edgar is called *clito*, the Latin equivalent of the English 'ætheling', a title conventionally bestowed upon members of the house of Wessex to signify that they were worthy of ascending the throne; according to an early twelfth-century source, Edgar was called ætheling by the Confessor himself.[26] By the end of the 1050s, therefore, and possibly as early as 1057, some people in England, including the ageing king, evidently considered that the problem of the succession had finally been solved.

But the political map of England continued to mutate. The death of Edward the Exile in the spring of 1057 was followed by that of Earl Leofric in the autumn and of Earl Ralph just a few days before Christmas, while the previous year had witnessed the passing of the king's other kinsman, Earl Odda. Once again there was huge change at the top of political society with far-reaching consequences. Ælfgar succeeded his father as earl of Mercia but to do so was obliged to give up the earldom of East Anglia. Ælfgar could hardly have objected to this in principle – after all, Harold had similarly surrendered the eastern shires on inheriting his father's earldom of Wessex – but he must have opposed the decision to award East Anglia to Gyrth, a younger brother of Harold and Tostig, apparently still in his teens. When a short time later the shires of the south-west Midlands that had belonged to Earl Ralph were awarded to yet another Godwine brother, Leofwine, we may reasonably suspect Ælfgar's anger boiled over. Probably he made some sort of defiant protest, for in 1058 he was again sent into exile. The details are almost completely lacking, but apparently what occurred was a rerun of earlier events. 'Earl Ælfgar was banished but soon returned with the help of Gruffudd', says the D Chronicle. 'It is tedious to tell how it all happened.'[27]

Sadly this taciturn attitude infects all three versions of the Chronicle during the next five years: an ominous silence descends as England becomes a one-party state under the Godwines. Between them the four brothers controlled every part of England except Mercia, where the embattled Ælfgar apparently continued to hold out. Recent scholarship has overturned the older notion, based on figures in the Domesday Book, that their combined income exceeded that of the king; revised calculations suggest that, in terms of the size of his estates, Edward probably retained the edge. But in pre-Conquest England, land and lordship were not automatically linked: a landowner could have tenants without necessarily being their lord, and a man could be 'commended' to a lord without necessarily holding any property from him. Edward owned lots of land but his lordship was seemingly lacking. The Godwines, by contrast, had an affinity that was vast, powerful and irresistibly expanding. Harold alone had a following measured in thousands, with scores of thegns commended to serve him in almost every shire.[28]

The Godwines also had powerful allies in the Church. When Archbishop Cynesige of York, appointed by Edward in 1051, went to take his place among the saints in 1060, the altogether more worldly and pro-Godwine Ealdred of Worcester was promoted to take his place, while Worcester itself went to Harold's friend and confidant, Wulfstan. The archbishopric of Canterbury, meanwhile, continued in the grip of Stigand, despite the pall that his appoint-ment had cast over the whole English Church. 'There was no archbishop in the land', commented the C Chronicle pointedly in the year after Stigand's elevation, and throughout the 1050s newly elected English bishops had avoided his taint by going overseas to be consecrated. The archbishop saw a chance to remedy matters in 1058 when an anti-reform party swept to power in Rome and installed the biddable Pope Benedict X, who obligingly sent Stigand a pallium of his very own. But the following year the reformers retook the papacy, denouncing Benedict as an antipope and leaving Stigand looking even more discredited than before. And yet, despite the shame he brought on England, the archbishop's worldly success meant he was unassailable. His annual income of £3,000 made him as rich as a great earl, and he was lord of over 1,000 thegns.[29]

Against this background it is hard to imagine that Edward the Confessor had any real power at all. The appointment in the winter of 1060–1 of two Lotharingian priests to the bishoprics of Hereford and Wells may indicate that the king retained some initiative in this area, but otherwise the impression is that, from the late 1050s, the Godwine brothers were governing the kingdom in his stead. Such is the unabashed admission of the *Life of King Edward*, the purpose of which was largely to justify this state of affairs and the family's unprec-edented accretion of power. Harold and Tostig in particular are depicted as the twin pillars of the realm, thanks to whose fortitude and diligence the Confessor is able to retreat into an existence free from all cares:

> And so with the kingdom made safe on all sides by these nobles, the most kindly King Edward passed his life in security and peace, and spent much of his time in the glades and woods in the pleasures of hunting. After divine service, which he gladly and devoutly attended every day, he took much pleasure in hawks and birds of that kind which were brought before him, and was really delighted by the baying and scram-bling of the hounds. In these and such like activities he sometimes spent the day, and it was in these alone that he seemed naturally inclined to snatch some worldly pleasure.[30]

In the early 1060s the power of the Godwines continued to increase. Earl Ælfgar appears to have died in 1062 – a year for which, suspiciously, the Anglo-Saxon Chronicle has no entries at all – and there is no sign in the immediate term that either of his sons succeeded him as earl of Mercia.[31] With their only English adversary finally gone for good, the Godwines decided that it was time to deal decisively with his former ally, Gruffudd ap Llywelyn: soon after Christmas 1062 Harold launched a surprise attack on the Welsh king's court at Rhuddlan. On that occasion Gruffudd managed to escape by ship, leaving Harold to vent his frustration by destroying the king's residence and the remainder of his fleet. But the following spring the earl unleashed a larger and more concerted assault, striking at the coast of south Wales with a fleet of his own while his brother Tostig led in a land army and overran the Welsh interior. So successful was their combined offensive that in early August Gruffudd was killed by his own men. His head was sent to Harold, who in turn sent it on to Edward the Confessor.[32]

But despite this belated nod to royal authority, there was no doubt to whom the victory in Wales really belonged. The E Chronicle tells us that it was Harold who appointed a new client king to rule in Gruffudd's place, while the historian Gerald of Wales, writing more than a century later, remarked that one could still see the stones raised all over the country to commemorate the various battles of 1063, inscribed HIC FUIT VICTOR HAROLDUS. Whereas the Confessor is all but absent from the historical record during the last decade of his reign, the eldest son of Godwine stands out as both conqueror and kingmaker.[33]

When we next encounter Harold, however, he is riding towards his manor of Bosham on the Sussex coast. He has a meal with his friends, takes a ship out into the English Channel, and somehow ends up as the guest of the duke of Normandy.

7

Hostages to Fortune

I f the years down to 1063 had been ones of glorious achievement
for Harold Godwineson, the same was equally true for William
of Normandy.

The duke's victory at Varaville in 1057 had not ended his war
with Henry I of France and Geoffrey Martel of Anjou: the following
year he pressed home his advantage against the French king, recovering the castle of Tillières that had been lost during his minority
and seizing Henry's own castle of Thimert; his struggle against Anjou,
meanwhile, ground on inexorably with no advertised losses or gains.
But 1060 proved to be a providential year – for William, that is. On
4 August Henry downed some medicine, disregarded his doctor's
orders not to drink any water, and died before the day was out.[1]
Around the same time Geoffrey Martel also fell ill, 'seized by an
incurable sickness that grew worse daily', according to an Angevin
chronicler. He died on 14 November, in great pain, surrounded by
his men.[2]

The near-simultaneous death of his two principal antagonists must
have come as a great relief to William, for it meant that the long-
standing threat of invasion was lifted. Henry I had been married
three times, but only his last queen had given him any children, and
in August 1060 his eldest son, Philip, was only eight years old. Power
in France passed to a regency council, headed by the widowed queen
and Henry's brother-in-law, Baldwin of Flanders – who also
happened, of course, to be William's father-in-law.[3] Matters in Anjou
fell out even more favourably for the Norman duke, since Geoffrey
Martel, despite no fewer than four marriages, had managed to produce

no children at all. The succession went to his sister's son, Geoffrey the Bearded, whose rule was contested from the first by his younger brother, Fulk. Their struggle, which lasted for several years, effectively ended Anjou's ability to compete with Normandy.

This was particularly evident in regard to the intermediate county of Maine. After his takeover of 1051, Geoffrey Martel had ruled Maine in the name of its rightful heir, Count Herbert II. According to William of Poitiers, at some point thereafter Herbert had escaped to Normandy in search of protection, in return for which he had provisionally made William his heir. Historians have been understandably sceptical of this story, which obviously contains strong echoes of the Norman claim to England. There is no reason why duplication by itself should automatically arouse suspicion: one could well argue that the similarity shows simply that this was the kind of arrangement that William favoured. Yet Poitiers' very insistence that he is telling the absolute truth, coupled with his vagueness on points of detail, do on this occasion raise serious doubts. Certainly, the Norman claim did not go uncontested in Maine itself. When Herbert died on 9 March 1062, having failed to beget any children of his own, the pro-Angevin party in Le Mans offered the succession to his uncle, Walter, and made ready to resist.[4]

But resistance was useless. Shortly afterwards William launched a relentless campaign of harrying on the countryside around Le Mans, 'To sow fear in its homes by frequent and lengthy visits,' as William of Poitiers unashamedly explains, 'to devastate its vineyards, fields and villages; to capture its outlying castles, to place garrisons wherever necessary, and thus everywhere and incessantly to inflict damage.' Walter and his supporters appealed for aid to their existing overlord, but despite making threatening noises the new count of Anjou failed to appear. And so, at length, the defenders decided to submit to William, and the gates of Le Mans were thrown open to admit him. Both Walter and his wife died soon after the city's fall, fuelling the rumour, first reported in the twelfth century, that they had been poisoned on the duke's orders. It remained only to capture the castle of Mayenne, a virtually impregnable stronghold to the south of Domfront whose lord had long been opposed to William's ambitions. The garrison there eventually surrendered after the Norman army succeeded in hurling fire at the castle and setting it alight.[5]

Thus, by 1063, William was in a triumphant position. Like Harold

Godwineson, he had witnessed the fortuitous deaths of his enemies and mounted a successful conquest of a neighbouring province. Nothing reflects this triumph today so well as the town of Caen, which was developed on the duke's orders during this same period. Caen had hitherto been a settlement of virtually no significance – indeed, it only enters the written record around the time of William's birth. But from the late 1050s the town was transformed out of all recognition, becoming the second greatest urban centre in Normandy after the capital at Rouen. The duke probably settled on Caen because of its proximity to the site of his providential victory at Val-ès-Dunes, which made it an ideal place to emphasize the God-given nature of his authority. But the location also boasted certain natural advantages, not least the rocky outcrop on which the duke established a castle. Sadly, although the outline of this extensive fortress-palace can be traced today, none of its original stone fabric has survived. The same is not true, however, in the case of the two abbeys that were founded by William and Matilda, probably in return for the pope's decision to lift the ban on their marriage. Her foundation was a house of nuns, begun around 1059 and dedicated to the Holy Trinity; his was a community of monks, started around 1063 and dedicated to St Stephen (St Etienne). Both, of course, were built in the Romanesque style, but William's church, despite being only slightly later, was far more sophisticated, its innovative design becoming a model for much that was to follow. Happily it was only little altered in later centuries and escaped the worst destruction of the Second World War, so its splendour can still be appreciated. After a great deal of insistent arm-twisting ('by a kind of pious violence', as William of Poitiers puts it) the duke persuaded his chief spiritual adviser, Lanfranc, to become its first abbot.[6]

Not long after the founding of St Stephen's, William received the exciting news that Harold Godwineson had landed on the north French coast.

Harold's Continental adventure is one of the most celebrated episodes in the story of the Norman Conquest, largely because it is the subject of the opening section of the Bayeux Tapestry. It is also one of the most controversial, for in spite of its extensive treatment in the Tapestry and also in chronicles written in Normandy, it goes entirely undiscussed in contemporary English sources such as the

Anglo-Saxon Chronicle and the *Life of King Edward*. As a result, the episode is difficult to date. Most historians are inclined to place it in the early summer of 1064, though it is just possible that it occurred at the same point in 1065. Fortunately, whichever of the two dates it was makes no difference to the story's significance.[7]

There is no doubt that it is a true story, for all versions, both contemporary Norman and later English, agree in broad outline about what happened. The Bayeux Tapestry provides the most detailed prologue, beginning, as we've seen, with Edward the Confessor. The king, white-haired, bearded and elderly, is shown in animated conversation with two men, one of whom we take to be Harold. The earl – now explicitly identified in a caption – then rides to his manor of Bosham in Sussex, accompanied by his mounted retainers and a pack of hounds, and carrying a hawk on his wrist. Once at Bosham they say a prudent prayer in the church (which still stands), and have a meal in the manor house, before setting out to sea. The Tapestry shows them hitching up their tunics as they wade out into the waves to climb aboard their ships.

While crossing the Channel, however, Harold and his men sail into a storm and only narrowly avoid being shipwrecked – a fact implied by the Tapestry and stated explicitly in all the chronicle accounts. Providentially they escape a watery grave, but end up putting to shore in Ponthieu, one of several small counties sandwiched between Normandy and Flanders. This is clearly not their intended destination: the Tapestry shows Harold being seized as soon as he disembarks by Ponthieu's ruler, Count Guy, and taken to be imprisoned at the castle of Beaurain. According to William of Poitiers, such brigandage was common practice in Ponthieu, and the count was planning to detain Harold and his companions until he obtained a large ransom.[8]

The scene then shifts to Normandy, where somehow news of Harold's arrival has reached the ears of Duke William. Possibly Harold himself managed to send the duke a message: the Tapestry, in a section that seems somewhat confused, shows a messenger whose moustache suggests he is an Englishman; in a later chronicle version, the earl gets word out by bribing one of his guards. However it came to pass, once William was aware of Harold's predicament he immediately sent messengers to Ponthieu to demand his release. William of Jumièges states that Count Guy was put under pressure, which seems entirely credible: the count had been captured at the Battle of Mortemer in 1054, and freed only after swearing fealty to the Norman duke. William of Poitiers, who evidently had a copy of Jumièges' chronicle in front of him, insists that Guy co-operated willingly, in return for which he received gifts of land and money. Bullied or bribed, the count brought Harold to the Norman border at Eu and handed him over to William, who escorted the earl and his men to the comforts of his palace at Rouen.[9]

During Harold's stay in Normandy, which by all accounts lasted some time, two significant things happened. Firstly, William fought a short and not particularly successful campaign in Brittany, described in detail by William of Poitiers and depicted at length on the Bayeux Tapestry. Harold accompanied his host on this mission, and the Tapestry shows him heroically rescuing some of William's men from the quicksands near Mont St Michel. Secondly, and more importantly, Harold at some point swore an oath to uphold the duke's claim to the English throne. According to William of Poitiers this happened at a specially convened council in the town of Bonneville-sur-Touques.[10] The Tapestry shows the earl touching holy relics as the oath is sworn.[11]

Such is the story of Harold's visit as told by our various sources. Although they differ over certain small details – where Harold swore his oath, for instance, or whether he swore it before or after the Brittany campaign – both the chroniclers and the Tapestry agree that this was how it happened.[12] Where they disagree totally, however, is *why* it happened.

According to Norman writers, the swearing of the oath had been the whole point of the exercise: Harold crossed the Channel because he had been sent by Edward the Confessor to confirm William's claim to the English throne. William of Jumièges, for instance, says that:

> Edward, king of the English, by the will of God having no heir, had in the past sent Robert, the archbishop of Canterbury, to appoint him heir to the kingdom given to him by God. But he also, at a later date, sent to him Harold, the greatest of all the earls in his realm in wealth, honour and power, that he should swear fealty to the duke concerning his crown and, according to Christian tradition, pledge it with oaths.[13]

William of Poitiers, who follows Jumièges' account, naturally endorses this statement, to the extent that he even copies bits of it word for word: Harold had been sent to protect William's position as Edward's heir. And so too do all later Norman chroniclers. 'The truth was', said Orderic Vitalis in the 1120s, 'that Edward had declared his intention of transmitting the whole kingdom to his kinsman, Duke William of Normandy, and had with the consent of the English made him heir to all his rights.'[14]

But the English themselves begged to differ. At the time, it is true, they seem to have preferred to stand on their silence. The Anglo-Saxon Chronicle carries no entries for the year 1064, and begins its discussion of 1065 with events that took place in August. The *Life of King Edward* also fails to make any reference to Harold's trip explicitly, although its author does make two comments which might be taken to allude to it. Later generations, however, were not so tight-lipped, and set out to deny the Norman claim directly. According to William of Malmesbury, for example, some Englishmen in the early twelfth century maintained that the earl had never intended to visit the Continent at all, but had been accidentally blown across the Channel having set out on a fishing trip.[15]

An altogether more credible alternative is offered by an early twelfth-century monk of Canterbury named Eadmer. According to Eadmer, Harold *had* set out for Normandy, but had done so on his own initiative, his purpose being to obtain the release of two relatives who were being held hostage at William's court. Here we are on much firmer ground, because this was indeed the case – even William of Poitiers admits to the hostages' existence. At some point during the crisis of 1051–2, the Godwines had handed over two of their number to Edward the Confessor: Eadmer names them as Wulfnoth, who was one of Harold's younger brothers, and Hakon, a son of Harold's older brother, the unlamented Earl Swein. Most likely they were surrendered in September 1051, when the family's power was collapsing and Swein was still an active participant in the drama. At some point in the year that followed they were evidently transferred to Normandy, the likeliest scenario being that they were taken back by William himself after his visit to England.[16]

Which, then, is more credible: Harold being sent to Normandy to confirm Edward's earlier promise, or the earl embarking on a mission of his own, trying to secure the liberation of his long-detained kinsmen? Do we prefer the testimony of William of Poitiers or that of Eadmer? Taken on their own merits there is little to help us decide between the two authors. William of Poitiers is more closely contemporary and provides a very detailed account of Harold's visit. He is seemingly well informed about the oath-taking ceremony, supplying not only its likeliest location but also the terms of the promises that the earl allegedly made. According to Poitiers, Harold swore firstly that he would act as William's advocate at Edward's court and, secondly, that when the king died he would use his wealth and influence to ensure the duke's succession. Thirdly, says Poitiers, the earl pledged to strengthen and garrison Dover Castle at his own expense for William's use and, fourthly, that he would similarly fortify and provision various other places in England as the duke directed.[17]

But then Eadmer, despite the fact he wrote a generation later, is also an apparently well-informed witness. He alone supplies us with the names of the two Godwine hostages, and contributes other convincing details (he knows, for example, the name of the estuary in Ponthieu where Harold made his landing). Eadmer, too, offers a detailed description of the earl's oath, mentioning both the pledge of personal support for William's claim and the fortification of Dover, and contributing the additional suggestion that the agreement was to be sealed by a marriage alliance, by which Harold's sister would marry a leading Norman magnate and the earl himself would wed one of the duke's daughters.[18]

At the same time, both Poitiers and Eadmer are evidently giving us biased accounts. Poitiers very obviously wants to do all he can to strengthen the Norman claim. Harold, he insists, swore his oath 'clearly and of his own free will', 'as the most truthful and distinguished men who were there as witnesses have told'. Such emphatic assurances from the pen of this particular chronicler immediately make us suspicious, and incline us to listen to Eadmer, who says that Harold realized that he was in a dangerous predicament, and effectively made his promises under duress: 'He could not see any way of escape without agreeing to all that William wished.'[19]

Eadmer, however, is an equally partisan informant. Like most Englishmen who lived through the experience, he regarded the Conquest as a terrible tragedy, and was as anxious to deny the Norman claim as Poitiers was to defend it.[20] In setting out his version of events he strains to avoid any mention of Edward's promise of 1051. Thus the cause of the king's quarrel with the Godwines that year goes unexplained, and the hostages are improbably handed over in 1052 once the Godwines are back in power. The effect of these suppressions and alterations is to absolve Harold of any blame. In Eadmer's account, the first the earl hears of the Norman claim to the English throne is after his arrival in Normandy, when William reveals that Edward promised him the succession during his exile.

All things being equal, it would be impossible to decide between two such manipulative writers. But when we consider their accounts in light of the wider context, it becomes obvious that we ought to reject Poitiers' explanation and accept that of Eadmer. Put simply, Eadmer's version of events accords far more convincingly with what we know about the political reality in England. By 1064, Harold and his brothers reigned supreme, whereas the authority of Edward the Confessor had been eroded to virtually nothing. It stretches credibility beyond its elastic limit to believe that the king, aged and powerless as he was, could have commanded the earl to do anything detrimental to his own interests, let alone to help resuscitate a scheme for the succession to which he and his family had always been vehemently opposed.[21]

By contrast, it seems perfectly reasonable to suppose that Harold, at the very height of his powers, would have been acutely embarrassed by the continued detention of two of his close relatives, and at the same time optimistic that he could use his influence to secure their release. Since they were being held to guarantee Edward's promise of 1051, the earl must have anticipated he would have to discuss the Norman claim, but must have felt confident that he could persuade William to drop it, either by tricking him or by paying him off. This is strongly implied in Eadmer's account, when Harold informs Edward that he intends to get the hostages back. 'I know that the duke is not so simple as to give them up to you,' cautions the king, 'unless he foresees some great advantage to himself.' But the earl disregards this advice and goes to Normandy anyway, taking with him a large amount of gold, silver and costly goods.[22]

There is one final piece of evidence which might be taken to support Eadmer's story, and that is the Bayeux Tapestry. The Tapestry is undoubtedly our most interesting source for the Norman Conquest, and also one of the most difficult to interpret. For the most part it appears to be a piece of Norman triumphalism, but the fact that it was created by English embroiderers seems to have affected its telling of the story. At critical moments where it could give us a decisive opinion on the Norman claim, the Tapestry is carefully ambiguous. To say this much is not to argue that it contains some hidden English code; simply that, as a piece of public art created very soon after the Conquest, the Tapestry seems to be trying deliberately to steer clear of controversy. In the opening scene, for example, we see Edward the Confessor talking to a figure whom we take to be Harold, but we are told nothing about the topic of their conversation. Norman observers would assume the king was ordering the earl to confirm William's succession. English observers could imagine that the discussion concerned Harold's plan to recover the hostages.

When it comes to depict the earl's return, however, the Tapestry seems rather less ambiguous. Both Eadmer and William of Poitiers tell us that Harold recrossed the Channel accompanied by his nephew, Hakon; his brother Wulfnoth remained in Norman custody. Had his objective been to free both hostages, therefore, his trip had been only a partial success. If, on the other hand, he had been charged with confirming William's position as Edward's heir, then the mission had been accomplished. Indeed, he ought to have been given a jubilant reception.[23]

Yet the Tapestry appears to show a different scene. 'Here Harold returns to England and comes to King Edward', says the caption, blankly, but the picture below shows the earl advancing towards the king with his head visibly bowed and his arms outstretched – a posture that looks very much like an act of supplication or apology. Edward himself, moreover, is no longer the genial figure he seemed at the start, but larger, sterner, and raising his index finger as if to admonish.

'Seems'; 'looks very much like'; 'appears'; 'as if'. This is of course a speculative reading of a single scene, which some historians would argue is as ambiguous as any other.[24] But Eadmer, who belonged to the same Canterbury tradition as the Tapestry's designer, was in no doubt about the nature of Harold's reception when he explained to the king what had happened. 'Did I not tell you that I knew William,' exclaims an exasperated Edward, 'and that your going might bring untold calamity upon this kingdom?'[25]

8

Northern Uproar

Harold had returned from Normandy by the summer of 1065 at the latest, for at that point the Anglo-Saxon Chronicle breaks its silence to inform us about his activities in south Wales. Before the start of August, we are told, the earl commissioned some building work at Portskewett, now a nondescript village on the Severn Estuary, a few miles south of Chepstow. His intention was apparently to invite Edward the Confessor there for a spot of hunting, to which end 'he got together there many goods'. Was this an attempt, one wonders, to curry recently lost favour?

If so, it was unsuccessful, for Harold's luck had not improved. On 24 August, when all the necessaries had been assembled and the building work was approaching completion, his new hunting lodge was attacked by the Welsh, still smarting from the earl's invasion of their country two years earlier. Almost all the people working on site were killed and all the carefully stockpiled provisions were carried off. 'We do not know', says the D version of the Chronicle, 'who first suggested this mischief', not for the first time infuriating us by hinting that there was some wider conspiracy at work, but failing to divulge anything in the way of details. As it happens, we know that there was indeed an anti-Godwine conspiracy underway in the summer of 1065. Its target, however, was not Harold, but his younger brother, the earl of Northumbria.[1]

Eleventh-century Northumbria was a lot bigger than its modern namesake. A former Anglo-Saxon kingdom, it originally extended, as its appellation suggests, north from the River Humber, and as such embraced all of Yorkshire and County Durham, as well as the region to the far north that now has exclusive ownership of the name. Once, in its glory days in the seventh century, Northumbria had extended even further still, to include the part of the Scottish lowlands known as Lothian, and as far west as the Irish Sea, to include all of modern Lancashire and Cumbria. During the tenth century, however, these outlying areas had been lost, or at least rendered highly debatable, thanks to the ambitions of rival rulers in Scotland and Strathclyde.

The kingdom of Northumbria, like all the Anglo-Saxon kingdoms except Wessex, had been brought to an end by the arrival of the Vikings. In the last third of the ninth century the Danes had conquered and colonized a large area of what is now northern and eastern England – a region referred to in later centuries as 'the Danelaw'. Yorkshire was extensively colonized by the invaders, and York itself became their capital. The former kings of Northumbria, meanwhile, continued to rule its northern rump – the far less productive territory north of the River Tees – from their ancient seat at Bamburgh, a rocky fastness surrounded by sea.[2]

The Viking kingdom of York did not last very long, falling in the middle of the tenth century to the all-conquering kings of Wessex, but the effects of the Danish invasion continued to be felt for generations beyond. Because of Viking settlement, Yorkshire was ethnically and culturally very different from the other parts of the newly forged kingdom of England. Its inhabitants, for example, persisted in using a Scandinavian counting system for their money, and commissioned tombs and memorial crosses of an unmistakably Nordic design. More significant still, they spoke a language that was barely intelligible to their southern neighbours, littered with Scandinavian loan words. In Yorkshire place names we commonly encounter the distinctive Danish '-by' (Grimsby, Kirkby). Elsewhere in England shires were divided into subdivisions called hundreds, and hundreds into hides; Yorkshire was divided into ridings, wapentakes and carucates. Even today, the major streets in York are designated by the Danish word 'gate' (Coppergate, Swinegate).[3]

As a result the north of England was politically divided. The Anglo-Danish magnates of Yorkshire naturally resented being ruled by their conquerors from Wessex. The members of the former royal dynasty based at Bamburgh, by contrast, although now reduced to the status of earls, were quite happy with the new situation. The exchange of a Viking ruler in nearby York for an extremely distant overlord in southern England meant that they were essentially left to look after their own affairs beyond the Tees, and more often than not appointed to govern Yorkshire as well. They were less happy (and their neighbours in Yorkshire correspondingly well pleased) when the Vikings returned to conquer England in 1016. After Cnut's takeover Yorkshire received its own Scandinavian earls, first Erik, then Siward, who became bitter enemies with the house of Bamburgh. Siward eventually ended the conflict in 1041 by arranging the murder of his northern rival and extending his authority across the whole of Northumbria.[4]

Such was the situation in northern England at the time of Siward's death in 1055. Divided culturally and politically, it was at the same time largely left to its own devices, for the good reason that it was a long way away and hard to reach. Thanks to the wide Humber Estuary and the bogs and swamps of Yorkshire and Cheshire, only a few roads linked the north to the south, and none of them were good: the 200-mile journey from London to York usually took a fortnight or more, assuming the roads were passable and that no robbers were encountered en route; by far the quickest and safest way to reach York from southern England was by ship. For this reason Northumbria was only subject to the lightest of royal super-vision. The king of England had very little land in Yorkshire; coins were minted in York bearing his face and name, but he himself was never seen there. Beyond the Tees, meanwhile, there was no permanent royal presence at all: no royal estates, no mints, no *burhs*, no shires. For most people in southern England, including the king, the north was a faraway country, where they did things differently, about which they knew and understood very little.[5]

This was one of the reasons that the appointment of Tostig Godwineson as Siward's successor had come as such a shock. As we have seen, Tostig's promotion in the spring of 1055 had caused a bitter rift in England south of the Humber, apparently provoking a showdown between the Godwine family and their rivals in Mercia. But within Northumbria itself his advancement must have caused equal if not greater consternation. In the century since the region had been absorbed into the kingdom of England, its earls had been

(*Above*) Edward the Confessor at the beginning of the Bayeux Tapestry.
(*Below*) William of Jumièges presents his history to William the Conqueror
(from a twelfth-century copy of the manuscript).

(*Left*) King Cnut and Queen Emma present a cross to New Minster, Winchester (from a contemporary manuscript).

(*Below*) Harold Godwineson rides towards Bosham.

(*Above*) English architecture before 1066. The early eleventh-century church tower at Earls Barton, Northamptonshire, shows how decoration took precedence over the order and precision of line beginning to be used on the Continent (see over).

(*Above*) The mighty castle at Arques, established during William's minority. The surviving masonry dates from the twelfth century.

Norman architecture before 1066. The Romanesque abbey churches of Jumièges (*below*), begun *c.* 1040, and St Stephen's Caen (*facing page*), begun *c.* 1063 (with twelfth-century vaulting).

(*Above*) The Norman invasion fleet crosses the Channel. The ship with the lantern on its mast is probably William's flagship, the *Mora*.

(*Below*) 'Skuldelev 3', datable to the eleventh century, on display in the Viking Ship Museum, Roskilde, Denmark.

(*Above*) Harrying in action: two Normans set fire to a house from which a woman and child flee.

The Battle of Hastings.
(*Above*) Norman knights charge the English shield-wall.
(*Below*) Bishop Odo rushes in to encourage the lads (*confortat pueros*).

either members of the house of Bamburgh or else Danes appointed by King Cnut. Only once, around the turn of the millennium, had the pattern been broken, when the earldom of York had gone to a Mercian named Ælfhelm, and his rule had not been a success. Yet in 1055 the Northumbrians were presented with Tostig, a twenty-something son of the late earl of Wessex, whose name was the only Danish thing about him. By birth, upbringing and political experience, Tostig was a southerner, and it showed.[6]

Complaints about Tostig's rule all date from a decade after his appointment, but evidently applied to the entirety of his period in office. According to the C version of the Anglo-Saxon Chronicle, the principal charge against him in Northumbria was that 'he robbed God first'. This is somewhat surprising and perhaps unfair (the C Chronicle, composed in Mercia, is a hostile source). The pro-Godwine *Life of King Edward* informs us that the earl was a notably pious individual, whose generosity to the Church was encouraged by his equally devout wife, Judith (a daughter of the count of Flanders, whom Tostig had married in 1051 during his family's Flemish exile), and this testimony is supported by later sources written at Durham Cathedral, which remember the earl and his countess as munificent benefactors. Just possibly the accusation of 'robbing God' is Tostig being tarred by association, for one of his first acts as earl had been to help replace Æthelric, the unpopular bishop of Durham, with his even more unpopular brother, Æthelwine. Both men, like Tostig, were southerners, and later remembered for having despoiled Durham and other northern churches in order to enrich their alma mater at Peterborough.[7]

If the Church did suffer directly at the hands of Tostig, it was more likely as a result of his tax policy, which was perceived to be disproportionately harsh. According to John of Worcester, another complaint against the earl in 1065 was that he had raised a 'huge tribute'. Exactly how excessive the earl's demands had been is impossible to say, but most likely the problem was one of differing expectations. Historically the north had paid very little tax at all: later records show that land was assessed at only one-sixth of the rate customarily applied in the south. This may have been in deference to the northerners' tradition of independence, or in recognition of the region's lower population and less productive economy. Perhaps Tostig had some grand scheme to improve revenues and bring the earldom into line with southern norms; more likely he simply tried to increase the tax yield to meet his own needs, and his expediency was seen as a nefarious attempt to introduce into the north the more onerous type of government to which the south had long been subject. Either way, Tostig's attempts to raise taxes above their traditional low levels plainly made him extremely unpopular.[8]

The same was true of his policy on law and order. Northumbria, says the *Life of King Edward*, was a notoriously lawless region, where even parties of twenty or thirty men could scarcely travel without being either killed or robbed; Tostig's sole intention, being 'a son and lover of divine justice', was to reduce this terrible lawlessness, to which end he killed and mutilated the robbers. The C Chronicle, conversely, says that Tostig simply killed and disinherited 'all those who were less powerful than himself'. Again, we might suspect that the truth lay somewhere in the middle, were it not for the fact that the author of the *Life*, rather less loyally, chose to report rather than refute such allegations. 'Not a few charged that glorious earl with being too cruel; and he was accused of punishing disturbers more for the desire of their confiscated property than for love of justice.' Elsewhere the same author ruefully remarks that Tostig was 'occasionally a little too enthusiastic in attacking evil'.[9]

Tostig, then, was unpopular because of what his friends chose charitably to regard as the overzealous execution of two of his principal duties, namely raising revenue and doing justice. By contrast, no contemporary complaint has come down to us about his discharge of a third and even more fundamental responsibility, namely the defence of his earldom from external attack. Indeed, the *Life of King Edward*, in a section that heaps praise on both Tostig and Harold, declared that just as Harold had beaten back the king's enemies in the south (i.e. the Welsh), so too his brother had scared them off in the north. The absence of contradiction here is surprising, in the first place because the *Life*'s statement was patently untrue, and, secondly, because Tostig's failure to defend his earldom led directly to the crisis that eventually engulfed him.[10]

Since the turn of the millennium, being earl of Northumbria had meant having to contend with the expansionist ambitions of the kings of Scotland. In the first half of the eleventh century the Scots had invaded northern England on three separate occasions, and on the last of these in 1040 they had laid siege to Durham. As we have already seen, Tostig's predecessor, Earl Siward, had dealt robustly with this problem, invading Scotland in 1054 and deposing its king, Macbeth. In his place the earl had installed Malcolm, son of the late King Duncan, the man whom Macbeth had famously murdered in order to ascend to the throne. Malcolm had apparently grown up as an exile at the court of Edward the Confessor, who seems to have backed Siward's scheme to reinstate him. The thinking, no doubt, was that a Scottish king who owed his position to the force of English arms would be less likely to pursue a policy of aggression against Northumbria.[11]

If that was the theory, it held good for only a short while. In the opening years of his reign Malcolm was preoccupied with his ongoing struggle against Macbeth (who, contrary to theatrical tradition, did not die after Dunsinane, but three years later, after the Battle of Lumphanan). But with Macbeth dead, and his stepson Lulach also killed in 1058, Malcolm reverted to type and, in the best tradition of his predecessors, began launching raids into northern England. The *Life of King Edward* explains that the new Scottish king was testing the even newer Earl Tostig, whose ability he held cheaply. But, the same source continues, the earl was too clever, and wore down his opponent 'as much by cunning schemes as by martial courage and military campaigns'. This was true, up to a point: in 1059, Tostig, aided by the bishops of Durham and York, somehow persuaded Malcolm to return to England for a personal interview with Edward the Confessor, who may have ventured across the Humber expressly for the purpose. A peace was agreed, hostages were exchanged and, as was the northern custom on such occasions, Malcolm and Tostig became 'sworn brothers'.[12]

But this was only half the story. Not long afterwards, in 1061, Tostig and Judith, accompanied by other members of their family and a number of English bishops, piously departed on a pilgrimage to Rome, thereby presenting Malcolm with what proved to be an irresistible open goal. That same year, says the twelfth-century chronicler Simeon of Durham, the Scottish king 'furiously ravaged the earldom of his sworn brother, Earl Tostig'. So thorough was the devastation that the Scots did not even deign to spare the Holy Island of Lindisfarne, the cradle of Christianity in northern England.

It was probably also at this moment that Malcolm invaded

Cumbria. Of all the debatable territories in the volatile north of England, none had been more frequently contested than this famously mountainous region on the north-west coast. Originally a British kingdom (its name derives from the same root as Cymru, the Celtic word for Wales), Cumbria had been absorbed into the English kingdom of Northumbria in the course of the seventh century, but lost around AD 900 to another British kingdom, Strathclyde, whose kings nominally ruled there for the next 120 years. During this time, however, Cumbria was invaded and settled by Norwegian Vikings operating out of Ireland, and then repeatedly conquered, ceded, harried and reconquered in a struggle for overlordship between the kings of England and Scotland. Latterly the region had been overrun by the Scots in 1018, an invasion which finally ended the rule of the kings of Strathclyde, but subsequently recovered for England during the rule of Earl Siward. Although the evidence is circumstantial, it seems fairly certain that Malcolm used the opportunity of Tostig's absence in 1061 to reverse the situation once again, and that Cumbria was reclaimed by the Scots.

The loss of Cumbria, not to mention the sacking of Lindisfarne and the devastation of the rest of his earldom, clearly demanded some sort of military response on Tostig's part. As far as we can tell, however, there was still no sign of the 'martial courage and military campaigns' ascribed to the earl by the *Life of King Edward*. On his return from Rome, Tostig appears to have accepted Malcolm's invasion as a fait accompli, for once again he sought out the Scottish king and offered to make peace. Cumbria, it seems, was going to remain a part of Scotland.[13]

But not everyone was as willing to let bygones be bygones. Among those likely to have been infuriated by Tostig's failure to defend his predecessor's conquests was Gospatric, a scion of the house of Bamburgh. Had the historical dice rolled differently, Gospatric, not Tostig, would have been earl of Northumbria. In ancient times, as we have noted, his ancestors had ruled the region as kings, and as recently as fifty years ago his father, Uhtred, had governed the whole province as earl. As we have also noted, however, the house of Bamburgh had lost out badly after the coming of Cnut. Earl Uhtred had been murdered in 1016 on Cnut's orders and the southern half of his earldom awarded to a Danish newcomer. Twenty-five years later, Gospatric's brother, Earl Eadwulf, was similarly betrayed and murdered at the behest of Earl Siward, who had subsequently taken over the remainder of the earldom. Gospatric, therefore, had ample excuse for feeling bitter about the way events had unfolded, but Siward had been smart enough to try to assuage such resentments. Soon after his taking over the house of Bamburgh's territory he had married Ælfflaed, a granddaughter of Earl Uhtred, thereby linking the fortunes of the defeated dynasty with his own. Around the same time, he had granted Gospatric a subordinate role in the running of the earldom by making him responsible for the government of Cumbria.[14]

Thus, while Tostig may have viewed the Scottish recovery of Cumbria with equanimity, for Gospatric it meant the loss of his consolation prize. We cannot say for certain that this was the cause of the subsequent bad blood between the two men – the earl was unpopular on so many other scores – but it certainly seems the likeliest one. We can see that fighting broke out between them soon afterwards, because in 1063 or 1064 Tostig is known to have invited two men, both members of Gospatric's affinity, to his hall at York for a peace conference – or so they thought. What the earl had actually arranged was an ambush of the kind practised by his Danish predecessors, and the two men were treacherously murdered. Their deaths probably prompted Gospatric to complain directly to the king, for at Christmas 1064 he was present at Edward's court. It was, however, his last appearance, for he had failed to take into account the loyalty of the Godwine family. On the fourth night of Christmas, Gospatric was himself assassinated on the orders of Tostig's sister, Queen Edith.

For a time it must have seemed that Tostig's decapitation strategy had worked: in the immediate wake of Gospatric's death the north seemed calm enough. But throughout the following year a far larger and more co-ordinated response to the earl's misrule was steadily gathering momentum. Had he been present in Northumbria Tostig might have read the signs. In March, for example, when the clerks of Durham staged a public protest by digging up and displaying the bones of King Oswine, a seventh-century Northumbria ruler who had died at the hands of his treacherous relatives. But such unsubtle propaganda seems to have passed Tostig by. The earl was frequently absent from his earldom, preferring to leave its day-to-day management to his deputies. Hence it was they rather than he who bore the immediate brunt of the northerners' fury.[15]

On Monday 3 October 1065, a group of thegns loyal to Gospatric entered York with a force of 200 armed men. John of Worcester, our best informed source, explicitly links their action to the treacherous betrayal of their master and his men. They seem to have taken the city by surprise, for on that Monday only two of Tostig's Danish housecarls are said to have died, hauled back and executed as they tried to escape. But the following day there was evidently a more hard-fought struggle with the rest of the earl's retainers, more than 200 of whom perished as a result. The rebels went on to smash open Tostig's treasury in York, seizing all his weapons, gold and silver.[16]

It was the beginning of a massive rebellion. The thegns from beyond the Tees, it is clear, had managed to defeat Tostig's sizeable retinue because they had been joined by the men of York – a remarkable testament to the earl's unpopularity, that the two traditionally hostile halves of his earldom should come together in order to oppose him. The rising was also clearly well co-ordinated and directed personally against Tostig. The *Life of King Edward* speaks of the slaughter of the earl's adherents wherever they could be found, not just in York but also on the streets of Lincoln, as well as on roads and rivers and in woods. 'Whosoever could be identified as having been at some time a member of Tostig's household was dragged to the torments of death without trial.'[17]

The rebels' plan, it transpired, was to replace Tostig with a young man named Morcar, the second son of the late Earl Ælfgar, formerly the Godwine family's most hostile opponent. According to the *Life*, Morcar and his older brother, Eadwine, had inherited all their father's ill will, particularly towards Tostig. It may be that for a time Tostig and Harold had contrived to keep Eadwine out of his paternal inheritance, for he does not appear in the record as earl of Mercia until the spring of 1065, some three years after his father's death. The speed with which the two Mercian brothers fell in with the rebels suggests that they had long been privy to the conspiracy. Morcar immediately accepted the proffered role as the rebels' leader and marched them south, raising the shires of Lincoln, Derby and Nottingham as he went. Meanwhile Eadwine assembled his men in Mercia, where he was also joined by his father's erstwhile allies, the Welsh. Everyone who had suffered as a result of the relentless rise of the Godwine family was uniting to try to end their monopoly.[18]

*   *   *

Tostig was at his brother-in-law's court when news of the revolt broke. Edward was in Wiltshire at the time, apparently for the rededication of the church at Wilton Abbey, childhood home of Queen Edith, who had funded its reconstruction. Since this was an important occasion, taking place in the heart of his own earldom of Wessex, we may assume with some confidence that Harold was also present. It was certainly Harold who was sent north to meet the rebels in order to negotiate.[19]

By the time the earl reached them, Eadwine and Morcar had united their forces in the town of Northampton. From Mercia, Wales and the whole of northern England, their army had 'gathered together in an immense body,' according to the *Life of King Edward*, 'like a whirlwind or a tempest'. Harold delivered the king's message, which was essentially that the rebels should desist, and that any injustices they could prove would in due course be corrected. This, unsurprisingly, failed to pacify his audience, who replied that Edward should dismiss Tostig, not merely from Northumbria but from the realm as a whole, or else he too would be regarded as their enemy. Such was the counter-offer that Harold conveyed back to the king in Wiltshire.[20]

Back in Wiltshire, Edward had summoned a council to his manor of Britford, a few miles east of Wilton, close to where the city of Salisbury now stands. When the meeting assembled there were ugly scenes. It was at this moment that many magnates charged Tostig with having ruled his earldom with excessive cruelty, effectively blaming him for having brought the crisis upon himself. It was, however, the demands that Harold brought back from Northampton that caused the greatest acrimony, for at this point Tostig accused his brother of being in league with the rebels; indeed, of having provoked the rebellion in the first place. The author of the *Life of King Edward*, who reports Tostig's accusation, personally professes not to believe it, and assures us that Harold cleared himself of the charge by swearing his innocence. At the same time, the same writer also slyly reminds us that an oath from Harold was not really worth very much (this seemingly an allusion to the earl's visit to Normandy).[21]

Despite this innuendo, it seems most unlikely that the earl was behind the plot to bring down his brother. If Harold had entertained such an idea, there were surely safer ways to go about it than provoking the kind of unpredictable storm that was now raging.

Since his departure from Northampton the rebels had begun harrying the countryside around the town, knowing that much of it belonged to Tostig. Not only did they kill people, says the Anglo-Saxon Chronicle, and put houses and barns full of corn to the torch, they also seized thousands of head of cattle and hundreds of human captives, all of which they subsequently led back to the north. They then advanced further south to Oxford, where the line of the River Thames marked the boundary between Mercia and Wessex, leaving no doubt that England was on the very brink of civil war.[22]

The more reasonable conclusion is that Harold, in his capacity as a negotiator, did all he could to try to appease the rebels and to save his brother. Such was the belief of John of Worcester, who insists that the earl had acted as a negotiator at Tostig's own request. What Harold was evidently not prepared to do was fight the rebels for his brother's restoration. According to the *Life of King Edward*, when the negotiations proved fruitless, the king ordered a royal army to crush the uprising. But no army was forthcoming. The *Life* blames the difficulty of raising troops on the winter weather that was already setting in, as well as a general reluctance to engage in a civil war. Yet the king and his court were in Harold's earldom, and in the end it must have been Harold's own refusal to commit his men to a suicidal struggle that condemned Tostig to his fate. It was Harold who on 27 October conveyed to the rebels in Oxford the king's acceptance of their demands, recognized Morcar as Northumbria's new earl and restored to the Northumbrians what the Chronicle calls 'the Laws of Cnut' – shorthand for the rights they had enjoyed in the good old days, before the novelties and taxes introduced by Tostig. Meanwhile, much to the grief of his mother and his sister, the queen, Tostig himself prepared to go into exile; on 1 November, the earl and his family, along with many of his loyal thegns, crossed the Channel to Flanders, where they were once again welcomed by his wife's father, Count Baldwin.[23]

The distress of the Godwine women, however, was as nothing compared to the grief of the king. As in 1052, when his demands for military action had similarly fallen on deaf ears, Edward's power-lessness had filled him with rage. 'He protested to God with deep sorrow', says the *Life*, 'that he was deprived of the due obedience of his men in repressing the presumption of the unrighteous; and he called down God's vengeance upon them.' Such was the king's mental anguish, the same source continues, that he fell sick as a result, and his sickness grew worse from day to day. It must have been clear to everyone that he would not live much longer, and so a dedication ceremony for his magnificent new church at Westminster was arranged to coincide with Christmas. The building work was almost complete, says the *Life*, with only the porch remaining unfinished, but new houses had to be hurriedly erected to accommodate the crowds of people that came to attend the festivities. On Christmas Day Edward apparently did his best to disguise his illness, sitting serenely at table but having no appetite for any of the fancy food that was served. Alas, on 28 December, the day scheduled for the new abbey's dedication, he was too unwell to attend, but at his insistence the service went ahead as planned with Edith acting as his proxy. Eight days later, attended by the queen and a few other intimates of his household, the old king died.[24]

The day after his death the Confessor's body was carried the short distance between his palace in Westminster and the adjacent abbey, there to be laid to rest. It was 6 January 1066. Later that same day, Harold Godwineson was crowned as his successor.

9

The Gathering Storm

How and why did Harold Godwineson come to succeed Edward the Confessor? What of the candidacy of Edgar Ætheling, son of Edward the Exile, whose claim by birth was manifestly superior? Had Harold long intended to wear his brother-in-law's crown, or did he accept it only at the last minute, in deference to the king's dying wishes? Was his accession a legitimate act or a usurpation? Was he spurred by ambition or rather a sense of duty? As ever, this pivotal moment in the history of the Norman Conquest raises many questions for which there can be no definitive answers.

Part of the difficulty, of course, is that in eleventh-century England there was no hard-and-fast set of rules governing the succession. At the start of the century the trend may have been in the direction of a hereditary principle, but that particular apple cart had been upset by the return of the Vikings, who had characteristically re-emphasized the importance of violence and opportunism. Cnut's grip on England, observed William of Poitiers, 'owed only to conquest by his father and himself and nothing else'.[1]

So what else was there? In the succession debate that followed Cnut's death we can discern three key factors. First, although there was no strict line of precedence, a close blood link with the previous king was still highly desirable – hence the unsubtle attempt to smear Harold Harefoot by suggesting that he was not really a son of Cnut at all but a low-born changeling. Second, it was also evidently considered beneficial for a prospective king to have been in some way designated as such by his predecessor. Thus the *Encomium Emmae Reginae* insists that Cnut had given Harthacnut everything under his control 'while he was still living', and maintains that Harthacnut had in turn invited Edward the Confessor to come to England in 1041 in order to hold the kingdom with him.[2]

The most important factor, however, in deciding who should be king was clearly election – not in the wide sense in which we use the term today, but in the sense of obtaining the approval of the majority of the kingdom's leading men. Harold Harefoot had plainly succeeded in 1035 because he was backed by just such a majority; Harthacnut, as the Anglo-Saxon Chronicle makes clear, had accepted the crown in 1040 at the invitation of a body of magnates. And Edward the Confessor, although he could claim descent from the ancient royal line and perhaps designation by his predecessor as well, ultimately owed his throne to the collective will of the English aristocracy, and in particular Earl Godwine.[3]

How, then, did Godwine's eldest surviving son manage to obtain the throne in January 1066? Clearly, in hereditary terms Harold's case was extremely weak. The earl was related to Edward the Confessor, but only by virtue of his sister's marriage. His claim therefore had to rest heavily on nomination by his predecessor and election by the magnates – which, according to some sources, is precisely what happened. 'Earl Harold', says the E version of the Anglo-Saxon Chronicle, 'succeeded to the kingdom of England just as the king had granted it to him, and also men chose him for it.' Similarly, John of Worcester, writing several decades later, says that Harold, 'whom the king had chosen before his demise as successor to the kingdom, was elected by all the principal men of England to the dignity of the kingship'.[4]

But both John of Worcester and the E Chronicle are written with a strong pro-Godwine bias; other sources are not nearly so sure about the legitimacy of Harold's elevation. Was he, for instance, really nominated by his predecessor? As it happens we have a very full account of the Confessor's last hours in the *Life of King Edward*. The old king, we are told, had been in bed for days, slipping in and out of consciousness and rarely saying anything intelligible. Of the small number of people who were with him, the author of the *Life* names just four: 'the queen, who was sitting on the floor warming his feet in her lap; her brother, Earl Harold; Robert, the steward of the palace, and Archbishop Stigand'.[5]

We can picture this scene more fully because it appears on the Bayeux Tapestry (which, moving seamlessly from Harold's return from Normandy, resumes its story at this point). Having shown us the Confessor's corpse being carried for burial in Westminster Abbey, it returns, as if in flashback, to the king's deathbed. The scene is so similar to that described in the *Life* that one source (probably the Tapestry) must have been inspired by the other. We see Edward, lying in bed, surrounded by four figures. A servant (perhaps Robert the Steward) props him up, while a weeping woman (presumably Queen Edith) sits at his feet. On the far side of the bed stands a tonsured cleric, whom we take to be Archbishop Stigand, while on the near side a fourth figure, who must be Harold, kneels and touches the king's outstretched hand with his own. 'Here King Edward, in bed, speaks to his faithful servants', says the caption.

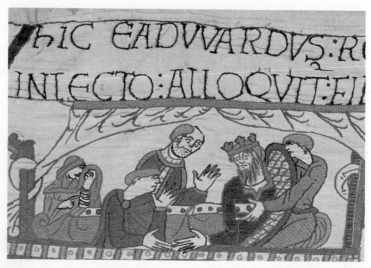

As usual the Tapestry gives us no idea what is actually being said, but the *Life of King Edward* purports to give us the Confessor's last words. 'May God be gracious to this my wife', he says to Edith, 'for the zealous solicitude of her service. For certainly she has served me devotedly, and has always stood by my side like a beloved daughter.' Edward then turns to address Harold ('stretching out his hand', says the *Life*, just as depicted on the Tapestry): 'I commend this woman and all the kingdom to your protection', he continues. 'Serve and honour her with faithful obedience as your lady and sister, which she is, and do not despoil her, as long as she lives, of any due honour got from me.'[6]

The heavy emphasis on Edith's welfare is hardly surprising, given that the *Life* was written at her behest. What *is* surprising is how casually the subject of the kingdom is introduced. Edward seems to mention it in passing, almost as an afterthought. As a result, his words fall a long way short of providing a clear and unambiguous designation of his successor. Indeed, all the king says is that he commends the kingdom to Harold's protection, which sounds rather more like the words one would use to nominate a regent. Of course, we don't have to believe that these were actually Edward's last words, any more than we have to accept the testimony of the pro-Godwine sources that insist Harold did receive his predecessor's blessing. The *Life of King Edward* was completed after the Norman Conquest, and as such suffers from hindsight. Had there been an unambiguous bequest to Harold, the author and his patron, living in a post-Conquest world, may have diplomatically decided to downplay it. Nonetheless, when all allowances have been made, it remains striking that our best-informed source for the Confessor's death is so reticent on the crucial subject of who he wanted to succeed him.[7]

Nor is the *Life* alone in using such guarded language. The E version of the Chronicle may insist that Edward 'granted' the kingdom to Harold, but the C and D versions say simply that the king 'entrusted' it to him – a significant verbal weakening which again suggests that Harold may have been empowered to take care of the kingdom only as a temporary measure. The Bayeux Tapestry might seem to offer something a little stronger, for immediately after Edward's death it shows Harold being handed the crown by two figures, one of whom points back to the deathbed scene, as if to indicate that the one event had legitimized the other. But, once again, the Tapestry is carefully ambiguous. Harold's supporters could interpret this scene as being the moment when the crown was bequeathed to him; his detractors, on the other hand, might see only the moment where Harold *claimed* the bequest had been made. Similarly, it is often argued in Harold's favour that the Norman chronicler William of Poitiers – a very hostile source – refers to Edward's deathbed bequest several times and, while he challenges its legitimacy, he makes no attempt to deny that it happened. This, however, proves nothing. Only a handful of people – those present by his bedside – could have actually *refuted* the suggestion that Edward, in his last hours, had nominated Harold. So far as we can tell, none of them did so. All we can say is, in the case of Queen Edith, she chose to describe it in a very non-committal way, and that such vagueness is also apparent in a number of other contemporary sources. Many people, it seems, harboured serious doubts about Harold's version of events.[8]

What of Harold's election? Was he, as the E Chronicle and John of Worcester maintain, chosen to be king by the English magnates, or did he, as William of Poitiers alleges, seize the throne 'with the connivance of a few wicked men'? Certainly Harold was in a good position to put his case to a wide audience because, as we've seen, Edward the Confessor had died just a few days after Christmas and the dedication of Westminster Abbey, the combination of which events would have ensured there was a crowd of magnates at court. This is confirmed, more or less, by a pair of charters in favour of the abbey, given on the day of the dedication (28 December 1065), which show that during his last days Edward was indeed surrounded by the most important men in his kingdom. On the spiritual side we see no fewer than ten bishops, including both archbishops, as well as eight abbots. On the secular side, we see five earls: Harold, his brothers Gyrth and Leofwine, and also the brothers Eadwine and Morcar.[9]

The presence of Eadwine and Morcar – and the glaring absence of Earl Tostig – reminds us immediately of the recent rebellion. Just eight weeks earlier, the two brothers had assumed the leadership of the largest uprising in living memory, and successfully brought about Tostig's downfall, despite the fact that he was supposedly the second most powerful man in England. Morcar was now the new earl of Northumbria, which meant that he and Eadwine (lately recognized as earl of Mercia) between them controlled almost half the kingdom. Clearly, for Harold's bid for the throne to have been the success that it was, it must have been essential to have secured their support. Harold, of course, had led the negotiations with the rebels in October, and ultimately accepted that Morcar should replace Tostig. Were any other deals, one wonders, struck at the same moment?

Certainly a deal was struck at some point, because by early 1066

Harold was married to Eadwine's and Morcar's sister, Ealdgyth. This was very obviously a political match; apart from anything else, Harold already had a long-term partner, after the Danish fashion, named Edith Swan-Neck. Irritatingly, we do not know when his wedding to Ealdgyth took place, so we cannot date the alliance it embodies. She had previously been the wife of Gruffudd ap Llywelyn, the Welsh king killed in August 1063, so in theory her marriage to Harold could have occurred at any point after her first husband's death. It is most unlikely, however, to have occurred before the rebellion of October 1065: whatever Tostig's assertions to the contrary, it is impossible to believe that Harold had prior knowledge of the rebels' plans, and far more plausible that the revolt itself obliged him to reach an accommodation with his brother's opponents. The question therefore becomes whether the deal was done before or after the Confessor's death. Given that the king's declining health must have been evident to everyone in the final weeks of 1065, a deal during those weeks would seem the likeliest scenario. Presumably, though, it was agreed in secret. Harold could hardly have married Eadwine's and Morcar's sister without revealing his intentions regarding the throne – especially if, as later chroniclers contend, he had earlier agreed to marry a daughter of the duke of Normandy.[10]

For how long had Harold harboured such intentions? Certainly the idea of becoming king had occurred to him well before his alleged designation by the dying Confessor.[11] That much is clear from the *Life of King Edward*, the original purpose of which was plainly to justify some sort of Godwine takeover once the Confessor was gone. What form this would have taken is uncertain: the author divides his praise fairly evenly between Harold, Tostig and his patron, Queen Edith. But since that plan, and the *Life*'s original purpose, was wrecked by the northern rebellion, we can safely date Harold's ambition for power earlier than October 1065. Some historians have suggested that it was spurred by his trip to Normandy, which revealed the undiminished hopes of Duke William. Yet if anything this episode pushes the seeds of the earl's ambition further back in time, for all our sources agree that at least part of his reason for going to Normandy was to effect the liberation of his brother and nephew – men whom William had long held hostage as a guarantee of his right to one day rule England. Harold's desire to put his kinsmen beyond harm's reach arguably indicates that his thoughts were already tending in the same direction.[12]

How Harold might have realized his ambition had the northern rebellion not happened, or been unsuccessful, is anybody's guess. But it is far from certain that, had Tostig remained in power as earl of Northumbria at the time of Edward's death, he would have stood in the way of his brother's accession. The rivalry between Tostig and Harold was a consequence of the October rising, not a cause of it. Indeed, if we look back at their careers before that point, all we can see is co-operation – Tostig's support of Harold's conquest of Wales being the most obvious case in point. Part of the reason for the Godwine family's success had always been their ability to stick together in both triumph and adversity. Based on past behaviour, it is more reasonable to suppose that Tostig, had he not been banished, would have supported rather than opposed his older brother's bid for the throne.

The real obstacle to Harold's ambition was neither Tostig nor William but Edgar Ætheling. The son of Edward the Exile, great-nephew of Edward the Confessor, Edgar was directly descended from the ancient dynasty that had ruled Wessex, and later England, since the beginning; the blood of Alfred and Athelstan, not to mention the celebrated tenth-century King Edgar, flowed in his veins. This fact, combined with the considerable efforts that had been required to secure his return from Hungary, must have led many to expect that the ætheling would in due course succeed his great-uncle. After all, his title, accorded to him in contemporary sources, indicates that he was considered worthy of ascending the throne. Moreover, according to one Continental chronicler with close connections to the English court, Harold himself had sworn to the Confessor that, when the time came, he would uphold Edgar's cause.[13] Whether this was true or not, the mere existence of this legitimate heir was singularly awkward for Harold. The saving grace was that in the autumn of 1065 Edgar was little more than a child, apparently no more than thirteen years old, and – owing to the Confessor's political weakness – with no power base of his own.[14] All Harold needed was enough of the other English magnates to agree that Edgar's rights should be set aside, which is what he must have obtained from Eadwine and Morcar. The incentive for them, of course, was Harold's marriage to their sister. As queen, Ealdgyth would produce children who would unite the fortunes of the two formerly rival houses, and a new royal dynasty would arise to take the place of the old.

No single fact points to a conspiracy of this kind more obviously than the circumstances of Harold's coronation, which took place on 6 January 1066, probably in Westminster Abbey. The Bayeux Tapestry shows the new king crowned and enthroned, holding his rod and sceptre, flanked on one side by two men who hand him a ceremonial sword, and on the other by the solitary figure of Archbishop Stigand. The inclusion of the excommunicate archbishop of Canterbury is almost certainly an underhand piece of Norman propaganda: it is far more likely that Harold's consecration was performed by Ealdred, the archbishop of York, as John of Worcester later insisted was the case. What *does* damn Harold, however, is the unseemly haste with which the ceremony was arranged. The new king was crowned the day after the Confessor's death, and on the same day as the old king's funeral. No previous king of England had demonstrated such a desperate hurry to have himself consecrated, for the good reason that in England the coronation had never been regarded as a constitutive part of the king-making process. Normally many months would pass between the crucial process of election and a new ruler's formal investiture. Edward the Confessor, as we have seen, had come to the throne by popular consent in the summer of 1042, but was not crowned until Easter the following year. Harold's rush to have himself crowned within hours of his predecessor's death was therefore quite unprecedented, and suggests that he was trying to buttress what was by any reckoning a highly dubious claim with an instant consecration. It is the most obviously suspect act in the drama.[15]

The last weeks of 1065, then, probably ran as follows. The king is clearly dying, and the greatest earl in the kingdom determines he will succeed him, having perhaps nurtured the hope of doing so for several years. He strikes a deal with his rivals in exchange for their support. The king dies, inevitably behind closed doors, and surrounded by only a handful of intimates, including the earl himself, his sister the queen and a partisan archbishop of Canterbury; afterwards it is given out that the old king, in his dying moments, nominated the earl as his successor. Before anyone can object – indeed, so fast that the dead king is barely in his grave – the new king is crowned, and is therefore deemed to be God's anointed.

Not everyone was convinced. Clearly many people were surprised by Harold's succession, not least because it required a far more legitimate candidate – Edgar Ætheling – be set aside. Half a century later, the historian William of Malmesbury wrote that Harold had seized the throne, having first exacted an oath of loyalty from the chief nobles. Malmesbury was hardly a hostile witness: in the same paragraph he praises Harold as a man of prudence and fortitude, and notes the English claim that the earl was granted the throne by Edward the Confessor. 'But I think', he adds, 'that this claim rests more on goodwill than judgement, for it makes [the Confessor] pass on his inheritance to a man of whose influence he had always been suspicious.'[16] More telling still is an account written in the 1090s for Baldwin, abbot of Bury St Edmunds, which described Harold's hasty coronation as sacrilegious, and accused the earl of taking the throne 'with cunning force'. Since Baldwin had formerly been Edward the Confessor's physician, and was therefore very likely present at his death, this testimony ought to be accorded considerable weight. It is also possible that there was opposition in the north of England at the unexpected enthronement of the earl of Wessex. We know that soon after his coronation Harold travelled to York, a destination far beyond the usual ambit of English kings. Perhaps the occasion was his marriage to Ealdgyth, planned secretly in advance and now publicly celebrated. Alternatively, Harold may have had to go there in order to quell opposition to his rule. William of Malmesbury says as much, and has it that the people of Northumbria initially refused to accept Harold as their king. Unfortunately, elements of his story suggest that he may have confused these events with the northern rebellion of the previous year. Nevertheless, the likeliest reason for Harold's trip to York was some sort of unrest. As the C version of the Anglo-Saxon Chronicle ruefully observed, there was little quiet in England while Harold wore the crown.[17]

Sadly we have few good contemporary sources for the immediate reaction in Normandy to the news of Harold's accession. The chronicler Wace, writing a century later, says that William was near Rouen, preparing to go hunting with his knights and squires, when a messenger arrived from England. The duke heard the message privately, and then returned to his hall in the city in anger, speaking to no one.[18]

Whatever the merits of this scene, we can surmise certain things. Edward the Confessor's final illness had been quite long-drawn-out, and so William must have known in the closing weeks of 1065 that the English throne was about to fall vacant. This has led some historians to wonder why he did not cross the Channel earlier, perhaps in time for Christmas, in order to push his candidacy when the moment arrived. In reality, though, this was not an option. If William had come in anticipation, however large an escort he might have been allowed to bring, he would still have been a stranger in a strange land, ill-placed to resist any parties that opposed his accession, and, moreover, vulnerable to the sort of deadly intrigues that went on at the English court. The only realistic option for William was to do precisely as he did: remain in Normandy and await an invitation to come and be crowned, as had previously happened in the case of Harthacnut and Edward the Confessor. More to the point, he already had someone who was supposed to be representing his interests in England, namely Harold Godwineson. During his trip to Normandy, says William of Poitiers, Harold had promised William 'that he would strive to the utmost with his counsel and with his wealth to ensure that the English monarchy should be pledged to him after Edward's death'. The news that Harold had made himself king was thus regarded by William as a betrayal, a violation of the fealty and the other sacred oaths he had previously sworn. According to William of Jumièges, the duke's immediate response was to send messengers to England urging Harold to renounce the throne and keep his pledges. Harold, unsurprisingly, chose to ignore these admonitions.[19]

From an early stage, therefore, it must have been clear that if William was going to obtain the English throne, he would have to mount an invasion of England – 'to claim his inheritance through force of arms', as William of Poitiers put it. Needless to say, this was an incredibly risky proposition, quite unlike the cautious kind of warfare that he had practised to such advantage during the previous two decades. Its only real parallel – in terms of risk rather than scale – is the battle he chose to fight at the start of his career, at Val-ès-Dunes, when threatened with extinction by his domestic enemies. From this we can reasonably conclude that Norman writers who emphasize the justice of William's cause – in particular his chaplain, William of Poitiers – accurately reflected the attitude of the duke himself. By choosing to embark upon a strategy of direct confrontation, William was effectively submitting that cause – along with his reputation, his life and the lives of thousands of fellow Normans – to the judgement of God.[20]

The duke's conviction in the righteousness of his cause is also reflected in his appeal to the pope. Very soon after learning of Harold's accession, he dispatched an embassy to Rome to put his case before Alexander II. Sadly, no text of this case survives, but there is no doubt that it was written down and circulated widely at the time, for it seems to inform several of the Norman accounts of 1066 (that of William of Poitiers in particular). Edward's promise and Harold's perjury were evidently the main planks of its argument, though it is likely that the Normans also alleged laxity against the English Church, epitomized by Archbishop Stigand. The pope clearly felt that the case was well founded (it may also have helped that he was a former pupil of Lanfranc), for he quickly decided that force would be legitimate. As a token of his decision, he sent William's ambassadors back from Rome bearing a banner that the duke could carry into battle.[21]

The support of the pope was all well and good, but what of support in Normandy itself? Another of William's initial moves in 1066 was evidently to summon a select meeting of the duchy's leading men: his half-brothers Robert and Odo and his friends William fitz Osbern and Roger of Montgomery are among the familiar names mentioned by Wace and William of Poitiers. According to Wace, these men, the duke's most intimate counsellors, gave him their full backing, but advised calling a second, wider assembly, in order to make his case to the rest of the Norman magnates. Again, although late, this is perfectly credible testimony: several other authors refer more vaguely to William taking consultation. William of Malmesbury, writing in the early twelfth century, says he summoned a council of magnates to the town of Lillebonne, 'in order to ascertain the view of individuals on the project'. Malmesbury also says that this was done after the duke had received the papal banner, which, if correct, would suggest that this wider council took place in the early spring.[22]

Patchy as our sources are, they suggest that at this meeting there was rather less enthusiasm for the projected invasion. 'Many of the greater men argued speciously that the enterprise was too arduous and far beyond the resources of Normandy', says William of Poitiers; the doubters pointed out the strength of Harold's position, observing that 'both in wealth and numbers of soldiers his kingdom was greatly superior to their own land'. Much of the Normans' anxiety seems to have hinged on the difficulties of crossing the Channel. 'Sire, we fear the sea', they say in Wace's account, while, according to William of Poitiers, the main concern was English naval superiority: Harold 'had numerous ships in his fleet, and skilled sailors, hardened in many dangers and sea-battles'.[23]

On this matter it is easy to sympathize with the naysayers. Although there is no way of making an accurate comparison between the naval resources of England and Normandy, the impression that

England was the superior power is entirely borne out by the sources. As we've seen, the military history of the Confessor's reign can be told largely in terms of ships. In the 1040s Edward had repeatedly commanded fleets for defence against Viking attack, and instituted a naval blockade of Flanders at the instance of the German emperor. The Godwines had forced their return in 1052 thanks to their ability to recruit a large fleet in exile, and Harold's victory in Wales in 1063 had been won in part because he was able to draw on naval support. By contrast, the history of Normandy in this period is about war waged across land borders; the only fleets we hear about are the ones raised by Edward and Alfred in the 1030s and, as some Normans might well have pointed out in the spring of 1066, none of these had resulted in success.[24]

Moreover, mounting a naval attack on England was not simply a matter of feasibility; there was, in addition, the question of obligation. According to Wace, those Normans who said that they feared the sea had also added 'we are not bound to serve beyond it'. Why should the Normans follow their duke on such a patently hazardous adventure? We know that in general terms William's subjects accepted that they owed him military service. The clearest statement of this fact comes in a document drawn up shortly after the Conquest (the so-called Penitential Ordinance) which refers at one point to those who fought because such service was owed.[25] Presumably these obligations in many instances had existed well before 1066, and explain in part how William was able to raise armies in the earlier part of his career. The frustrating thing is we don't know on what basis military service was rendered. Historians used to argue that the Normans had a precociously developed feudal system, wherein many if not all major landowners recognized their obligation to serve the duke with a fixed number of knights. The problem is that there is virtually no evidence at all for the existence of such quotas prior to 1066.[26]

The first time, in fact, that we get a clear indication of formal obligations being discussed is in 1066 itself, during the build-up to the invasion of England. Wace speaks of individual negotiations between William and each of his vassals, during which he begged them to render double what they normally owed and reassured them that this extraordinary service would not be drawn into a precedent. 'Each said what he would do and how many ships he would bring.

And the duke had it all recorded at once, namely the ships and knights, and the barons agreed to it.'[27]

This would all seem pretty thin – Wace was writing a century later – were it not for the fact that William's written record, or at least a redaction of it, has survived. It amounts to a short paragraph of Latin, copied in an early twelfth-century hand, and it fills only a single page of a much larger manuscript. Historians call it the Ship List, because it is simply a list of fourteen names and the number of ships that each agreed to provide for William in 1066. For a long time it was regarded as inauthentic on the grounds that such precise statements of military service are otherwise unknown at such an early date. Nowadays scholars are inclined to regard it as a genuine résumé of the arrangements made that year, drawn up very soon after the Conquest. In other words, it bears witness to a key moment not only in the preparation for William's expedition but also in the development of the duke's relationship with his vassals. The extraordinary demands of 1066 itself seem to have set the Normans on the road to the more exacting form of feudalism for which they are famous.[28]

Precisely how William won over the more sceptical of his subjects is unknown. Wace has it that they were tricked into offering additional service by William fitz Osbern, who led the negotiations on the duke's behalf. No doubt much was made of the injury to the duke's right, the justice of his cause, and the permission he had obtained from the pope: if Malmesbury is correct about the timing of the assembly, William would have been able to display the papal banner and assure his audience that God was most definitely on their side. Certainly one of the inducements that was put forward to the Normans was the enormous material rewards that would come to them should the plan succeed. According to William of Poitiers, the duke pointed out that Harold could offer his men nothing in victory, whereas he, William, was promising those who followed him a share of the spoils. This may explain why, in the end, the Normans agreed to having the terms of their service written down, for the greater the service rendered, the greater the eventual reward.[29]

It was one thing to pledge large amounts of service, another to deliver it. The figures listed on the Ship List must have been minimum requirements, but even so their scale impresses. William fitz Osbern and Roger of Montgomery, the duke's intimate advisers since the start of his career, both appear on the list, pledged to provide sixty ships apiece; William's half-brothers, Odo and Robert, were respectively required to find 100 and 120. How these men, great as they were, proposed to procure these personal armadas is, like so much else, a mystery. The Bayeux Tapestry gives the impression that the entire Norman fleet was constructed from scratch. 'Here Duke William ordered ships to be built', it says, and immediately we see men with axes hacking down trees and shipwrights turning the timber into boats. Given the very large numbers required, and the very limited time available, we do not have to believe that every vessel was obtained in this way. The duke and his magnates must have had some ships of their own already to hand, and others could have been purchased or requisitioned, either in Normandy itself, or from places further afield, such as Flanders. Nevertheless, in the spring of 1066 there must have been much frenzied activity in the forests and shipyards of Normandy as men struggled to meet the demands of the duke's great project that was now underway.[30]

News of these preparations must have travelled quickly across the Channel – William of Poitiers tells us that Harold had sent spies to Normandy, and in any case activity on such a scale could hardly have been kept secret. By Easter, at which point the new English king returned south from his mysterious trip to York, fears of foreign invasion must already have been mounting.

It was, therefore, unfortunate that his return to Westminster co-incided with a rare celestial phenomenon. 'Throughout all England', says the Anglo-Saxon Chronicle, 'a portent such as men had never seen before was seen in the heavens.' Every night during the last week of April, an extraordinary star was seen blazing across the sky. Some people, says the Chronicle, called it 'the long-haired star', while others called it a comet. It was, in fact, the most famous comet of all; the one which, six and a half centuries later, the astronomer Edmond Halley calculated came round every seventy-six years. But to men and women living through the uncertain events of 1066, it seemed wholly unprecedented, and as such was regarded as a terrible omen. 'Many people', said William of Jumièges, 'said that it portended a change in some kingdom.' On the Bayeux Tapestry, an anxious crowd of Englishmen point to the comet in wonder, while in the next scene King Harold is told what is evidently disturbing news.

Beneath his feet, in the Tapestry's border, a ghostly fleet is already at sea.[31]

And indeed, no sooner had the comet disappeared than news came that southern England was being attacked by a hostile fleet – but not a Norman one. The attacker was Harold's estranged brother, Tostig, last seen being driven into exile as a result of the previous year's rebellion. Precisely what he had been up to in the meantime is an insoluble mystery. A thirteenth-century Icelandic writer called Snorri Sturluson (of whom more later) maintains that the exiled earl travelled to Denmark and tried to persuade its king, Swein Estrithson, to help him conquer England. Orderic Vitalis, writing considerably closer to events, has it that Tostig visited Normandy and had actually returned to England as an agent of Duke William. Both these authors, however, make major factual errors in telling their stories, which should caution us against giving them too much credence.[32] All we can say for certain is what the Anglo-Saxon Chronicle and the *Life of King Edward* tell us: that when Tostig left England in 1065 he sailed to Flanders, where he was received by his brother-in-law, Count Baldwin. Most probably it was from Flanders that he launched his assault.[33]

According to the Chronicle, Tostig and his troops landed first on the Isle of Wight, which they plundered for money and provisions, and then sailed eastwards along the coast, raiding as they went, until they reached the port of Sandwich. Their wider objective is unclear. Possibly, in view of his rancorous split with Harold, Tostig was hoping to unseat his brother and replace him as king. More plausible, perhaps, is the notion that the younger Godwine was simply aiming to recover the estates and position he had lost the previous autumn, much as his father had done in similar circumstances fourteen years earlier, using almost identical tactics.

Whatever Tostig's hopes might have been, they were ultimately dashed. Harold set out for Sandwich at once to confront his brother, and Tostig, hearing this news, put to sea again, taking with him the town's shipmen. 'Some went willingly, others unwillingly', says the Chronicle, suggesting that enthusiasm for the exile's cause, in the south at least, was at best mixed. Nor did his fortunes improve as he sailed north. Having reached the River Humber he raided southwards into Lincolnshire, 'slaying many good men' and perhaps intentionally trying to provoke his arch rivals, Eadwine and Morcar. If so he was not kept waiting long, for the two earls soon appeared leading land levies. Whether or not any actual fighting subsequently took place is unclear; the Chronicle says simply that the Mercian brothers drove Tostig out. Clearly one of the decisive factors that counted against him was the desertion of the press-ganged shipmen of Sandwich, and the extent of this haemorrhage is captured by the D Chronicler, who noted that the earl had sailed into the Humber with sixty ships, but left with only twelve. No doubt to his immense frustration, Tostig had found that support for his several rivals – Harold, Eadwine and Morcar – was far stronger than anticipated. From the Humber he sailed the remnant of his fleet further north and sought refuge with his sometime adversary, King Malcolm of Scotland.[34]

Having successfully seen off his troublesome younger brother, Harold turned his mind to the far greater threat looming across the Channel, and began preparations to resist the planned Norman invasion. Tostig's attack may have caused him to begin mobilizing his forces rather sooner than he might otherwise have done, and Harold, having arrived in Sandwich too late to intercept his brother, remained there waiting for his troops to muster. The reason for the delay may well have been the scale of the operation. 'He gathered together greater naval and land armies than any king in this country had ever gathered before', says the C Chronicle, clearly impressed.

Perhaps the host approached the notional maximum of 16,000 men that the recruitment customs recorded in the Domesday Book suggest. The gathering sense of national emergency, the fear of imminent foreign invasion, must have helped to swell the king's ranks, and Harold, like English leaders in other eras faced with similar crises, no doubt played on such sentiments in his military summons. Several decades later John of Worcester penned a roseate picture of the king, for the most part formulaic in its praise, but probably authentic in recalling how Harold had ordered his earls and sheriffs 'to exert themselves by land and sea for the defence of their country'.[35]

Having assembled his host at Sandwich, probably in the month of May, Harold took the unusual decision to break it up again. As the Chronicle explains, the king decided to station levies everywhere along the coast.[36] Perhaps he feared that William, when he came, would repeat Tostig's tactics, raiding along the shoreline in search of supplies and support. These troops would also have been able to provide an effective lookout for Norman sails, and no doubt there was some plan to enable the whole army to reassemble if a large enemy force made a landing. Harold himself sailed from Sandwich to the Isle of Wight (another decision possibly inspired by his brother's attack) and established his headquarters there. Then he and the thousands of men spread out across England's south coast did all they could do in such circumstances: they watched, and waited.

On 18 June 1066 William and his wife Matilda stood in the abbey of Holy Trinity in Caen, surrounded by a crowd of nobles, bishops, abbots and townspeople. It was the day of the abbey's dedication, and we can picture the scene because it is described in a charter given on the day itself. Founded by Matilda some seven years earlier, Holy Trinity can hardly have been finished by the summer of 1066; as with Westminster Abbey a few months earlier, the rapid turn of political events had evidently prompted a dedication ceremony in advance of the church's completion. Here was another public occasion for William and Matilda to demonstrate their piety, and to seek divine approval for the projected invasion. As the charter attests, as well as giving lands and rights to the new abbey, the couple also presented one of their daughters, Cecilia, to begin life there as a

nun. Nor was it just the duke and his consort making such dona-
tions: the charter (properly speaking a pancart) also records the gifts
made to the abbey by several Norman magnates, and elsewhere in
Normandy we can see other individuals making gifts to religious
houses around this time as part of their spiritual preparations for
the coming conflict. A certain Roger fitz Turold, for instance, made
a grant of land to Holy Trinity in Rouen, confirmed by a charter
which stated that he was 'about to put to sea with Count William'.
At some point during the summer, William himself gave a charter
to the ducal abbey of Fécamp, promising its monks the future possession of land at Steyning in Sussex 'if God should grant him victory
in England'.[37]

As such spiritual preparations suggest, by mid-June the Normans
were nearing a point where the planned invasion would be possible.
The fleet to transport them across the Channel, begun several months
earlier, must have been nearing completion, with ships – bought,
borrowed or newly built – being assembled at the mouth of the
River Dives in the port of Dives-sur-Mer. As both Wace and the
Bayeux Tapestry make clear, they were all different shapes and sizes:
some were warships, akin to the familiar Viking longboats, which
could have measured anywhere between fifteen and thirty-six metres
(49 to 118 feet); others were cargo vessels with deeper draughts,
suitable for transporting large quantities of food and wine, or for
fitting with stalls for the transport of horses. The closest surviving
examples are the ships sunk at Skuldelev in Denmark towards the
end of the eleventh century, excavated in the 1960s and now on
display in the Viking Ship Museum at Roskilde. Wace also writes
of smaller boats and skiffs that were used to ferry arms, harnesses
and other equipment.[38]

How large this highly miscellaneous armada was remains a matter
of conjecture. The Ship List, arguably our surest guide, states that
William's magnates had furnished him with 1,000 ships, though the
actual total of its individual quotas comes to only 776. It also states
that the duke had many other ships from other men, though it is
highly unlikely that these uncounted extras would be sufficiently
numerous to create the kind of monster fleet imagined by some
chroniclers: William of Jumièges, for instance, who offers the utterly
incredible figure of 3,000 vessels. Interestingly, Wace, writing a century
later, expressed his doubts about such inflated figures because they

conflicted with the oral tradition that had come down to him. 'I heard my father say, and I remember it well, although it was before I was armed as a knight, that there were seven hundred ships less four.' A figure of 696 (which, Wace makes clear, included even the little boats and skiffs) fits far better with the evidence of the Ship List, and still constitutes a very big fleet.[39]

A big fleet was necessary because William, like Harold, was in the process of recruiting a very large army. The Ship List suggests that, as with the ships, individual Norman magnates had agreed to support the invasion with a certain number of knights, but sadly it records such quotas in only four cases. Clearly, many more Normans must have agreed to serve, either in fulfilment of existing obligations to the duke or in exchange for new inducements. Moreover, it was not just Normans that were turning out for William. 'Foreign knights flocked to him in great numbers', explains William of Poitiers, 'attracted by the well-known liberality of the duke, but all fully confident of the justice of his cause.' Liberality, of course, is a polite way of saying that William was recruiting mercenaries: 'men with a lust for war', as Orderic Vitalis put it, 'panting for the spoils of England'. They came from all over Francia and possibly even further afield – between them these two chroniclers mention the men of France, Brittany, Maine, Aquitaine, Poitou, Burgundy, 'and other peoples north of the Alps'.[40]

Alas, we cannot say with any certainty how many men William eventually recruited. Medieval chroniclers are notoriously bad guides when it comes to estimating troop numbers. William of Poitiers, for example, offers us the figure of 50,000 men, and then a few pages later increases it to 60,000; Orderic Vitalis, who may have taken his information from Poitiers, suggests that there were 50,000 knights 'and a great company of foot soldiers'. Other chroniclers put the total even higher: at least two say that it was 150,000. No medieval armies were ever so large. The peak figures in Britain during the Middle Ages, derived from muster rolls rather than monastic observation, occurred during the reign of Edward I, whose largest armies numbered around 30,000 men. Needless to say, if this was the maximum for a king of England in the more populous and prosperous thirteenth century, it would have been difficult for an eleventh-century duke of Normandy to match, let alone exceed it. Modern historians have tried to arrive at better estimates for

William's invasion force, but invariably end up basing their figures on conjecture (extrapolating, for example, from the number of ships, a pointless exercise if ever there was one, since their size and number are also unknowable).[41]

The best we can do in such circumstances is to look at comparable situations in subsequent centuries. When it came to crossing the Channel, no English king in the later Middle Ages ever managed more than 10,000 men. Given the disparities in power and population mentioned above, if William managed to assemble an army of even half that size he would have been doing extremely well. The consensus among Victorian scholars – who, whatever their other faults, knew a thing or two about landing cavalry forces on foreign shores – was that the Norman army may have measured around 7,000 men. Despite recent attempts to dismiss it, this is a conclusion that remains valid and compelling.[42]

To judge from comments made by William of Poitiers, the Norman invasion force, both army and fleet, was fully assembled by the first week of August, but the duke's desire to set sail was frustrated for a whole month thereafter by unfavourable winds. In recent times, historians have been very sceptical of this statement. What William was actually doing, they aver, was waiting for Harold's army to disband, either because its supplies had run out or else because the majority of men would have had to return home in time for the harvest. There are good reasons, however, for rejecting such scepticism. In the first place, comparative evidence suggests that delay in crossing the Channel due to contrary winds occurred all the time. In later, better-documented centuries, we see armies and ambassadors held up for weeks on end by bad weather, or dashed to pieces at sea when in desperation they attempt a crossing in such conditions. Experts with greater nautical experience tend to the opinion that, had the wind been blowing in the right direction that August, William would have been extremely foolish had he not seized the moment and got on with it. More to the point, the question of resources cuts both ways. Waiting for Harold's army to run into difficulties and disband was all very well, but it would only have worked if William could keep his own equally large army well supplied and disciplined for the same duration.[43]

This was no mean feat. Some years ago, an American scholar named Bernard Bachrach wrote a paper looking at the logistics involved in keeping the Norman invasion force supplied during its month-long stay at Dives-sur-Mer. For unconvincing reasons (essentially, the testimony of an obscure contemporary chronicle) he assumed an army of 14,000 men, i.e. twice the generally accepted figure, but even if we halve his totals, they remain arresting. Supposing the men subsisted only on grain (highly unlikely, of course), it would have required fourteen tons a day to keep them fed, and a similar amount to feed an estimated 2,000 horses. Between them the men and their mounts would have also needed around 30,000 gallons of fresh water *every day*, and the horses, in addition, would have needed four to five tons of straw a day for their bedding. The resulting totals for a whole month are mammoth: thousands of tons of food and water, all of which had to be transported to the encampment, either ferried down the Dives or carted along rutted roads. Equal forethought, of course, had to be given to sanitation. That many men and horses would have produced a mountain of manure and a river of urine (2,000 tons and 700,000 gallons are Bachrach's respective figures for the horses alone). Lastly, of course, they all required shelter: tents for the men, stalls for the horses. These, it bears repeating, are minimum requirements for keeping people alive for a month, more in keeping with a refugee camp than a volunteer army. To keep his men together, and to maintain their morale, William would have had to have found many more items – meat, fish, wine and ale – in similarly colossal quantities.[44]

Just to keep his army supplied, therefore, was a major undertaking – but one which William evidently managed to pull off. 'Such was his moderation and wisdom that abundant provision was made for the soldiers and their hosts', says William of Poitiers, who was also at pains to stress that the duke had forbidden his army from plundering the local people. 'The crops waited unharmed for the scythe of the harvester, and were neither trampled by the proud stampede of horsemen nor cut down by foragers. A man who was weak or unarmed could ride singing on his horse wherever he wished, without trembling at the sight of squadrons of knights.' Even if, as usual, Poitiers is laying it on here with a trowel, his overall claim must be broadly true. The Norman army could not live off the land while it remained in Normandy. Order and discipline had to be maintained.[45]

At last, on 8 September, the stalemate was broken, when Harold was forced to stand down his army. 'The men's provisions had run out', explains the Chronicle, 'and no one could keep them there any longer.' The troops, we are told, were given permission to return home. The king, still on the Isle of Wight, sent his fleet back to London, and then set out for the city himself. As the Chronicle says, he had managed to keep his army together for the whole summer, and he must have hoped that whatever was delaying his opponent would continue to detain him a little while longer. Very soon it would be too late in the year for William to attempt a crossing.

On arrival in London, however, Harold was greeted with terrible news. Hostile sails had at last been sighted on the horizon; an invasion fleet had landed. But, once again, it was not the enemy he had been expecting.[46]

It was Tostig, come back for a second try. And this time he had brought some Vikings.

10

The Thunderbolt

Contemporaries, it is clear, stood in awe of Harold Sigurdson. 'The thunderbolt of the North', was how Adam of Bremen, who wrote in the 1070s, remembered him; 'the strongest living man under the sun', said William of Poitiers (albeit reporting the words of somebody else). A half-brother of King Olaf II of Norway, born around 1015, Harold had been forced to flee from his native country while still in his teens, and ended up spending several years at the court of Yaroslav the Wise, king of Russia. From there he ventured south, like countless generations of Vikings before him, to Constantinople, capital of Byzantium, the eastern rump of the Roman Empire, and rose to great power and eminence by rendering military service to successive emperors. His reputation and his fortune won, he returned to Scandinavia in the mid-1040s and used his well-honed skills to make himself king of Norway, where he subsequently reigned with a fist of iron, fighting his neighbours and executing his rivals. Small wonder that when later Norse historians looked back on his life they dubbed him 'the Hard Ruler', or Hardrada.[1]

The fact that his famous nickname was not recorded until the thirteenth century, however, alerts us immediately to an inescapable problem. Harold's contemporaries may have been impressed by his epic tale, but they did not write it down – unsurprisingly, for eleventh-century Scandinavia was still for the most part a pagan society and hence largely illiterate. The first sources to deal with his reign in any detail are Norse sagas dating from the late twelfth and early thirteenth centuries, almost 150 years after the events they purport to describe. The most celebrated account of all – the so-called *King Harold's Saga* – was told by an Icelandic historian called Snorri Sturluson, who died in 1241 and wrote in the 1220s and 1230s – that is, almost two centuries after Harold's own time.

How much trust can we place in such late sources? On the positive side, we can see from similarities in his text that Snorri drew on earlier sagas, as well as oral traditions. He also considered himself to be an objective writer, and in several passages seeks to reassure his readers of his conscientiousness as a historian. Halfway through *King Harold's Saga*, for example, he explains that he has omitted many of the feats ascribed to his protagonist, 'partly because of my lack of knowledge, and partly because I am reluctant to place on record stories that are unsubstantiated. Although I have been told various stories and have heard about other deeds, it seems to me better that my account should later be expanded than that it should have to be emended.'[2]

There is no reason to doubt Snorri's sincerity but, alas, we cannot set as much store by his stories as we could with a contemporary source, especially when it comes to points of detail. Take, for instance, his account of Harold's adventures in the east. On the one hand, we can be absolutely certain that the future king went to Constantinople, and that he rose to a position of prominence there, because he appears in contemporary Byzantine sources (as 'Araltes'). These same sources confirm Snorri's statements that Harold fought for the emperor in Sicily and Bulgaria, and show that he ultimately obtained the rank of *spatharocandidate*, just three levels below the emperor himself. But, on the other hand, when it comes to the details of Harold's eastern adventures, the same local sources show that Snorri was often wrong. Sometimes he gives events in the incorrect order, and at other times he gets the names of key individuals confused. Harold, for instance, is said by Snorri to have blinded Emperor Monomachus, whereas contemporary sources show that the true victim was the previous emperor, Michael Calaphates.[3] This leads us to a general conclusion about the value of Snorri's work. The broad thrust of his story may well be true, but on points of detail it has to be regarded as very suspect, and all but useless unless it can be corroborated by other, more reliable witnesses.

Harold apparently returned from his adventures in the east in 1045, at which point he intruded himself in the struggle for power in Scandinavia between his nephew, King Magnus of Norway, and the king of Denmark, Swein Estrithson (discussed above, Chapter 4). If there is any truth in Snorri's version of events, the former *spatharocandidate* employed the same underhand and unscrupulous methods that had worked so effectively in Byzantium, siding first with Swein, but then defecting to Magnus in return for a half-share of the latter's kingdom. When Magnus died in 1047 he reportedly bequeathed all of Norway to Harold and declared that Swein should be left unmolested in possession of Denmark. His uncle, however, was not the kind of man to settle for such half-measures, and soon the war between the two countries was resumed.[4]

According to some modern historians, Hardrada from the start of his reign also had similar designs on England. There is, however, precious little evidence to support such a view, either in the contemporary record or, for that matter, in the later sagas. It is often said that the new Norwegian king considered himself to have a claim to the English throne on account of the alleged deal between Magnus and Harthacnut that each should be the other's heir. Whether this deal, first reported by a mid-twelfth-century writer, had any basis in fact or not, Magnus certainly behaved as if England was his by right. As we have seen, Edward the Confessor took the threat from Norway very seriously during the early years of his reign, setting out every summer with his fleet to defend his coast from invasion.[5]

In the case of Harold Hardrada, by contrast, there is scant evidence to indicate a similarly hostile intent. Historians have made much of an obscure Norwegian raid that took place somewhere in England in 1058, led by Hardrada's son, Magnus, because an Irish annalist described it as an attempt at conquest. In reality it can have been little more than a young man's luckless quest for adventure and booty. It finds no mention in any of the Norse sagas, and was barely noticed by the Anglo-Saxon Chronicle ('A pirate host came from Norway', says the D version, briefly and uniquely, as a coda to its description of Earl Ælfgar's rebellion that year). Beyond this there is nothing in our English sources to suggest that an invasion from Norway was either anticipated or feared. Edward the Confessor, far from sailing out from Sandwich each summer, disbanded his fleet in the early 1050s and cancelled the geld which paid for it. Later in the reign, when the Godwine brothers were effectively running the kingdom, neither demonstrated any concern with Scandinavian attack. Tostig concentrated on securing peace with Scotland, and Harold on carrying war into Wales, and both felt sufficiently confident to leave England for trips to the Continent. Of course, one could argue that, by dealing with their Celtic neighbours, the Godwines were strengthening the kingdom generally, and hence improving its ability to withstand any future Viking assault, but that would seem to be a fairly roundabout way to prepare were such an assault really regarded as imminent. The reasonable conclusion is that it was not regarded as such. Prior to 1066, Harold Hardrada is mentioned only once in the Anglo-Saxon Chronicle – at the start of his reign, when he sent messengers to England in order to make peace.[6]

The truth is that, from the moment of his accession onwards, the Norwegian king was entirely preoccupied with his struggle against Swein Estrithson for control of Denmark; not until 1064 did he agree to a permanent peace, and even after that he had to contend with opposition within Norway because of his oppressive rule.[7] Both the Scandinavian and English sources, in short, point to the same conclusion, which is that the idea of invading England was not seriously entertained by Harold Hardrada until the year 1066 itself. And the reason it took root that year, most likely, was because it was planted by Tostig Godwineson.

Tostig, as we've already seen, had not responded well to the prospect of a life in permanent exile. We know that after his banishment from England in November 1065 he had fled to Flanders, and most likely it was from Flanders that he returned in the spring of 1066, raiding along the southern and eastern coasts before eventually retiring to Scotland. According to the Anglo-Saxon Chronicle, he remained in Scotland as the guest of King Malcolm for the rest of the summer.[8]

Precisely how and when he established contact with Harold Hardrada is therefore something of a mystery. One possibility is that he did so early in the year, ahead of his spring raid. Such was the belief of Snorri Sturluson, and it finds some support in other sources. A twelfth-century English chronicler called Geoffrey Gaimar, for example, informs us that most of Tostig's own troops in the spring had been drawn from Flanders, but also says that some ships had joined him from Orkney, a territory then under Norwegian control.[9]

This has led some historians to see Tostig as the mastermind of an elaborate strategy in 1066. In this view, his initial raid was not a failure at all, but rather a clever diversionary tactic, a preliminary feint intended to focus English attention on the south coast, away from the larger assault he was planning to launch from the north.[10] While this is possible, it does smack somewhat of reading events backwards, and ascribing to Tostig's cunning a course of events that could easily have been determined by contingency. An alternative reading is that the earl simply secured some sort of tacit co-operation from Hardrada ahead of his spring attack, then, when that attack failed, turned to him again in search of more substantial support.

Whenever it was that the two of them agreed to collaborate, it seems very likely that in order to broker the alliance Tostig travelled to Norway to meet Hardrada in person. Partly this is because it is hard to conceive of such an alliance being struck without a personal meeting, but mainly it is because Tostig's arrival in Norway forms such a central plank of the story as told in the Norse sagas. In Snorri's account, and also in the accounts of his known sources, Tostig first visits Denmark to seek the help of King Swein, but his proposal is rejected. Disgruntled but undeterred, he pushes on to Norway where he meets Hardrada at Oslo Fjord (appropriately, since the city of Oslo was Hardrada's own foundation). The Norwegian king is at first aloof and suspicious, telling Tostig that his subjects will not be keen to participate. Tostig, however, proceeds to talk Hardrada around, reminding the king of his putative claim, and plying him with compliments ('Everyone knows that there has never been a warrior in Scandinavia to compare with you'). He also stresses that the conquest of England will be easy on account of his own involvement, telling the king: 'I can ensure that the majority of the magnates there will be your friends.' Of course, we do not have to accept any of the specifics here – Snorri is dramatizing, and the speeches must be made up. Yet, for all the invented detail, one suspects that the essence of his account is true. Hardrada had built a career on opportunism and violence; the prospect of one last great adventure, of replicating the success of King Cnut, or simply of recapturing the flavour of his glory days in the Mediterranean, must have been extremely enticing. Moreover, the expectation of support from within England itself would have made the enterprise seem feasible. The Scandinavian tradition that

Tostig's visit to Norway set Hardrada's invasion in motion is, in short, very hard to dismiss. Nor is it unsupported by earlier sources: Orderic Vitalis, writing in the early twelfth century, says much the same thing, explaining that the earl's proposal greatly pleased the covetous Norwegian king. 'At once he ordered an army to be gathered together, weapons of war prepared, and the royal fleet fitted out.'[11]

If Tostig went to Norway from Scotland, he was clearly back in Scotland by the end of the summer: when Hardrada set sail towards the end of August, his English ally was not with him. The king was accompanied, however, by several members of his own family, including his queen, Elizabeth, two of his daughters and one of his younger sons. His eldest son, Magnus, he left behind in Norway to act as regent, having first taken the precaution of naming him as his heir in the event of his non-return. As to the size of his fleet, we have a predictable variety of estimates. The contemporary Anglo-Saxon Chronicle suggests it contained 300 ships, while John of Worcester later increased the figure to 500. Snorri, from whom we might expect even greater exaggeration, says that Hardrada assembled a great host, reported to have contained more than 200 ships, plus smaller craft for carrying supplies: a useful reminder that even a fleet of this size constituted an enormous deployment, and a caution against believing the far larger numbers offered by other chroniclers for fleets in this period. If each of the Norwegian king's 200 ships carried a modest average of forty passengers apiece, this would still have given him an army of 8,000 men.[12]

Snorri says quite credibly that Hardrada sailed first to Shetland and then to Orkney, where he was joined by the local earls and where he left behind his wife and daughters. From the Northern Isles he proceeded down the east coasts of Scotland and Northumbria until he reached the River Tyne, where (according to the most detailed English sources) he met up again with Tostig. Whether the earl had managed to add to the meagre flotilla of twelve ships that had limped to Scotland with him at the start of the summer is unknown; but even if King Malcolm had increased the naval resources of his some-time sworn brother, it would have been apparent to all that Tostig was very much the junior partner. Hardrada had come in great force to conquer England and make himself its new ruler. On his arrival, says the Chronicle, the earl swore allegiance to him as his new sovereign. Together they then set out on the last leg of the voyage, sailing and raiding along England's north-eastern coast (Snorri, for what it's worth, describes significant encounters at Scarborough and Holderness), before eventually turning up in the estuary of the Humber, and then making their way up the River Ouse. Eventually they landed at Riccall, a settlement on the Ouse's north bank, some ten miles south of their principal target: the city of York.[13]

Although they cannot have planned it with any great precision, the invaders had apparently timed their arrival to perfection. We have no certain dates for their progress around the Northumbrian coast, but the testimony of the Anglo-Saxon Chronicle suggests it occurred in the first week of September. Any earlier and news of their coming would have reached southern England before 8 September – the day on which, according to the Chronicle, Harold Godwineson dismissed the great army and fleet he had held in readiness since the start of the summer. At the same time, the Norwegian invasion can hardly have begun any later in September, because the Chronicle also says that Harold received the terrible news as soon as he reached London, presumably just a few days after he had left the Isle of Wight. The inescapable conclusion – and how utterly galling it must have been for the English king – is that he must have disbanded his army at more or less exactly the moment that the invaders had disembarked.[14]

This dramatic turn of events, more than anything else, shows how totally unexpected an attack from the north had been. Harold had spent the whole summer preparing for an assault from Normandy; all his resources were directed southwards. This alone suggests that the notion, advanced in many modern history books, that a Scandinavian invasion of England had been long anticipated is simply an assumption, without any evidence to recommend it. All the evidence, both direct and circumstantial, actually points in the opposite direction, and indicates that the invaders had kept their intentions well concealed. Orderic Vitalis, for example, claims that nothing had been known in Normandy about Hardrada's preparations, and the Anglo-Saxon Chronicle reports that the Norwegian fleet had arrived in England '*unwaran*' – unexpectedly.[15]

It was obviously imperative that Harold speedily reassemble his forces. The fleet which he had sent back to London was apparently still intact, although according to the Chronicle many ships had been lost as they had made their way around the south coast, presumably due to bad weather in the Channel. The king would also still have had with him his housecarls, ready as ever to form the nucleus of any new army. But he had no time to wait while such an army regrouped in London. Harold can have paused in the city for only a few days before setting out for Yorkshire and, as he did so, messengers must have ridden in all directions, recalling the thegns who had been dismissed only days beforehand. The English king, says the Chronicle, 'marched northwards day and night, as quickly as he could assemble his levies'.

What had been happening in Yorkshire during the second week of September is altogether unclear. Hardrada and Tostig had made their camp at Riccall, and must have sent their troops out into the surrounding countryside to plunder it for provisions; as yet, however, there had apparently been no assault on York. All we know for certain is that during this period the earls of Mercia and Northumbria, Eadwine and Morcar, began raising an army of their own with which to confront the invaders, and that by the third week of September they obviously felt sufficiently confident in their numbers to risk an engagement. On 20 September the two sides met just to the south of York, on the east side of the Ouse, at a place called Fulford.[16]

Sadly, despite modern attempts to reconstruct this battle, the truth is that we can say next to nothing about it. Even its location was not recorded until the twelfth century, and Snorri's account is so demonstrably inaccurate as to be virtually worthless. He does provide the colourful detail that Hardrada advanced behind his famous banner, 'Land-waster', which earlier in the saga is said to have had the magical property of guaranteeing victory to its bearer. It evidently worked its magic that day at Fulford, for the only certain fact about the battle is that Eadwine and Morcar were defeated. The C version of the Anglo-Saxon Chronicle, compiled at a Mercian monastery, tried its best to preserve the honour of its patrons, reporting that they inflicted heavy casualties on the invaders, but could not disguise the final outcome. 'A great number of the English were slain or drowned or driven in flight,' it lamented, 'and the Norwegians had possession of the place of slaughter.' Eadwine and Morcar themselves must have been among the fugitives, for (despite Snorri's assertions to the contrary) both brothers survived the battle.[17]

In the wake of their victory, the Norwegians entered York. We might imagine that the city would have been put to the sack, but this was clearly not the case. 'After the battle,' says the C Chronicle, 'King Harold of Norway and Earl Tostig went into York with as large a force as suited them, and they were given hostages from the city as well as provisions.' This sounds very much as if the citizens of York had surrendered without a fight and obtained good terms. John of Worcester, when he later rewrote this section of the Chronicle, actually stated that there was an *exchange* of hostages between the two sides, with 150 townspeople being swapped for an identical number of Norwegians. Here indeed was the friendly collaboration that Hardrada had been led to expect. Tostig may have been the target of Northumbrian hostility the previous year, but he could evidently call upon the support of at least some sections of society in Yorkshire – especially now he had a victorious Viking army at his back. The Anglo-Danish aristocracy of York had always worn its loyalty to the south lightly; faced with the choice between a new Scandinavian ruler or a recently crowned earl of Wessex, they readily chose the former. According to the Chronicle, discussions were held between the citizens and Hardrada with a view to concluding a lasting peace, 'provided that they all marched south with him to conquer the country'.[18]

Having been favourably received in York and won the support of its citizens, the Norwegians withdrew to their ships at Riccall. Before they set out to conquer the south, however, it had been agreed that there would be another meeting, at which hostages from the rest of Yorkshire would be handed over. For reasons that remain obscure,[19] the location selected for this meeting was neither Riccall nor York, but a small settlement eight miles to the east of the city, a crossing of the River Derwent known as Stamford Bridge. Hardrada and Tostig were waiting there on 25 September in expectation of a final round of submissions before they advanced to subdue the rest of the kingdom.

What they encountered in the event was Harold Godwineson at the head of a new royal army. The English king had advanced northwards and reassembled his host far more quickly than his opponents had anticipated. After leaving London around the middle of the month, he had arrived in the Yorkshire town of Tadcaster on 24 September, having covered the intervening 200 miles in little more than a week. According to the Chronicle, he had expected to find Tostig and Hardrada holding York against him and had drawn up his forces against an attack from that direction. But the following morning he discovered that his brother and the Norwegian king had left for their appointment at Stamford Bridge, evidently quite oblivious to his approach. It was an opportunity not to be missed. Harold marched his men straight through York and out towards the crossing on the Derwent, a distance of some eighteen miles. The day must already have been well advanced by the time the English king fell upon his unsuspecting enemies.[20]

The accounts of the Battle of Stamford Bridge are not much better than those for the encounter at Fulford five days before. Snorri is once again on fine (i.e. unreliable) form, giving an account of the preliminaries entirely at odds with that of the Chronicle, including an improbable interview between the two King Harolds before the onset of hostilities (notably for its oft-quoted line that Hardrada would be granted only 'seven feet of ground'). One element of Snorri's account which does merit attention, however, is his claim that the Norwegians had gone to Stamford Bridge wearing their helmets and carrying their weapons, but without their mail shirts because the weather was warm and sunny. Special pleading, you might think, but the story is corroborated by a contemporary chronicler called Marianus Scotus. The C version of the Anglo-Saxon Chronicle contributes a few more details, confirming that the English king caught his enemies 'unawares', describing the fighting as 'fierce' and adding that it lasted until late in the day. It concludes with a story, added in the twelfth century and repeated by several other writers, of how the English were for some time prevented from crossing the bridge over the Derwent by a single Norwegian warrior, apparently wearing a mail shirt, until at length an inspired Englishman sneaked under the bridge and speared the Viking in the one place where such armour offers no protection. This was supposedly the turning point of the battle: Harold and his forces surged over the undefended bridge and the rest of the Norwegian army were slaughtered. Both Hardrada and Tostig were among the fallen.[21]

It was, said the D Chronicle, 'a very stubborn battle'. When the remaining Norwegians tried to flee back to their ships at Riccall, the English attacked them as they ran. Some drowned, says the Chronicle, some burnt to death, and others died in various different ways, so that in the end there were very few survivors. The author of the *Life of King Edward*, weeping for the death of Tostig, wrote of rivers of blood: the 'Ouse with corpses choked', and the Humber that had 'dyed the ocean waves for miles around with Viking gore'. Only those who made it back to Riccall – the D Chronicle names Hardrada's son, Olaf, among them – were given any quarter, their lives spared in exchange for a sworn promise never to return. Above all, the scale of the Norwegian defeat is indicated by the Chronicle's comment that it took just twenty-four ships to take the survivors home.[22]

After the battle, the bodies of thousands of Englishmen and Norwegians were left in the field where they had fallen; more than half a century later, Orderic Vitalis wrote that travellers could still recognize the site on account of the great mountain of dead men's bones. But the body of Tostig Godwineson was recovered from the general carnage and carried to York for an honourable burial; William of Malmesbury, who had a fondness for such human details, reports that it was recognized on account of a wart between the shoulder blades (the implication being that all the earl's other distinguishing features had been too badly maimed). His older brother, it is as good as certain, also returned to York in the aftermath of his victory. Apart from anything else, he would have wanted to have a serious conversation with its citizens about the alacrity they had shown in supporting his Norwegian namesake. Quite possibly, therefore, Harold Godwineson was present at Tostig's funeral, whipped by the wind that continued to blow from the north.[23]

Two days after the battle, however, the wind changed direction.

11

Invasion

I f we believe William of Poitiers, the late summer of 1066 must
have been a time of immeasurable frustration for the duke of
Normandy and his army of would-be invaders. Although apparently ready since the start of August, the fleet that was supposed to
carry them across the Channel to England had been unable to put
to sea, its departure indefinitely delayed by bad weather and adverse
winds. As late as the second week in September, the 700 ships were
still beached and anchored in the port of Dives, leaving the thousands of knights, soldiers and horses idling in the nearby
encampment.

If we believe most modern historians, on the other hand, this is
simply nonsense. A delay of that length, they maintain, must have
been deliberate; William of Poitiers, not for the first time, is twisting
the facts to fit his own sensationalist agenda. What the duke was
really doing during these weeks, say the sceptics, was waiting for
Harold's army to disband, so that the Normans could land in England
unopposed.[1]

It is easy to see why this argument has commanded so much
credence: apart from anything else, it seems well supported by the
timing of subsequent events. Harold stood down his army, the Anglo-
Saxon Chronicle tells us, around 8 September. Very soon afterwards
– just four or five days later, as far as we can determine – William's
fleet finally put to sea. And yet, a closer examination of the evidence
suggests that the sceptical line is unjustified. The duke, it seems, *was*
delayed by contrary winds. For once, William of Poitiers appears to
have given us the unvarnished truth.

The principal reason for believing Poitiers is that his testimony is corroborated by a new source – the so-called *Carmen de Hastingae Proelio*, or 'Song of the Battle of Hastings'. The *Carmen*, as it is known for brevity's sake, has a controversial history of its own. An epic poem, 835 lines long, it was discovered in 1826 in the Royal Library in Brussels. The text as it stands is anonymous, but it was quickly ascribed to Guy, bishop of Amiens, a contemporary of the Conqueror, chiefly because Orderic Vitalis, writing a couple of generations later, tells us that the same Bishop Guy had written just such a poem about the Battle of Hastings. Doubts about this attribution, and indeed the poem's authenticity, have persisted almost since the moment of its discovery; such academic scorn was poured upon it in the late 1970s that many books and articles written soon thereafter simply ruled it out of court as evidence. Latterly, however, the *Carmen*'s fortunes have been greatly revived. Scholars are now inclined to accept that it *was* the poem described by Orderic, and, since he tells us that it was composed before the spring of 1068, it is reckoned as one of the earliest sources we have for the events of 1066. It remains, of course, a poem, with all the potential for artistic licence that that implies, but nevertheless the *Carmen* is now regarded as one of the key texts for the study of the Conquest.[2]

One thing that makes the *Carmen* especially interesting is that it was apparently written for the ears of William the Conqueror himself (the first 150 lines or so are written in the second person, i.e. 'You did this, you did that'). This, of course, is true for some of our other sources, such as William of Jumièges and William of Poitiers; the difference in the case of the *Carmen* is that its author, Bishop Guy, was not himself a Norman. The city of Amiens lies in the neighbouring county of Ponthieu, and Guy himself was a scion of Ponthieu's ruling house. As such, while he clearly sets out to praise William and the Normans, Guy does so with a greater sense of detachment, and far less sycophancy, than, say, William of Poitiers. Another thing that makes the *Carmen* an interesting source is that William of Poitiers had clearly read it. At various points in his own history we can see Poitiers responding to Bishop Guy's poem, sometimes borrowing a word or phrase by way of endorsement, other times implicitly denying its account by substituting his own alternative version of events.[3]

What bearing does all this have on whether or not William's delay in sailing was deliberate or not? The answer is that the *Carmen* – an early, independent source, addressed to the duke himself – begins by describing the adverse weather conditions that prevailed in the late summer of 1066: 'For a long time tempest and continuous rain prevented your fleet from sailing across the Channel . . . You were in despair when all hope of sailing was denied you. But, in the end, whether you liked it or not, you left your shore and directed your ships towards the coast of a neighbour.'[4]

William of Poitiers, following the *Carmen*'s lead, elaborates: 'Presently', he says, 'the whole fleet, equipped with such great fore-sight, was blown from the mouth of the Dives and the neighbouring ports, where they had long waited for a south wind to carry them across, and was driven by the breath of the west wind to moorings at Valéry.'[5] Poitiers is probably being slightly economical with the truth here in blaming the mishap entirely on the weather – presumably the ships did not simply break their anchors and drift out to sea. What must have happened, and what the chronicler has judiciously excised from his account, is that the duke decided to set sail in less than favourable conditions. Having waited a month or more for a south wind that never came, he would have learned soon after 8 September that the English army had disbanded. It must have seemed an opportunity too good to miss, and in any case his carefully stockpiled provisions at Dives could hardly have lasted much longer. Probably around 12 or 13 September, William took a chance and launched his expedition, with near disastrous results.

'The rough sea compelled you to turn back', says the *Carmen*, candidly. The Norman fleet ended up, not in England as they intended, but (as William of Poitiers indicates) in the port of St Valéry, a hundred miles further east along the north French coast – 'a dangerous rock-bound coast', as the *Carmen* accurately describes it. William had, in truth, been very lucky to have escaped a more comprehensive disaster. Poitiers speaks of 'terrible shipwrecks', and tells us that men began to desert from the duke's army. Although his comment that William tried to maintain morale by burying the bodies of the drowned in secret looks somewhat suspect (Xerxes once did something similar), Poitiers' testimony is in general terms perfectly plausible. Indeed, it draws support from a fact we have already seen, namely that the disbanded English fleet, sailing back to London at the same time, suffered similar losses.[6]

In mid-September, therefore, William's planned invasion hung precariously in the balance. His fleet was diminished by losses, his supplies were dwindling. He was no longer in his own duchy – St Valéry lies in the neighbouring county of Ponthieu (hence the *Carmen*'s credibility for these events). And the weather continued to be against him. Guy of Amiens describes the duke not only visiting the shrine of St Valéry, but anxiously watching the weathercock on top of the church's steeple for signs of a change in the wind. 'You were forsaken', says the *Carmen*, 'It was cold and wet, and the sky was hidden by clouds and rain.' With the heavens set against them, there was nothing else the Normans could do except seek divine intervention. William himself prayed and made offerings at St Valéry's shrine; he also (as subsequent records show) vowed to found a new church dedicated to the saint in England, should the invasion be successful. When these personal overtures had no discernible effect, he decided to get the whole army involved. According to William of Poitiers, the duke had Valéry's body removed from its shrine and carried out of the church, in what was clearly a large-scale, open-air ceremony. 'All the assembled men-at-arms', says the chronicler, 'shared in taking up the same arms of humility.'

They had to wait a further fortnight, but eventually their prayers were answered. 'At length', says Poitiers, 'the expected wind blows. Voices and hands are raised to heaven in thanks and, at the same time, a tumult arises as each man encourages the other.' The Bayeux Tapestry shows men carrying and carting weapons and wine to the ships in a somewhat sedate fashion. It is the *Carmen* that best captures the jubilant but frantic atmosphere that followed:

> Immediately, all were of one mind and purpose – to entrust themselves to the sea, now calm at last. Although dispersed, all arrive rejoicing, and run instantly to take up position. Some step the masts, others then hoist the sails. Many force the knights' horses to clamber on to the ships. The rest hasten to stow their arms. Like a flock of doves seeking their lofts, the throngs of infantry rush to take their places on the boats. O what a great noise suddenly erupts from that place as the sailors seek their oars, the knights their arms![7]

Frustratingly, conflicting dates in our source material means we do not know on what day this dramatic scene took place. Most probably it was 27 September, though just possibly it was 28 September. We can, however, estimate the time of day by looking at the tides. The Normans would have needed to embark on a rising tide, and to have departed soon after high tide, in order for their heavily laden ships to have sufficient clearance. On 27 September 1066 low water at St Valéry occurred at around 9 a.m., high tide at around 3 p.m., and the sun set just before 5.30 p.m. This fits very well with the *Carmen*'s comment that 'the day was already closing in, the setting sun departing' when the ships finally cast off their moorings, and the duke's own vessel raced ahead and took the lead.[8]

As luck would have it we have a description of William's ship. A few lines added to the end of the Ship List tell us it was called the *Mora*, and that it been prepared for him by his wife, Matilda. Sadly, we can't say for certain what the ship's name signified (though all manner of suggestions have been put forward). The List also tells us about a finishing touch that Matilda had caused to be added: at the prow of the vessel stood the figure of a small, gilded boy, holding a horn to his lips with one hand and pointing towards England with the other. A similar figure appears on one of the ships depicted on the Bayeux Tapestry.[9]

Once the ships reached the open sea, says William of Poitiers, they immediately dropped anchor. Partly this must have been to enable the fleet to establish the 'orderly formation' described by the *Carmen*, but it was also, as Poitiers explains, 'for fear that they might reach the shore to which they were bound before dawn, and run into danger in a hostile and unknown landing place'. There would, of course, have been no shortage of sailors who had made the same crossing hundreds of times before on hand to advise on timings. The English coast lies about sixty miles from St Valéry; if they maintained a speed of between three and four knots the voyage would take at least twelve hours – bringing them to England, as Poitiers indicates, before the sun had risen. For several hours, therefore, they idled outside the estuary while night fell. As the stars filled up the heavens, says the *Carmen*, so the ocean filled with glowing torches. At length – probably around 9 p.m. – a lantern was lit on William's ship, a trumpet sounded, and the fleet sailed on.[10]

When the sun rose the next morning, at around 6 a.m., there was apparently intense anxiety on board the *Mora*. As William of Poitiers explains, during the night the duke's flagship had raced ahead of the others ('trying to equal his ardour by its speed'); at daybreak its occupants discovered they were quite alone, with no other sails in sight. The duke himself, naturally, was unperturbed, and quelled the nerves of his companions by calmly sitting down to an abundant meal, 'as if he were in his hall at home'. It is a scene worthy of the classical authors that Poitiers sought to emulate, but not directly copied from any of them and so impossible to dismiss completely. Of course, by the time William had finished his hearty breakfast – washed down, we are told, with spiced wine – the crisis was over. 'On being asked again', says Poitiers, 'the lookout saw four ships following; the third time he exclaimed that there were so many they resembled a dense forest whose trees bore sails.'[11]

Some three hours later, around 9 a.m., the Norman fleet landed on the English coast. Their port of arrival was Pevensey, and this was almost certainly intended. The town itself was insubstantial, but it boasted the attraction of a former Roman fort (Anderitum) which afforded the invaders some immediate protection. More importantly, aiming his ships at Pevensey meant that William could make use of Pevensey Bay, a suitably extensive landing ground for his several hundred ships. The Bayeux Tapestry shows the horses being unloaded from the ships, and Norman knights racing to occupy the town of Hastings, a dozen miles further east along the coast. Here too they seized an ancient fortification, in this case the Iron Age hill fort that stands on the cliffs high above the town. 'You repair the remnants of earlier fortifications and set guards to protect them', says the *Carmen*: the fort at Hastings, like the one at Pevensey, was immediately customized to meet the Normans' requirements. As we can see from the surviving remains, the invaders dug ditches and raised ramparts to reduce the size of both sites, transforming each from an old-style communal fortress into that modern French phenomenon, the castle. At Hastings, the Tapestry shows teams of diggers labouring to create that most distinctive of early castle features, the motte.[12]

Thus William landed in England, probably on the morning of 28 September, possibly the morning after. When did Harold learn of his arrival? The answer depends, of course, on where the English king was, and here our sources leave us somewhat in the dark. We know that he fought and won the battle of Stamford Bridge on 25 September, but what he did in the days that followed is uncertain.

One possibility is that, still anxious about the Norman threat, he immediately rounded up the remnant of his army and set out southwards, but this does not seem at all probable. Having won his great victory over the Vikings, it is far more likely that Harold would have remained in Yorkshire for a few days, resting his men and attending to the region's pacification. We know that he negotiated with the Norwegian survivors and granted them safe passage home, and we can reasonably assume that he would have wanted to reimpose his authority on the citizens of York. As we've seen, William of Malmesbury claims that the body of Tostig Godwineson was taken to the city for burial, an occasion for which his brother is likely to have been present. Another twelfth-century writer, Henry of Huntingdon, says explicitly that Harold was holding a celebratory feast in York when news arrived of the Norman landing.[13]

The king's location is important because it determines how much time he had to react. From Pevensey to York is approximately 270 miles: if the Normans landed in the morning of 28 September, news can hardly have reached him before 1 October. Looking ahead for a moment to our one indisputable date (and not, I hope, giving too much away), the Battle of Hastings took place on 14 October. Harold, in other words, moved from Yorkshire to the Sussex coast in barely a fortnight. Moreover, as all the chronicles attest, he spent some of that time paused in London – six days, if we believe Orderic Vitalis. All of which means the king must have travelled south from Yorkshire very quickly – much more quickly than he had travelled on his outward journey, which usually attracts greater admiration. If Orderic is right, Harold must have covered the 200 miles between York and London in just four or five days. Obviously he cannot have marched infantry at a rate of forty or fifty miles a day; most likely the foot soldiers who had fought at Stamford Bridge were dismissed in the wake of their victory. The conclusion must be that the king rode south, as fast as he could, accompanied only by mounted men. As they rode, fresh orders must have been sent to the shires, with orders to assemble a new army in London.[14]

Back in Sussex, the Normans themselves must have been anxious for news of their enemy – not least who their enemy was. As we have seen, it is highly likely that William's original departure from Dives, around 12 September, had been inspired by news that Harold had stood down his army a few days earlier. It is also likely that, in the days that followed, the Normans learned about the arrival in Yorkshire of Tostig and Harold Hardrada. They cannot, however, have heard about the battle of Stamford Bridge on 25 September before their departure from St Valéry just two or three days later. It is a fact that has been noted by historians many times in the past, but is no less arresting for all that: William arrived in England not knowing which Harold he was going to have to fight.

News of Stamford Bridge must have reached William within a few days of his arrival – probably around the same time that Harold was made aware of the Norman landing. According to William of Poitiers, the messenger who brought the news was sent by Robert fitz Wimarc, a Norman who had come to England many years earlier in the company of Edward the Confessor and served in the former king's household (he is the 'Robert the Steward' who was present at the Confessor's death). If Poitiers can be believed – and here we must bear in mind his desire to dramatize events – the message sent by this sympathetic Norman was not encouraging. Harold had defeated and killed both Tostig and Hardrada, destroying their huge armies, and was now heading south to confront William. The duke was advised to stay behind his fortifications.[15]

Harold was thus aware of William's arrival, and William of Harold's return to London. As such, we have little difficulty in believing the various chroniclers who tell us that in the days that followed messages were exchanged between the two men. Both the *Carmen* and William of Poitiers purport to give the content of these messages as spoken by the monks who delivered them; what they are actually doing is rehearsing the arguments of both sides for possession of the English throne. In the case of William of Poitiers, in particular, his account becomes a rhetorical exercise to justify the Norman invasion; quite probably he was drawing on the legal case that had earlier been prepared for the pope. We hear, once again, of a grateful Edward the Confessor making William his heir; of oaths sworn and hostages given; of Harold's visit to Normandy and his promise to uphold the duke's claim. In fairness to Poitiers, we also hear Harold's counter-argument, namely the story of the Confessor's deathbed bequest and its historic legitimacy. Naturally we don't have to believe that all of these arguments were revisited in the course of these exchanges, though no doubt some of them were. Certainly we can believe the *Carmen* that offers were made by both sides in the hope of avoiding conflict. William, we are told, offered to let Harold hold the earldom of Wessex if he resigned the kingship; Harold, rather less generously, promised to let William return to Normandy unmolested if he made reparations for the damage he had caused.[16]

That the Normans had already caused extensive damage is beyond doubt. 'Here the horses leave the boats', says the Bayeux Tapestry, above the fleet's arrival, 'and here the knights hurry to Hastings in order to seize food.' While they waited in France, William's army had been forbidden to live off the land; once in England, they could start to plunder the surrounding countryside. On the Tapestry this requisitioning operation looks fairly innocuous; more space is devoted to the preparation of the tasty sit-down meal than the manner in which it was obtained. Of course, as with the creation of castles at Pevensey and Hastings, the damage involved in the search for food could be considered as collateral, but our sources leave no room for doubt that the Normans were also engaged in deliberate and indiscriminate destruction. In the *Carmen*, Harold is informed that William 'has invaded the land, wastes it and sets it on fire'. The Tapestry famously shows two Norman soldiers torching a house from which a woman and a child are seen trying to flee.[17]

Indiscriminate it may have been, but this was devastation with a purpose. William, for the first time in his career, was engaged in a battle-seeking strategy. Had Harold decided to remain in London, the duke would have been in a difficult fix. His only option would have been to leave the security of his camp and lead a march into hostile territory, with all the dangers that implied. An army forced to live off the land would be vulnerable to attack as it spread out to forage, or death from disease or hunger if it failed to do so. Far better, then, from William's point of view, to have the English king come to him and decide their dispute in a decisive battle. In William's devastation, therefore, we discern a deliberate attempt to provoke a fight. It no doubt helped in this regard that the Normans had landed in Harold's own territory, and were therefore terrorizing the king's own tenants.

Harold, it seems, rose to the bait. In the opinion of several sources, the English king set out from London too soon: 'before all his host came up', says the E version of the Anglo-Saxon Chronicle, a comment later amplified by John of Worcester to 'half his host'. Another later writer, Orderic Vitalis, relates a dramatic conversation in London between the king and the rest of his family. His mother Gytha, already lamenting the loss of Tostig, tried to dissuade Harold from riding to war for a second time. His brother Gyrth also urged caution, saying 'You have just returned worn out after the war against the Norwegians; are you now hastening to move against the Normans?' According to Orderic, Gyrth volunteered to lead the army on Harold's behalf, on the rather unlikely grounds that he had sworn no oath to William. These representations, however, came to nothing: Harold flew into a violent rage, rebuked his relatives and hurried off to do battle.[18]

It has been fairly observed that all of these sources are English (or, in Orderic's case, has clear English sympathies), and it might therefore seem reasonable to assume that all were making excuses for Harold ahead of his impending defeat. Yet it is William of Poitiers who tells us that 'the furious king was hastening his march all the more because he had heard that the lands near to the Norman camp were being laid waste'. Naturally Poitiers, given his own sympathies, does not endorse the view that a speedy departure in any way diminished Harold's fighting strength; like the other Norman writers, he maintains that the king's army was enormous. But it is precisely the fact that Poitiers so often disagrees with our English sources at other times that makes his agreement on the point of Harold's haste so significant, and suggests that the king did indeed set out too soon.[19]

Besides his desire to stop the Norman devastation, Harold set out at speed to confront William for another reason. He was, according to William of Jumièges, 'hastening to take him by surprise'. As William of Poitiers explains more fully, the English king 'thought that in a night or surprise attack he might defeat [the Normans] unawares'. We should have no difficulty in believing these statements. Harold had just won a great victory at Stamford Bridge by launching exactly such a surprise attack on his enemies. Of course, the situation differed somewhat in that the Norwegians appear to have been wholly unaware of the king's approach. Yet the fact that William and Harold exchanged messages with each other in the days before the battle does not preclude the possibility of the English launching an attack sooner than expected, or falling on the Normans under cover of darkness. Harold could still hope to catch William off guard, especially if he moved quickly.[20]

William, however, got wind of his opponent's intentions. According to the *Carmen*, it was the duke's own envoy, returning from a final parley with the king, who revealed the plan, saying 'Harold hopes to be able to catch you unawares. He is preparing for a great offensive on both land and sea. He is reported to have sent five hundred ships to obstruct our passage home.' William of Poitiers, while he echoes the story about the ships, rather more credibly attributes the duke's foreknowledge to good military practice. 'Experienced knights, who had been sent out scouting, reported that the enemy would soon be there.' (It is important to remember in what follows that Poitiers had himself once been a knight.)[21]

With each side trying to outfox the other, it is hardly surprising that our sources give no clear account of the timings involved. The likeliest scenario is that Harold set out from London around 11 October, and was drawing near to Hastings on 13 October when William learned of his approach. According to William of Jumièges, the duke, 'taking precautions in case of a night-time attack, ordered his army to stand to arms from dusk to dawn'. But the night-time attack never came, and early the next morning William set out in search of his enemy.[22]

Harold's army had reached a spot about seven miles north-west of Hastings which at that time had no very obvious name. The D version of the Anglo-Saxon Chronicle, uniquely, says that the English were at 'the grey apple tree' – presumably a significant landmark, long since lost. Orderic Vitalis, writing over fifty years later, insisted that the place had been known since ancient times as 'Senlac', though nobody else favoured the term until it was adopted by Freeman in the nineteenth century. After 1066, most people referred to the place by the name that it still bears today – Battle.[23]

For it was here that the Norman army surprised Harold's men on the morning of 14 October. 'William came upon him unexpectedly, before his army was set in order', says the D Chronicle unequivocally. The duke, thanks to his good reconnaissance, had succeeded in turning the tables. Harold had intended to surprise William by attacking his camp at Hastings, but William had discovered this just in time and advanced to meet him. Although some historians contend he must have set out sooner, the obvious inference from our sources is that the duke left Hastings at sunrise on the morning of 14 October – a Saturday – and came upon Harold's army a few hours later, around 9 a.m. The truly insoluble question is which side was more exhausted. Few modern commentators accept William of Jumièges' statement that the English had ridden through the night to arrive at the battlefield at dawn, but whenever they arrived the speed of their advance must have taken its toll. At the same time, the Normans, having reportedly stood to arms all night and marched several miles in the morning, can scarcely have been better rested. William of Malmesbury, writing many years later, famously recorded the rumour that the English had spent the whole night singing and drinking, while the Normans had been confessing their sins. Scurrilous, no doubt, but it does fit well with the notion that the English were taken by surprise and the Normans knew what was coming.[24]

Although William had turned the tables by advancing on Harold, it is clear that this did not enable the Normans to ambush the English. Both sides had spotted each other in advance and there was a sudden rush to arms. Possibly it was only at this stage – i.e. after their early-morning march – that William's men donned their heavy shirts of mail, or hauberks. According to a story reported by several chroniclers (William of Poitiers alludes to it in passing) the duke, in his haste, put his own hauberk on back to front, and had to laugh off what others took to be a bad omen. He also, says Poitiers, fortified himself spiritually by hanging around his neck the relics on which Harold had sworn his oath.[25]

There was just enough time for a pre-battle speech. 'Here Duke William exhorts his knights to prepare themselves manfully and wisely against the English', reads the caption on the Bayeux Tapestry. Poitiers, who admits with unusual candour that he is paraphrasing, purports to give us the gist: William reminded the Normans of their past victories and his own unbroken record, and exhorted them to prove their valour. He also stressed, with good reason, the do-or-die nature of the imminent conflict, reminding his men that retreat was not an option. Lastly, he played down the martial reputation of the English, saying they had been defeated many times in the past. 'Never were they famed for the glory of their feats of arms.' Not terribly fair, of course, but precisely the sort of denigration of an opponent we might expect from a commander about to lead his men into battle.

Poitiers uses the same speech to imply that the Normans were outnumbered by the English, saying 'men who are inexpert in warfare could easily be crushed by the valour and strength of a few'. It is a line of dubious worth, largely because it is adapted from a maxim of Vegetius, a Roman authority on military matters (though Poitiers may have borrowed it from the *Carmen*, which says something similar). As we have seen, the English sources make comparable excuses for the size of the English army, with comments to the effect that Harold went into battle before all his host had been drawn up. Both sides would argue over this point for years to come. William of Malmesbury, incensed by the suggestion that Harold had lost despite having a large army, insisted that the English 'were few in number but brave in the extreme'. Several decades later, the Norman writer Wace found it equally hard to accept that William had fielded the bigger army, and concluded that both armies had been much the same size. As ever with numbers, it is impossible to pronounce with any certainty. No doubt an opposing army often seems daunting to those about to confront it. The most reasonable conclusion, given the nature of the battle that followed, is that Wace was right, and the two sides were more or less evenly matched.[26]

Fortunately there is less disagreement over where the battle was fought. William had advanced from Hastings by the only viable route, namely the high ground known as The Ridge; the ground to either side would have been mostly impassable forest. The English, once aware of the Norman approach, had moved from the forest and seized a nearby hill – so says Poitiers and so says the *Carmen*. The hill is easily identified today because, some years later, William caused an abbey to be erected on the site, and its substantial ruins still remain.

Having seized the hilltop, the English arranged themselves in their favoured formation. 'They dismounted and left their horses in the rear', says the *Carmen*, with a hint of incredulity. 'For that people, unskilled in the art of war, spurn the assistance of horses: trusting to their strength they stand fast on foot.' This was, indeed, the way in which English armies had traditionally deployed for centuries – standing in a long line, several men deep, shields to the fore, forming the so-called 'shield-wall'. Harold, we are told, took his place in the centre of the line, planting his standard on the summit of the hill. According to a local tradition dating back to the late twelfth century, this spot is marked by the abbey's high altar.

William, at the foot of the hill, had adopted a more sophisticated arrangement – three lines, according to the knowledgeable William of Poitiers. The first line, at the front, consisted of foot soldiers 'armed with arrows and crossbows' (in other words, the archers). The second line also consisted of foot soldiers 'but more powerful and wearing hauberks' (i.e. mailed men-at-arms, probably carrying swords). Finally, says Poitiers, came the cavalry – 'the squadrons of mounted knights' – in the middle of which rode the duke himself, 'so he could direct operations on all sides with hand and voice'. Poitiers, naturally, describes this deployment as 'a well-planned order', and perhaps that was the case. For the record, however, the *Carmen* implies that William had originally intended to place the cavalry behind the archers – i.e. in the second line – 'but was prevented from doing so from the onset of battle'.[27]

That onset was signalled on both sides by 'the harsh bray of trumpets', says Poitiers, and followed by a thick cloud of arrows – 'a shower of blows like a storm of hail', in the words of the *Carmen*. To read the accounts of both writers, one might assume that the use of arrows was confined exclusively to the French side, for neither mentions English archers. Some later chroniclers went even further, and insisted that the English did not know about archery at all: Baudri of Bourgeuil, for example, spoke of the English at Hastings dying by 'the arrow, which they had not known before'. Of course, this is patently ridiculous – cavemen hunted with bows and arrows – and hence historians have tried to square the circle by assuming that Baudri was talking about crossbows, which were indeed something of a novelty in 1066. But this is to put a rather strained reading on the evidence. Most likely Baudri *had* come to believe that at the time of Hastings the English knew nothing of conventional archery – probably because earlier accounts of the battle, like the *Carmen* and William of Poitiers, not only fail to mention English archers, but also insist that the English were ignorant when it came to military matters. Thus Henry of Huntingdon, also writing in the twelfth century, has Duke William describe the English in his pre-battle harangue as 'a people accustomed to defeat, a people devoid of military knowledge, a people that does not even possess arrows'. In fact, the silence about English archers at Hastings is not quite total: the Bayeux Tapestry shows a man armed with a bow and arrow lining up with the soldiers who formed the shield-wall. At the same time, this lone figure is the only evidence that Harold had brought any bowmen with him, compared with the abundant references to French archers in the chronicle accounts, and indeed the two dozen Normans depicted with bows on the Tapestry. The reasonable conclusion is that the English king, perhaps because of his haste, had not managed to assemble archers in any great numbers.[28]

The shower of arrows thus fell disproportionately on Harold's men, striking and destroying shields (says the *Carmen*), killing and maiming many (Poitiers). Yet the English remained, in the *Carmen's* words, 'rooted to the ground'. They were not about to rush down the hill and forsake the advantage of the high ground – the point of the shield-wall was that it should remain intact and impenetrable. Hence it was the Normans who were obliged to advance in order to engage the English in hand-to-hand fighting. Once the volley of arrows had ceased, the Norman heavy infantry ('helmeted soldiers', as the *Carmen* calls them) rushed forward 'to crash shields against shields'. According to Poitiers, these men immediately got into difficulty, for the English 'resisted bravely, each one by any means he could devise. They threw javelins and missiles of various kinds, murderous axes and stones tied to sticks.' The Norman cavalry therefore rode to the rescue, engaging the enemy with their swords. 'The loud shouting, here Norman, there foreign, was drowned by the clash of weapons and the groans of the dying', says Poitiers. 'So for a time both sides fought with all their might.'[29]

At some point during this initial clash, according to the *Carmen*, there was a remarkable episode. A Norman knight named Taillefer rode in front of the duke's army, encouraging them both with his words and with his dextrous swordplay, for as he spoke he juggled his sword, throwing it high into the air. These antics so irritated one Englishman that he broke ranks and ran forward to attack the juggler, but Taillefer was too quick: he turned, spurred his horse at his assailant and ran him through with his lance. Then, to the delight of his watching comrades, he hacked the fallen man's head from his body and held it aloft in triumph.[30]

Even if this episode really occurred, the Normans had little else to celebrate. As William of Poitiers explains, 'the English were greatly helped by the advantage of the higher ground'. The hilltop position that Harold had selected seemed unassailable. Not only was it practically impossible to mount an effective cavalry charge up such a steep slope, the terrain itself was also unfavourable – Poitiers refers at one point to 'the roughness of the ground', while the *Carmen* speaks of 'land too rough to be tilled'. Unable to mount a mass charge, the Norman horsemen were forced to engage the English at close quarters, riding up to hurl their javelins, or closer still to hack with their swords. These methods (both of which can be seen on the Bayeux Tapestry) naturally exposed the attackers themselves to far greater risk. When Poitiers refers allusively to English weapons 'which easily penetrated shields and other protections', he is presumably talking about the great battleaxes which we also see on the Tapestry, being brandished by heavily armed English housecarls. 'They strongly held or drove back those who dared to attack them with drawn swords', says Poitiers. 'They even wounded those who flung javelins at them from a distance.'[31]

This bloody business, with the Normans trying but failing to break through the English line, must have continued intermittently for hours: we know that the Battle of Hastings went on all day. At some stage, however, presumably several hours into the conflict, there came a crucial turning point, though the *Carmen* and William of Poitiers offer different versions of how it happened. According to Poitiers, it began with a near disaster. Because of the ferocity of the English resistance, he says, some troops on the left wing of the French army turned tail and started to flee. At the same time, a rumour ran through the entire army that William himself had been killed, which in turn led to 'almost the whole of the duke's battle line giving way'. The situation was only retrieved by an act of personal heroism by William, who rushed towards the fugitives, shouting 'Look at me! I am alive, and with God's help I will conquer! What madness is persuading you to flee? What way is open to escape?' At these words, says Poitiers, the Normans recovered their courage. Following the duke's lead, they turned to face the English who had been pursuing them, and killed them all in a moment.

The *Carmen* tells it somewhat differently. In this version, the episode begins with the French *pretending* to run away – it is a plan, intended to lure the English out from their impenetrable shield-wall. And at first it is successful: the English take the bait and run down the hill in pursuit of what they take to be a retreating enemy, only to have the French turn around and start attacking them. But soon thereafter, the plan goes awry, when the English fight back with unexpected vigour, compelling their attackers to run away for real. 'Thus', says the *Carmen*, 'a flight which had started as a sham became one dictated by the enemy's strength.' It is at this point that William rides to the rescue, rallies the deserting troops and leads them in a successful counter-attack.[32]

Clearly, something like this must have happened. The two stories are quite similar in places, particularly in the crucial role they attribute to William. In the *Carmen*, just as in Poitiers' version, the duke removes his helmet to dispel the rumour of his death, and this same scene is also depicted on the Bayeux Tapestry. (Although, as ever with the Tapestry, the true hero appears to be Bishop Odo, who rides in brandishing his baculum 'to encourage the lads'.) The essential difference is that, in the *Carmen*, what begins as a ruse almost results in disaster, whereas in Poitiers' account it begins as a disaster which in turn gives rise to a ruse. For, as Poitiers has it, the Normans soon realized their moment of crisis had given them a rare opportunity to kill Englishmen. 'They remembered how, a little while before, their flight had brought about the result they desired.' And so they fled again, only this time as a trick. The English, as before, rushed after them in pursuit, only to have the Normans wheel around their horses and cut them down.[33]

There is not much to help us choose between the two accounts. Our first instinct might be to believe Poitiers, the man with military experience. Yet there are strong hints in his text that the old soldier was here writing more in his capacity as ducal propagandist, trying to improve on the version of events related by the *Carmen*. In the latter account, for instance, it is unclear exactly who was responsible for the flight that nearly caused the disaster, but we are clearly told 'the Normans turn tail; their shields protect their backs'. Poitiers, by contrast, blames the initial flight on 'the Breton knights and other auxiliaries on the left wing'. If the Normans did run away, he says, it was only because they believed their leader was dead, so there was no shame in that; even the army of the Roman Empire, he continues, fled occasionally in such circumstances. This all smacks of protesting rather too much, and we might therefore prefer to believe the *Carmen* when it speaks of a deliberate stratagem that went badly wrong. Certainly it is hard to credit Poitiers when he claims that a subsequent fake flight was inspired by the original retreat, as if the Normans had discovered this trick during the course of the battle. Despite the doubts expressed by many armchair generals over the decades, feigned flight was a ruse that French cavalry forces had been employing for centuries. The Normans themselves are described as having used it to good effect against invading French forces in 1053, in the course of the struggle for Arques.[34]

One flight or two, real or ruse, the outcome was the same: substantial numbers of English soldiers were slaughtered, and the integrity of the English shield-wall was compromised. 'Up to now', says William of Poitiers, 'the enemy line had been bristling with weapons and most difficult to encircle', the obvious implication being that this was now no longer the case. The English grew weaker, he tells us, as the Normans 'shot arrows, smote and pierced'. Arrows may well have become the crucial factor: at this point on the Bayeux Tapestry, the lower margin fills with archers. 'The dead, by falling, seemed to move more than the living', says Poitiers. 'It was not possible for the lightly wounded to escape, for they were crushed to death by the serried ranks of their companions. So fortune turned for William, hastening his triumph.'[35]

What ultimately decided the battle, everyone agrees, was the death of King Harold. Day was already turning to night, says the *Carmen*, when the report 'Harold is dead' flew throughout the battlefield, causing the English to lose heart. Poitiers concurs: knowing that their king was dead, 'the English army realized there was no hope of resisting the Normans any longer'. William of Jumièges, in his brief account of the battle, tells us that 'when the English learned that their king had met his death, they greatly feared for their own lives, and turned at nightfall to seek refuge in flight'. The Bayeux Tapestry puts it in typically telegraphic terms: 'Here Harold was killed, and the English turned in flight.'[36]

But how did Harold die? The established story, as everyone knows, is that the king was felled by an arrow that hit him in the eye. The Tapestry famously shows him gripping a shaft that has lodged in his face, and this depiction is seemingly backed up by several chroniclers. 'A shaft pierces Harold with deadly doom', wrote Baudri of Bourgeuil; 'his brain was pierced by an arrow', says William of Malmesbury. 'The whole shower sent by the archers fell around King Harold', says Henry of Huntingdon, 'and he himself sank to the ground, struck in the eye.'[37]

But there are problems. The Tapestry, as is well known, is debatable, principally for two reasons. First, there is debate over which figure is actually Harold. Is he the upright figure grasping the arrow (whose head, after all, interrupts the word 'Harold' in the caption); or is he the falling figure immediately to the right, being hacked down by a horseman, under the words '*interfectus est*' ('was killed')? Some critics solve the riddle by saying that Harold is represented by both these figures, and that the Bayeux Tapestry artist does this kind of thing on numerous other occasions; others have demurred that, if this is really the case, Harold manages the neat trick of losing his shield and acquiring an axe in the act of dying.

Even if, however, we accept that the first figure represents Harold, there is controversy over the arrow itself. The Tapestry was heavily restored in the mid-nineteenth century, and the death of Harold is one of the areas where the restorers may have taken considerable liberties. Some experts contend, from an analysis of the embroidery and an examination of the earliest drawings of the Tapestry in its (apparently) unrestored state, that the first figure is actually holding not an arrow but a spear, ready to hurl at his attackers.[38]

Even if the Tapestry artist did intend to depict an arrow, can we be sure that he was depicting what really happened? On many occasions we can see that the Tapestry includes images which are not truly original, but which have been copied and adapted from other illustrated manuscripts that the artist had to hand, and it looks very much like this process was at work in Harold's death scene. Immediately before the king dies, we see a Norman soldier about to decapitate an unarmed Englishman. This otherwise inexplicable image seems to have been lifted more or less unaltered from an illustrated version of an Old Testament story, namely the fate of King Zedekiah and his sons, one of whom is shown being beheaded in exactly this manner. This artist may have lighted on this particular image because of the resonance of the story – Zedekiah and his family were punished because he had broken his oath of fealty to his overlord, and Zedekiah's own punishment was blinding. It could well be, therefore, that the arrow in Harold's eye is simply a piece of artistic licence based on nothing more than an allusion to this particular Bible story, and that blinding was felt to be a fitting end for a king who was similarly foresworn.[39]

Lastly, we have to consider the fact that the Tapestry is our only *contemporary* source to suggest that Harold was hit in the face by an arrow. True, a similar report is carried by an Italian chronicler, Amatus of Montecassino, writing about 1080, but his account is compromised by the fact that the Latin original is lost – it survives only in a fourteenth-century French translation, heavily interpolated in places, and hence of negligible worth.[40] These two questionable sources apart, the story that Harold was felled by an arrow occurs in later works (Baudri of Bourgeuil, William of Malmesbury and Henry of Huntingdon are all twelfth-century). Contemporary accounts, by contrast – the *Carmen*, William of Poitiers, William of Jumièges and the various versions of the Anglo-Saxon Chronicle – make no mention of it. In the case of the last two, this omission is not very remarkable, given the brevity of their accounts; in the case of William of Poitiers and the *Carmen* it is altogether more striking. Poitiers offers us the longest and most detailed account of the battle, yet makes no mention of the manner in which Harold died. Possibly this was because he did not know. Alternatively, it may have been because he knew full well, having read the *Carmen*'s version, and did not care to endorse it.

For the *Carmen* – our earliest source for the battle – offers an entirely different account of how Harold met his end. According to the *Carmen*, the battle was almost won – the French were already seeking spoils of war – when William caught sight of Harold on top of the hill, hacking down his foes. The duke called together a cohort of men, including Count Eustace of Boulogne, Hugh of Ponthieu and a certain 'Gilfard' ('known by his father's surname'), and set out to kill the king. In this they were successful, and the *Carmen* gives a graphic description of the injuries each inflicted on Harold, who was pierced with a lance, beheaded with a sword and disembowelled with a spear. His thigh, we are told (possibly a euphemism for his genitalia) was hacked off and carried away some distance.[41]

Historians have always had huge problems with this story, and still tend to reject it outright. One of the foremost experts of the last century, Professor R. Allen Brown, found it impossible to believe that William had been personally involved in Harold's death; not because the duke was uninvolved in the fighting, for everyone accepts that fact. Rather, his objection was that, had William really been involved so directly in Harold's death, 'the feat of arms would have been bruited abroad in every court and *chanson* in Latin Christendom and beyond'.[42]

This argument, however, assumes that everyone in Christendom would have regarded the premeditated butchery of a crowned king as acceptable behaviour, which was not necessarily the case. The *Carmen* insists that Harold's killers acted 'in accordance with the rules of war', a statement which by itself suggests that others may have felt that these rules had been broken. One person who may have thought as much was William of Poitiers. In general he is not afraid to contest points of detail with the *Carmen* and offer his own version of what happened. When it comes to Harold's gory end, however, he offers no denial and no alternative scenario: he simply lapses into silence. With most writers, their silence on a particular point would be a poor foundation on which to build an argument. But with a writer as erudite as William of Poitiers, we can reasonably read more into it. Poitiers wanted to present the duke as measured, merciful and just in all his dealings, and in particular in his pursuit of England's throne. He did not want to show his hero, whose mission had been sanctioned by the pope, hacking his opponent into pieces. The suspicion that Poitiers tried to suppress the *Carmen*'s version of Harold's death is reinforced by his similar failure to include the episode involving Taillefer the juggler. Perhaps he thought it unreliable; more likely he considered it shameful – a piece of bloodthirsty barbarism that cast the Normans in a bad light. More pertinent still is the fact we have caught Poitiers at this kind of *suppressio veri* once before, in his account of the taking of the town of Alençon. His source, William of Jumièges, tells us that the duke mutilated the town's defenders by lopping off their hands and feet, but Poitiers omits all mention of this from his own account. In the case of Harold's death, therefore, the silence of William of Poitiers, far from undermining our faith in the *Carmen*'s version, could instead be considered to strengthen its credibility. That credibility is also enhanced by the fact that the poem's author, Guy of Amiens, had close connections with the men he tells us were William's accomplices.[43]

Of course, we cannot say for certain how Harold died. Our sources, as ever, are contradictory, and each of them can be regarded as in some way compromised (because they are based on biblical or classical motifs; because they are inherently biased; because they are better regarded as imaginative works of art rather than sober reportage). We know that at various points in the battle the Normans showered the English with arrows and crossbow bolts, so it is not unlikely that Harold was hit, perhaps fatally, perhaps in the eye. At the same time, we cannot lightly disregard the *Carmen* (as historians have usually done) when it tells us that Harold died in a very different way, deliberately cut down by his enemies. Apart from anything else, a deliberate killing accords well with William's assumed war-aim. He had risked everything to get an army to England and to bring Harold to battle. After a long day's fighting, with the autumn light starting to fade, it would have been quite possible for the English king to withdraw, enabling him to fight another day. William could not take that risk; for him it was imperative that his opponent should die before the day was out. Given this fact, it would not be at all surprising if the duke, in the closing stages of the conflict, decided to risk all and lead just the kind of death squad that the *Carmen* describes. By the same token, with the deed accomplished, it would be equally unsurprising if the Normans in general, like William of Poitiers in particular, sought to keep these details quiet. An anonymous arrow in the eye accorded better with the idea that, in the final analysis, Harold's death had been down to the judgement of God.

12

The Spoils of Victory

The night after Hastings was almost as terrible as the day itself. William of Poitiers paints a vivid picture of the English fleeing from the battlefield, 'some on horses they had seized, some on foot; some along roads, others through untrodden wastes'. These, he makes clear, were the fortunate ones, the lucky unscathed or the lightly wounded. More pitiful is his description of those who wanted to flee but could not: the men lying helpless in their own blood, the maimed who hauled themselves a short distance only to collapse in the woods, where their corpses blocked the escape of others. The Normans pursued them, says Poitiers, slashing at their backs, galloping over their bodies, 'putting the last touches to the victory'. Yet even the victors died in large numbers that night, their pursuit turning to disaster when they rushed headlong into an unseen obstacle. 'High grass concealed an ancient rampart', explains Orderic Vitalis, 'and as the Normans, fully armed on their horses, rode up against it, they fell, one on top of the other, thus crushing each other to death.' The chronicler of Battle Abbey records that this pit was afterwards known locally as the Malfosse.[1]

Thus when the sun came up the next morning it revealed an appalling scene. 'Far and wide the earth was covered with the flower of the English nobility and youth, drenched in blood', says Poitiers, noting that among them lay Harold's two brothers, Leofwine and Gyrth, whose bodies were said to have been found close to the king's own. Beyond this, however, Poitiers gives us a fairly sanitized account. He says little, for instance, of Norman casualties, which must have been considerable. (The Anglo-Saxon Chronicle speaks of 'great slaughter on both sides'.) Similarly, we hear nothing about the routine medieval practice whereby the dead were deprived of their valuables, yet we know from other sources that this had been happening even before the end of the battle. (The Bayeux Tapestry, for example, shows in its margins men being stripped of their expensive mail shirts.) Most interestingly, we see Poitiers implicitly contesting a statement made by the author of the *Carmen*, who says that while William buried his own dead, he left the bodies of the English 'to be eaten by worms and wolves, by birds and dogs'. Nothing too surprising there, you might think, considering the labour that burying thousands of Englishmen would entail, but Poitiers was determined to depict his master in the best possible moral light, however much it contradicted military common sense. Leaving the dead unburied, we are told, 'seemed cruel' to the Conqueror, who accordingly allowed any who wished to recover their relatives' remains to do so.[2]

But not the remains of Harold. As Poitiers and several other sources make plain, the king's corpse was in a very bad state, stripped of all its valuables, and so hacked about the face that it could be recognized only by 'certain marks'. According to the twelfth-century tradition at Waltham Abbey, the task of confirming his identity required the presence of Harold's sometime partner, Edith Swan-Neck, 'for she had been admitted to a greater intimacy of his person'.[3] In contemporary accounts, by contrast, it is the king's mother, Gytha, who appears amid the carnage to plead for the return of her son's body. Despite allegedly offering its weight in gold (a detail provided by the *Carmen* and kept by Poitiers), her request was refused, William angrily replying that it would be inappropriate for Harold to be interred while countless others lay unburied on his account. This directly contradicts the later tradition that the king was buried at Waltham, and both Poitiers and the *Carmen* state that his remains were buried on the summit of a nearby cliff, under a mocking inscription which suggested that he could in this way still guard the seashore. It is not impossible that Harold was removed to Waltham at some later date; but had he been granted a Christian burial in 1066, we can be sure that William of Poitiers in particular would have let us know about it.

So the king was dead; long live the king? The *Carmen* says that, with Harold thus entombed, William 'renounced the title of duke

[and] assumed the royal style', but Poitiers once again offers a pointed rebuttal: the victor *could* have gone on immediately to London, placed the crown on his head and rewarded his followers with the booty, slaying Englishmen or driving them into exile; *but*, we are told, 'he preferred to act more moderately, and rule with greater clemency'. Both comments, of course, are equally nonsensical. There was no rule that said the man who killed a king must automatically replace him, nor was William in any position to march on Westminster. He had won a great victory, and succeeded in what we take to be a deliberate strategy of decapitation. But when Poitiers, even in what is obviously a rhetorical passage, suggests that 'the forces of Normandy had subjugated all the cities of the English in a single day', the effect is unintentionally comic. The truth was that, apart from Pevensey and Hastings, every town and city in England still remained to be taken.[4]

In London, for example, the streets were teeming. 'A crowd of warriors from elsewhere had flocked there', says Poitiers in a more prosaic mode, 'and the city, in spite of its great size, could scarcely accommodate them all.' Some of these men were doubtless the troops summoned by Harold that had not arrived by the time of his premature departure. Others were survivors from Hastings – 'the obstinate men who had been defeated in battle', as the *Carmen* calls them. Their collective mood was determined and defiant. The *Carmen* speaks of their 'hope of being able to live there in freedom for a long time', while Poitiers goes even further, saying 'it was indeed their highest wish to have no king who was not a compatriot'.[5]

With Harold gone, there was only one plausible candidate. 'Archbishop Ealdred and the citizens of London wished to have Edgar Ætheling as king', says the Anglo-Saxon Chronicle, 'as indeed was his right by birth.' The great-nephew of Edward the Confessor, last of the ancient royal line, Edgar did indeed have a better claim than anybody else. Yet, as events at the start of the year had shown, a teenager with a strong claim could easily be elbowed aside by a powerful man with a weak one. Support from the archbishop of York, who had led the mission to bring Edgar's father home from Hungary, was useful, as was the allegiance of the Londoners. But for the boy to have any hope of success he would need friends with more muscle.

The only individuals in London that autumn in a position to

lend such strength were Eadwine and Morcar, the brother earls of Mercia and Northumbria, last seen losing the battle of Fulford several weeks earlier. What they had been doing in the meantime is frustratingly unclear: contemporary sources make no mention of them until this point, and later ones are contradictory. Orderic Vitalis, for example, states categorically that they had not fought at Hastings, whereas John of Worcester implies that they had, but withdrew before its bloody conclusion. On reaching London their first thought was reportedly to get Harold's widow, Ealdgyth – their sister – out of harm's way, to which end they sent her north to Chester; but they also gave their backing to Edgar Ætheling. 'Eadwine and Morcar promised they would fight for him', says the Anglo-Saxon Chronicle.[6]

None of this, of course, can have been known to William in the days immediately after the battle. Having buried his own dead, the duke had withdrawn to Hastings, where he waited, in the words of the Chronicle, 'to see if there would be any surrender'. According to the *Carmen* he stayed there for a fortnight, but no surrender came. 'When he realized that none were willing to come to him', says the Chronicle, 'he marched inland with what was left of his host.'

William began his march by heading east along the coast. His first stop was the town of Romney, where, says Poitiers, 'he inflicted such punishment as he thought fit for the slaughter of his men who had landed there by mistake' – an interesting, belated indication of the dangers the Normans had risked by crossing the Channel at night. Presumably leaving the charred remains of Romney behind him, the duke proceeded further along the coast to Dover. 'A great multitude had gathered there', says Poitiers, 'because the place seemed impregnable', and both he and the *Carmen* devote several lines to describing the defensive advantages of the rocky headland on which Dover Castle now stands. As the Normans approached, though, the defenders lost heart and surrendered. More burning followed when the town was occupied, which Poitiers insists was accidental, and blames on the lower ranks of the duke's army, greedy for plunder.

William remained at Dover for some time: a month according to the *Carmen*, though Poitiers, perhaps more credibly, implies it might have been just over a week. One reason was his reported desire to strengthen the site's existing defences (some historians would date the origins of Dover Castle from this point); another may have been the need to wait for the 'reinforcements from overseas' referred to by the D Chronicle. Despite the losses suffered at Hastings, William's army was clearly still formidably large. Too large, perhaps: during their stay at Dover, some of his men resorted to drinking water and eating freshly killed meat, which led to an outbreak of dysentery and in due course many deaths. Their high-risk diet indicates that supplies of more suitable foodstuffs must have run short, and reminds us of a fundamental point: the Normans were living off the land, and needed to keep foraging and ravaging in order to remain alive. A short time later, Poitiers tells us, William himself fell ill, but despite the concern of those close to him he pushed on, 'lest the army should suffer from a shortage of supplies'.[7]

Leaving a garrison at Dover, as well as those too ill to continue, William set his sights on London. As he advanced, representatives of other cities approached him and offered their submission. The citizens of Canterbury did so, says Poitiers, fearful of total ruin if they resisted further. The *Carmen*, meanwhile, carries the uncorroborated but entirely credible story that the duke sent troops to demand the surrender of Winchester, the site of the royal treasury and hence a highly desirable prize. Since the start of the year the city had been held by Edward the Confessor's widow, Edith, as part of her dower, and this, says the *Carmen*, meant that its inhabitants were treated leniently, with William requiring only a profession of fealty and a promise of future rent – terms which the former queen and the city fathers chose to accept. Other towns and cities evidently had to make their submission on such terms as they could get, which generally involved the payment of large tributes. 'Just as hungry flies attack in swarms wounds brimming with blood', says the *Carmen*, 'so from all sides the English rush to dance attendance on the king. Nor do they come with hands empty of gifts. All bring presents, bow their necks to the yoke, and kiss his feet on bended knees.'[8]

But not the citizens of London. If he had not known before, by now William had heard about the election of Edgar Ætheling. 'When he learnt what had been done in London', says the *Carmen*, 'contrary to justice and by fools, he ordered his troops to approach the walls of the city.' Unfortunately at this point the *Carmen* becomes an unreliable guide, describing a siege of London which is at odds with the accounts of all other writers. We seem to be on surer ground with William of Poitiers, who explains how the approach of an advance party of Norman knights triggered an English sortie. Poitiers does not say so, but since the city lies on the north side of the Thames and the Normans were approaching from the south, the defenders must have crossed the river to meet their enemies, which presumably means they used London Bridge. The sortie was unsuccessful, with the English forced into a retreat, back across the bridge and inside the walls. The Normans vented their fury by torching all the houses on the south bank.[9]

With his army on one side of the Thames and London's recalcitrant citizens safely ensconced on the other, William faced a major problem: how to induce a surrender without attempting a suicidal direct assault. The solution was the kind of terror campaign he had used in similar circumstances earlier in his career, most recently in the case of Le Mans. The Norman advance from Hastings to London can hardly have been the peaceful progress that some later chroniclers pretended; apart from anything else, the need to forage for food would have meant much violent appropriation. Even William of Poitiers, although he makes some prefatory noises about clemency and moderation, could not avoid mentioning the punishing of Romney and the burning of Dover. These actions, however, Poitiers evidently felt could be justified or excused as accidental; when, by contrast, he comes to describe the army's actions after the confrontation on the south bank, he retreats into one of his telling silences, saying only that the duke proceeded 'wherever he wished'. It is our English sources, despite their habitual terseness, that furnish us with a fuller picture. William, says the Anglo-Saxon Chronicle, 'harried that part of the country through which he advanced'. From this moment, if not before, foraging became outright ravaging – wilful and deliberate destruction, intended to sow fear among those who had not yet submitted. Some idea of the extent of the campaign is provided by John of Worcester, who wrote that the Normans 'laid waste Sussex, Kent, Hampshire, Middlesex and Hertfordshire, and did not cease from burning townships and slaying men'.[10]

As to precisely where they went, we cannot know. More than a century ago, a scholar called Francis Baring suggested that the route of William's devastating march could be recovered by looking at the depreciation of land values recorded in the Domesday Book. It all seemed very clever and well substantiated, and one can still find books written in the not too distant past that cite Baring's reconstruction with approval. Latterly, however, the Baring method has been discredited, not least because even its staunchest advocates are unable to agree on the same conclusion.[11] The truth is that we can only recover the general direction of the duke's route from the information recorded in the chronicles. We can be fairly sure that, having decided against a direct assault on London, William headed west. If John of Worcester is right, the Normans harried into Hampshire, then turned north, burning their way through Berkshire and on into Oxfordshire, before coming to a stop at Wallingford. As its name implies, Wallingford was a convenient place for the Normans to cross the Thames (apparently the first place they could have crossed the river without recourse to boats or bridges). It may also have had an additional importance as a military target: the town's entry in the Domesday Book contains a passing reference to land 'where the housecarls lived'. To judge from the comments of the chroniclers, William stayed in Wallingford for several days – even the brief account of William of Jumièges says that the duke ordered his troops to pitch camp there – and one naturally suspects that during this time, as at Dover, work commenced on the town's new castle.[12]

According to William of Poitiers, it was at Wallingford that the archbishop of Canterbury, Stigand, came and did homage to William, at the same time renouncing Edgar Ætheling. While we have no particular reason to doubt that this was the case, we might suspect that Poitiers exaggerates the archbishop's role in the English resistance. In his account, Stigand is portrayed as the leader of the Londoners at the time of Edgar's election; Ealdred, whom the English sources identify in that role, receives no mention. Very likely Poitiers is altering the past here, conscious of the subsequent fortunes of the two men, protecting Ealdred's reputation by making Stigand the scapegoat. (He may have done much the same with the coronation of Harold at the start of the year.) The submission of the archbishop of Canterbury was, of course, significant. But the opposition in London, for the time being, continued.[13]

And so therefore did the harrying. Having crossed the Thames at Wallingford, the Norman army resumed its devastating progress, turning north-east so that the line of their march began to encircle the capital. Probably following the ancient path along the Chilterns known as the Icknield Way, William and his men passed through Buckinghamshire and on into Hertfordshire (as John of Worcester indicates), where they established another camp (and possibly the great motte-and-bailey castle) at Berkhamsted.

By now the mood in London must have been quite despondent. Apart from the terrifying spectacle of the Norman progress, English spirits had been dealt a crushing blow by the desertion of Eadwine and Morcar. The two earls, says John of Worcester, 'withdrew their support and returned home with their army', presumably meaning that at some point during the autumn they had left London and gone north to their earldoms. As a result of this action, Eadwine and Morcar have long been cast, probably unfairly, in the role of arch traitors. In the early twelfth century, for example, William of Malmesbury described them as 'two brothers of great ambition', and stated, quite inaccurately, that they left London because the citizens had refused to elect one of them as king: as we have seen, our most closely contemporary source, the D Chronicle, indicates that the earls had initially promised to fight for Edgar Ætheling, and says nothing about their departure for the north. At the same time, the D Chronicle, brief as it is, conveys vividly the collapse of hope among the English in London in the weeks that followed, as they contemplated fighting in the name of a child king against the terrible enemy that was wasting the land beyond their walls. 'Always when some initiative should have been shown, there was delay from day to day, until matters went from bad to worse, as everything did in the end.'[14]

And so the English in London – or at least those who had championed the cause of young Edgar – decided to surrender. As the darkest days of the year drew in, Edgar himself, accompanied by a delegation of magnates and bishops, began the thirty-mile journey from London to Berkhamsted in order to submit to William's superior might. They went, says the Anglo-Saxon Chronicle, 'out of necessity, after most damage had been done – and it was a great piece of folly that they had not done it earlier'. When at last they came before the Conqueror, 'they gave hostages, and swore oaths to him, and he promised them that he would be a gracious lord'.

Did this mean that William was England's new king? To English minds, the answer must have been yes. As we've seen, English kingship was elective: a ruler's reign began the moment he was accepted by the magnates. This means, of course, that the ætheling must have been regarded as king as well. Although the Anglo-Saxon Chronicle is understandably very coy about saying so, Edgar's rule had clearly been proclaimed in the days immediately after Hastings. We are told, for example, that after the death of their abbot from wounds sustained in the battle, the monks of Peterborough had sent his successor to Edgar for confirmation, and – more to the point – Edgar had 'gladly consented'. William of Poitiers is even more explicit: 'They had chosen Edgar Ætheling, of the noble stock of King Edward, as king.' Evidently Edgar, like the Confessor before him, had not been crowned in the early days of his reign, but in English eyes this did not matter. Coronation, to repeat, was simply confirmation – it conferred God's blessing, but not the kingship itself.[15]

The Normans, however, saw matters differently. On the Continent, a king was created at the moment of his coronation, not before. The Edgar episode, of course, gave them good reason for insisting on this point: the boy had not been crowned; ergo he was not king. The English may have thought this was rather irregular, but they were clearly in no position to debate constitutional practice, and so fell quickly into line with Norman thinking. At the same time, they realized that this new logic left the country in an anxious state of limbo: England would have no king until William was crowned. Hence, says William of Poitiers, 'the bishops and other leading men begged him to take the crown, saying that they were accustomed to obey a king, and wished to have a king as their lord'. The Normans, too, urged their leader to take the throne quickly, albeit for different reasons. 'They wished their gains and honours to be increased by his elevation.'[16]

But, according to Poitiers, William himself hesitated. It was not seemly, he said, to rush when climbing to the topmost pinnacle. Given that this had been the whole point of the Conquest, we might assume that this scene is Poitiers' own invention – a conceit designed to emphasize his master's thoughtfulness and modesty, and hence ultimately his suitability to rule. Yet unseemliness is not the only argument that the Conqueror is said to have put forward. What chiefly dissuaded him, he told his closest companions, was the confused situation in England: some people were still rebelling; also, he had wanted his wife to be crowned with him, and she, of course, was still in Normandy. These arguments seem quite credible. At this point only the south-eastern part of the country was under William's control. It would have been perfectly understandable had he wished to complete his military takeover, and to have all Englishmen submit to him, so that he and Matilda could experience an orderly coronation at some future date. In this respect at least, his attitude towards the ceremony was not so very different from that of his Anglo–Saxon predecessors.

Eventually, having put the matter to a meeting of his magnates, William was talked around. 'After carefully reconsidering everything', says Poitiers, 'he gave way to all their requests and arguments.' Apparently the key argument that persuaded him to change his mind was the military one. 'Above all, he hoped that once he had begun to reign, any rebels would be less ready to challenge him and more easily put down.' The decision taken, says Poitiers, William sent some of his men ahead to London to make the necessary preparations.[17]

By the time William himself reached London some days later, the situation there must have been incredibly tense. The city, as we have noted, had been swelled by the survivors of Hastings. They, and the relatives of the thousands who had fallen, can hardly have looked upon the arrival of the Normans with anything other than abhorrence. According to William of Jumièges, the advance guard that the Conqueror had sent ahead 'found many rebels determined to offer every possible resistance. Fighting followed immediately and thus London was plunged into mourning for the loss of her sons and citizens.' Jumièges may not be the most reliable witness here, but the resistance he describes is implicitly acknowledged by the better-informed William of Poitiers, who tells us that the advance guard had been ordered to build a fortress in the city, 'as a defence against the inconstancy of the numerous and hostile inhabitants'.[18]

The coronation itself took place on Christmas Day. Given the situation in London, there can have been little appetite for the kind of processions through the streets that we know preceded later ceremonies. If the *Carmen* can be believed (and, sadly, most of its account of this episode has to be rejected), William may have taken up residence in Edward the Confessor's palace at Westminster in the days immediately prior to the ceremony. We know that the ceremony took place in the Confessor's new church at Westminster Abbey, and we also know that the audience included both English and Normans. Since there can only have been space inside for a few hundred people, the majority of London's citizens must have remained at home, and the bulk of the Norman army camped elsewhere (perhaps in the new castle in the city's south-eastern corner). A number of armed and mounted Normans, however, were stationed outside the abbey as a precaution against ambush.[19]

As for the ceremony itself, we know enough to see that it followed a conventional form. Historians continue to debate which order of service was followed, but all agree that, despite the novelty of regarding it as the king-making moment, William's coronation adhered to long-standing English traditions. Anthems in praise of the king were sung, just as they had been in the Confessor's day, and the service was conducted by an English archbishop. As at the start of the year, this was Ealdred, archbishop of York, rather than Stigand, the pariah archbishop of Canterbury. In describing the ceremony, English sources, for obvious reasons, emphasized the first part, wherein the new king swore the traditional oath to govern his subjects well, according to the best practice of his predecessors. As John of Worcester explains, William promised to defend the Church and its rulers; to govern the whole people justly; and to establish and maintain the law, totally forbidding 'rapine and unjust judgements'.[20]

The English in the audience must have been particularly keen to hear the last part, in light of recent events. William of Poitiers gives the impression that the days between the submissions at Berkhamsted and the coronation had been peaceful ones: had the Conqueror wished, we are told, he could have spent all his time in hunting and falconry. The D Chronicle, by contrast, tells a different story. Having noted William's promise at Berkhamsted to be a gracious lord, it adds bitterly that 'nevertheless, in the meantime, they harried everywhere they came'. As the English had feared, the Normans had continued to behave during these weeks as if they were still at war. Now, at last, as their new king swore his oath, they could hope the ravaging would cease.[21]

But evidently someone had forgotten to explain the significance of this moment to those Normans who were standing guard outside. As William of Poitiers explains, the next part of the service involved asking the audience whether or not they would accept the rule of the new king – a question which had to be put twice, first in English by Ealdred, and again in French by the Norman bishop of Coutances. Naturally everyone answered in the affirmative, shouting out in their respective tongues, but, unfortunately, says Poitiers, the guards outside the church thought that this loud clamour was some sort of last-minute English treachery, and responded by setting fire to the nearby houses.

As modern historians have observed, this is William of Poitiers at his most unconvincing: if the guards had really thought there was trouble in the church, surely they would have rushed inside. What we seem to have is a clumsy attempt to excuse yet more burning and pillaging, even as the coronation service was in progress. At the same time, the fact that Poitiers felt compelled to mention this incident at all suggests it must have been serious, and that suspicion is confirmed by the later but fuller account provided by Orderic Vitalis. As the fire spread rapidly, says Orderic, 'the crowd who had been rejoicing in the church took fright, and throngs of men and women of every rank and condition rushed outside in frantic haste'. Some, we are told, went to fight the flames, while others went to join in the looting. Meanwhile, in the abbey, only the bishops and a few monks and clergy remained to complete the coronation service. Archbishop Ealdred, as was customary, anointed William with holy oil, placed the crown upon his head, and seated him on the royal throne. The churchmen were reportedly terrified, and one can well believe it: at the very moment they had called upon God to bless their new king and grant him a peaceful rule, the scene outside was mayhem. By the end of the ceremony, we are told, even the Conqueror himself was trembling from head to foot. It was, as Orderic observes, an inauspicious beginning.[22]

For a few days after his coronation William remained in London. His first royal act, if we follow William of Poitiers' account, was the distribution of rewards to those who had supported him. This was the moment his men had been itching for, and the reason they had echoed the English cry for an early coronation. Naturally, Poitiers does his best to put a positive spin on the process. The new king, he says, 'distributed liberally what Harold had avariciously shut up in the royal treasury', though he cannot avoid admitting, belatedly, that this munificence was also made possible by the large tributes that had been received during the preceding months. We are next assured that, while some of the spoils went to 'those who had helped him win the battle', the greater and more valuable part was given to monasteries. Whatever the truth about the ratio, that many churches received gifts from William is well established. Needless to say, Poitiers is speaking here of Continental churches, and particularly those which had offered prayers for the success of the Conquest. Some, we are told, received large golden crosses, wonderfully jewelled, while others were given golden vessels or vestments. The obvious inference (made all the more obvious by Poitiers' later attempt to deny it) is that these items had been obtained by plundering English churches. The choicest gifts of all were reserved for William's greatest spiritual supporter, Pope Alexander, who was sent 'more gold and silver coins than could be credibly told, as well as ornaments that even Byzantium would have considered precious'. These included Harold's own banner, with its image of an armed man embroidered in gold, presumably a quid pro quo for the banner Alexander had bestowed on William to signal his support for the invasion.[23]

The needs of the English at the start of the reign were not entirely ignored: Poitiers assures us that, immediately after his coronation, William 'made many wise, just and merciful provisions', some for London, some for the country as a whole. In the case of London, at least, this statement is supported by an original writ, almost certainly drawn up during these dramatic early days, and still preserved at the London Metropolitan Archives, in which the new king promises the city's leading men that their laws will be maintained as they had been 'in the time of King Edward'. In general terms, however, Poitiers' repeated insistence on the fairness of his master's actions ('he condemned none save those whom it would have been unjust not to condemn'; he accepted 'nothing which was contrary to fair dealing') reads like a response to complaints that the new king had been anything but fair. In particular, his comment that William 'set a limit that was not oppressive to the collection of tribute' needs to be set against the opinion of the D Chronicle, which juxtaposes the king's coronation oath to govern justly with the comment 'nevertheless, he imposed a very heavy tax on the country'.[24]

This glaring contradiction between the Norman and English accounts is also apparent with regard to an important meeting that took place early in the new year 1067. As William of Poitiers explains, the king, having gained the measure of London's citizens, decided it would be better to stay elsewhere until his new fortress was finished, and so withdrew from the city to nearby Barking. It was while he was there, says Poitiers, that earls Eadwine and Morcar, 'perhaps the most powerful of all the English', came to submit to him. Along with 'various other wealthy nobles', the two brothers 'sought his pardon for any hostility they had shown him, and surrendered themselves and all their property to his mercy'.[25]

But what happened to that property? According to Poitiers, 'the king readily accepted their oaths, freely granted them his favour, restored all their possessions, and treated them with great honour'. Other sources, however, suggest that William's favour was anything but free. 'Men paid him tribute, and gave him hostages', says the E Chronicler, '*and then redeemed their lands from him* [my italics]'. Similarly, the Domesday Book refers casually on more than one occasion to 'the time when the English redeemed their lands'. Englishmen, in other words, were obliged to buy back their estates from the Conqueror, and we can assume he charged them handsomely.[26]

Many Englishmen, of course, were no longer in a position to strike such a bargain, having perished on the field at Hastings. The fate of their lands is revealed in a writ, almost certainly issued at the very start of William's reign, in which the king insists that the abbot of Bury St Edmunds should surrender to him 'all the land which those men held . . . who stood in battle against me and there were slain'. The fact that the list of the fallen included some of the greatest landowners in the kingdom – not only the late King Harold but also his brothers Leofwine and Gyrth – meant that the amount of land forfeited was massive. Much of it in the first instance the Conqueror kept for himself, but some of it was quickly redistributed as rewards to his closest followers. To his half-brother Odo, for instance, William gave all of Kent, formerly the property of Leofwine, along with the castle of Dover; William fitz Osbern, meanwhile, received the Isle of Wight and lands in adjacent Hampshire; soon after the Barking meeting, the king travelled to Hampshire in person, and began building a castle at Winchester for fitz Osbern to hold on his behalf.[27]

The concentration of power implicit in these gifts to his two most trusted advisers was appropriate, because William intended them to act as his regents. Although just a few weeks had elapsed since the start of his reign, the new king wanted to return to Normandy. In March he travelled to Pevensey, where he had landed his troops the previous September. Now, barely six months later, he was ready to let them leave. Substantial numbers of knights and soldiers remained to guard England in his absence, but the majority were paid off at this point, rewarded for their role in his mighty victory.

Also assembled at Pevensey by the king's command were a crowd of high-ranking Englishmen: Archbishop Stigand, Edgar Ætheling and earls Eadwine and Morcar are the most notable names. 'Those whose loyalty and power he particularly suspected', as Poitiers describes them, were to join William for his homecoming, 'so that during his absence no revolt instigated by them might break out, and the general populace, deprived of their leaders, would be less capable of rebellion'. They were, in other words, hostages, which is what the Anglo-Saxon Chronicle calls them, and indeed is a word that Poitiers himself found impossible to avoid. But although these men were held 'almost as hostages', we are assured that 'they were not led about as captives, but accompanied their lord the king in his retinue, so as to have greater favour and honour'.[28]

Thus the Conqueror, accompanied by victorious Frenchmen and vanquished Englishmen, returned home. For William of Poitiers, this was a culminating moment, and he misses no trick in describing it: the weather was unseasonably bright and sunny; the crossing of the Channel was made easy by a favourable wind and tide. For several pages we are treated to an extended comparison of William with Julius Caesar, much to the king's advantage and to Caesar's detriment. Hence when we are told that the Norman ships were fitted with new white sails for their return journey, after the fashion of the conquering fleets of antiquity, we might suspect that fact is shading into fable. Nevertheless, we can believe our source when he tells us that the strict observances of Lent were forgotten that spring, and everyone in Normandy behaved as if it were a time of high festival. Wherever William went, people from remote parts crowded to see him; in his principal city of Rouen, men, women and children shouted out his name. The churches of Normandy were showered with precious objects generously donated by their English counterparts. The duke, now a king, was reunited with his consort, now a queen, and the rest of the family and friends he had left behind. When he celebrated Easter at Fécamp, William was surrounded by not only a crowd of bishops and abbots from Normandy, but also a delegation of nobles from neighbouring France.

All gazed in awe at the new king and his entourage, decked out in their clothes encrusted with gold, accompanied by their handsome, long-haired English guests. At the banquet that followed the Easter service, they drank only from horns gilded at both ends, or goblets of silver and gold.[29]

Such is the picture that Poitiers paints of his master's return: exaggerated in places, airbrushed in others, but overall capturing brilliantly the exultation of a duke and a duchy whose fortunes had been in every sense transformed by his astonishing victory. 'Nothing which ought to have been done in celebration of such honour was left undone', says the chronicler, and we can see that festivities continued well into the summer. On 1 May, for example, the new abbey church at St-Pierre-sur-Dives, begun a generation earlier, was consecrated on William's orders and in his presence, and a similar ceremony followed at Jumièges on 1 July. At some other point during the summer the king visited Caen, and his own foundation of St Stephen's, bringing gifts so precious 'that they deserve to be remembered until the end of time'. 'A light of unaccustomed serenity seemed suddenly to have dawned upon the province', says Poitiers; William 'spent that summer and autumn, and part of winter, on this side of the sea, devoting all his time to love of his native land'.[30]

But the onset of winter brought ominous intelligence from the other side of the Channel: an English conspiracy to kill the Norman occupiers and undo the recent Conquest.

The Godwine family, it seems, were planning another comeback.

13

Insurrection

We have encountered the chronicler Orderic Vitalis on several earlier occasions. A monk at the Norman abbey of St Evroult, not far from the town of L'Aigle, Orderic began writing in the early twelfth century, but is a valuable source for events well before his own day. He is, for example, one of our best informants for the troubled years of William the Conqueror's boyhood, because he possessed a keen ear for the stories told to him by local aristocrats about the deeds of their ancestors.[1] Similarly, his monumental *Ecclesiastical History*, despite its title, is one of our principal sources for the Norman Conquest of England – but for rather different reasons.

Although he had lived at St Evroult since his childhood, Orderic had not been born in Normandy. 'I came here from the remote parts of Mercia as a ten-year-old English boy', he explains at the start of his fifth book. More specifically, he came from Shropshire: as he goes on to tell us, he was born on 16 February 1075, baptized at St Eata's Church in Atcham, and named after the local priest. At the age of five he was sent to learn his letters in Shrewsbury, before being packed off by his father to St Evroult five years later, 'an ignorant stranger of another race'. This might seem a strange fate for a Shropshire lad so soon after the Conquest, but it is explained by the fact that his father was a Norman – a priest who had come to England in the wake of William's victory. We infer that Orderic's mother (whom he never mentions) must have been English, and it was from her that he derived his identity as an Englishman.[2]

The fact that he was the product of a mixed, Anglo-Norman

marriage makes Orderic's thoughts on the Norman Conquest doubly interesting. Like a lot of medieval writers, he copied freely from earlier sources, and his account of the Conquest draws heavily on that of William of Poitiers (it is, indeed, precisely because Orderic acknowledges this debt that we know anything about Poitiers' own career).[3] Sometimes he is content to copy more or less verbatim, losing a word here, inserting a sentence there. At other times he makes more substantial changes, and occasionally he makes it very clear that he has departed from his source material because he disapproves of its anti-English sentiment. On the eve of the Battle of Hastings, for example, Poitiers describes King Harold as 'a man soiled with lasciviousness, a cruel murderer, resplendent with plundered riches, and an enemy of God and the just'. In Orderic's version Harold becomes 'a brave and valiant man, strong and handsome, pleasant in speech, and a good friend to his own followers'.[4]

Orderic is also uniquely valuable for the years immediately following the Conquest because, sadly, the end of William of Poitiers' history is lost. We know, thanks to Orderic, that it originally covered the period up to the start of the year 1071, but the only copy that has come down to us breaks off mid-sentence in 1067. Part of the fun of reading Orderic, therefore, is trying to guess where he is copying Poitiers, where he might be adding new information gleaned from other sources, and where his sensibilities as an Englishman have been sufficiently affronted that he has been prompted to offer his own alternative version.

Consider, for instance, the different accounts offered by the two writers of events in England during William's absence. As we have seen, before his return to Normandy, the newly crowned king had committed the government of England to Odo of Bayeux and William fitz Osbern, respectively based at Dover and Winchester. Shortly before his manuscript breaks off, William of Poitiers ceases his description of his master's triumphal homecoming and resumes the story in England:

> Meanwhile Odo, bishop of Bayeux, and William fitz Osbern were administering their prefectures in the kingdom . . . They burned with a common desire to keep the Christian people in peace, and deferred readily to each other's advice. They paid the greatest respect to justice, as the king had admonished, so

that fierce men and enemies might be corrected and brought into friendship. The lesser officials were equally zealous in the castles where each had been placed.

Orderic, confronted by this passage, replaced it with his own:

Meanwhile, the English were groaning under the Norman yoke, and suffering oppressions from the proud lords who ignored the king's injunctions. The petty lords who were guarding the castles oppressed all the native inhabitants of high and low degree, and heaped shameful burdens on them. For Bishop Odo and William fitz Osbern, the king's vicegerents, were so swollen with pride that they would not deign to hear the reasonable plea of the English or give them impartial judgement. When their men at arms were guilty of plunder and rape they protected them by force, and wreaked their wrath all the more violently upon those who complained of the cruel wrongs they suffered.[5]

Clearly, not much common ground. The only point on which Poitiers and Orderic seem to agree is that the newcomers were based in castles. The Normans, as we've seen, had started digging in from the moment of their arrival. We hear of new fortifications being established at Pevensey, Hastings, Dover, London and Winchester, and we can make a strong circumstantial case for supposing they were also begun at other places, such as Canterbury, Wallingford and Berkhamsted. What form these castles took is a matter of debate. As every schoolchild knows, the common-or-garden model in Norman England was the so-called 'motte and bailey' – a giant mound of earth to support a wooden tower, paired with a shallower but more extensive enclosure to house and protect the castle's other buildings; around three-quarters of all known sites conform to this type. It could be that the Normans were establishing such castles from the first – the Bayeux Tapestry shows men erecting a motte at Hastings, and a motte can still be seen on the site today. But, then again, the Tapestry depicts *every* castle in this way, so it could be that drawing a motte was simply a convenient artistic shorthand. While there are surviving mottes at Canterbury, Wallingford and Berkhamsted, excavation has shown that the one at Winchester was added a few years after the Conquest, and at Pevensey, Dover and London there were evidently never any mottes at all. Construction on this scale would have required weeks running into months, so it may be that the very earliest Norman castles were simply enclosures (or 'ringworks' as they are often termed): the one on Castle Hill near Folkestone is a good example.[6]

Whatever form they took, the important point – quite obvious from the fact that the Normans felt obliged to build so many from the moment of their arrival – is that castles in England were a new phenomenon. England, for all the woes that it had suffered in the eleventh century, remained a strong, united kingdom. It had not experienced anything like the political fragmentation that had engulfed the principalities of western Europe. Its coinage, its courts and its laws were all part of a long-established royal monopoly, and so too were its fortifications – the *burhs* established by the conquering kings of Wessex in the tenth century. The private dwellings known as *burhgeats*, associated with thegnly status and claimed by some historians to be castles in all but name, were clearly nowhere near as strong and defensible as the true castles we find on the Continent.[7] In England we do not read of rebellions based on fortresses, or find the king besieging his greater subjects in their own homes. When English magnates fall from grace they flee into foreign exile, and resist if they can by raising fleets.

The exception that proves the rule is a tiny handful of castles constructed in the years immediately prior to 1051 by some of the French friends of Edward the Confessor. One was apparently built at Clavering in Essex, and three others were built in Herefordshire as part of an attempt (quite unsuccessful) to keep the Welsh at bay. Their novelty is suitably underlined by the fact the Anglo-Saxon Chronicle, describing the situation in Herefordshire in 1051, employs the earliest recorded example of the word 'castle' in English. The word, like the thing itself, was a foreign import. Beyond this there was nothing in England that could be meaningfully regarded as a castle. As Orderic Vitalis later put it in a justly famous passage, 'the fortifications that the Normans called castles were scarcely known in the English provinces, and so the English – in spite of their courage and love of fighting – could put up only a weak resistance to their enemies'.[8]

Consequently, we sense the shock in the English sources when castles suddenly start appearing in large numbers. As in France, so too in England, their introduction went hand in hand with oppression. The foreigners who built the castle in Hereford, says the Chronicle, 'inflicted all the injuries and insults they possibly could upon the king's men in that region'. This may have been because the local population were forced to build them, or because their homes were demolished to make way for them, or simply because they served as bases for soldiers and knights who would ride out each day to cow the surrounding countryside into submission, indulging in the acts of plunder, rape and violence that Orderic Vitalis describes. Orderic's account of the activities of the Conqueror's regents during his absence in 1067 accords far better with our English sources than the panegyric of William of Poitiers. 'Bishop Odo and Earl William were left behind here,' groans the Anglo-Saxon Chronicle, 'and they built castles far and wide throughout the land, oppressing the unhappy people, and things went ever from bad to worse. When God wills may the end be good!'[9]

Small wonder, then, that the English, as Orderic puts it, 'plotted ceaselessly to find some way of shaking off a yoke that was so intolerable and unaccustomed'.[10] During the year 1067 we hear of several local risings by the English against their new castle-building overlords. In Herefordshire, one of the most powerful English thegns, the aptly named Eadric the Wild, fought back with some success against the new Norman garrisons installed in those original pre-Conquest castles. According to John of Worcester, they frequently devastated his lands, but whenever they attacked him they lost many of their knights and soldiers. At length, in mid-August, Eadric joined forces with two Welsh kings, Bleddyn and Rhiwallon, with whom he ravaged Herefordshire 'up to the bridge of the River Lugg', and 'brought back great spoil.'[11]

Around the same time, or perhaps a little later, a potentially more serious rebellion took place in the south-east. The men of Kent, either 'because they hated the Normans' (William of Poitiers) or 'goaded by Norman oppression' (Orderic Vitalis), sent emissaries across the Channel in an effort to persuade Eustace, count of Boulogne, to help them seize Dover Castle. This might seem a surprising appeal, given their relations in the not too distant past – it was Eustace's attack on Dover in 1051 that had sparked the great crisis of that year, and the count had also fought for the Normans at Hastings: he is, indeed, one of the four individuals credited by the *Carmen* with the killing of King Harold. Yet his relations with Normandy were not as close or cordial as this might suggest: in 1053 Eustace had joined the rebellion that had tried to topple William and, when it failed, had been forced to surrender his son as a hostage. At some point in the first half of 1067 the two men had fallen out again, for reasons unknown; Orderic refers simply to jealousy between them, while Poitiers says only that, *were* he to go into details, he would easily convince us that William was in the right. Modern historians tend to assume, in lieu of any better explanation, that the count had been disappointed by the amount of land he had received as reward.

Whatever the reason for the rift, it predisposed Eustace to accept the Kentish offer: he assembled an invasion force and sailed across the Channel at night, intending to take Dover by surprise at dawn. His intelligence was seemingly good, because both Odo of Bayeux and the castle's commander, Hugh de Montfort, were far away at the time, on the other side of the Thames, and had taken with them most of their troops. The men of Kent were already up in arms, says Poitiers, and would have been joined by rebels from other regions, had the siege lasted as long as two days; but Eustace and his English allies found Dover's defenders to be more doughty than expected. Rather than wait for more attackers to assemble, the Norman garrison sallied out of the gates and put their foes to flight. Eustace himself, familiar with the terrain, managed to find his way back to a boat and the safety of Boulogne, but many of his men were pursued to the cliffs and plunged to their deaths. The English, meanwhile, scattered in all directions, their plan of replacing one foreign lord with another having come to nothing.[12]

Lastly there had been trouble in Northumbria. Notionally the north of England remained under the command of Earl Morcar, elected by the northerners themselves in the wake of the successful rebellion against Tostig Godwineson in 1065 (the new earl was at least still in possession of his title in the period immediately after the Conquest). From the very first, however, Morcar had been obliged to share power with others. As we have seen, the 1065 rebellion had been triggered by the murder of Gospatric, head of the house of Bamburgh, and Morcar, mindful of this, had immediately ceded authority above the Tyne to Gospatric's nephew, Oswulf.

But at the start of 1067, just before his return to Normandy, William had upset this arrangement by granting the earldom of Northumbria, or at the very least its northern half, to a Yorkshire thegn called Copsig. It was an astonishing appointment, for Copsig had previously been Tostig's lieutenant, and was no less hated in the north than his former master. He had, however, submitted to the Conqueror in a way that Oswulf evidently had not, and by some unknown magic had convinced the king that, when it came to controlling the north, he was the best man for the job. ('He was', says William of Poitiers, 'entirely favourable to the king and supported his cause.') As it was, the confidence of both parties turned out to be seriously misplaced: within just a few weeks of his arrival in Northumbria, Copsig was ambushed and killed by Oswulf, who personally hacked off his rival's head. Oswulf might therefore have expected some future day of reckoning with the Conqueror or his regents, but at some point in the autumn of 1067 he too came to an untimely end, run through by the lance of a robber.[13]

It was none of these risings or rebellions, however, that caused William to return to England, but reports of some wider conspiracy. The details are sketchy, and have to be reconstructed forensically from the often allusive comments of the chroniclers. The general conclusion, however, seems clear: in the last weeks of 1067, the Conqueror learned of a conspiracy against him, organized by the surviving members of the Godwine family.[14]

Orderic Vitalis gives us the general context. During his stay in Normandy, he says, the king was disquieted by intelligence which intimated that the troops he had left behind in England were about to be massacred as part of an English plot. William of Jumièges provides the more specific but uncorroborated information that the plotters' intention was to attack the Normans on Ash Wednesday, the beginning of Lent, when they would be walking barefoot to church. In 1068 this day fell on 6 February.

William, therefore, hurried to cross the Channel before the end of 1067, sailing from Dieppe on 6 December despite the rough sea and wintry weather, and arriving safely at Winchelsea the following morning. From there he made straight for London, where he celebrated Christmas and tried to sniff out the conspirators. According to Orderic, he was very gracious to the English lords and bishops who attended him, granting them favours and offering them the kiss of peace. Such behaviour, explains the chronicler, often brings back to the fold persons whose loyalty is doubtful, but at the same time William warned his Norman followers, behind the backs of the English, not to relax their guard for a moment.

Early in the new year, William received the certain intelligence he had been seeking: the conspiracy was based in the south-west of England, in the city of Exeter. The king's suspicions must already have lain in that direction. Before leaving Normandy he had apparently sent some of his knights across the Channel to investigate the rumours, and those who had gone to Exeter had been 'ill-treated'. Confirmation came in 1068 when Exeter sent messages to other cities, urging them to join the rebellion – messages which William intercepted. The plot uncovered, the king sent a message of his own, demanding that Exeter's citizens swear fealty to him.

Orderic Vitalis, presumably following William of Poitiers, says nothing about the identity of the plotters. It is only from the terse accounts of this episode in our English sources that we can see that the ringleaders were the surviving members of the Godwine family, and, in particular, Harold's mother, Gytha. Last reported bargaining with the Conqueror over Harold's body, Gytha had evidently gone west after the battle to lick her wounds and plan her revenge. We can well imagine the intensity of her hatred: besides Harold, she had lost three other sons in 1066 (Tostig, Leofwine and Gyrth), and her sole surviving son, Wulfnoth, still languished in a Norman prison.

Gytha evidently had her hopes pinned on a new generation of Godwine men. Harold, of course, had been married to his queen, Ealdgyth, for only a short time before his death; had this match produced any children – one later chronicler claims it produced a son – then they would still have been babies at this point. But the dead king had been married earlier, according to Danish custom, to Edith Swan-Neck, by whom he had multiple offspring – no fewer than five children, at least three of whom were boys.[15] These young men, probably in their late teens or early twenties in 1066, had also fled west in the wake of their father's death, crossing the sea to Ireland. Their plan, along with Gytha, was evidently to restage the successful Godwine comeback of 1052: a mercenary fleet from Ireland, a fifth column in England – and perhaps also an invasion from Scandinavia. William of Poitiers says that the plotters had 'repeatedly sent envoys to the Danes or some other people from whom they might hope for help', while Orderic says the plot was 'supported by the Danes and other barbarous peoples'.[16]

William was evidently determined to stop this plan before it started. When Exeter refused his demand for fealty, he raised an army and began to march westwards. Orderic notes that in doing so the king for the first time demanded military service from his English subjects. Naturally William still had many Norman troops by his side and stationed elsewhere around the country. But summoning Englishmen to fight by his side had wider implications. It made the rebellion in the West Country a litmus test for loyalty: those who did not aid the king in crushing it would themselves be counted as rebels.

At first it seemed that there would be no struggle at all. As the royal army drew near to Exeter, a delegation of leading citizens rode out to sue for peace, much as other urban leaders had done in 1066. They promised to open their gates to William and to obey his commands, guaranteeing their good faith by handing over hostages. Yet on their return to the city, says Orderic, these men 'continued their hostile preparations, encouraging each other to fight for many reasons'.[17]

What were the reasons for this eccentric behaviour? One possibility is that the delegates were simply playing for time, and hoping to hold out until the arrival of their overseas allies. The other scenario, perhaps more likely, is that differences of opinion existed within the rebel ranks. Gytha and the other ringleaders had evidently been able to attract widespread popular support during William's absence, and perhaps also for a time thereafter. One of the king's first actions on his return, says John of Worcester, had been the imposition of 'an unbearable tax', and this was clearly a key factor for many in Exeter. According to Orderic, even as they defied William, the citizens indicated that they would be willing to pay tax at the customary rate. Some rebels, in short, were merely hoping for better treatment from the Conqueror; others remained determined to see him toppled. For the time being, it seems, the will of the diehards had carried the day.[18]

Inevitably, therefore, the matter was decided by violence. Exeter was a walled city and on his arrival William found the rebels manning the whole circuit of its ramparts. In a final attempt to induce a surrender he ordered one of the hostages to be blinded in view of the walls, but, says Orderic, this merely strengthened the determination of the defenders. Indeed, according to William of Malmesbury, one of them staged something of a counter-demonstration by dropping his trousers and farting loudly in the king's general direction. The siege that followed was evidently hard-fought. Orderic says that for many days William attempted to storm the city and undermine its walls; 'a large part of his army perished', adds the Anglo-Saxon Chronicle.

At length, after eighteen days, the citizens agreed to surrender. Orderic, no doubt toeing the line established by William of Poitiers, says that they were compelled to do so because of the Normans' relentless assault. William of Malmesbury claims that the king's forces gained entry after a section of wall collapsed – a break which he attributes to divine intervention after the fashion of Jericho rather than any Norman mining operations. The English chroniclers, by contrast, suggest that the surrender came about because of the desertion of the Godwine faction. Gytha, says John of Worcester, 'escaped with many in flight from the city', while the D Chronicle, apparently describing the same incident, says that the citizens surrendered 'because the thegns had betrayed them'. Accompanied by 'many other distinguished men's wives', Gytha sailed into the Bristol Channel and took refuge on the tiny island of Flat Holm. Presumably these pro-Godwine women remained hopeful that their husbands and grandsons would soon be crossing from Ireland.[19]

With the Godwine party gone, there was nothing to stop the more moderate of Exeter's citizens from seeking terms of surrender. According to Orderic and Poitiers, these were very favourable: William refrained from seizing their goods and guarded the gates in order to prevent any post-siege plunder. The Chronicle, predictably, offers a more acid assessment: the king 'made fair promises to them, and fulfilled them badly'. The truth probably lies somewhere in the middle, but that the surrender was negotiated rather than dictated seems clear. On one point, at least, the citizens seem to have got their way: the Domesday Book shows that in 1086 Exeter paid the same tax as it had done 'in the time of King Edward'.

After the surrender William spent more time in the south-west attending to security. A castle was established in Exeter itself and very likely others were erected elsewhere. Orderic tells us that the king led his army on into Cornwall, 'putting down every disturbance that came to his attention', and it was probably at this time he handed command of the region to a Breton follower called Brian. At length William disbanded his Anglo-Norman army and returned to Winchester, in time to celebrate Easter.[20]

With the defeat of the conspiracy and the flight of the Godwine faction, William no doubt felt more secure. He also had more rewards to distribute, for the property of Gytha and her followers, like the lands of those who had fought at Hastings, was now deemed forfeit. The chronicler at Abingdon Abbey, writing in the twelfth century, remembered how 'the mother of the slain king . . . had with her in her company the priest Blæcmann, together with many others . . . and whatever had been his was taken back into the king's hand, as that of a fugitive'.[21]

One of the principal beneficiaries of this fresh round of redistribution was the king's long-term friend, Roger of Montgomery. Having remained in Normandy in 1066 to assist the regency government headed by Matilda, Roger had accompanied William on his return to England the following year, and had immediately been rewarded with lands in Sussex. It must have been at this time that the county was sliced up into new Norman lordships – the so-called 'rapes' which endured as administrative units into modern times. Stretching from the county's northern border southwards to the sea, these long, narrow lordships were in each case named after the castles their new owners created just a few miles inland. Roger of Montgomery, for example, held the castles and rapes of Chichester and Arundel, while another of the Conqueror's closest companions, William de Warenne, was responsible for the rape and castle of Lewes. Their purpose was clearly military: to protect the quickest routes to Normandy, and to tighten the Norman grip on what had been the Godwine heartland.[22]

At the same time, the Normans did not enjoy a total monopoly of royal favour. 'Very many Englishmen received through his generous gifts what they had not received from their kinsmen or previous lords', says William of Poitiers – speaking, admittedly, of the period immediately after the coronation, and no doubt exaggerating his case. Nonetheless, we find some evidence of Englishmen, or at least non-Normans, being rewarded for their loyalty in the eighteen months that followed. In 1067, for example, Regenbald, a Lotharingian priest formerly in the service of Edward the Confessor, had been granted lands that had previously belonged to King Harold, while the following year another Lotharingian, Bishop Giso of Wells, was similarly granted estates that the late king had confiscated. Perhaps the most striking example, however, of William's continued willingness to work with the natives was his settlement of affairs in the north. At some point after his return to England the king received a visit from Gospatric, a scion of the house of Bamburgh, who came in the hope of obtaining the earldom of Northumbria lately vacated by his kinsman, Oswulf. Given that Oswulf, as we have seen, had been personally responsible for murdering the king's preferred candidate, Earl Copsig, Gospatric must have proceeded with some caution. Yet his mission was a success, and William agreed to sell him the earldom for what Simeon of Durham calls 'a great sum'. Such were the pragmatic deals that the Conqueror was still willing to strike in the hope of a peaceful settlement.[23]

William's increasing sense of security by Easter 1068 is revealed by his decision at that point to send messengers across the Channel to fetch his wife. Matilda, says Orderic, came at once, accompanied by a great company of vassals, noblewomen and clergy, and a few weeks later, on the feast of Whitsun, she was crowned at Westminster. This coronation, so far as we can tell, passed with none of the unplanned excitement that had marred the king's own ceremony. Chronicle accounts of the occasion are perfunctory, but we possess a valuable snapshot of proceedings thanks to a royal charter drawn up on the day itself ('when my wife Matilda was consecrated in the church of St Peter at Westminster', to quote its dating clause). The content of the grant is unimportant, but its witness-list allows us to see the composition of William's court at this particularly crucial juncture. Besides the king himself and his newly crowned queen stand the two English archbishops, Ealdred (once again officiating) and Stigand. The other bishops come next, a fairly even mix of English and Normans, with Leofric of Exeter, for example, lining up alongside the likes of Odo of Bayeux. When we reach the secular magnates, too, we see a similar degree of balance being maintained, with Roger of Montgomery and William fitz Osbern rubbing shoulders with Eadwine and Morcar. Significantly, the charter is a bilingual document, drawn up in both English and Latin. We seem, in short, to be looking at the kind of Anglo-Norman modus vivendi that the Conqueror had been hoping to achieve.[24]

Behind this facade of unity, however, a new and more dangerous tension was building. Among the English at court and across the country there was great and mounting anger, the principal reason for which was the redistribution of land that had occurred since 1066. Dispossessing the dead of Hastings was all very well, but what of their sons, brothers, uncles, nephews and cousins – those who lived on but whose expectations had thereby been dashed? It is easy to imagine a figure like Gytha, perhaps, being motivated purely by thoughts of revenge, but most of her supporters, and perhaps even her grandsons, were probably fighting in the hope of regaining their lost inheritances. And, of course, it was not just the dead and their heirs who had been dispossessed. *All* those who had fought against the Conqueror at Hastings, including the survivors, were deemed to have forfeited, and the same applied to those who had recently fled from Exeter. There was even a growing group of Englishmen whose lands had been confiscated because they were unable to pay the two heavy gelds that had been levied in the short time since William's accession. That disinheritance was the principal English grievance is suggested by all our chronicle sources. The E version of the Anglo-Saxon Chronicle, for instance, woefully brief for the years immediately after the Conquest, sums up the six-month period after William's return from Normandy in a single sentence: 'When he came back he gave away every man's land.' Describing events that occurred a little later, Orderic attributed English anger against the Normans to 'the killing of their kinsmen and compatriots' and 'the loss of their patrimonies'. William of Poitiers, meanwhile, merely confirms the criticism of his master's actions with a typically clunky rebuttal. 'Nothing was given to any Frenchman which had been taken unjustly from any Englishman', he says, a line that Orderic Vitalis found so ridiculous he deliberately left it out.[25]

Even those Englishmen whom William had apparently tried to appease were becoming dangerously disaffected. The brothers Eadwine and Morcar may have harboured resentment over their compulsory trip to Normandy as the king's honoured guests, but what must have rankled more was the steady erosion of their authority in England. In Morcar's case, the north of his earldom, thanks to William's grant to Gospatric, remained outside his control; but in

Yorkshire, too, the young earl may have exercised very little power. A late but local source tells us that, after the brothers' defeat at Stamford Bridge, Harold had handed control of the region to Mærleswein, the sheriff of Lincolnshire, and it seems quite likely that the same man was still in charge there two years on.[26]

As for Eadwine, he may have felt even more disillusioned, given the gulf between what he had been promised and what he had actually received. According to Orderic (here showing his Mercian roots), when William had made his peace with Eadwine he had granted him 'authority over his brother and almost a third of England, and had promised to give him his daughter in marriage'. But none of this had come to pass. Far from being enlarged, Eadwine's existing authority in Mercia had been undermined. Along the border between England and Wales, for example, the king had established a buffer zone, with new earldoms based on Hereford and Shrewsbury. The first, which had gone to William fitz Osbern, seems also to have included Worcester, which had previously been Eadwine's concern. As for the second, lately given to Roger of Montgomery, there was no question: Shropshire was a constituent part of Mercia, now taken away from its English governor. The king's desire was doubtless to create a cordon sanitaire between the western counties of England and kingdoms of Wales – this was, after all, the very area where Eadric the Wild and his Welsh allies remained active – but in doing so he had driven a wedge between himself and the greatest surviving English earl. As for William's promise of his daughter's hand in marriage, this too had been denied. 'Listening to the dishonest counsels of his envious and greedy Norman followers', says Orderic, 'he withheld the maiden from the noble youth, who greatly desired her and had long waited for her.'[27]

And so, says Orderic, Eadwine and Morcar rose in rebellion, and many others with them. 'A general outcry arose against the injustice and tyranny inflicted on the English . . . All were ready to conspire together to recover their former liberty, and bind themselves by weighty oaths against the Normans.' Orderic mentions only a few by name: King Bleddyn of Wales, for example, the erstwhile supporter of Eadric the Wild, now came out to support the two Mercian brothers. But from other sources we can piece together a longer list of rebels, and it is impressive. The fact that Morcar exercised little true power in Northumbria, for instance, hardly mattered, because the true leaders of northern society rallied to the cause. Mærleswein, the actual governor of Yorkshire, threw his lot in with rebels, as did Gospatric, the new earl beyond the Tyne, despite the fact that he had submitted to William only a few months earlier. Archbishop Ealdred, who had crowned the Conqueror in 1066 and his queen just a few weeks before the rebellion's outbreak, reportedly tried to quell the discontent in his city of York, but entirely without success. The bishop of Durham, by contrast, appears to have supported the rebellion.[28]

The most significant name of all, however, was that of Edgar Ætheling. Despite the fact that (according to William of Poitiers at least) the Conqueror counted him amongst his dearest friends on account of his kinship to Edward the Confessor, and had 'endowed him with ample lands' as a compensation prize, Edgar joined the rebels and thereby gave them a legitimate cause. They prepared to defend themselves, says Orderic, in woods, marshes and cities. 'The king was informed', says the Anglo-Saxon Chronicle, 'that the people in the North had gathered together, and meant to make a stand against him if he came.'[29]

William wasted no time in coming. Orderic goes on to explain how the king responded by marching northwards, building new castles as he went (this is the precise context of his famous quote about the English not having castles and therefore being unable to resist). To read his account (based, remember, on that of William of Poitiers), one would almost think that the campaign that followed was a purely defensive measure. 'The king rode to all the remote parts of the kingdom and fortified strategic sites against enemy attacks', we are told. We can reasonably assume, however, that as the Norman war machine advanced it blazed its typical trail of destruction; the Anglo-Saxon Chronicle for this year says at one point 'he allowed his men to harry wherever they came'.[30]

The scale of the violence can also be inferred from the speed of the rebels' submissions. As soon as William had planted his first new castle at Warwick, Eadwine and Morcar – ostensibly the leaders of the revolt – surrendered. When Nottingham fell, and another new castle arose, the citizens of York were sent into a terrified panic, and hurriedly dispatched hostages along with the keys to the city. William arrived there soon afterwards, planting a third new castle (the site now known as Clifford's Tower), at which point the remaining rebels in Northumbria also gave up the fight. Some, like the bishop of Durham, approached the king and sought his pardon. Others, including the leaders Mærleswein, Gospatric, and Edgar Ætheling, fled northwards, and sought refuge in Scotland. According to Orderic, King Malcolm had been backing the rebels from the start and was preparing to send forces in their aid. But, seeing how quickly the rising had collapsed, he now decided, to paraphrase Orderic, that he preferred peace to war. When envoys arrived from William demanding his submission, the Scottish king sent back representatives to swear fealty and obedience on his behalf. Satisfied, William departed from York, leaving a large garrison to guard the new castle there. As he marched his army back south, more new castles were established at Lincoln, Huntingdon and Cambridge.[31]

While William had been campaigning in the north, the sons of King Harold had decided to launch the invasion that had been frustrated at the start of the year by the pre-emptive strike on Exeter. Seizing what seemed to be a second chance, the three young men (John of Worcester names them as Godwine, Edmund and Magnus) landed in Somerset, and began ravaging around the mouth of the River Avon. (Their point of landing suggests that they may have travelled via Flat Holm, where their grandmother still lurked.) Having failed to take Bristol, they returned to their ships with such booty as they could grab (which would almost certainly have included slaves) and began raiding further south along the Somerset coast, but there they were confronted by local levies in a battle that saw heavy casualties on both sides. According to John of Worcester, the Godwine boys had the victory, and for an encore went on to raid in Devon and Cornwall, before returning to Ireland with their spoils. But if this was intended to be an attack to re-establish the Godwine family in England, it was a dismal failure.[32]

The summer months of 1068 had clearly been terrible ones – and not just for the English. 'Ill fortune held victors and vanquished alike in its snare', says Orderic, 'bringing down on them war, famine and pestilence.' In a particularly revealing passage, normally quoted only for its amusement value, the historian goes on to explain how at this moment many Normans were thinking of quitting England altogether:

Certain Norman women, consumed by fierce lust, sent message after message to their husbands, urging them to return at once, and adding that unless they did so with all speed, they would take other husbands. For they dared not join their men themselves, being unaccustomed to the sea-crossing and afraid of seeking them out in England, where they were engaging in armed forays every day and blood flowed freely on both sides.

What we see here, of course, apart from the casual misogyny of the medieval celibate, is a crude attempt to excuse faint-heartedness on the part of male Normans (one suspects that this passage originated with William of Poitiers). The desperate circumstances in England were clearly leading to widespread desertion: Orderic tells us that at this point the keepers of the castles at Winchester and Hastings, and many others besides, decided to abandon their posts and return home. Given the ongoing level of violence, one might suppose that even unmarried men (or men with less wanton wives) were having second thoughts about the whole enterprise, and concluding that the rewards were simply not worth the risk.

Such desertions, of course, put the Conqueror himself in a difficult bind. 'The king,' says Orderic, 'with so much fighting on his hands, was most anxious to keep all his knights about him, and made them a friendly offer of lands and revenues and great authority, promising them more when he had completely rid the kingdom of all his enemies.' This was an understandable reaction, but promising ever greater rewards to those Normans who stayed the course meant depriving ever greater numbers of Englishmen of their estates, and causing more of the disinheritance that seems to have inspired the rebellion in the first place. Both sides, in short, were being drawn into an increasingly vicious circle.[33]

Nevertheless, by the autumn of 1068, William may well have thought that the circle had been squared. In the course of the year he had defeated major rebellions in the south-west, the Midlands and the north, and in each case his enemies had submitted to his mercy or fled in the face of his wrath. A string of new castles had been established in strategic towns and cities, securing his grip on the country as far as York. Moreover, he could draw hope for the future from the fact that many Englishmen were evidently willing to fight, even to die, defending his authority: the sons of King Harold had been beaten off in the first instance by the citizens of Bristol, and the forces that had subsequently met them in battle had been captained by Eadnoth the Staller, a sometime servant of Edward the Confessor. Once the campaign against the rebels was over, says Orderic, the king assembled his mercenary soldiers and, having rewarded them royally, allowed them to go home. It was a further mark of his confidence that, as the end of the year approached, William himself crossed the Channel and returned to Normandy.[34]

The peace did not last long. William evidently remained anxious about the security of northern England, and with good reason. The concessions he had wrung from the king of Scots during the campaign of 1068 had clearly been limited. Malcolm may have offered his personal submission, but there is no suggestion that he had surrendered any of the English rebels who had taken refuge at his court. Mærleswein, Gospatric and Edgar Ætheling, to name just the three most important, remained at large, either in Scotland or in the far north of England.[35]

At the start of the new year 1069, therefore, the English king decided to tighten his grip on the north by appointing yet another new earl. His experiment with Gospatric having failed, William reverted to his original strategy and appointed an outsider. Robert Cumin, as this new appointee was named, is a man about whom we know next to nothing. A later writer says he came to England at the head of a band of Flemings, so it may well be that Robert himself hailed from the Flemish town of Comines. The Flemish connection also implies his men were probably mercenaries. No doubt conscious of the fate of his predecessor, Earl Copsig, Cumin came north in considerable force: the chroniclers give estimates of between 500 and 900 armed men.[36]

The fullest account of what followed is provided by the local chronicler, Simeon of Durham. According to Simeon, the new earl advanced leaving a trail of destruction, allowing his men to ravage the countryside by pillaging and killing. His remit was apparently to govern the territory beyond the River Tyne, and when they heard of his coming, the people of this region left their homes and prepared to flee. But, says Simeon, 'suddenly there came such a heavy fall of snow and such harsh winter weather that all possibility of flight was denied'. With their backs against the wall, the Northumbrians decided they had no choice, and resolved that they would either kill the earl or die trying. At this point the bishop of Durham – only recently reconciled after his dalliance with rebellion the previous year – hurried to meet Cumin and urged him to halt his advance. The earl, predictably, spurned this advice, and proceeded to enter Durham itself, where he planned to spend the night. Inside the city, his men continued their killing and looting in their quest for quarters.

The outcome was equally predictable. 'At first light', says Simeon, 'the Northumbrians who had banded together burst in through all the gates, and rushed through the whole town killing the earl's companions.' The streets, we are told, were choked with bodies and awash with blood. Cumin himself was staying in the house of the bishop, where the Flemings were able to put up some effective resistance. But, driven back by the defenders' javelins, the attackers simply set the building on fire. 'Some of those inside burned to death,' says Simeon, 'others rushed out through the doors and were cut down. Thus the earl was killed on 31 January.'[37]

The massacre of Cumin and his men acted as a trigger for a new general rising. A short time later the governor of the new castle at York was slaughtered along with many of his men. (From what follows it seems clear that he must have been away from the castle at the time.) 'The English now gained confidence in resisting the Normans, whom they saw as oppressors of their friends and allies', says Orderic Vitalis. Seeing that a new and spontaneous uprising was underway, the leaders of northern England returned from their Scottish exile. As Orderic explains, Mærleswein, Gospatric and Edgar Ætheling, along with many others, joined forces with the insurgents and led them in an attack on York, where the Norman sheriff and his men were still holding out. Somehow he managed to get a message to the king, explaining that unless York was relieved quickly he would be forced to surrender.[38]

William was almost certainly back in England by this date, for once again he arrived on the scene with a suddenness that left the rebels reeling. 'Swift was the king's coming', says Orderic, while the Anglo-Saxon Chronicle confirms that the Conqueror came upon his enemies 'by surprise, with an overwhelming army'. Many were captured, says Orderic, and more were killed, while the rest were put to flight. The Chronicle speaks of the whole city of York being ravaged, and York Minster being made 'an object of scorn'.

Mærleswein and Gospatric evidently managed to escape, though where they fled to is unclear. Edgar Ætheling, we are told, returned to Scotland. The king, says Orderic, remained in York for a further eight days, during which time a second castle was constructed. (The surviving earthworks can still be seen on the west bank of the River Ouse.) Finally, as a further mark of his seriousness, he committed the city to the custody of William fitz Osbern, before returning south to Winchester in time to celebrate Easter on 13 April.[39]

William was clearly under no illusion that the rebellion was over. After his return south the castles at York were subjected to a renewed attack, which fitz Osbern and his men managed to beat off, but which suggests that the rebels had not retreated very far; north of York the Normans can have exercised almost no meaningful authority at all. According to Simeon of Durham, the king at some point sent 'a certain duke with an army' into Northumbria to exact revenge for the death of Robert Cumin, but when these men reached Northallerton they found themselves surrounded by a fog so dense that they could hardly see each other. An unnamed individual subsequently appeared and explained to them that Durham was protected by a powerful saint, and no one could harm its citizens with impunity, at which point they decided to return home. The story is obviously suspect (note the total lack of names and dates) and clearly intended to demonstrate nothing apart from the awesome power of St Cuthbert. If it has any basis in truth, however, it also demonstrates that the Normans were learning to approach northern England with greater caution.[40]

Surrounded by the storms of war on all sides, according to Orderic, William himself was taking no unnecessary risks. At some point after his return south the king sent his wife back to Normandy, 'away from English tumults'. These included the return of the sons of King Harold, who sailed from Ireland at midsummer 1069 and landed on the north Devon coast near Barnstaple. Their second coming may well have been more serious than their first: even the laconic William of Jumièges, writing in Normandy, devotes several lines to describing it, and his sixty-six-ship fleet accords well with the sixty-four ships reported by the Anglo-Saxon Chronicle. As before, the Godwine boys were defeated – beaten in battle by Brian, the local Breton count – but not without the shedding of much blood on both sides: Jumièges puts the death toll at 1,700 men,

'some of whom were magnates of the realm'. The Godwines themselves escaped back to their ships and returned to Ireland, and it
may have been at this point that their grandmother, the indomitable
Gytha, left her fastness on Flat Holm and sailed to Flanders.[41]

If in retrospect the Godwine family seem such a spent force, that
was not necessarily the way it appeared to the Conqueror in the
summer of 1069. William might well have been alarmed to discover
that Gytha, after a short stay in Flanders, had sailed on to Denmark.
Almost from the minute of his coronation, Englishmen had been
sending messages across the sea, attempting to solicit aid from the
Danish king, Swein Estrithson. Prior to this point, Swein had shown
little enthusiasm for adventures in England; in the early months of
1066 he had apparently turned down similar invitations from Earl
Tostig. In the wake of the Norman victory, however, he had started
to display a keener interest. According to Orderic, clearly following
William of Poitiers, this was partly because the Danish king had
sent some troops to help Harold at Hastings, whose deaths he now
wished to avenge. Both aspects of this story seem highly unlikely.
What is altogether more probable is that, as time wore on, Swein
became increasingly convinced that an invasion of England would
have a fair chance of success. By 1069, anyone could see that Norman
rule, especially in the north of England, was hugely unpopular, and
besides, it was a region with strong historical and cultural ties to
Scandinavia. The English envoys can have had little difficulty in
convincing Swein that if he invaded he would be able to draw upon
a huge groundswell of support.[42]

And so, throughout the summer of 1069, the Danish king started
to assemble a great invasion force, just as the duke of Normandy
had done three years earlier. 'He strained all the resources of his
kingdom', says Orderic, 'as well as amassing numerous troops from
neighbouring regions which were friendly towards him: Poland,
Frisia and Saxony all helped.' It was probably also at this point that
Swein took another leaf out of William's book and started putting
it about that he had been promised the English throne many years
earlier by Edward the Confessor: the historian Adam of Bremen,
who visited the Danish king around this time, credulously included
the claim in his chronicle, to be followed by other historians down
to the present.[43]

It was late in the summer when the Danish fleet finally sailed:

the E Chronicle says they arrived between the two feasts of St Mary, 15 August and 8 September. Orderic, doubtless following the upbeat assessment of Poitiers, gives the impression that they were successfully driven off from Dover, Sandwich, Ipswich and Norwich. This seems unlikely, since the Danish fleet was reportedly huge (the D and E versions of the Chronicle give figures of 240 and 300 ships). What the Danes were doing was following the route of Viking fleets of old, raiding their way up England's eastern seaboard as a prelude to invasion. When they reached the estuary of the Humber they were joined by their English allies, led, as ever, by Mærleswein, Gospatric and Edgar Ætheling. Quite how Edgar's aspirations were going to be reconciled with those of the Danish king is unclear, but the problem may have been shelved in the short term because Swein had elected not to take part in his own conquest, and had given command of the Danish fleet to his brother, Asbjorn. Whatever the plan was, nothing was allowed to dampen the mood in the English camp, which was clearly euphoric. The D Chronicle describes how the rebel leaders set out 'with all the Northumbrians and all the people, riding and marching with an immense host, rejoicing exceedingly'. The days of Norman rule in England appeared to be numbered.[44]

William, says Orderic, was hunting in the Forest of Dean when he first heard news of the Danes' arrival. Their decision to raid the east coast gave him sufficient time to send messengers to York, warning his men to be prepared and instructing them to send for him if necessary. Surprisingly, given the circumstances, the garrisons of York replied confidently that they could hold out without help for a year. Elsewhere the news caused greater dismay. Ealdred, the city's elderly archbishop, reportedly became so distressed on learning of the Danish invasion that he fell ill, and died on 11 September.[45]

A week or so later – perhaps having ascertained the size of the approaching army – York's Norman defenders appear to have become rather more desperate. According to John of Worcester, who provides the fullest account, on Saturday 19 September they began setting fire to the houses that stood adjacent to the castle, fearing that their timbers could be used to bridge its defensive ditch. Inevitably the blaze ran out of control, and soon the whole city (including York Minster) was alight. Two days later, with the fires still burning, the Anglo-Danish army arrived. In desperation the garrison sallied out of the castle to engage them, but were quickly overwhelmed. More than 3,000 Normans were killed, says John of Worcester, and only a few, such as the sheriff of York and his family, were spared and taken prisoner. Having destroyed the two castles and plundered the rest of the city, the Danes then returned to their ships.[46]

News would have reached southern England within a matter of days. 'Rumour exaggerated the fearful numbers of the enemy', says Orderic, 'who were said to be confidently awaiting battle with the king himself.' This last report, however, proved to be false. When William, 'filled with sorrow and anger', in due course raised an army and set out to confront the Danes, he discovered that they had abandoned York altogether, and had crossed to the other side of the Humber. They were now camped in Lincolnshire, holed up in the marshy and inaccessible region known as the Isle of Axholme. Whatever the Danish strategy was, seeking battle clearly formed no part of it.

According to Orderic, the king set about flushing his enemies out from their hiding places, putting some to the sword and forcing others to flee. Yet no sooner had he embarked on this course of action than news arrived of rebellions in other parts of the kingdom. The castle of Montacute, close to Yeovil on the Dorset–Somerset border, was being attacked by the men of both counties; meanwhile Exeter was similarly being besieged by the men of Devon and Cornwall. More serious than either of these, it seems, was the situation in Shrewsbury, where the town's new castle was subjected to a combined assault from the Welsh and the men of Chester, as well as the local population – Orderic mentions 'the powerful and warlike Eadric the Wild and other untameable Englishmen'. All William's enemies, it seems, were seizing the chance to shake off his lordship.

The seriousness of the rising in the west Midlands is suggested by the royal response, with the king detaching William fitz Osbern and Count Brian from his side and sending them west to suppress it. The western rebels, however, proved as elusive as their northern counterparts: at the approach of the king's deputies they set fire to Shrewsbury and scattered, only to reassemble once the Normans had moved on to Exeter. In the end the Conqueror was obliged to deal with this insurrection in person, deputing the struggle on the Humber to his half-brother, Robert, and eventually defeating a large force of rebels at Stafford. 'In all these battles', says Orderic, 'much blood had flowed on both sides, and combatant and non-combatants alike were reduced to great wretchedness by the disturbances . . . Massacres of wretched people increased, souls were imperilled by the sins of envy and anger, and swept away to Hell in their thousands.'[47]

On his way back to Lincolnshire, William discovered that the Danes had again disappeared. 'It was rumoured that these brigands had returned to York', says Orderic, 'to celebrate Christmas and prepare for battle.' If the first reason seems rather unlikely (earlier we are told that the invaders still worshipped Wodin, Thor and Freya), it does at least remind us that many weeks had passed since the start of the invasion in August. Probably it was around mid-November that the king received this intelligence and turned his army northwards. More time was lost when they found that they could not cross the River Aire in Yorkshire, probably because the bridge they were expecting to use had been deliberately broken (this is the earliest reference to the town of 'Ponte-fract'). Unwilling to build a new bridge lest they were attacked, it was not until three weeks later that the Normans finally found a place further upstream where the river could just about be forded, and even then they had to fight off defenders on the opposite bank. It must have been early December, having struggled through woods and marshes on account of their diversion, that they at last drew near to York – only to discover that the Danes had once again fled.[48]

By this point it must have been amply clear that, despite the persistent rumours, the Danes had absolutely no intention of meeting William in battle. At the same time, they seemed in no hurry to leave England either. So what were they up to? From subsequent events we can infer that their objective was probably to occupy northern England, creating a bridgehead in anticipation of the coming of King Swein himself the following year. One modern historian has argued that they had planned to remain in York but found that the fire had made the city indefensible; yet it was the Danes themselves, we are told, who had destroyed both the castles. The simplest solution is to look again at our sources. The Danish situation seems desperate in the pages of Orderic Vitalis, but then Orderic is almost certainly parroting the positive comments of William of Poitiers (in which enemies always flee, whereas Normans strategically withdraw).

Our other sources suggest that it was the Normans rather than the invaders who were experiencing the greater difficulty. The D Chronicle, for instance, says that the Danish fleet 'lay all the winter in the Humber, where the king could not get at them'.[49]

William had been fighting a desperate campaign, dragged here and there across the country in pursuit of his enemies and still unable to defeat them. Orderic tells us that once the king had entered York he assigned men to begin rebuilding the castles. But would their garrisons hold out once he and his army withdrew? Twice before he had left his men in Yorkshire, only to have them massacred; this was his third visit to the north in less than eighteen months. Experience had taught him that as soon as he headed south, the rebels would simply re-emerge from their hiding places and retake the city. Meanwhile he could not get at the Danish fleet, and the Northumbrians, we are told, had also withdrawn to their homes.[50]

William's solution was twofold. In the first place, he sent messengers to the Danes and offered them generous terms. According to John of Worcester, Earl Asbjorn was 'secretly promised a large sum of money, and permission for his army to forage freely along the coasts, on condition that he would leave without fighting at the end of the winter'. Much to the chronicler's disgust, the Danish commander, 'exceedingly greedy for gold and silver', agreed.[51]

Having bought off his main opponent, William embarked on the second part of his plan. As Orderic explains, the king left York and divided his army into smaller contingents that could comb the mountains and forests where the rebels were hiding. They spread out, we are told, over more than a hundred miles of territory, slaying many men and destroying the lairs of others. This, however, was only the beginning of William's strategy. 'In his anger', continues Orderic, 'he commanded that all crops and herds, chattels and food of every kind should be brought together and burned to ashes with consuming fire, so that the whole region north of the Humber might be stripped of all means of sustenance.' The Conqueror's aim was to ensure that no future army, English or Danish, would be able to support itself against him and, as Orderic makes clear, this scorched-earth policy was brutally effective. 'As a consequence, so serious a scarcity was felt in England, and so terrible a famine fell upon the humble and defenceless people, that more than 100,000 Christian folk of both sexes, young and old alike, perished of hunger.'[52]

This terrible episode – the so-called 'Harrying of the North' – has established itself as one of the most notorious incidents not only of William's reign but of English history as a whole, and used to damn the king and the Normans down the ages. In recent years there have been attempts to downplay its severity. In particular, attempts have been made to show that the devastation described by the chroniclers is not supported by the economic information recorded in the Domesday Book. As we shall see, these arguments can easily be set aside.[53] Moreover, even if we dismiss the most lurid chronicle evidence, what remains is both credible and compelling. John of Worcester, for example, tells us that the famine was so severe that people ate human flesh as well as horses, cats and dogs. Others, adds Simeon of Durham, sold themselves into perpetual slavery to preserve their own existence. At Evesham Abbey in distant Worcestershire, the monks long remembered how large numbers of starving refugees arrived in search of food, but (like concentration-camp survivors in modern times) died from eating too ravenously. Every day, says the abbey's chronicler, they buried five or six more bodies.[54]

The last word on the subject, therefore, must still go to Orderic. As we noted at the outset, when Orderic wrote his account of these events he had in front of him the relentlessly pro-Norman words of William of Poitiers, and we have seen that for much of the time he was content to repeat them without demur. When he reached Poitiers' account of the Harrying, however, Orderic stopped copying. Because the end of the original is lost, we can never know what arguments the Conqueror's chaplain devised to justify his master's actions that winter, but they elicited this reaction from the man who had been born in Mercia just five years later:

My narrative has frequently had occasion to praise William, but for this act which condemned the innocent and guilty alike to die by slow starvation I cannot commend him. For when I think of helpless children, young men in the prime of life, and hoary greybeards perishing alike of hunger, I am so moved to pity that I would rather lament the grief and sufferings of the wretched people than make a vain attempt to flatter the perpetrator of such infamy.

Moreover, I declare that assuredly such brutal slaughter cannot remain unpunished. For the almighty Judge watches over high and low alike; he will weigh the deeds of all in an even balance, and as a just avenger will punish wrongdoing, as the eternal law makes clear to all men.[55]

14

Aftershocks

As the year 1069 drew to a close, and with the countryside all around him still smouldering, the Conqueror left his army in camp and went to keep Christmas in York. After the recent waves of violence, and particularly the uncontrollable fire started by the Norman garrisons in September, there can have been few buildings in the city left standing. The cathedral church of York Minster was in a terrible state, 'completely laid waste and burnt down', in the words of the Anglo-Saxon Chronicle, its ornaments and documents, according to a later writer, either lost or destroyed. Yet it was almost certainly in the church's charred remains that William, to quote Orderic Vitalis, 'celebrated the birth of our Saviour'. He was also, of course, celebrating the third anniversary of his own coronation, and this coincidence was not allowed to pass unnoticed. As Orderic explains, at some point during the fighting the king had sent to Winchester for his crown and regalia, and he wore them both in York that Christmas. His northern subjects, so fickle of late in their loyalty, were being reminded that William's authority was not based simply on overwhelming military might; he was also their legitimate king, anointed by the Holy Church, chosen by God.[1]

The military might was nevertheless rapidly reapplied. Soon after Christmas William learned the location of some of the English rebel leaders and set out to confront them. When they in turn fled he pursued them across the unforgiving landscape of North Yorkshire, 'forcing his way through trackless wastes, over ground so rough that he was frequently compelled to go on foot'. At length he came to the banks of the River Tees, where he camped his army for a fortnight, during which time there were significant submissions. Some prominent rebels, says Orderic, appeared in person and swore an oath of fealty; Earl Gospatric stayed away but swore through proxies. Others, such as Mærleswein and Edgar Ætheling, evidently fled further north, eventually finding their way back to Scotland. It is not entirely clear whether the king himself followed them, but, according to Simeon of Durham, his army 'spread over all the places between the Tees and the Tyne'. Everywhere they went, though, the Normans 'found only one continued solitude'. The people of Durham had fled to the woods and the mountains; they had heard about Yorkshire's terrible fate.[2]

Towards the end of January 1070, therefore, William decided to abandon the hunt. Returning to York he spent some time rebuilding the castles and re-establishing order, before setting off to deal with the remaining rebels in Mercia. Orderic says simply that he suppressed the risings there 'with royal power', but we can safely infer that more harrying occurred: the Domesday Book shows a dramatic drop in values for the counties along the Welsh border. The rebel siege of Shrewsbury was raised and more new castles were constructed at Chester and Stafford. All of this must have taken several weeks, and so it must have been well into March before the king reached Salisbury, at which point his troops were finally dismissed.[3]

After almost two years of fighting, the English revolt was over. Thousands, probably tens of thousands, had died – the total figure will forever remain unknown, but it must have been far in excess of the death toll at Hastings. The English themselves, of course, had suffered appallingly, cut down in battle or killed indiscriminately as part of the brutal process of repression. Many more had been condemned to a slower death because of the Harrying, and would continue to perish from hunger for months to come. 'In this year there was great famine', says the Anglo-Saxon Chronicle for 1070, passing over in silence the fact that much of it had been artificially induced.[4]

It is important to recognize, however, that for the Normans too these had been terrible days. They had also fallen in battle, or been massacred in great numbers when their castles were overrun. They too had experienced horrendous conditions. Consider, for example, the description of the Conqueror's march from York to Chester during the early weeks of 1070 given by Orderic Vitalis:

> He pushed on with determination along a road no horseman had attempted before, over steep mountains and precipitous valleys, through rivers and rushing streams and deep abysses. As they stumbled along the path they were lashed with rain and hail. Sometimes all were obliged to feed on horses which had perished in the bogs.

For some of the king's followers this proved too much to stomach. Even before they had set out for Chester,

> The men of Anjou, Brittany and Maine complained loudly that they were grievously burdened with intolerable duties, and repeatedly asked the king to discharge them from his service. They urged in defence of their conduct that they could not obey a lord who went from one hazard to the next and commanded them to do the impossible.

Orderic is clearly copying William of Poitiers here – witness the telltale attempt to blame this dissent on the non-Norman elements in the army. Yet the fact that Poitiers felt compelled to include it at all is highly significant, for it implies a protest so serious that not even the Conqueror's principal apologist felt able to sweep it under the carpet. During the winter of 1069–70 conditions in William's army were clearly so bad that there appears to have been something approaching a mutiny; there was certainly widespread desertion, because we are later told that the king 'counted any who chose to desert him as idle cowards and weaklings'. As before, there was only one inducement that William could offer to the waverers. 'He promised that the victors should enjoy rest when their great labours were over, assuring them that they could not hope to win rewards without toil.'[5]

Some may have wanted land, and the king had plenty to spare. A few English rebels, such as Gospatric, had submitted in January and had their estates restored. But many more had been killed or exiled, which meant there had been a new round of confiscations. Those who lost their lands at this point probably included Edgar

Ætheling, and certainly his fellow exile Mærleswein, whose estates were transferred en bloc to a Norman called Ralph Pagnell. Other Normans who received lands around this time included William de Percy, who was active in restoring order to Yorkshire after the rebellion, and Hugh fitz Baldric, who became the county's new sheriff.[6]

Yet not everyone can have been rewarded with land, nor can everyone have wanted it. Even the hardiest and hungriest of Normans might have thought twice about accepting estates on such a wild and desolate frontier, and having to wonder whether each day might bring a new English rising or Danish invasion. By the end of the campaign, many of William's troops would doubtless have preferred to receive the kind of reward they could carry back home to the Continent. Here, however, there seems to have been more of a problem. Land may have been superabundant, but money and other moveable wealth was in short supply. This was hardly surprising, given the huge amount that had already been extracted since 1066 in the form of tribute and taxes. Getting more by such methods was clearly going to be difficult: in many areas of the country the economy had been completely devastated. And yet, at the same time, mercenaries must be paid.

The solution, it seems, was the eleventh-century equivalent of a raid on the bank. As John of Worcester explains, precisely because of the ravaging and violence, many rich Englishmen had secreted their money in monasteries – the assumption being, of course, that valuables would be safer in such theoretically inviolable spaces. But during Lent (i.e. after 17 February 1070) the king 'ordered that the monasteries all over England be searched, and that the wealth deposited in them be seized and taken to his treasury'. (The idea, we are told, was the brainchild of William fitz Osbern.) The twelfth-century chronicler at Abingdon Abbey relates much the same story, but explains that it was not just the secular stashes that were confiscated. 'In addition, very many precious goods which could be found within the monks' precinct – a wealth of gold and silver, vestments, books, and vessels of diverse types, assigned to the use and honour of the church – were indiscriminately taken away.' There can be little doubt, given the timing of the raid, that this loot became the 'lavish rewards' distributed to the king's troops when they were dismissed at Salisbury a short while later. Such expedients, while they solved the immediate problem of mercenary expectations, can hardly have done much to improve relations between the conquerors and the conquered.[7]

At Easter 1070 William was crowned for a second time. The ceremony, which on this occasion took place in Winchester, passed without any reported hitches, and was designed, like the recent crown-wearing in York, to provide an emphatic statement of the Conqueror's legitimacy. Some time earlier, the king had petitioned his friend and supporter, Pope Alexander, for assistance in bolstering his rule, and Alexander had responded by sending to England a legation composed of two cardinals and a bishop. It was these men, explains Orderic Vitalis, who solemnly re-crowned William that Easter, underscoring his position as the pope's most cherished son.[8]

A new coronation was not the only reason for the cardinals' visit; another was the Normans' pressing need for atonement. Even by the competitive standards of the eleventh century, the king and his fellow warriors had been responsible for spilling an exceptionally large amount of blood. Indeed, it seems possible that some of the opposition the Conqueror faced during the campaign of 1069–70 might have been due not merely to physical hardship but also to moral objections. Orderic Vitalis names at least one Norman who returned home at this point declining to have any further part in the Conquest, and chronicle accounts of the Harrying suggest that, even in an age familiar with such atrocities, the scale of the human suffering was felt by some to be shocking.[9]

William was acutely conscious of such criticism and the need to diffuse it. At an earlier stage in the Conquest, probably on the occasion of his victorious homecoming at Easter 1067, the bishops of Normandy had instituted a set of penances for those who had participated in the Hastings campaign; they survive in a fascinating document known today as the Penitential Ordinance. Since this was a highly unusual measure, and the Conqueror's control over the Norman Church is well established, we can reasonably assume that he personally approved it, and regard it as a reflection of his ongoing desire to have his actions seen as legitimate.[10]

In general the penances imposed by the Ordinance seem fairly heavy: 'Anyone who knows that he killed a man in the great battle must do one year's penance for each man he killed . . . Anyone who wounded a man, and does not know whether he killed him or not, must do penance for forty days for each man he struck': by these reckonings the more practised warriors in William's army were going to be doing penance for an extremely long time. There were, however, other clauses designed to lighten the burden in certain circumstances. Archers, for example, who could not possibly know how many they killed or wounded, were permitted to do penance for three Lents. In fact, as another clause made clear, *anyone* unable to recall his precise body count could, at the discretion of his local bishop, do penance for one day a week for the rest of his life; alternatively, he could redeem his sin by either endowing or building a church. This last, of course, was the option chosen by William himself. At some point in the early years of the Conquest, the king caused Battle Abbey to be founded on the site of the field of Hastings, its purpose both to commemorate the victory and atone for the bloodshed.[11]

The provisions of the Ordinance also extended into the post-Hastings period, acknowledging that William's men may have faced resistance when looking for food, but imposing stiffer penances for those who killed while in pursuit of plunder. The cut-off point was the coronation: any killings carried out thereafter were deemed to be regular homicides, wilfully committed, and hence subject to regular (i.e. stricter) penalties. But once again there was an exception: the same special penances would apply even *after* the coronation, if any of those killed were in arms against the king. This, of course, meant that the Penitential Ordinance, although probably drafted in the months after Hastings, could also cover the years of violence that had followed, and the fact that it survives only in English sources in connection with the papal legation of 1070 strongly suggests that it was confirmed or reissued at this point – again, doubtless on the express orders of the king.[12]

The principal reason for the legates' visit, however, was neither legitimization nor atonement but reform. 'They took part in much business up and down the country, as they found needful in regions which lacked ecclesiastical order and discipline', says Orderic Vitalis. The lax state of the English Church had been one of the main arguments put forward by William to secure papal support for the Conquest, so it was hardly surprising to find the legates engaged in such work. In one sense this was simply a policy intended from the outset, delayed by the years of rebellion.

At the same time, the rebellion itself clearly influenced the nature of the reform that was undertaken. At the start of his reign the Conqueror had promised to uphold established law and custom, and had confirmed the majority of his subjects in their lands and titles. But if the period 1068–70 had proved one thing, it was that Englishmen could not be trusted. Time and again William had forgiven certain individuals, only to have them rebel again once his back was turned. With laymen he was able to take a tough line by confiscating their estates and thus depriving them of their place in society, but with churchmen the task was not so simple. The most recalcitrant clergy had already removed themselves, either by dying in battle or fleeing into exile, while a few others appear to have been subject to summary sentences – most notably Æthelric, the former bishop of Durham, and his brother, Æthelwine, the sitting bishop, respectively arrested and outlawed during the summer of 1069, presumably for having supported the northern rebels.[13] But kings could not simply start deposing and replacing senior churchmen, however culpable or untrustworthy they seemed.

Papal legates, on the other hand, could. Soon after Easter, in a specially convened council at Winchester, reform of the English Church began with the dismissal of Archbishop Stigand. In many respects, of course, it was surprising that Stigand had not been removed sooner. He was, after all, the Godwine candidate for Canterbury, uncanonically installed in 1052 after the flight of his Norman predecessor, Robert of Jumièges, and this indeed formed part of the charge sheet against him at Winchester. The other main plank of the prosecution's case – one which was impossible to contest – was pluralism: despite his promotion to Canterbury, Stigand had continued to serve as bishop of Winchester. Since he had already been excommunicated on these grounds by the pope it can hardly have been a surprise that he was in due course deposed by the legates. His survival prior to this point was probably due to the wealth and influence attributed to him by William of Poitiers, and also his advanced years: a career that had started in 1020 could not have been expected in 1066 to last very much longer. By 1070, however, William had clearly grown tired of waiting for the inevitable and had abandoned any pretence of deferring to English sentiment: the archbishop was an embarrassment and therefore had to go.[14]

But Stigand was far from being the only casualty. Either in the same council at Winchester, or else during a second synod held a few weeks later at Windsor, three other English bishops were similarly expelled from office. In the case of Leofwine, bishop of Lichfield, we know that part of the case against him was a charge of 'carnal incontinence': he had a wife and children. A similar case may have been brought against Æthelmær of East Anglia, for he too was a married man. As for Æthelric, bishop of Sussex, we have no idea what the charge was, but it cannot have been very convincing: the following year the pope ordered the case be reviewed and the bishop reinstated (an order which was ignored).

It is amply clear from both their concentration and their timing that these depositions were political. Æthelmær and Leofwine may have been married, but so too were countless other clerics (including, in Æthelmær's case, the man appointed as his successor). The real reason for their dismissal is apparent from their connections: Leofwine was a leading light in the affinity of the earls of Mercia; Æthelmær was Stigand's brother. What William was doing in 1070 was sweeping the board clean of bishops whose loyalties he considered to be suspect. The moral or canonical case against Æthelric of Sussex was clearly very weak, but in the king's eyes he must have constituted a major security threat, for he was not only deposed but imprisoned: 'kept under guard at Marlborough', in the words of John of Worcester, 'even though he was guiltless'.[15]

It was, of course, a virtual replay of events in Normandy sixteen years earlier, when Archbishop Mauger of Rouen had been removed from office in the wake of a rebellion in which he was suspected of being complicit. On that occasion, too, William had been careful to follow procedure, and the accused had been condemned on account of his supposed moral failings by a council headed by a papal legate. Indeed, if the English episcopate had been paying any attention to the Conqueror's earlier career, they might have read the writing on the wall from the moment of the legates' arrival in 1070, for the bishop in charge of proceedings was none other than Ermenfrid of Sion, the same man who had presided over Mauger's downfall.[16]

That said, the exercise in 1070 was conducted on a far larger scale; it was not just the bishops who were purged at Winchester and Windsor. 'Many abbots were there deposed', says John of Worcester, and although he names no names it seems likely that the cull included the abbots of Abingdon, St Albans and St Augustine's Canterbury, all of whom lost their positions – and in some cases their liberty – around this time. The king, says John, 'stripped of their offices many bishops and abbots who had not been condemned for any obvious cause, whether of conciliar or secular law. He kept them in prison for life simply on suspicion (as we have said) of being opposed to the new kingdom.'[17]

Naturally, their replacements were Normans. For obvious reasons William preferred to promote men he knew personally, and so turned in the first instance to the clerks of his own chapel. The bishoprics of Winchester, East Anglia, Sussex and Lichfield were in each case filled by former royal chaplains, as was the archbishopric of York, vacated the previous year by the death of Ealdred. Only in the case of Durham did the king depart from this practice, installing instead a Lotharingian priest by the name of Walcher. The net result of these new appointments was that the higher echelons of the English Church were transformed, just as surely and swiftly as the secular aristocracy had been transformed by the Battle of Hastings and the subsequent rebellions. By the time the purge of 1070 was over, only three of England's fifteen bishoprics were held by Englishmen.[18]

The plunder of its monastic riches during Lent; the deposition of many of its leaders during the spring: clearly 1070 was already shaping up to be an *annus horribilis* for the English Church. But in the course of the same year, it seems, the Church had to absorb yet another blow, when the Conqueror imposed on many of its bishoprics and abbeys the novel burden of military service.

Military service was something that all medieval rulers expected from their subjects. In Normandy, as we've noted, there is scant evidence to indicate how it was obtained before 1066, but enough to suggest that the duchy was moving in an increasingly 'feudal' direction, with magnates being made to understand that they held their estates at the duke's discretion in return for supplying him with, among other things, a specific number of knights whenever he demanded. In England, as we've also noted, a somewhat different system was used, whereby individual lords were required to contribute a certain number of soldiers to the royal host, the number apparently determined by the amount of land they owned as measured in hides. Since the start of his reign in England, William had been granting out new estates to his Norman followers and also, in some cases, allowing English lords to redeem their existing lands. The assumption, based on later evidence, is that the king must have seized the unique opportunity afforded by this fresh start to define precisely how much military service each man owed, expressed as a quota of knights.[19]

In the early years of the reign such new demands were apparently not imposed on the English Church. Whereas in Normandy it was quite common for monasteries to be expected to provided benefices for their founders' military followers, in England it was more common for the monks to wave a charter, granted by some obliging former monarch, conveniently excusing them from all such secular burdens. William, given his professed intention at the start of his reign to abide by the laws and usages of his English predecessors, appears initially to have accepted the validity of such exemptions.

Four years into his reign, however, the Conqueror changed his mind. 'In the year 1070', says the chronicler Roger of Wendover, 'King William imposed military service on all the bishoprics and abbacies which had, until that time, been free from all secular authority', adding that the king 'had written down how many knights he wanted each to provide to him and his successors in time of hostility'. Wendover is, admittedly, a late source, writing in the early thirteenth century, which has led some historians to doubt the worth of his words. (There are few more controversial topics relating to the Norman Conquest than the introduction of knight service.) But his comments are supported by those of other chroniclers writing in the twelfth century and, more tentatively, by a copy of an original writ which, if genuine, can have been issued no later than 1076. Despite the controversy, most historians accept that the Conqueror did make new military demands of the English Church at this moment.[20]

If we ask why he did so, the answer is self-evidently because he felt that such additional service was required. William may have been content to uphold the promises of his predecessors at the start of his reign, but since that time his new kingdom had been shaken by three years of almost constant rebellion. We know that during these years he had summoned Englishmen to fight in his armies, who presumably turned out on the basis of their existing pre-Conquest obligations; but we can also see that he made extensive use of mercenaries from the Continent, rewarding them with the proceeds of two heavy gelds. As the desperate expedient of plundering the monasteries in 1070 shows, the maintenance of an army by such methods was unsustainable; indeed, one could speculate that the cash-flow crisis at the start of the year might well have suggested to the king and his advisers the necessity of finding new ways to pass on the burden to his subjects. The rebellions may have been over by the spring of 1070, but the need for military service remained pressing. William no longer had a grand army in his pay, but over the previous two years he had founded dozens of new castles, all of which required permanent garrisons. Who was going to pay for this dispersed army of occupation from one week to the next, until some unforeseen time in the future?

The answer, clearly, was the English Church. According to the twelfth-century chronicler at the abbey of Ely, William informed all his abbots and bishops that 'from then on, garrisons for the kings of England were to be paid for, as a perpetual legal requirement, out of their resources . . . and that no one, even if supported by the utmost of authority, should presume to raise an objection to this decree'. Similarly, and more specifically, the twelfth-century Abingdon Chronicle says 'this abbey was ordered by royal command to provide knights for guard duty at Windsor Castle'. Of course, in some cases the heads of these houses were Normans appointed as a result of the recent purge, and who could hardly have been expected to take up their posts without investing in such protection. At Abingdon, it was later recalled that the new Norman abbot, Adelelm, 'went nowhere in the first days of his abbacy unless surrounded by a band of armed knights . . . For at that time many and widespread rumours of conspiracies against the king and his kingdom boiled up, forcing everyone in England to defend themselves.'[21]

And, indeed, soon after the council at Windsor was over, a fresh military crisis erupted – or rather the embers of an old one were kindled back into flame. Despite the deal struck the previous year, the Viking army sent by King Swein of Denmark had not returned home. Their plan all along, it seems, had been to establish a base in northern England from which Swein could personally lead an outright conquest, and, at some point towards the end of May 1070, the Danish king finally arrived, joining his brother Asbjorn at the mouth of the River Humber. His reception, according to the Anglo-Saxon Chronicle, was rapturous. Although the English leaders had either fled or surrendered at the start of the year, the local people came out in support of the invader, assuming that he would carry all before him. Swein himself seems to have remained near the Humber, but Asbjorn and a force of Danish housecarls immediately moved south into East Anglia and seized the town of Ely. Here too there was reportedly a great surge of goodwill among the natives, and optimism about what portended. 'Englishmen from all over the fenlands came to meet them', says the E Chronicle, 'thinking that they were going to conquer the whole land.'[22]

One Englishman who was particularly enthusiastic about the prospect of a Danish takeover was Hereward, known to posterity as 'the Wake'. Of all the figures who chose to resist the Normans, Hereward is arguably the most famous, but sadly his fame derives almost entirely from stories written down several generations after his own day, by which stage they had already taken a legendary turn. The twelfth-century *Gesta Herewardi*, for example, contains a few elements that appear to have some basis in fact, but too many escapades involving witches, princesses and monsters to be taken seriously as a historical source. Even Hereward's arresting cognomen, once taken to indicate an exceptional level of alertness, is not recorded until the thirteenth century, and probably signifies nothing more than his supposed connection with the Wake family of Lincolnshire. The most we can say about Hereward is that, despite an uncertain ancestry, he seems to have been a man of noble status; apparently in exile at the time of the Conquest, he had returned to England at some point after 1066 to discover the Normans had killed his brother and seized his estates. Certainly when he enters the historic record in the summer of 1070, Hereward is already an outlaw.[23]

Having described the arrival of the Danes in East Anglia, the E version of the Anglo-Saxon Chronicle reports that 'Hereward and his gang' were planning to plunder the monastery at Peterborough (where the E chronicle was later copied and interpolated, hence its detailed description of these events). It seems that they were motivated not only by the Danish invasion, but also by the knowledge that Peterborough had recently been committed to a new Norman abbot. Determined to score another victory against his oppressors, Hereward resolved to ransack the abbey ahead of the newcomer's arrival. Despite the best efforts of the monks, who sent for help and resisted for as long as they could, Hereward and his followers eventually forced their way into the town of Peterborough and reduced much of it to ashes. They then entered the abbey church and seized its treasures – crosses, altar-fronts and shrines, all made of gold and silver, as well as money, books and vestments – which they carried off in triumph to the Danish camp at Ely. 'They said they had done this out of loyalty to this monastery', says the E Chronicle with evident bitterness. Hereward and his companions appear to have convinced themselves, if not the monks, that they were acting like prototype Robin Hoods, confiscating the abbey's valuables to save them from expropriation by rapacious Normans. It was not, to be fair, a wholly implausible pose: Hereward and his men were tenants of the abbey, and the Conqueror's raid on English monasteries at the start of the year was still fresh in everyone's memory.[24]

Having torched the town and looted the abbey, there may have been some talk among the outlaws and their Danish allies of holding Peterborough against the Normans. The E Chronicle says that 'the Danes, thinking they would get the better of the French, drove out all the monks'. Yet when the new incumbent, Abbot Turold, arrived a short time later, he found the place deserted, the raiders having returned to their ships. Turold, it must be said, was no ordinary monk: William of Malmesbury later described him as acting 'more like a knight than an abbot', while the Chronicle calls him 'a very ferocious man', and reveals that he arrived to take up his post accompanied by no fewer than 160 fully armed Frenchmen. All the same, it says little for the reputation of the Danes and their English allies that they chose to flee from a monk, however fearsome, and what was, in relative terms, a small Norman force.[25]

In truth, Danish dreams of conquest had probably died many weeks earlier. It seems likely that on his arrival in England Swein had found the forces under his brother's command in an extremely sorry state. Orderic Vitalis provides a long description of the privations they had suffered during the winter as a result of storms and starvation. 'Some perished through shipwreck', he says. 'The rest sustained life with vile pottage; princes, earls and bishops being no better off than the common soldiers.' This is almost certainly a borrowing from William of Poitiers, for it is clearly heavily biased. At one point, for example, we are told that the Danes could not leave their ships for fear of the inhabitants, which is hardly the impression given by the Anglo-Saxon Chronicle. Moreover, the same account misleadingly omits all mention of Swein's own arrival, saying only that the remains of the Danish army returned home to tell the king the sad story of their losses. Nevertheless, even when all such allowances are made, the essential point that the Danes were in trouble is likely to be true enough. In the wake of the Harrying it must have been very difficult for these men to have found sufficient food to sustain themselves.[26]

Swein must have quickly realized that the remnants of his great fleet were inadequate for mounting a conquest: seen in this light, his decision to send Asbjorn into East Anglia looks less like the start of a military campaign, and more like a conventional Viking raid intended to recoup costs. At some point soon after the attack on Peterborough (which occurred on 2 June), William offered terms, and the Danish king readily accepted. His fleet sailed around the east coast, put into the Thames for two nights, then sailed back to Denmark. By midsummer, barely a month since his arrival, Swein was gone, leaving his English supporters high and dry, their hopes of regime change once again confounded. If Hereward and his fellow outlaws had ever truly regarded themselves as simply the temporary trustees of Peterborough's treasures, now was the moment that they were disabused. 'The Danes left Ely', says the E Chronicle, 'taking all the aforementioned treasures with them.' The monks had to console themselves with the knowledge that their plunderers did not go unpunished. On its return voyage the Danish fleet was scattered by a great storm, so that only a small fraction of the booty ended up in Denmark, and even that little was lost to fire a few years later. Earl Asbjorn, meanwhile, was accused of having compromised the invasion by accepting William's bribes, and sent into exile.[27]

William, certainly, seems to have thought that Swein's departure marked the end of the matter. At some point towards the end of the summer or in the early autumn, the king left England and sailed to Normandy. On the Continent, trouble was brewing: in particular, there was disturbing news from neighbouring Flanders, his wife's homeland, where a succession dispute was threatening to descend into civil war. On the other side of the Channel, by contrast, all seemed quiet. 'At this time,' say Orderic Vitalis, 'by the grace of God, peace reigned over England, and a degree of serenity returned to its inhabitants now that the brigands had been driven off . . . No one dared to pillage, and everyone cultivated his own fields in safety and lived contentedly with his neighbour.'[28]

'But', adds Orderic, 'not for long.' He was obliged to qualify his remarks because, once again, a new revolt was fanned from the ashes of the old. William seems to have assumed that, with the departure of the Danes, their English supporters would melt away, or be easily mopped up by local commanders like the redoubtable Abbot Turold. But the English resistance in the Fens proved extremely difficult to eradicate. It was no accident that the Danes had chosen to establish their camp at Ely, for in the eleventh century (and for many centuries thereafter) the town was an island, surrounded on all sides by marshes and accessible only by boat. With the Danes gone, Ely's inhabitants were left feeling nervous, imagining that their collaboration would be punished with violent repression. According to the *Gesta Herewardi* (a far from reliable witness, but the only source that attempts to explain the genesis of the revolt), the abbot of Ely feared that he would soon join the growing list of English churchmen ousted in favour of Normans. Naturally, the monks looked to Hereward himself for help, and he in due course came to their assistance. But, as subsequent events show, it was not only the local hero and his band who responded to Ely's call. From all across the kingdom, other desperate men began to converge on the Fens. 'Fearing subjection to foreigners', says the *Gesta*, 'the monks of that place risked endangering themselves rather than be reduced to servitude, and, gathering to themselves outlaws, the condemned, the disinherited, those who had lost parents, and suchlike, they put their place and the island in something of a state of defence.'[29]

One of these desperate men was Æthelwine, erstwhile bishop of Durham. Æthelwine has something of the reluctant rebel about him. Implicated in the revolts of 1068–9 and subsequently outlawed, he had fled from the Conqueror's armies during the Harrying and led the people of his bishopric to a temporary refuge on Lindisfarne. By the spring of 1070 he had returned to the mainland but, according to Simeon of Durham, he did not intend to stay for long. 'Observing the affairs of the English were everywhere in confusion, and dreading the heavy rule of a foreign nation, whose language and customs he knew not, he determined to resign his bishopric and provide for himself wherever a stranger might.' But even here Æthelwine met with no luck. When, later in the summer, he set sail from Wearmouth, hoping to reach Cologne, a contrary wind drove his ship to Scotland, where he found himself in the company of Edgar Ætheling, Mærleswein and their dwindling band of fellow exiles. A short while afterwards news must have reached them of the stand being made at Ely. By this stage the bishop must have felt that he had little left to lose: his brother Æthelric had been arrested the previous year, and his own outlawry had probably been confirmed by the papal legates during the spring. The fact that a new rebellion was being mounted at Ely may perhaps have exerted some emotional pull, for Æthelwine was a native of the Fens, having come to Durham from Peterborough. Whatever the precise cause, the bishop abandoned his plan of leaving England and elected to throw his lot in with the rebels. At some point early in the new year 1071, he sailed from Scotland to Ely, taking with him a northern English magnate named Siward Barn and several hundred other exiles, all determined to make a stand.[30]

The Ely revolt might still not have amounted to much had it not been for the simultaneous action taken by earls Eadwine and Morcar. The two brothers had played no part in the English rebellions since their speedy submission in the summer of 1068. Indeed, they had played no discernible part in politics of any kind, all but vanishing from the subsequent historical record. A royal charter, probably drawn up in the spring of 1069, shows they were still at court and being accorded their titles. But to have called Eadwine 'earl of Mercia' or Morcar 'earl of Northumbria' must have been tantamount to mockery, for they plainly exercised no real power at all in their respective provinces. Rule in the north was now split between the Norman castellans of York and the recently rehabilitated Gospatric. Mercia, meanwhile, was governed by its new Norman sheriffs, supported by the garrisons of new castles at Warwick, Nottingham, Shrewsbury and Stafford. As early as 1068 Eadwine's authority had been seriously compromised by the establishment of rival earldoms centred on Hereford and Shrewsbury for William fitz Osbern and Roger of Montgomery; since the start of 1070 it had been dealt a further and probably fatal blow with the creation of another new earldom based on Chester and given to Gerbod, one of the Conqueror's Flemish followers. A comment by Orderic Vitalis that the two brothers had received the king's forgiveness in 1068 only 'in outward appearance' rings true; one suspects that thereafter they may once again have had some form of restriction imposed on their freedom. Whether William's return to Normandy in 1070 heralded some temporary weakening of such constraints, or whether because, as John of Worcester has it, they feared being placed in stricter custody, Eadwine and Morcar decided to make a break. At some point during the winter of 1070–1 they stole away in secret from the king's household and set about trying to raise rebellion.[31]

It soon became apparent, however, just how far their fortunes had sunk, for it seems that no one rallied to their cause. Since the Norman takeover the brothers had failed in that most fundamental of a lord's tasks, namely protecting their own men. Where had Eadwine been when the Conqueror's armies had ravaged the Midlands, or Morcar when the north was harried? In this respect their behaviour compares unfavourably with that of Earl Godwine, who refused a royal order to sack his own town of Dover in 1051, or with King Harold, who rushed to Hastings in 1066 partly because his own tenants were being terrorized. During the years 1068–70 the two earls had left their followers to face either death or dispossession at Norman hands. The fact that the brothers probably had little freedom of action in this time might engage our sympathy, but can have been no consolation to those who had lost their lands or their relatives.[32]

The failure of the earls' rebellion reduced them to the status of fugitives; the Anglo-Saxon Chronicle says evocatively that the brothers 'travelled aimlessly in woods and moors', and at length, says John of Worcester, they elected to go their separate ways. Eadwine went north, intending to reach Scotland and the other English exiles; Morcar went east to join the rebellion at Ely. It seems very likely, judging from the proximity of their lands in Lincolnshire, that Morcar counted Hereward among his commended men. If so, the outlaw was one of the few men on whom the earl could still count.[33]

The flight of Eadwine and Morcar and the latter's arrival at Ely were probably the crucial factors that decided William to return to England in 1071 in order to deal with the revolt personally. Sadly we are extremely poorly informed about the king's movements during this particular year, so we cannot say precisely when this happened. Nor do we have any precise account of the military action that ensued. The Anglo-Saxon Chronicle, followed closely by John of Worcester, says that William called out both naval and land forces in order to mount an attack from all directions: ships were used to blockade the island on its eastern, seaward side, while to the west his army constructed a causeway or pontoon bridge to enable an assault across the marshes.[34] When it comes to the details of the assault, however, our reliable sources are unforthcoming. According to the *Gesta Herewardi*, the Normans made several attempts to storm the island but on each occasion were driven back by the superior military skill of Hereward and his followers. By way of total contrast, another twelfth-century source, the *Liber Eliensis*, would have us believe that the Normans, led by William himself, mounted an entirely successful attack across the bridge and put the defenders to flight. There is little to be said for either of these two accounts: the *Gesta* is compromised by its determination to entertain its audience and to cast Hereward in a favourable light, while the *Liber* is simply a horrendous Frankenstein's monster of a text, stitched together from bits and pieces of other chronicles wrenched out of their original context. Its account of the storming of Ely is interesting only because it seems to draw on the lost ending of William of Poitiers. (Who else would start their account by seeking to assure us that Eadwine and Morcar had never enjoyed greater favour and honour than they had received at William's court?) It may be, therefore, that there is something to be said for the story that the Normans mounted a successful attack.[35]

The *Liber* apart, however, our sources agree that the siege was ended by an English surrender. 'The king took their ships and weapons and plenty of money', says the Anglo-Saxon Chronicle, 'and did as he pleased with the men.' Bishop Æthelwine was placed in custody at the abbey of Abingdon, where he died the following winter. Earl Morcar was also held in captivity for the rest of his life, a sentence that lasted far longer. As for the others who submitted to William, says John of Worcester, 'some he imprisoned, some he allowed to go free – after their hands had been cut off and their eyes gouged out'. The only figure of note to escape these punishments was Hereward, who refused to surrender, and contrived a remarkable escape, stealing away undetected through the Fens with those who wished to go with him. 'He led them out valiantly', says the contemporary D Chronicle, demonstrating that Hereward's heroism was not merely the product of later legend.[36]

Orderic Vitalis, when he read William of Poitiers' account of the fall of Ely, rejected it entirely. Morcar, he maintains, had been doing no harm to the king, who had tricked him into surrendering with false promises of peace and friendship. Orderic goes on to tell us that Earl Eadwine, when he heard the news of Ely's fall, vowed to continue the fight, and spent six months touring England, Wales and Scotland in search of the support that would help him free his brother. But here Orderic is almost certainly wrong, relating a legendary pro-Mercian version of the story that may have been circulating for some time. Other more closely contemporary sources, such as the Chronicle, suggest that even before the siege of Ely had started, Eadwine was dead. The theme common to all accounts is treachery. 'Three brothers who were his most intimate servants betrayed him to the Normans', says Orderic, in what sounds like a passage borrowed from an epic poem. The earl, we are told, was caught beside a rising tidal stream which prevented his escape, and killed along with his small band of followers, 'all fighting desperately to the last'. So ended the house of Leofric, brought down by those they had failed to protect, who could see no further hope in resisting the Normans.[37]

15

Aliens and Natives

With the benefit of hindsight, we can see that the surrender of Ely and the fall of earls Eadwine and Morcar constitute an important milestone in the history of the Norman Conquest; from that time on, there were no English rebellions of any consequence. But King William, surveying the situation in the immediate wake of the revolt, enjoyed no such long-term perspective. Ely represented another region tamed, another royal castle established, and another costly garrison installed, while the fall of the Mercian brothers meant another massive windfall of land, the most substantial since the eclipse of the Godwines five years earlier. Yet the struggle for England's security was not over, for there was still one problem that the Conqueror felt compelled to address.[1]

Where had the majority of the rebels originated from, besides Ely itself? In which direction had Eadwine been fleeing before he was overtaken? Where, above all, did the last remaining representative of the English royal line still lurk, biding his time in the hope of better circumstances? The answer, of course, was Scotland, and the court of King Malcolm. The Scottish king, an irritant from the first, had recently compounded his offence by harrying northern England as far as Durham, and also by marrying Margaret, the sister of Edgar Ætheling. In retrospect the threat posed by Edgar and his supporters might seem negligible but, again, this was by no means obvious to contemporaries. After all, the story of the Conquest is not short of sudden reversals of fortune, and young men in apparently hopeless situations bestirring themselves to greatness.[2]

William therefore decided to nip this potential plot line in the bud, and in the summer of 1072 launched an invasion of Scotland. This was a bold undertaking, for it meant waging war a long way from his power base in southern England. Only one previous English king – the mighty Athelstan in AD 934 – had ever ventured so far north. It must have been one of the great campaigns of William's military career, yet we know virtually nothing about it. William of Poitiers, who doubtless could have furnished us with a gripping account, stopped his story at the fall of Ely. Orderic Vitalis, who had followed Poitiers closely up to this point, becomes chronologically rudderless thereafter, and makes no mention of these events. All we have to go on are a few short sentences in the Anglo-Saxon Chronicle and some supplementary facts from John of Worcester. Like Athelstan before him, William invaded using naval and land levies, blockading the Scottish coast with his ships and personally leading an army across the River Forth. The Chronicle, with its characteristically dismissive turn of phrase, comments 'he found nothing there that they were any better for'. Presumably the king engaged in the normal business of devastating the countryside until eventually his opponent decided to submit. Malcolm came to meet the Conqueror at Abernethy, near the Firth of Tay, swore to become his vassal and gave him hostages – including, it seems, his eldest son, Duncan. Beyond this we are ignorant of the terms agreed, but they must have included a promise on Malcolm's part to stop sheltering English exiles. We hear nothing of Edgar Ætheling at this time, but it seems most likely that he fled at the news of his enemy's advance. The next time we have news of him we find he is living in Flanders.[3]

Having put Malcolm in his place and sent the ætheling scurrying, William returned south. As he did so he took steps to improve the security of northern England. The previous year he had appointed the Lotharingian priest, Walcher, to be the new bishop of Durham, and now as he passed through the city the king built a castle, right beside the cathedral, for the bishop's greater protection. Clearly William was mindful of the fate of Robert Cumin and his men, massacred in Durham almost four years earlier, for at this same moment he deprived Cumin's English successor, Gospatric, of the earldom of Northumbria. Allowing Gospatric to retain his lands and title after his submission in January 1070 had evidently been an act of political expediency. Now the king was able to exert a more direct influence in the north, he could afford to dispense with a man whose loyalty had always seemed dubious. Gospatric was condemned for having participated in the massacre of the Norman garrisons at York in September 1069, and also for having been complicit in the attack on Durham at the start of the same year. Presumably he was sentenced *in absentia*, for such charges would surely have merited indefinite detention; he avoided this fate by fleeing in the first instance to Scotland, but Malcolm must have made it clear that he was no longer in a position to receive luckless Englishmen, and so the earl followed the ætheling into Flemish exile.[4]

One might assume that Gospatric's removal owed something to a growing prejudice on William's part against Englishmen in general, but this was clearly not the case, for the earl was replaced by a member of his own family. Waltheof, a younger member of the house of Bamburgh, was in one respect well qualified to govern the north, for he was the surviving son of Earl Siward, the pugnacious earl of Northumbria appointed by King Cnut, and Ælfflaed, the grand-daughter of Earl Uhtred; that is, the fruit of a union that had been arranged to nurture peace between the Bamburgh dynasty and the Danes of York. A teenager at the time of his father's death in 1055, Waltheof had been passed over in favour of Tostig Godwineson but compensated a few years later with a smaller earldom in the east Midlands.[5] Because of his youth, however, Waltheof had made no impact on politics prior to 1066 – he first enters the story the following year, when several chroniclers noticed him among the hostages that the Conqueror took home to Normandy. During this time he must have worked hard to win William's trust and affection (he appears as a witness to a ducal charter, unlike his fellow hostages Eadwine and Morcar).[6] Indeed, the strength of Waltheof's friendship with William can be gauged by the fact it survived his subsequent involvement in the English rebellion of 1069. After his submission at the start of the following year, the earl was not merely forgiven but shown greater favour, being married at some point thereafter to the king's niece, Judith. This really was a unique distinction – one recalls that a similar match promised to Earl Eadwine had never taken place – and under-lines the esteem and confidence in which Waltheof continued to be held. With family connections to both the English house of Bamburgh and the new Norman dynasty, he must have seemed the best possible candidate to serve as the new earl of Northumbria: an Anglo-Norman magnate in the truest sense, who might act as a bridge between the two peoples.[7]

With the security of the north seemingly in better shape, William focused his attention on the Continent, where problems had been multiplying for some time. As the flight of his enemies to Flanders suggests, relations between Normandy and her north-eastern neighbour had recently taken a turn for the worse. The cordiality established by William's marriage to Matilda had survived the death of her father, Baldwin V, in 1067, but had been thrown into doubt by the untimely death of his son, Baldwin VI, just three years later. A bitter succession dispute had erupted in 1070 and the Normans had backed the losing candidate. William had weighed in on the side of primogeniture, supporting the younger Baldwin's teenage son, Arnulf. But victory had gone to the late count's brother, Robert, who defeated and killed his rival at the Battle of Cassel in February the following year. It was a double blow for William, for to deal with Flanders he had dispatched his most trusted lieutenant, William fitz Osbern, and the earl had also been among the fallen. Thus the king not only found himself suddenly having to worry about a hostile power on Normandy's border, he was also left mourning the loss of one of his closest advisers, a friend since his earliest youth and one of the principal architects of the Norman Conquest.[8]

Nor was it just Flanders. In almost every other significant quarter, the fortuitous conditions that had obtained during the previous decade – conditions without which the conquest of England would scarcely have been feasible – had become far less clement. In the spring of 1069, for example, there had been a rebellion against Norman rule in Maine, with the citizens of Le Mans driving out William's garrisons. By itself this must have seemed bad enough, occurring as it did at a time when the king was wholly preoccupied with crushing rebellion in England. It was made much worse, however, by the reviving political fortunes of both Anjou and France. Both powers had been in eclipse for several years following the almost simultaneous deaths of Geoffrey Martel and Henry I in the autumn of 1060 – in Anjou's case because of a disputed succession, and in France's case because its new king was only a child. A decade on, however, and the eclipse had ended. The struggle in Anjou had been resolved decisively in favour of a new count, Fulk Réchin, after he defeated and imprisoned the rival contender, his brother. In France, meanwhile, the new king, Philip I, had emerged from the political tutelage of his mother (Anna of Kiev, who had given him his unusual Greek name), and was consciously pursuing the anti-Norman policy developed by his father. In 1072 Philip, now turned twenty, nailed his colours firmly to the mast by marrying Bertha, the half-sister of Robert of Flanders. In the same year, the rebels in Maine appealed to Fulk of Anjou for help, and the count responded by invading and occupying the county. It was as if the clock had been turned back twenty years: on every side Normandy was menaced by enemies.[9]

We should put this into perspective by observing that the situation in 1072 was not as serious as it had been a generation earlier. After the Conquest of England William was the most feared warrior in Europe, while his adversaries were young men of little or no reputation. He was also, as king of England, able to draw on far greater resources than at the start of his career. In 1073 he led a large English army across the Channel and reconquered Maine in a matter of weeks. But while there is no sense of crisis in the early 1070s, these developments were highly distracting. Increasingly William would have to spend more and more of his time defending his duchy's borders, refighting old battles against new, more youthful adversaries.[10]

Thus the government of England had to be entrusted to others. We know that during his first period of absence in 1067, the Conqueror had left William fitz Osbern and Odo of Bayeux in charge of his new kingdom, and it may be that Odo continued to act alone in this capacity after fitz Osbern's death. The Anglo-Saxon Chronicle, in a retrospective review of William's reign, tells us unequivocally that his half-brother 'was master of the land when the king was in Normandy'. Yet there is no evidence to indicate that the bishop was filling this role during the early 1070s, and we know that for at least some of the time he was with William on the other side of the Channel. Other sources, meanwhile, suggest that the principal figure in England during these years was a man of altogether different qualities.[11]

In August 1070, after some four months of argument, William had finally succeeded in appointing a new archbishop of Canterbury. It was clearly felt important to banish the memory of the worldly and excommunicate Stigand, and thus, as far as the king was concerned, there was only one man suitable for the job: Lanfranc, his long-time friend and spiritual adviser, the most celebrated scholar in Europe. Lanfranc himself, however, was equally determined that he was not going to accept it. Seven years earlier he had been pressured into becoming the abbot of William's new monastery of St Stephen's in Caen, and this time he was adamant: he was not going to move to Canterbury. As he explained to Pope Alexander II a short time later, 'although that duke, now king of the English, endeavoured in many ways to bring this about, his labours were in vain'. It was only when Alexander, at William's urging, commanded Lanfranc to accept the archbishopric that the abbot had finally and reluctantly agreed. He was appointed on 15 August 1070 and consecrated in Canterbury a fortnight later, almost certainly in the king's own presence.[12]

Lanfranc protested that he was not up to the scale of the task. 'When I was in charge of the monastery at Caen, I was unequal to ruling a few monks', he told Alexander, 'so I cannot conceive by what judgement of almighty God I have at your insistence been made the overseer of many and numberless peoples.' Much of his reluctance must have stemmed from the fear that, as in Normandy, he would be made responsible for more than these people's spiritual welfare, and so it proved. It was probably an exaggeration for his twelfth-century biographer to describe Lanfranc as the 'chief and keeper' of England during William's absences, for other men clearly helped share the burden of secular government. Nonetheless, the archbishop's letters, laced as they are with phrases like 'instructing you in the king's name and my own', indicate that he was exercising something like vice-regal power on his master's behalf. The letters themselves, collected within a few years of Lanfranc's death, are one of our most valuable windows on to life in England immediately after the Conquest.[13]

Although he was periodically called upon for purposes of state, Lanfranc's principal concern was the Church. Historians continue to argue about the condition of the English Church on the eve of the Conquest, with some maintaining that everything was essentially fine. Both Lanfranc and William, however, saw an institution in desperate need of reform. 'Before my time,' the king declared in a writ of the early 1070s, 'episcopal laws were not properly administered in England according to the precepts of the Holy Canons.' The writ went on to address the fundamental problem of overlapping jurisdictions. In

Anglo-Saxon England, spiritual crimes such as blasphemy and adultery had been tried in secular courts – a situation that seemed scandalous to reformers like Lanfranc. In future, William explained, they would be heard in special Church courts, before the bishop or his deputy. This meant other changes necessarily had to follow: bishop's deputies, or archdeacons, had hardly been known in England before 1066; now, because of this new workload, their numbers began to increase dramatically.[14]

William's writ also highlights another important innovation, for the king begins by saying he has acted on 'the common counsel of the archbishops, bishops, abbots and all the magnates of my kingdom'. In pre-Conquest England there had been no reforming councils of the kind familiar in Normandy, but in the Conqueror's reign they became regular events, with no fewer than five held in the period 1070–6. As the decrees of these councils make clear, Lanfranc was not simply introducing change for its own sake; administrative reform was a necessary first step to correcting people's religious beliefs. 'Soothsaying, divination or any such works of the devil should not be practised,' declared the eighth canon of the Council of London in 1075, 'as all such things the sacred canons have forbidden, and those who practise them will be excommunicated.' Of course, the fact that such practices were condemned does not prove that they were any more prevalent in England than elsewhere in Europe, or that the situation in Normandy was any better. When in 1072 the archbishop of Rouen, John of Avranches, decided to take a firm line on clerical celibacy, declaring in a council that married priests must put away their wives, the result was a riot. According to Orderic Vitalis, the archbishop was stoned from his cathedral, crying 'O God, the heathen are come into thine inheritance!' Lanfranc, perhaps mindful of this episode, took a softer line in England, allowing existing priests to keep their partners, but forbidding clerical marriages in future.[15]

One important area in which Lanfranc led not so much by prescription but example was architecture. Three years before his appointment, in December 1067, the cathedral church of Canterbury had been gutted by fire (a disaster which reportedly coincided with William's return to England at that very moment). The new archbishop immediately moved to set matters right, commissioning a brand-new building in the latest Romanesque style. Little of this work now remains, but from its floor plan we can see that it was closely modelled on Lanfranc's former abbey of St Stephen's in Caen, a building which was itself so new that construction work had not yet been completed.[16]

Where the archbishop led, other churchmen followed. Almost at once the new Norman abbot of St Augustine's Abbey in Canterbury demolished his old Anglo-Saxon church and commissioned a Romanesque replacement, while in 1072 construction began on a new cathedral at Lincoln, deliberately designed to be as defensible as the nearby castle. During the same decade, other new cathedrals or abbey churches were also started at Salisbury, Chichester, Rochester, St Albans and Winchester (the last two in particular still retaining substantial amounts of their original Norman masonry). It was nothing less than an architectural revolution. Prior to 1066 England had only one comparable structure in the shape of Edward the Confessor's Westminster Abbey; after 1070, it seems, every bishop and abbot had to have one. These were grand buildings, expensively fashioned in stone (large quantities of which had to be shipped from Caen for the finely carved details) and completed in astonishing time. Lanfranc's new cathedral was advanced enough to be dedicated in 1077. As William of Malmesbury later declared 'you do not know which to admire more, the beauty or the speed'.[17]

It was not just the buildings that were new. In several instances the Normans seized the opportunity to transfer the seat of an ancient English bishopric to a different location. The bishop of Lincoln, for example, had been based before the Conquest at Dorchester-upon-Thames; the bishop of Salisbury had previously operated out of Sherborne, and the bishop of Chichester had earlier resided in the coastal village of Selsey. All were moved during the 1070s, as were the bishops of Lichfield (to Chester) and East Anglia (moved from Elmham to Thetford, and thence, eventually, to Norwich). Again, before the Conquest this had happened only once, when the bishop of Crediton had moved his see to Exeter; after 1070 it became a matter of policy. 'Episcopal seats should not be in villages, they should be in cities', agreed the Council of London in 1075, when three of these transfers were approved and others mooted. This was ostensibly for pastoral reasons: being based in urban areas meant that bishops were closer to a greater proportion of their flocks. But security was clearly also a consideration, for cities were safer places for foreigners, especially if they had castles. The new cathedral at Salisbury (Old Sarum, as it eventually became known) was situated within the castle's defensive perimeter.[18]

The architectural results may now seem splendid but, as the concerns about security imply, such changes were not universally welcomed by the natives. Consider, for example, Lanfranc's rebuilding of Canterbury Cathedral. As a necessary prelude to reconstruction, the new archbishop caused all the shrines and relics to be removed from the old fire-damaged church and kept in other buildings (at one stage they were placed in the monks' refectory). But there was more to this action than careful stewardship. As he explained in 1079 to his fellow scholar (and eventual successor), Anselm of Bec, Lanfranc had serious reservations about Canterbury's collection of bones. 'These Englishmen among whom we are living have set up for themselves certain saints whom they revere', he confided, 'but sometimes when I turn over in my mind their own accounts of who they were, I cannot help having doubts about the quality of their sanctity.' Anselm, in response, spoke up for St Ælfheah, the archbishop murdered by the Danes in 1012, and Lanfranc in this particular instance softened his stance, allowing that Ælfheah could be included in Canterbury's liturgical calendar, albeit celebrated with a feast of the second order. But other long-established local saints – including the most revered of all, St Dunstan – were purged from the community's commemorative round. Nor is there any sign that the shrines of either Ælfheah or Dunstan were replaced in the new cathedral during Lanfranc's lifetime. Indeed, it seems likely they remained, along with all the other relics, secreted in an upstairs room above the church's north transept.[19]

By acting this way, the new archbishop may not have felt he was doing anything particularly controversial. Like other reformers, Lanfranc wanted to direct popular devotion away from local saints with dubious credentials and focus instead on the figure of Christ himself. Thus when his new church was dedicated in 1077 the ceremony took place not on Dunstan's feast day but on Palm Sunday, and when the monastic community processed through Canterbury they carried the Eucharist – i.e. the body of Christ – rather than Dunstan's bones. Yet some Englishmen took considerable offence at the archbishop's actions. Eadmer of Canterbury, the historian who preserved the above anecdote about Lanfranc's sceptical attitude towards English saints, prefaced it by saying that sometimes the archbishop had altered English customs for no reason other than to assert his own authority.[20]

Moreover, if Lanfranc caused offence at Canterbury, it was nothing compared to that caused elsewhere by some of his subordinates. Adelelm, the new Norman abbot of Abingdon, was remembered in the twelfth century not only for having despoiled his church of its valuables, but also for having dismissed his saintly predecessor, Æthelwold, as an 'English rustic'. Similarly Lanfranc's nephew, Paul, who became abbot of St Albans in 1077, was said to have referred to his forebears as 'uncouth illiterates', and – following his uncle's example – to have removed their tombs from the abbey church. There were worse examples. William of Malmesbury describes how the Norman appointed to his monastery in 1070, Abbot Warin, 'looked with scorn on what his predecessors had achieved, and was governed by a proud distaste for the bodies of the saints'. The pre-Conquest custom at Malmesbury had apparently been to place the bones of bygone abbots in two stone receptacles that stood either side of the altar, the bones themselves carefully kept separate by means of wooden partitions. 'All these Warin piled up like a heap of rubble, or the remains of worthless hirelings', says William, 'and threw them out of the church door.' The bodies of the saints, meanwhile, were removed to the lesser of the abbey's two churches and sealed off with stone. A similarly shocking story was recorded at Evesham about the actions of Abbot Walter, who, after his arrival in 1078, reportedly found it difficult to reconcile the sheer number of English saints with the fact of the Norman victory, and so proceeded – on Lanfranc's orders – to test the sanctity of the abbey's relics by submitting them to an ordeal by fire. The archbishop's connection to several of these cases (he was also involved in vetting certain saints at Malmesbury) make it look as if the attitude of Norman newcomers to the English Church was part of an official programme; at the very least it suggests a collective mindset.[21]

Much of the misunderstanding between the conquerors and the conquered must have been down to language. One of the main arguments Lanfranc had advanced against his promotion to Canterbury was his ignorance of English, and one suspects that it was an ignorance shared by most if not all of the new bishops and abbots, not to mention the new Norman sheriffs and castellans. Of course, some Englishmen must have spoken French, and some Normans probably learned a little English as a means of getting by without always having to rely on interpreters. According to Orderic Vitalis, the Conqueror himself began to learn English in the hope of being better able to govern his new subjects, but had to abandon the effort as his problems began to multiply.[22]

In one crucial respect, however, the Normans deliberately spurned the linguistic tradition they encountered. As we've already noted, English was highly unusual in being a written as well as spoken language. In England, not only were books and chronicles composed in the vernacular; so too were official documents – the charters, writs and diplomas issued in the name of the king. But in or around 1070 the use of English for such documents suddenly ceased. This must have been a decision taken at the highest level, and the coincidence of its timing with the arrival of Lanfranc might lead us to identify him as the prime suspect. That said, the purge of the Church hierarchy that same year, along with the steady attrition of English secular officials, must have made the abandonment of written English a fairly obvious development: what, after all, would have been the point of addressing orders to Continental newcomers in words they could not understand? From 1070 onwards, therefore, all royal documents were written in Latin, a language that was familiar to both literate Normans and educated Englishmen. Nevertheless, even if it was a necessary switch, it was a switch that had been rendered necessary by the fact of the Conquest, and may therefore still have been perceived by many Englishmen as yet another attack on their native culture.[23]

Such cultural attacks, real or imagined, could lead to tension which spilled over into violence. The most notorious example occurred at Glastonbury in 1083, when the new Norman abbot, Thurstan, fell out with his monks over a number of matters (among other things, he insisted that they abandon their accustomed Gregorian chant in favour of the version used at Fécamp). Eventually the argument escalated to such an extent that Thurstan tried to silence his critics by sending in a group of armed knights. The Anglo-Saxon Chronicle, normally so laconic, in this case lamented at length:

The Frenchmen broke into the choir and threw missiles towards the altar where the monks were, and some of the knights went to the upper storey and shot arrows down towards the shrine, so that many arrows stuck in the cross that stood above the altar: and the wretched monks were lying round the altar, and some crept under it, and cried to God zealously, asking for His mercy when they could get no mercy from men. What can we say, except that they shot fiercely, and the others broke down the doors there, and went in and killed some of the monks and wounded many there in the church, so that the blood came from the altar on to the steps, and from the steps on to the floor. Three were killed there and eighteen wounded.

This was clearly an extreme episode in every sense: the king himself intervened and Thurstan was sent back to Normandy in disgrace.[24] Yet there are other recorded instances of similar discord, albeit less violent, between English monks and their Norman masters. A letter from Lanfranc to Adelelm, the unpopular abbot of Abingdon, refers to an unspecified row that had caused several of the brothers to abscond, and implies that the disagreement was partly Adelelm's own fault. Meanwhile Lanfranc himself at one time clashed with the monks of St Augustine's over their refusal to accept the rule of a new French abbot. To reduce the rebels to obedience, the archbishop imprisoned some of them in chains, but even this was not enough for one especially obdurate individual. 'Would you kill your abbot?' asked Lanfranc. 'Certainly I would if I could,' replied the monk – an answer which resulted in him being tied naked to the abbey door, whipped in view of the people and driven from the city.[25]

That exchange exposes one of the great fears for the Normans immediately after the Conquest – that Englishmen, given half the chance, would surreptitiously slaughter them the moment their backs were turned. That much is made clear by a new law introduced by William, known as 'murdrum', to deal with precisely such circumstances. By this law, if a Norman was found murdered, the onus was placed on the lord of the murderer to produce him within five days or face a ruinous fine. If the culprit remained at large despite his lord's financial ruin, the penalty was simply transferred to the local community as a whole, and levied until such time as the murderer was produced. Clearly the aim was to deter both lords and communities from granting protection and anonymity to such killers, and the obvious inference is that this is exactly what they had been doing. The murdrum fine conjures the vivid picture of Englishmen up and down the country, frustrated by the failure of the major rebellions, continuing to vent their anger against their Norman occupiers by picking them off individually whenever the opportunity presented itself.[26]

Writing to Alexander II in the early part of 1073, Lanfranc described the situation in England as unbearably awful. 'I am continually hearing, seeing and experiencing so much unrest among different people, such distress and injuries, such hardness of heart, greed and dishonesty, such a decline in the Holy Church, that I am weary of my life, and grieve exceedingly to have lived in times like these.' It is notable that, in describing England's woes, the archbishop does not seek to apportion blame between the English or the Normans. As his letters show, Lanfranc was not afraid to upbraid Frenchmen if he felt they had strayed from the path of righteousness. The bishop of Thetford received a stern admonition to curb his licentious lifestyle, while the bishop of Chester was severely criticized for his harassment of the monks of Coventry. Lanfranc's correspondence with the bishop of Rochester, meanwhile, shows the Normans in a poor light when it refers to the problem of Englishwomen who had fled to nunneries 'not for love of the religious life but for fear of the French' – a line that rubbishes William of Poitiers' glib assertion that during the Conquest 'women were safe from the violence which passionate men often inflict', and proves that Orderic Vitalis had been right to speak of Norman rape.[27]

Nevertheless, it seems likely that, in one important respect, the archbishop probably did see the English as more culpable than their conquerors. The problem with Englishmen was not just that they killed Normans on the quiet when no one was looking; it was also that they frequently resorted to killing each other. There was a long tradition in England of solving political problems or family disputes by resorting to murder. Confining ourselves to only eleventh-century examples, we could point to the purges that had been carried out at the court of King Æthelred, or the aristocratic bloodbath that had attended the accession of King Cnut. Earl Godwine had famously killed Edward the Confessor's brother, Alfred, Earl Siward had arranged the murder of his rival, Eadwulf, and Tostig had similarly ordered the deaths of his Northumbrian enemies. Even Godwine's daughter, Queen Edith, was said to have contrived the assassination of her brother's bête noire, Gospatric, when he was staying peacefully at her husband's court. Monastic chroniclers may have bewailed such behaviour, but it was clear that secular society tolerated it as a usual and useful part of the political process.[28]

In Normandy this was not the case. The Normans may have been famously violent and rejoiced in their reputation as masters of war, but by 1066 both their warfare and politics adhered to a different set of rules. During the eleventh century it had become usual practice in northern France for noblemen to spare the lives of their enemies once they had them at their mercy. Society had become, in a word, chivalrous. The Normans seem to have embraced this new attitude in the course of the Conqueror's own lifetime. The last time we witness political killings in Normandy is during his minority, when the duchy's leading families had engaged in a murderous struggle for control of the young duke. Since he had come of age, however, such behaviour had ceased. His own warfare was still appallingly violent, and many innocent people perished when it was prosecuted; also, when all else failed, the duke resorted to blinding and maiming his opponents. But, significantly – and in stark contrast to Æthelred, Cnut et al. – he refrained from killing them, and even the blinding and maiming does not seem to have been inflicted in the case of high-status individuals. Aristocrats who rebelled against William were either imprisoned or exiled; occasionally they were even forgiven.[29]

William had applied these same principles in England after the Conquest. Of course the Conquest itself had been extremely bloody. Constant campaigning down to 1070 had led to indiscriminate slaughter, especially in the north, and revolts had occasionally been resolved by the maiming of low-status rebels. But no Englishman is known to have been executed after his surrender. Earl Morcar was committed to prison after his capture; so too was his fellow rebel from Ely, Siward Barn. Gospatric of Northumbria was at first forgiven and then later banished, while his replacement, Earl Waltheof, was not merely forgiven but promoted. From an English point of view this was quite remarkable – good grounds, it has been observed, for regarding William as the first chivalrous king of England. His biographer, William of Poitiers, certainly seems to have thought so: on one occasion he breaks off his story to address the English directly, drawing an implicit contrast between his master's behaviour and that of earlier English kings:

> And you too, you English land, would love him and hold him in the highest respect . . . if putting aside your folly and wickedness you could judge more soundly the kind of man into whose power you had come . . . Cnut the Dane slaughtered the noblest of your sons, young and old, with the utmost cruelty, so that he could subject you to his rule and that of his children.[30]

Yet the inclusion of this impassioned plea clearly indicates that, at the time Poitiers was writing in the mid-1070s, the English did not appreciate William's finer qualities. As far as they were concerned he was responsible for the death of Harold and countless thousands of their fellow countrymen; the fact that he had spared those who surrendered seems to have made no difference to his popularity. Nor, it seems, did it have much impact on attitudes towards killing among the English themselves, who in some cases continued to behave exactly as before. The family of Earl Waltheof, for example, had for most of the eleventh century been engaged in a long and murderous bloodfeud. In brief, the earl's great-grandfather, Uhtred, had been ambushed and killed by his rival, Thurbrand, who was in due course killed by Uhtred's son, Ealdred, who had accordingly been slain by Thurbrand's son, Carl. And there the matter had rested for over three decades – until the winter of 1073–4, when Waltheof himself saw an opportunity for vengeance, and sent his retainers to slaughter Carl's sons and grandsons as they were sitting down to dinner in their hall at Settrington. Despite his marriage to William's niece and his implicit acceptance into the new chivalrous world order, the earl in this instance had chosen to act in a traditional English manner. Such conduct must have seemed appalling to the Normans; it may be behaviour of this sort that led several Continental commentators in the 1070s, including both William of Poitiers and Archbishop Lanfranc, to describe the English as 'barbarous'.[31]

It will be obvious by now that evidence about conditions in England during the 1070s, and relations between the English and Normans, is largely anecdotal, and as such open to different interpretations. Lanfranc, for example, insisted that the situation in 1073 was dreadful, but he clearly wanted to paint as bleak a picture as possible, for he immediately went on to ask the pope to allow him to resign his post and return to a peaceful monastic life in Normandy. Similarly, his letter which mentions the flight of English women to nunneries in order to avoid Norman rape was written in response to a question from the bishop of Rochester, who wanted to know what to do in the case of those women who now wished to abandon their veils. In other words, by the time this letter was written (some point after 1077), conditions were far better than they had been in 1066.

One can marshal other evidence to suggest that Anglo-Norman relations were improving as time wore on. Within just a few years of the Conquest, says Orderic Vitalis, 'English and Normans were living peacefully together in boroughs, towns and cities, and were intermarrying with each other. You could see many villages or town markets filled with displays of French wares and merchandise, and observe the English, who had previously seemed contemptible to the French in their native dress, completely transformed by foreign fashions.' Of course, this too is anecdotal evidence, and many modern historians have argued that Orderic, writing several decades after the events he describes, gives an impression which is altogether too roseate. Nevertheless, it is as well to remember that Orderic, born in 1075, was himself the product of an Anglo-Norman match. It may also be the case, as his quote suggests, that intermarriage was more common in urban areas.[32]

There are other anecdotes that speak of co-operation between the English and their conquerors. Earl Waltheof, as well as marrying into the Norman world, was also seen to be working well with the new Lotharingian bishop of Durham. 'Bishop Walcher and Earl Waltheof were very friendly and accommodating to each other', recalls Simeon of Durham, 'so that he, sitting together with the bishop in the synod of priests, humbly and obediently carried out whatever the bishop decreed for the reformation of Christianity in his earldom.'[33]

There were also political developments that led to improved relations. Waltheof's predecessor, Gospatric, who soon returned from Flanders to Scotland and therefore might have continued to pose a threat, appears to have died between 1073 and 1075. Far more significantly, the other Flemish exile, Edgar Ætheling, decided during this same period that it was time to submit. For a while he had cherished the idea of continuing his fight against the Conqueror on the Continent; the young king of France, Philip I, offered him the castle of Montreuil-sur-Mer as a base from which to harass Normandy's northern border, and in 1074 Edgar returned to Scotland in order to marshal the resources necessary for such a move. But thereafter the plan went disastrously wrong: en route to France the pretender was shipwrecked, losing all his treasure and very nearly his life. When he eventually limped back to Scotland, his brother-in-law King Malcolm suggested it was perhaps time for Edgar to make peace with William. 'And so indeed he did,' says the Anglo-Saxon Chronicle,

> and the king granted his request and sent for him. King Malcolm and his sister again gave countless treasures to him and to all his men, and sent him once more from their domain in great state. The sheriff of York came to meet him at Durham, and accompanied him the whole way, and arranged for food and fodder to be obtained for him in every castle they came to, until they came across the sea to the king.

Here indeed was proof that the English were conscious of the Conqueror's chivalry, for in earlier times no sane ætheling would have surrendered in this way for fear of execution. William, by contrast, was the very model of chivalrous courtesy. Edgar was received 'with great ceremony, and he then remained at the king's court there, and accepted such privileges as he granted him'.[34]

The clearest indication of improved Anglo-Norman relations, however, is a new revolt that erupted in 1075. Although often ranked with earlier rebellions against the Conqueror, this revolt differed in the important respect that its leaders were French rather than English. The prime mover, it seems, was a young man called Ralph de Gaël, who was by birth and upbringing a Breton (Gaël was his lordship in Brittany). The Bretons in general were not popular with the Normans, but Ralph's father (also named Ralph) had been one of the Continental courtiers of Edward the Confessor, and had been rewarded after the Conquest with the earldom of East Anglia, vacated by the death of Gyrth Godwineson. By 1069, if not before, Ralph senior was dead and Ralph junior had arrived in England to take up his father's title. Very soon he was plotting rebellion.[35]

And he was not alone. The new earl of East Anglia found a willing co-conspirator in Roger, earl of Hereford, son and successor (in England) of no less a person than William fitz Osbern. The two young men cemented their alliance, probably in the spring of 1075, when Ralph married Roger's sister, Emma – the wedding took place at Exning, near Newmarket in Suffolk, and it was there that the plot was hatched. 'That bride-ale', said the Anglo-Saxon Chronicle, 'led many to bale.'[36]

Precisely what their grievances were is impossible to say. John of Worcester says that William had forbidden the marriage to take place, which might be construed as a reason, albeit a weak one, were it not for the fact that the Chronicle says that, on the contrary, the king had approved the match. Orderic Vitalis puts a long list of complaints into the mouths of the two earls, most of which are either familiar (e.g. William's bastardy) or clearly the chronicler's own (e.g. the invasion of England had been unjust). There may, however, be something in Orderic's ventriloquism when he makes the earls say that lands given out soon after the Conquest had been either wholly or partially confiscated. Immediately after his coronation the Conqueror had appointed new earls on the existing English model. Odo of Bayeux, William fitz Osbern and the older Earl Ralph had taken over the vast commands vacated by the Godwinesons, with authority in each case stretching across several counties. Yet when the king came to create his own earldoms a short while later – for example, at Shrewsbury and at Chester – they were smaller affairs, based on a single shire, and thus closer in extent to a Continental county. What appears to have happened in the case of both Roger and Ralph is that, when they succeeded to their father's estates, their scope of their authority was much reduced, bringing their old 'super-earldoms' into line with William's more modest model. We can see from a letter of Lanfranc that Roger in particular was angered by the fact that royal sheriffs were holding pleas within his earldom, the obvious inference being that this had not happened during the time of his father.[37]

Whatever their grievances, the two earls were clearly trading on the assumption that any rebellion against the Conqueror would be supported by the English. That much is suggested by their decision to approach the last Englishman of any power and standing. Earl Waltheof was a guest at the wedding in Exning and it was there that he was invited to join the conspiracy. According to Orderic, Roger and Ralph held out the prospect of a kingdom split three ways, with one man taking the crown and the other two ruling as dukes – an altogether unlikely story, given that we know from other sources that the plotters had appealed for help from the Danes. Yet Orderic is surely correct to assume that the point of the rebellion was to get rid of William. As the Anglo-Saxon Chronicle puts it, 'they plotted to drive their royal lord out of his kingdom'.[38]

But in assuming that the English would automatically rise up and join them, the earls badly miscalculated. What the events of 1075 prove, above all else, is that there was no further appetite for rebellion among the natives. Earl Waltheof, according to John of Worcester, quickly came to his senses and confessed all to Lanfranc. Whether this was true or not, the archbishop soon discovered that castles were being strengthened and troops raised against the king. His response can be charted from a series of letters he sent soon afterwards to Roger of Hereford. At first Lanfranc tried to appease the earl, reminding him of his father's outstanding loyalty, informing him that his dispute with the king's sheriffs would be investigated, and offering to meet him in person so that they could discuss matters further. Evidently this olive branch was rejected, for the archbishop's next letter begins, 'I grieve more than I can say at the news I hear of you.' Roger was again reminded of his father's great integrity and urged to come and talk his problems over. But the rebel could not be persuaded, and so Lanfranc changed his attitude entirely. 'I have cursed and excommunicated you and all your adherents', he says in his final letter, adding 'I can free you from this bond of anathema only if you seek my lord the king's mercy.'[39]

In the meantime the king's more warlike lieutenants in England were marshalling forces with which to crush the rebellion – forces which, in every account, bear witness to extensive Anglo-Norman co-operation. According to John of Worcester the rebels raised by Earl Roger in Herefordshire were prevented from crossing the River Severn by armies under the command of Bishop Wulfstan of Worcester and Abbot Æthelwig of Evesham, along with 'a great multitude of people'. The Anglo-Saxon Chronicle tells us that Earl Ralph and his men were similarly frustrated in East Anglia, because 'the castle garrisons in England [i.e. the Normans] and all the local people [i.e. the English] came against them and prevented them from doing anything'. John of Worcester adds that Ralph was camped at Cambridge when he encountered 'a large force of English and Normans', ready for battle, while Orderic maintains that a battle actually took place at the nearby manor of Fawdon, in the course of which the rebels were routed by 'an English army'.[40]

And so the ill-conceived revolt of the earls was thwarted. Ralph fled back to his base in Norfolk and from there took ship to Brittany, leaving his new wife and his Breton followers to defend the mighty royal castle at Norwich. This suggests he was hoping to return, either with fresh forces raised on the Continent or in the company of his Danish allies. But after a long siege – three months, if Orderic is to be believed – Emma and the rest of the Norwich garrison sought terms of surrender. In exchange for a promise of life and limb, they agreed to leave England and never to return. 'Glory be to God on high,' wrote Lanfranc to his royal master, 'your kingdom has been purged of its Breton filth.'[41]

As the archbishop's letter implies, William was still in Normandy at the time of the surrender. Earlier in the crisis he had evidently been ready to cross the Channel, but Lanfranc had dissuaded him ('You would be offering us a grave insult were you to come to our assistance', the king was firmly told). William did return soon afterwards, however, having discovered that in one respect the rebels' plan had met with success. 'The Danes are indeed coming, as the king has told us,' wrote Lanfranc to the bishop of Durham that autumn, 'so fortify your castle with men, weapons and stores: be ready.' But this too turned out to be a passing storm. A fleet of 200 Danish ships in due course arrived but, says the Anglo-Saxon Chronicle, 'they dared not fight with King William', and contented themselves with plundering York before returning home.[42]

William was therefore able to spend Christmas at Westminster, dealing with the rebellion's aftermath. 'There all the Bretons who were at the wedding feast were sentenced', says the Anglo-Saxon Chronicle. 'Some of them were blinded, and some of them were banished.' Tough sentences, as one would expect for men who had plotted treason, but note that, in keeping with proper chivalric practice, none of them were executed. Roger of Hereford, who was captured soon after the king's return, was sentenced to lose his lands and liberty, but not his life. Like Earl Morcar, he would spend the rest of his days in prison, contemplating the folly of rebelling against William the Bastard.[43]

That left Earl Waltheof, who had been implicated in the rebellion but to a degree that was uncertain, even to contemporaries. According to both the Chronicle and John of Worcester, the earl was essentially innocent. Forced to swear an oath while at the wedding, he had immediately gone to Lanfranc for absolution, and then, on the archbishop's advice, crossed to Normandy to seek similar forgiveness from the king. By contrast, in Orderic's account (which seems in many respects less reliable), Waltheof was made party to the plot, disapproved of it, but told no one. Thus, although he did not participate in the rebellion, he could be charged with the crime of concealment.

The judges, says Orderic, could not agree on a verdict, and the earl was held at Winchester for several months until they reached a decision. Clearly the worst that could happen would be that, like Earl Roger, he would remain in captivity forever, but Orderic says it was generally supposed that Waltheof would be released. He was, after all, married to the king's niece. The earl may even have hoped that, as in the case of Edgar Ætheling, his timely surrender might count in his favour and enable his rehabilitation.[44]

If so he was gravely disappointed. Six months later, judgement was finally passed on Waltheof, who was found to be as guilty as any of the other conspirators. His sentence, however, was different. As Orderic explains, Roger of Hereford was a Norman and had hence been judged 'by the laws of the Normans'. Waltheof on the other hand was an Englishman and was sentenced according to 'the law of England'. On the morning of 31 May 1076, while the city's other inhabitants were still asleep, the earl was led out of Winchester to the top of St Giles Hill and beheaded. Despite Orderic's description of his prayers and tears, it is difficult to feel a great deal of sympathy for Waltheof – here, after all, was a man who had recently arranged the murders of his political rivals as they were sitting down to enjoy their evening meal. By his own actions, the last English earl had proved the chronicler's point that the conquerors and the conquered did indeed play by different rules. Yet while such differences existed, there can have been little hope of reconciliation.[45]

16

Ravening Wolves

In the summer of 1076, with Earl Roger in prison and Earl Waltheof dead, the Conqueror crossed the Channel in pursuit of the one remaining conspirator, the elusive Earl Ralph. This might suggest a thoroughness on William's part bordering on the obsessive, but Ralph was no wandering exile. Back in his native Brittany, the earl had ensconced himself in the castle of Dol, from where he and his men were able to menace Normandy's western marches. And not just *his* men either: local chronicles reveal that some of the garrison had been supplied by the count of Anjou. Ralph, in other words, was in league with the king's other enemies on the Continent, which raises the possibility that this had been the case even before his rebellion in England, and thereby casts that rebellion in a new and more serious light. Like Edgar Ætheling before him, Ralph may have been part of a wider plot to topple William from power, orchestrated by the count of Anjou, the count of Flanders and the king of France.[1]

If anything William seems to have underestimated the scale of the threat. In September 1076 he advanced into Brittany, terrorizing Ralph's lordship and subjecting Dol to a sustained siege. But the defenders proved more resolute than anticipated and held out for many weeks. Then, with the onset of winter, the king of France came to their aid, surprising William and forcing him into what sounds at best like a hasty retreat, if not quite a total rout. 'King William went away', says the Anglo-Saxon Chronicle, 'and lost both men and horses and incalculable treasure.' It was the first recorded setback of the Conqueror's military career. Fifty years later, Orderic

Vitalis saw it as the workings of divine justice, with God punishing William for Waltheof's death.[2]

During the remainder of 1077, therefore, peace negotiations took place with both France and Anjou, with William for once in the uncomfortable position of not having the upper hand. No doubt significantly, the summer and autumn of that year saw the dedication of several major new churches in the duchy, including the king's own foundation of St Stephen's in Caen. Perhaps William was worried about divine displeasure and was seeking to make amends. What he was certainly seeking was an alternative means of advertising the full extent of his power. The dedication of St Stephen's was attended not just by the king, the queen and all the magnates then in Normandy; also there by special arrangement were the most powerful Norman barons from England, as well as Archbishop Lanfranc and Thomas, the archbishop of York. Here was an attempt, surely, to remind Continental observers that the Normans, although preoc-cupied in many cases with affairs in England, were far more powerful as a result of their Conquest, and, although divided by the Channel, were not divided in their loyalties. Unfortunately, it was not true in every instance, and least of all within William's own family.[3]

Since their marriage in or around 1050, William and Matilda had produced at least nine children – four sons and (probably) five girls. If we have not mentioned them before, it is because next to nothing is known about their lives before they reached adulthood. The second son, Richard, had died in a hunting accident during his teens, leaving three surviving brothers. Henry, the youngest child of all, had been born either in 1068 or 1069, while William, known as Rufus on account of his red hair, had been born around 1060 and was there-fore just emerging from adolescence. But the firstborn son, Robert, was probably the oldest of all the nine children, and was already long past this stage. By 1077 he was very much a young adult male, and that was precisely the problem.[4]

Robert, according to Orderic Vitalis, 'was talkative and extravagant, reckless, very courageous in battle, a powerful and sure archer with a clear, cheerful voice and a fluent tongue. Round-faced, short and stout, he was commonly nicknamed "fat-legs" and "shorty-pants".' This last nickname was the one that stuck, and, rendered into Norman French as 'Curt-hose', has echoed down the ages. If, as William of

Malmesbury implies, it was a designation used, and perhaps even devised, by the Conqueror himself, then one might observe that it hardly sounds like a term of endearment. As Orderic and other writers make clear, there was little love lost between William and Robert, who together faced the perennial problem of medieval rulers and their male offspring.[5]

Robert, like virtually every heir apparent known to history, craved a greater share of his father's power. During his mid-teens this had seemed an imminent prospect, for on the eve of his departure for England in 1066 William had taken the precautionary measure of recognizing Robert as his successor and swearing all the Norman magnates to do likewise. Since that time, however, the prospect had gradually faded. William routinely left Matilda to act as his regent in Normandy, supported by a council of older, experienced men. The young duke-in-waiting was probably allowed some role in government, for he appears occasionally as a witness to ducal acts. But like every young man, what he wanted was not the exercise of delegated authority, but actual independence – the ability to pick and choose his own followers, and the lands and money with which to reward them. Matters were not helped by the fact that his transition to manhood coincided with the re-emergence of serious threats to Normandy's security; just at the moment that Robert might have expected to be granted more power, he found instead that his father was almost always present in the duchy to direct affairs in person. According to Orderic, Robert asked to be given Normandy and Maine, but William refused, telling him to wait for a more opportune moment. Robert, says Orderic, 'took offence because he could get nothing out of his father, and arrogantly came to blows with him on a number of occasions'.[6]

The crunch came not long after the dedication of St Stephen's in September 1077, which is the last date we can place William and Robert in each other's company. At some point soon thereafter, the king was staying in the town of L'Aigle, preparing a military expedition on his southern frontier, when a brawl broke out between Robert and his younger brothers. As Orderic tells it, William Rufus and Henry

> came to the town of L'Aigle, where Robert had taken up residence in the house of Roger Cauchois, and began to play

dice in the upper gallery, as soldiers do. They made a great noise about it, and soon began to pour down water on Robert and his sycophants underneath. Then Ivo and Aubrey of Grandmesnil said to Robert, 'Why do you put up with such insults? Just look at the way your brothers have climbed above your head and are defiling you and us with filth to your shame. Don't you see what this means? Even a blind man could. Unless you punish this insult without delay it will be all over with you: you will never be able to hold your head up again.' Hearing these words Robert leaped to his feet in a towering rage, and dashed to the upper room to take his brothers unawares.

We might be justly suspicious of this story. In particular, the image of Rufus and Henry 'climbing above' Robert suggests at first glance that Orderic has simply constructed a rather laboured metaphor for the brothers' later political fortunes. But in other respects the story convinces. Why, for instance, are we told that it was Ivo and Aubrey de Grandmesnil who egged Robert on, or that they were staying in 'the house of Roger Cauchois', a figure otherwise unknown to posterity? The answer, surely, is that Orderic was well informed about the incident: L'Aigle lies just a few miles from his monastery of St Evroult, and the family of Grandmesnil were the abbey's founders. The chronicler goes on to tell us that the noise of the fracas quickly brought the king to the spot (William 'was lodging in Gunher's house') and for the time being the quarrel was repaired. The next night, however, Robert and his followers deserted the king's army and rode hurriedly to Rouen, where they attempted, without success, to seize the city's castle. When William heard the news he flew into a terrible rage and ordered all the conspirators to be seized, at which point Robert and his adherents fled into exile.[7]

Orderic's pejorative opinion of Robert (he is 'reckless' whereas his father is 'prudent') should not lead us to underestimate the enormous seriousness of this rebellion. Among the men who followed the heir apparent into exile (Orderic's 'sycophants') were the eldest son of Roger of Montgomery, Robert of Bellême, and the eldest son of William fitz Osbern, William of Breteuil (the latter doubtless dismayed by the recent imprisonment of his brother Roger). With them went many other members of the younger generation. The struggle between William and Robert, in short, had split the entire Norman aristocracy along similar father–son lines, leaving family loyalties strained and divided. The king's reaction, predictably, was to try to stamp out the flames. The rebels in the first instance fled to the castle of Rémalard, just across Normandy's southern border, and William in due course mustered an army and besieged them there. So Robert fled again, this time into the embrace of his father's enemies: first to his uncle, the count of Flanders, and ultimately to the court of the king of France, who must have been overjoyed at his good fortune. Having spent years trying to find a convincing figure around whom an anti-Norman alliance could coalesce, Philip suddenly and unexpectedly found himself playing host to the Conqueror's own son and heir. It was a card to trump all others.[8]

The inevitable result of this family rift was that, once again, William was wholly preoccupied with a Continental crisis, and England was once again left to the rule of others. As was the case in the early 1070s, Lanfranc continued to play a pivotal role. In every surviving letter that the king sent to England from Normandy, the archbishop always heads the list of addressees. At the same time, it seems that during the later 1070s there was another, even more powerful figure in England, in the shape of William's half-brother, Odo of Bayeux.[9]

Odo, it almost goes without saying, was a very different character to Lanfranc. He too, of course, was a bishop – his splendid new cathedral at Bayeux had been another of the dedications during the summer of 1077 – and, if we believe William of Poitiers, he was intelligent and eloquent in discussions about Christian worship. But Odo, unlike Lanfranc, had never been a monk, and did not crave a return to the quiet of the cloister. On the contrary, he appears to have revelled in his role as a man of the world, readily accepting the secular position of earl of Kent bestowed on him by William immediately after the Conquest. For Poitiers this made him 'the kind of man best able to undertake both ecclesiastical and secular business'; for Orderic it merely proved he was 'more given to worldly affairs than spiritual contemplation'. A man of God, a man of the world, Odo was also clearly a man of war. His own seal depicted him on one side as a bishop holding his crosier, but on the other side as a mounted warrior brandishing a sword. This makes rather a mockery of Poitiers' claim that Odo 'never took up arms, and never wished to do so', and his self-evidently preposterous assertion that the bishop had been present at Hastings only because of the strength of his affection for his half-brother ('a love so great that he would not willingly be separated from him even on the field of battle'). Against such nonsense we also have the magnificent testimony of the Bayeux Tapestry, almost certainly commissioned by Odo himself, which shows the bellicose bishop charging into battle on a black horse, rallying the Normans at the crucial moment. Whatever reservations others may have had about his behaviour, Odo clearly had no problems with the dual nature of his role.[10]

Odo's pre-eminent position in England during the late 1070s is not apparent from surviving royal letters (he is addressed in only two) but from the testimony of the chronicles. 'He was the foremost man after the king', says the Anglo-Saxon Chronicle, 'and was master of the land when the king was in Normandy', while Orderic tells us that Odo 'had greater authority than all the earls and other magnates in the kingdom'. Just how extraordinary his authority was is revealed in the pages of the Domesday Book, where a series of entries show that he was able to redistribute land and settle disputes about landholding on his own authority, without reference to anyone, including the king. In this respect his power was virtually unique – Domesday shows that William fitz Osbern had occasionally exercised similar power up to his death in 1071, but by the late 1070s Odo was evidently the only figure allowed to handle such business. When, for example, the abbot of Abingdon purchased a new manor at Nuneham Courtenay, he took care to advise Odo of the price and obtain the bishop's approval. As the abbey's chronicler explains, this happened when 'the king was in Normandy and his brother, Odo, bishop of Bayeux, was governing the kingdom'. Orderic states the situation even more plainly. Odo, he says 'was dreaded by Englishmen everywhere, and able to dispense justice like a second king'.[11]

Interestingly, the period during which the bishop was in charge coincides with a major change in the way land was allocated. As we've seen, the Conqueror's closest companions – men such as Odo himself and William fitz Osbern – had been granted land in England immediately after the coronation, while other favourites such as Roger of Montgomery had been rewarded in this way soon after the king's return the following year. In each case these men had been given consolidated blocks of territory – Odo received Kent, fitz Osbern the Isle of Wight, Montgomery the county of Shropshire – which paid no attention to pre-existing landholding patterns. This was most obvious in the case of Sussex, where the new rapes cut clean across the boundaries of earlier estates. Since all of the lands distributed in this way were located on the periphery of William's realm, the assumption is that the king's chief concern was security.[12]

But these early grants to his closest followers seem to have been the exception to the general rule. In other areas, away from the coast and the borders, we find land was allocated on a different basis, with individual Normans being rewarded with the lands of individual English lords. Take, for example, the case of Ansgar the Staller, who was one of the richest men in England below the rank of earl. Ansgar seems to have fought at Hastings (he may, indeed, have been Harold's standard-bearer) and looks to have received mortal injuries there: the last reference to him comes in the *Carmen*'s account of the surrender of London, which Ansgar negotiated, despite being seriously injured. Soon thereafter his position as 'portreeve' of London – the equivalent to the later position of mayor – was in the hands of a Norman, Geoffrey de Mandeville, who, at the time of the Domesday Book, was holding all of Ansgar's lands. Geoffrey, in other words, appears simply to have stepped into the place his predecessor had vacated.[13]

A similar situation occurs with Englishmen who rebelled between 1068 and 1071. The estate of Mærleswein, sometime sheriff of Lincoln and, until his flight in 1070, one of the leading rebels, passed unbroken to his Norman successor, Ralph Pagnell. So too with Siward Barn, who was imprisoned after the fall of Ely; all his lands went to a Norman called Henry de Ferrers. Orderic provides us with the names of several other individuals involved in the English revolt, and in each case we can see from the Domesday Book that their lands passed intact to a new Norman holder. Moreover, the same process seems to have continued beyond the period of rebellion and into the early 1070s. We know, for instance, that the northern thegn called Thurbrand died in the winter of 1073–4, because he was one of the sons of Carl killed at Settrington on the orders of Earl Waltheof. In Domesday all his lands in Lincolnshire and Yorkshire are recorded as belonging to the Norman lord Berengar de Tosny.[14]

At some point thereafter, however, we can discern a switch. No longer are individual Englishmen succeeded by individual Normans. Instead we witness the return of territorial grants – great blocks of land of the kind given out in the immediate aftermath of the Conquest. As an example, consider the case of William's other half-brother, Robert of Mortain. At some stage before 1086, when it is recorded in the Domesday Book, Robert received a large swathe of territory in Yorkshire. Tenurially speaking it is a total mess – the lands within it were formerly the property of dozens of individual Englishmen; there are whole estates in some places and bits of estates in others. In territorial terms, however, Robert's new lordship is precisely defined, because its boundaries are formed by the existing administrative subdivisions of the county (what in the south would be called hundreds, but what in the north were known as wapentakes). Clearly it was these boundaries, and not the existing land-holding arrangements, that provided the basis of the grant.

At the same time, Robert's territorial dominance within this well-defined area is not quite total, because it is interrupted in one or two places by estates held by other Norman newcomers – men who have acquired their lands on the principal of tenurial succession. The obvious inference is that these men were given their lands first, and Robert's grant has been made afterwards. We appear, in short, to be looking at a situation where Robert has been assigned an area of territory, demarcated by administrative boundaries, and told 'take whatever's left'.[15]

This is a scenario we see repeated elsewhere in England: large blocks of territory, granted out on the principle of 'whatever's left'. It is particularly noticeable in the counties of the north Midlands and beyond – the areas largely untouched by the first wave of Norman settlement. Precise dating of the creation of these lordships is impossible, but the evidence suggests that several of the lords who held in this way were in place by around 1080, and we have seen that straightforward succession on the earlier model appears to have continued up to 1073–4. At some point between these two dates, someone decided on a radical change of policy.[16]

The most obvious candidate for making such a decision is the Conqueror himself – after all, the distribution of land is about as important a task as one can imagine. If so, the likeliest time for the change would have been the last weeks of 1075 or the early months of 1076, when we known that William was in England to deal with the revolt of the earls and its aftermath. That revolt, like its predecessors, meant more major confiscations as earls Roger, Ralph and Waltheof were dispossessed. At the same time, the decision to grant out land on a different basis may have been due to other factors. If William had been doling out the property of Englishmen on the basis of strict succession for almost a decade, by the mid-1070s there can have been few great estates left with which to reward loyal followers. Also, those followers may have preferred to have the kind of compact territories established immediately after the Conquest, rather than the various manors of an English predecessor, which were often scattered across several counties. But the change may simply have been dictated by politics and pragmatism. By the mid-1070s, William was increasingly embroiled in events on the Continent, and may have decided that grants needed to be made, once again, on the basis of security, rather than in deference to existing patterns of English landholding. If England was in the hands of reliable men, William's own hands would be free to fight battles elsewhere.

The alternative, of course, is that this change in policy was caused by a change in personnel at the top. It is just conceivable that the switch to territorial grants was the brainchild of Bishop Odo, acting in his capacity as regent. This, after all, was the basis on which his own lordship of Kent had been created, and we know from other evidence that he had wide-ranging powers to decide on matters of landholding. At the very least Odo must have been responsible for implementing the new policy, and in some cases we can see that the recipients of territorial grants in the north were drawn from the ranks of his own followers.[17]

By the mid-1070s William and Odo were not the only ones granting out lands. Just as the king or his regent granted out territory to men who had served them well, so too these men began in turn to grant it out to their dependants. This process – modern historians call it 'subinfeudation' – is not well documented, especially in the case of laymen. Orderic Vitalis provides a vague description of how Roger of Montgomery distributed positions of authority in Shropshire to his 'brave and loyal men'.[18] However, since the monasteries had been informed in or around 1070 that they too would have to supply the king with a set number of knights, we find better descriptions in the pages of monastic chronicles. The Abingdon Chronicle records how, in the initial years of his rule, the new Norman abbot, Adelelm, 'securely protected the monastery entrusted to him with a band of armed knights':

> At first indeed, he used paid troops for this. But after the attacks had died down, and when it was noted by royal edict in the annual records how many knights might be demanded from bishoprics, and how many from abbeys, if by chance compelling need arose, the abbot then granted manors from the possessions of the church to his followers (who had previously been retained by gifts), laying down for each the terms of subordination for his manor.[19]

For lay lords, especially if they had received a generous grant of land from the king, distributing a portion of it among their followers made good sense, for it was probably more cost-effective than maintaining such men permanently within a baronial household. For the monasteries and bishops the incentive was probably even stronger, for accommodating a troop of knights was not only ruinously expensive but highly disruptive. Bishop Wulfstan of Worcester, recalls William of Malmesbury, was obliged to maintain an array of knights that drained his resources, and stayed up late in his hall, drinking and brawling into the night.[20]

The quid pro quo for a grant of land was that the recipient would furnish the donor with military service. One of the earliest charters enshrining such an arrangement, by which Robert Losinga, the Norman bishop of Hereford, gave land to a knight called Roger fitz Walter, is helpfully explicit. 'Previously the said bishop held this land as his own demesne and for the sustenance of the church', it says at one point, 'but the bishop, by the counsel of his vassals, gave [Roger] this same land in return for a promise that he would serve the bishop with two knights, as his father did, whenever the need arose.'[21]

In many cases, as we've seen, the king also required his tenants to supply men to guard his castles, and, again, the same expectation existed between a lord and his own subtenants. Whether he had simply stepped into the tenurial shoes of an English predecessor, or received a block of territory that paid no regard to previous landowning patterns, the first act of a new Norman lord was invariably to establish a castle. If it were the former case, he might well choose to erect the earthworks over his predecessor's existing residence; several Norman mottes have proved on excavation to be built on top of Anglo-Saxon halls.[22] Equally – and especially in the case of those who received territorial grants – he might plant the castle wherever he chose in order to assert his lordship. The point of a castle was to dominate the surrounding countryside – to control road and water routes for economic and military purposes – and to protect its Norman occupants. Some territorial lordships are specifically referred to in the Domesday Book as 'castleries', indicating that the entire district was arranged around the castle at its centre. In other cases this is evident from the way a lordship has been organized. At Richmond in Yorkshire, for example, we can see that lands were granted out in such a way that castle-guard was performed on a rota basis, each subtenant serving for a period of two months, so that the castle was kept in a permanent state of defensive readiness.[23]

Described in this way, the Norman settlement and colonization of England can sound like a fairly orderly process: the king grants land to his leading men in return for military service; they keep some themselves and distribute the rest to others. There is disruption and upheaval at a local level as castles are built, especially if these castles are the centre of new territorial lordships. Yet the impression of order remains, both in the way land is distributed and the way that new patterns of landholding are imposed.

It is without doubt a misleading impression, for it masks the considerable chaos and confusion that the process of settlement entailed. Obviously, the fact that land was granted out on two different principles meant that there was huge potential for conflict between incoming Norman lords, with some claiming all the land with a certain administrative district, and others insisting that they held particular manors within it as the heirs of English predecessors. But this confusion was magnified many times over owing to the complicated nature of Old English lordship. In pre-Conquest England, a man could be bound to a lord in a number of different ways; he *might* hold land from him, but then again he might not. In some cases a lord could have jurisdiction over certain men but not be their landlord. In other cases, the lord–man relationship could be one of 'commendation', a tie which was purely personal, and had neither tenurial nor jurisdictional content. Some land was held of no lord at all, which explains the frequent statement in the Domesday Book that a particular Englishman 'could go with his land where he wished'. In Normandy, by contrast, the tenurial bond was much stronger. Although land and lordship did not automatically go together, the general assumption was that they should, because the trend had been in this direction for many decades. Hence there was ample scope for confusion and disagreement after 1066 when the Normans encountered the tangled strands of English lordship. An aggressive newcomer, for example, might try to treat men who had merely been commended to his predecessor, or under his predecessor's jurisdiction, as if they were his tenants; in so doing, he would provoke not only protests from the men themselves, but also opposition from other Normans who regarded their rights of lordship to be superior.[24]

So the Normans interpreted (or, rather, wilfully misinterpreted) the rights of their English predecessors in their own interests and pushed them as hard as possible. They also, in many cases, simply grabbed whatever they could. There is abundant evidence to show that, while much land was given out by the king and entered into legally, a considerable amount was acquired by less legitimate methods – extortion, intimidation and violence. In certain areas of the country – the east Midlands and East Anglia – the Domesday Book shows no clear pattern of land-distribution, which has been interpreted as indicating that the Norman settlement in these regions was something of a free-for-all. More concretely, Domesday also preserves the testimony of local jurors that certain Normans had helped themselves. Take, for instance, Richard fitz Gilbert. A long-standing friend of the Conqueror (he was the son of William's ill-fated guardian, Count Gilbert), Richard was rewarded soon after the Conquest with a large, territorial lordship based on Tonbridge in Kent – he erected the mighty motte-and-bailey castle that still dominates the town today, and later styled himself 'Richard of Tonbridge'. But, in the years that followed, he continued to extend and add to his lordship at every available opportunity. Domesday jurors swore in 1086 that he had illegally seized three manors in neighbouring Surrey, while a compensation package later agreed by his son reveals that Richard had also relieved the monks of Rochester of several properties in the same county.[25]

Confronted by a figure like Richard fitz Gilbert – who, by 1086, was one of the ten richest men in the kingdom – to whom could a dispossessed Englishman turn? Of old he might have appealed to the king's representative in the shire – the 'shire reeve', or sheriff. After all, sheriffs had been introduced during the reign of Æthelred the Unready as a means of checking the influence of the king's mightier servants, the earls. But, since the Conquest, the English sheriffs had been for the most part swept away and replaced by Norman newcomers. Like the men they supplanted, these Normans tended to be men of very modest backgrounds but, by comparison with their English predecessors, they seemed altogether more determined to raise themselves higher. And, with the earls themselves gone, who was going to stop them? Plentiful evidence exists to show that, when it came to land and landholding, the supposed gamekeepers were the worst poachers of all. As Henry of Huntingdon later put it, 'the sheriffs and reeves, whose function it was to preserve justice and legality, were fiercer than thieves or robbers, and more savage to all than the most savage'. Every monastic house seems to have suffered at the hands of its local sheriff. According to William of Malmesbury, the new Norman sheriff of Worcester, Urse d'Abetôt, planted his castle so close to Worcester Cathedral priory that its ditch cut through the monk's cemetery (provoking a celebrated put-down from Ealdred, the city's erstwhile bishop: 'Thou art called Urse – have thee God's curse!'). The monks of Ely, meanwhile, had it even worse, since their support for Hereward the Wake and his fellow fenland rebels earned them lasting royal displeasure. Many local Normans seem to have assumed thereafter that it was open season on the abbey's estates, and none more so than Picot the Sheriff. Such was the scale of his appropriations from Ely that the monks remembered him in the twelfth century as 'a hungry lion, a roving wolf, a crafty fox, a filthy pig, a shameless dog'.[26]

The tide of complaint from the monastic chronicles gives the impression that the Church suffered far more than the laity, but in actual fact this is likely to be the reverse of the truth. The Church certainly suffered but, being blessed with institutional continuity and possessed of copious documentation, armed with the spiritual weapon of excommunication and having access to friends in high places, including the king and the pope, senior churchmen were often able to obtain redress if their rights were violated. In 1077, for example, King William himself wrote to his leading magnates in England (Richard fitz Gilbert is among the addressees), requiring them and the sheriffs to return any Church property they had seized by intimidation or violence.[27]

One suspects that English laymen, by contrast, had rather less luck. Surrounded by land-hungry Norman neighbours and predatory sheriffs, the small English landholder had few remaining options. He might, perhaps, try to put himself and his lands under the protection of a sympathetic local abbot: the chronicler of Evesham Abbey recalled how, immediately after the Conquest, Abbot Æthelwig 'attracted knights and men to him with their land . . . promising them protection against the Normans'. But protection, in this instance at least, lasted only as long as the abbot. When Æthelwig died in 1078 he was replaced by Abbot Walter, who (in addition to barbe-cuing the abbey's relics) began to grant out estates entrusted to the abbey's protection to his Norman friends and relatives.[28] The only alternative open to the defenceless lay landowner, therefore, was to make the best of a bad deal – to approach the new lord or sheriff and try to secure the right to one's own property, even it meant sacrificing a part of it, or holding it on unfavourable terms.

This is the darker side of the Norman settlement of England – not merely confused and chaotic, but violent, rapacious and in many cases unjust. It was, one might argue, an inevitable part of any military takeover, only to be expected in circumstances where aggressive men, expectant of reward and greedy for spoils, are unleashed on a vanquished people. Yet it cannot have helped matters that, in the late 1070s, the worst offender of all was the man in charge. Odo of Bayeux, it seems, was from the first a great believer in self-help:

> He established himself in the county of Kent very strongly and exercised great power therein. Moreover, because in those days there was no one in that shire who could resist so powerful a magnate, he attached to himself many men of the archbishopric of Canterbury, and seized many of the customary rights which pertained to it.

So begins a report, written at Canterbury, of a great assembly held at Penenden Heath near Maidstone, probably in 1072. It goes on to explain how Archbishop Lanfranc, after his appointment in 1070, discovered the extent of Odo's usurpations and complained to the king, who in turn arranged the meeting at Penenden as a means of investigating the matter. So numerous were the lands in dispute, we are told, that the hearing went on for three days, by the end of which Canterbury's rights were vindicated.[29]

But while the archbishop managed to reclaim some of his lost property from the earl, other churchmen were not so successful. 'Holy monasteries had good cause to complain that Odo was doing them great harm,' says Orderic Vitalis', 'violently and unjustly robbing them of ancient endowments made by pious Englishmen.' This must have applied in particular to the period during the late 1070s when the bishop apparently governed England with unfettered power. At Evesham Abbey, for example, it was remembered that the bishop 'ruled the country at that time under the king like some tyrant'. Odo, the abbey's chronicler complained, preyed on Evesham's estates 'like a ravening wolf', packing the courts with hostile witnesses to deprive the monks of no fewer than twenty-eight properties, 'more by his own evil influence than by legitimate means'. Again, if the Church, which to some degree had the ability to resist such encroachments, suffered in this way, then the laymen who came up against Odo must surely have suffered more. Such indeed is the impression given on folio after folio in the Domesday Book, with jurors complaining time and again that the king's half-brother had obtained lands to which he had no legal right.[30]

'Read the scriptures, and see if there is any law to justify the forcible imposition on a people of God of a shepherd chosen from among its enemies.' The words, if we believe Orderic Vitalis, of Guitmund, a pious and learned Norman monk, summoned to England by King William soon after the Conquest and offered a plum position in the English Church. 'I deem all England to be the spoils of robbery, and shrink from it and its treasures as from consuming fire.' Historians have been rightfully sceptical of this scene, pointing out that the opinions expressed in the speech are Orderic's own, and that any monk who had actually been so frank before the Conqueror would most likely have been found hanging by his cowl from the nearest tree. At the same time, there may be a kernel of truth in the story. Guitmund was most certainly a real person, a noted theologian who for some reason felt compelled late in his career to leave Normandy and seek alternative employment at the papal court; he ended his days as bishop of the Italian city of Aversa.

Other evidence suggests that some Normans did have reservations about participating in what was descending into a colonial carve-up. But they were clearly outnumbered by the legions of other men, secular and religious, who were rushing across the Channel to join in the scramble for worldly goods and riches.[31]

17

The Edges of Empire

While Odo lorded it over the English, William was still struggling to bring his errant eldest son to heel. The king of France had taken full advantage of his enemy's discomfort, installing Robert in the castle of Gerberoy, a fortress close to Normandy's eastern frontier, from where the frustrated young man and his followers – now supplemented, says Orderic Vitalis, by many common knights and mercenary French barons – made frequent raids into his father's duchy. Finally, soon after Christmas 1078, William moved against him and a bitter stand-off ensued. As the various chronicle accounts make clear, it was yet another occasion where the once invincible warrior was worsted. After enduring a three-week siege, Robert led a sortie against his father, at one point fighting him in person and wounding him in the hand. The Conqueror's other adult son, the loyal William Rufus, was also injured in the clash, while many other men were killed or taken prisoner. When the king's horse was shot from under him, the man who tried to bring him a replacement was felled by a second bolt. According to John of Worcester, William escaped only because Robert recognized his voice and, giving up his own horse, commanded his father to ride away.[1]

Unsurprisingly, therefore, the wounds from this encounter took a long time to heal. William was evidently very sore, his humiliation compounded by the discovery that Matilda, 'feeling a mother's affection for her son', had been secretly supporting Robert by sending him large sums of silver and gold. (Such as least is the story told by Orderic.) For most of 1079 there can have been little movement in the direction of reconciliation, despite repeated efforts on the part of the queen, the bishops and the most senior Norman magnates to intercede with William on Robert's behalf, hoping 'by fair speech and pleading to soften his harshness'. It was not until the early months of the following year that a breakthrough was achieved:

> Finally, the stern king yielded to the pressure of all these great persons, and, surrendering to paternal duty, became reconciled with his son and his son's confederates. And by the advice of his chief men he again granted Robert the duchy of Normandy after his death, as he had once before granted it to him . . . The people of Normandy and Maine welcomed the restoration of peace with rejoicing, for they had been weakened and impoverished by several years of war.

This reconciliation must have happened shortly before Easter 1080, for that is the first occasion when we see William and Robert together again, witnessing a charter in the company of a great crowd of Norman magnates, in what was no doubt a deliberately contrived show of unity. At long last, the dispute that had threatened to tear the duchy apart was over. By 8 May the news had reached Rome, and the pope wrote a congratulatory letter to Robert, rejoicing that the rift had been repaired, and quoting him some choice passages from Scripture on the subject of filial duty.[2]

The end of the dispute meant that William could finally turn his attention to England. He did not return immediately, presumably because (as Orderic implies) there remained much work to be done in restoring peace to Maine and Normandy. But at some point after July, the Conqueror crossed the Channel once more, returning to his kingdom for the first time in over four years.[3]

Having been away for so long, William probably returned for no other reason than to make his presence felt, and to satisfy himself that affairs in England had been handled satisfactorily in his absence. Nevertheless, by the summer of 1080 there were at least two urgent items on the agenda, both of which concerned the north. The previous August King Malcolm of Scotland had raided into Northumbria, thus violating the peace agreed at Abernethy seven years earlier. Meanwhile, as recently as May 1080, the bishop of Durham had been murdered. Possibly the two events were connected: Bishop Walcher had been de facto earl of Northumbria since the fall of Waltheof in 1075; it may be that the devastation of the region he was supposed to be defending exposed the weakness of his rule and provoked a plot to end it. According to a long and detailed account by John of Worcester, however, the bishop was brought down by a personal quarrel between two of his servants, one of whom killed the other, thus triggering a bloodfeud which ended badly for all involved. Walcher tried to negotiate with the dead man's kin, but they opted instead for revenge, slaughtering him and a hundred of his followers at Gateshead as they tried to take refuge in a church. Thus what appears to have started as a feud ended up resembling an out-and-out rebellion, an impression the bishop's killers reinforced when they went on to Durham and attempted, without success, to capture the city's castle.[4]

Both the Scottish raid and Walcher's murder cried out for reprisals, and William did not hesitate to inflict them. At some point after July 1080 he dispatched into Northumbria that altogether more strenuous prelate, Odo of Bayeux, who demonstrated what William of Poitiers would no doubt have called his skill in secular affairs by leading an army into the region and laying it to waste. According to Simeon of Durham, Odo killed, maimed and extorted money from the guilty and innocent alike, before helping himself to some of the cathedral's treasures, including an ornate pastoral staff. Later in the same autumn Robert Curthose was sent on a similar mission into Scotland, as if to demonstrate to King Malcolm that his attempt to make hay during the recent father–son rift had been a short-sighted mistake. Simeon was dismissive of his efforts, but it seems that Robert succeeded in reimposing the terms of the earlier Anglo-Scottish peace. On his return journey he also gave additional substance to Norman rule in the north by establishing a permanent outpost near the site of Walcher's murder at Gateshead – a 'new castle' upon the Tyne.[5]

William's decision to delegate northern affairs to Odo and Robert may indicate that he did not actually return to England until late in the year – the first definite evidence of his having crossed the Channel comes at Christmas, when he appears at Gloucester. This destination was partly traditional: Edward the Confessor had generally celebrated Christmas in the same city, drawn there by the hunting to be had in the nearby Forest of Dean, and the same attraction would have appealed to William, who was notoriously addicted to the joys of the chase. 'He loved the stags as much as if he were their father', says the Anglo-Saxon Chronicle.[6]

Such, indeed, was William's love of hunting that he imported the very concept of 'the Forest' into England – the word occurs for the first time in an English context in the Domesday Book. We tend to think of forests as heavily wooded areas, but originally the term could be applied to land of any sort. It probably derived from the Latin word *foris*, meaning 'outside', for the Forest's defining aspect was that it was a jurisdiction apart: an expanse of land reserved for the king's own recreation, with its own rigorously enforced law. 'He set aside a vast deer preserve and imposed laws concerning it', says the Anglo-Saxon Chronicle. 'Whoever slew a hart or a hind / Should be made blind.'[7]

William caused forests to be made in many places, but the most famous was the one he established in Hampshire, appropriately still known as the New Forest. It was evidently created early in the reign, for the king's second son, Richard, died there at some point in the late 1060s or early 1070s. Later chroniclers saw this death as divine retribution for the suffering that the forest's creation had entailed. 'In past times,' says John of Worcester, 'that area was fruitfully planted with churches and people who worshipped the lord. But on King William's command, men were expelled, homes were cast down, and the land was made habitable only for wild beasts.' In fact, as historians have long pointed out, the sandy soil of the New Forest could never have supported the kind of densely populated society that the chroniclers imply, and the Domesday Book shows that the greater part of the area – about 75,000 acres – had indeed been uncultivated before 1066. But Domesday also shows that William had added a further 15,000–20,000 acres, an extension which involved the clearance of some twenty villages and a dozen hamlets, containing approximately 2,000 people. The chronicles had exaggerated, but the essence of their story was true.[8]

Another reason for the king's decision to keep Christmas at Gloucester in 1080 would have been the city's proximity to Wales.

In general Wales had proved far less problematic for William than Scotland, largely thanks to the victories of his immediate predecessor. Although the Conqueror may not have cared to acknowledge it, Harold's success in toppling the all-powerful Gruffudd ap Llywelyn in 1063 had returned Wales to its usual state of disarray, with multiple rulers vying against each other for supremacy. By the time the Normans arrived in the region soon after 1066, much of their work had already been done for them.

William had created three new earldoms along the border as a means of separating English rebels from potential Welsh allies, and before long their holders were expanding their power westwards. As earl of Shrewsbury Roger of Montgomery had pushed across the ancient frontier of Offa's Dyke and begun colonizing parts of the Welsh interior, founding a castle and town that he named Montgomery in honour of his home in Normandy, while his men advanced further along the Severn Valley, establishing castles of their own in similar fashion. To the north Earl Hugh of Chester (successor of the short-lived Earl Gerbod) had achieved even greater territorial gains by terrorizing the natives. 'He went about surrounded by an army instead of a household', recalls Orderic Vitalis, and as a result 'wrought great slaughter among the Welsh'. Castles were planted as far west as the River Conwy, and raids conducted further west still, into the heart of Snowdonia.[9]

In south Wales, by contrast, a rather different situation had emerged. The earl of Hereford, William fitz Osbern, had also struck hard at the Welsh, crossing the River Wye to establish towns and castles, possibly as bridgeheads for further expansion, but in the event there had hardly been any advance beyond the existing frontier. With so many responsibilities elsewhere, fitz Osbern appears to have decided to reach an accommodation with the local Welsh rulers, recognizing their rights in return for an admission of his superior lordship. After the earl's death in 1071, the same policy was evidently continued by his son, Roger of Breteuil, for the following year we find Norman knights fighting in the service of the native ruler Caradog ap Gruffudd. Caradog had been a force to reckon with in south-east Wales for some time – the destruction of Harold's hunting lodge at Portskewett in 1065 had been his handiwork – and saw the Normans as useful allies against his Welsh rivals. In 1072 this alliance enabled him to defeat and kill the king of neighbouring Deheubarth, thereby fulfilling a long-cherished ambition to make himself master of Glamorgan. Such, indeed, was the strength of the understanding between him and his Norman overlord that, in the wake of Roger's disastrous rebellion of 1075, Caradog received some of the earl's fugitive supporters into his protection.

It was Roger's rebellion that caused the Conqueror to become directly involved in the region, for the earl's fall meant that his estates were forfeit: from 1075 the king himself held the earldom of Hereford and with it the overlordship of south Wales. Naturally Caradog's reception of some of the rebels had not gone down well with William, who had sent an army against him to punish the offence. But afterwards the status quo was soon restored and the accommodating relationship was maintained.

If William went west at the end of 1080 partly to cast a supervisory eye over the affairs of south Wales, subsequent events a short time later caused him to return there in a far more dramatic fashion. At some point in 1081, probably during the early months of the year, the rivalry between the various rulers of Wales culminated in a single great battle. On one side fought Caradog and his Welsh and Norman allies; on the other the kings of Gwynedd and Deheubarth, supported by Irish and Danish mercenaries. They met somewhere to the north of St David's, on a hill called Mynydd Carn, in a clash that proved bloody and decisive. Caradog and his allies were defeated, and power in south Wales passed to the king of Deheubarth, Rhys ap Tewdwr.

This upset called for urgent action on William's part: the king needed to establish over Rhys the same kind of control he had maintained over Caradog. Accordingly, at some point later in the year (possibly as early as the spring), the Conqueror moved into south Wales. Despite its cursory notices in the chronicles, this was clearly a major intervention: William travelled all the way across the country, stopping only when he came to St David's, the westernmost place in Wales, beyond which there is only the Irish Sea. This destination prompted the native chronicle known as *The Brut* to describe the royal progress as a pilgrimage; if so, it was a heavily armed one, for the Anglo-Saxon Chronicle says 'the king led levies into Wales'. This was a demonstration of military might, pure and simple, intended to put Rhys in his place and reduce him to client status. On his return journey, William left a permanent reminder of his presence by founding a new town and castle in the ruins of a Roman fort called Cardiff.[10]

Besides telling us that William 'led levies into Wales', the Anglo-Saxon Chronicle gives us one further fact about the 1081 expedition by adding that the king 'there freed many hundreds'. Since we know that some Norman troops had fought and lost alongside Caradog, our first assumption might be that the men the king was liberating were his own. This, however, is a highly unlikely scenario, for the Welsh, like the English, did not hesitate to kill their enemies, even when they had them at their mercy. 'Trahaern was pierced in the middle until he was on the ground dying, biting the long grass with his teeth, and groping about to come upon his weapons; and Gwcharis the Irishman made bacon of him as of a pig.' Such is the exultant description of the death of one of Caradog's allies at the Battle of Mynydd Carn, penned by a Welsh author in the mid-twelfth century. At the same time, it would be inaccurate to say that the Welsh took no prisoners: after the battle, the victorious king of Gwynedd 'set out towards Arwystli and destroyed and slew the common folk there; and he burned its houses, and bore into captivity its women and maidens'.[11]

The Welsh, in other words, took slaves. Here too, of course, they were no different from the English, or for that matter the Scots and the Irish: slavery, slave-raiding and slave-trading were accepted institutions across the whole of the British Isles. In England, nothing had changed in this respect since the days of Cnut. Confining ourselves to reports in the Anglo-Saxon Chronicle, we see that Godwine sold some of Alfred's followers for money in 1036; that Harold seized both men and cattle from Somerset on his return from Ireland in 1052, and – lest it be thought that the Godwines were running a family monopoly – that the Northumbrian rebels in 1065 'took many hundreds of captives, and carried them off north'. Right up to the eve of the Conquest, the slave trade in England was flourishing. William of Malmesbury, looking back from the 1120s, offers a vivid description of its operation out of the port of Bristol. A full seven centuries before their better-known involvement in the buying and selling of Africans, the merchants of Bristol

> would buy up people from all over England and sell them off
> to Ireland in the hope of profit, and put up for sale maidservants

after toying with them in bed, making them pregnant. You would have groaned to see the files of the wretches of people roped together, young persons of both sexes whose beautiful appearance and youthful innocence might move barbarians to pity, being put up for sale every day.[12]

Once upon a time you could have groaned at similar scenes in Normandy too. Back when the Normans had been Norsemen there had been a constant traffic in human cargo from northern France back to Scandinavia, with a thriving slave market in the centre of Rouen. But during the first half of the eleventh century this trade had died out: the last reference to the Rouen market occurs in the late tenth century, and the last references to slavery occur in the 1020s. Traditionally historians have put its disappearance down to economic factors, but more likely it was due to moral objections, as the dukes of Normandy came increasingly under the influence of reforming churchmen. Significantly, the decline of slavery coincides with the rise of chivalry, suggesting that in Normandy and elsewhere in northern France, those in power had come to place a higher value on human life.[13]

The attitude of the Normans towards slavery in England shows signs of having been initially ambivalent. William of Poitiers, comparing his hero with Julius Caesar, insists that the Conqueror returned to Normandy in 1067 'not bringing a crowd of captives in the Roman fashion'; the *Carmen*, by contrast, casually (and perhaps ignorantly) states that William seized people as well as cattle at the time of his landing in 1066. Whatever the truth, William's own attitude is reported to have changed after the arrival in England of his long-term moral tutor, Lanfranc, in 1070. According to William of Malmesbury, it was at the archbishop's insistence that the king 'frustrated the schemes of those rascals who had an established practice of selling their slaves into Ireland', although the Conqueror was reluctant to do so 'because he enjoyed a share of the profits from this traffic'. Other evidence confirms that Malmesbury was right on both scores. The king's financial interest is confirmed by the Domesday Book's description of the slave market at Lewes in Sussex which paid him fourpence for each slave sold. But the so-called Laws of William the Conqueror show that at some point the king nevertheless acted to stop the slave trade, cunningly preserving some profit as he did so. 'I prohibit the sale of any man by another outside the country,' says the ninth law in the list, 'on pain of a fine to be paid in full to me.'[14]

Banning the slave trade, of course, was not the same as banning slavery itself: with ten per cent of the population classed as slaves, such a move would have been nigh-on impossible. But banning the slave trade was still immensely significant, and shows that William was in step with the humane thinking of the reformed Church, even if it cost him financially. It is very likely, therefore, that when the Anglo-Saxon Chronicle tells us that on his progress through Wales the king 'freed many hundreds', it was speaking of the manumission of slaves: those taken captive in the wake of the recent war, chained, roped or caged in readiness for sale abroad, who unexpectedly found themselves set at liberty by a Conqueror.

As William returned from Wales to England, he almost certainly passed through the town of Chepstow, one of the new boroughs founded soon after the Conquest by William fitz Osbern. Fitz Osbern had founded a priory there, too, and also a castle, raised high on a rocky promontory overlooking the River Wye. As the ditches cut into the cliff at either end of its site suggest, the castle had been established primarily with a view to defence, an outpost established in expectation of trouble. But at some point after he acquired the lordship of Chepstow – perhaps as he passed through in 1081 – the Conqueror ordered a substantial new building to be added: a giant stone hall which seems to have been built with different concerns in mind. The hall, which still stands today, has no obvious defensive advantages, nor the domestic features (kitchens, latrines, etc.) that would indicate it was intended to be used as a residence. What we seem to have is a building designed to serve as a ceremonial space: an audience chamber, perhaps, where the king or his representatives could receive the newly subjugated rulers of Wales (we know from Domesday that Rhys ap Tewdwr had agreed to pay William a tribute of £40 a year). Whatever specific purposes it was intended for, the Conqueror's magnificent new hall at Chepstow proclaimed the establishment of royal authority in Wales, just as surely as Newcastle upon Tyne advertised its advance into Northumbria.[15]

Chepstow was not the only grandiose project of this kind; by 1081 major building work was also underway at two other sites. At

Colchester in Essex another stone tower was rising, in this case far larger than its counterpart in Wales (the tower there, which also survives, measures a gargantuan 110 by 151 feet at base). William's reasons for commanding the construction of this behemoth remain obscure: apart from his brief post-coronation visit to Barking there is no evidence that the king ever ventured into Essex. Conventional opinion holds that the castle was built as a defence against Viking raids, but this seems unconvincing: the Danes may have raided eastern England after the Conquest, but their activities were concentrated further north, in Norfolk, Lincolnshire and Yorkshire. The likeliest explanation for the tower at Colchester is the pull of the past, for it was built on the foundations of an earlier Roman temple. William of Poitiers, as we have seen, draws frequent comparison between the Conqueror and the heroes of Ancient Rome; the king himself, it seems, was keen to make the same connection. At Chepstow, too, the new royal hall had similar Roman resonances, its horizontal band of orange tiles reused from the ruins at nearby Caerwent.[16]

The Conqueror's other major building project was, of course, the Tower of London. Built on the site he had selected for a castle in the days before his coronation, the Tower was begun in the 1070s and remained unfinished at the time of William's death, to be eventually completed during the reigns of his sons. As this implies, the result was a truly monumental building, three storeys high, a royal palace that would overawe the populace of the kingdom's principal city. Clear similarities with Colchester (most notably the projecting apsidal chapel) suggest that both buildings were designed by the same individual, identified in a twelfth-century source as Gundulf, a companion of Lanfranc who later became bishop of Rochester. Like Colchester and, indeed, the great hall at Chepstow, the Tower heralded a new dawn in English secular architecture. Construction on this scale had not been seen in Britain since the days of the Roman emperors whom William was so eager to emulate.[17]

Towards the end of May 1081, the king went to Winchester in order to celebrate Whitsun, which fell on the last day of the month. Here too, in England's second greatest city, the Conqueror was making his mark. A decade earlier he had begun to build a new royal palace, distinct from the old Saxon hall it replaced and the new Norman castle, and by this point presumably finished. At the time of his visit in 1081 the great building project in Winchester was the city's new cathedral, begun two years earlier by its new Norman bishop, Walkelin. The cathedrals and abbeys built by the Normans in England before this date had been conceived, without exception, on a bigger and more ambitious scale than their predecessors in Normandy. Compare, for instance, the naves of Jumièges (140 feet) and St Stephen's (156 feet) with those at Canterbury (185 feet), Lincoln (188 feet) and St Albans (210 feet). At Winchester, however, the gulf with the past was rendered even greater still, its nave laid out to stretch an astonishing 266 feet. Not only did this make it the largest church in England by a very considerable margin; it also meant it was larger than virtually every other church in Europe, including the giant cathedrals erected earlier in the century at Speyer and Mainz by the emperors of Germany, from which it borrowed many of its architectural features. Winchester, in fact, stood second only to St Peter's in Rome, erected seven and half centuries earlier by the emperor Constantine. As with their great towers, therefore, so too with their cathedrals: William and the Normans were building on a scale and to a design that corresponded to contemporary and ancient expectations of what it meant to be an imperial power.[18]

This kind of architecture gives us a good indication of the way William perceived himself by the time of his triumphant return to England in 1080–1 – a great king, on a par with German and Roman emperors. Here was a man safeguarding his gains, defining his borders, and proclaiming his achievement. It was probably during the course of this visit that he decided to reform the country's minting practices, sweeping away the elaborate English system by which the weight of the coinage had been periodically altered, and introducing instead a heavier type of coin, the weight of which would thereafter remain fixed (*steor* in Old English, from which we get 'sterling'). At Gloucester at Christmas 1080 he had ceremoniously worn his crown, and he did so again on his visit to Winchester at Whitsun.[19]

Orderic Vitalis provides us with a glimpse of the king's court at this very moment, revealing something of its grandeur. The chronicler describes how Mainer, the then abbot of St Evroult, crossed to England in 1081 and went to Winchester. He was well received by the king and his magnates, all of whom were happy to make gifts to St Evroult because of the immense wealth that had come to them as a result of the Conquest. William confirmed these gifts to the

The field at Hastings.
Battle Abbey, built on the ridge, marks the spot where Harold fell.

(*Above*) Berkhamsted Castle, Hertfordshire. A giant motte-and-bailey, almost certainly started by William himself in the final weeks of 1066 (the masonry was added later).

(*Below*) Pickering Castle, Yorkshire. An artist's impression of how such an earth-and-timber castle would have appeared in the eleventh century.

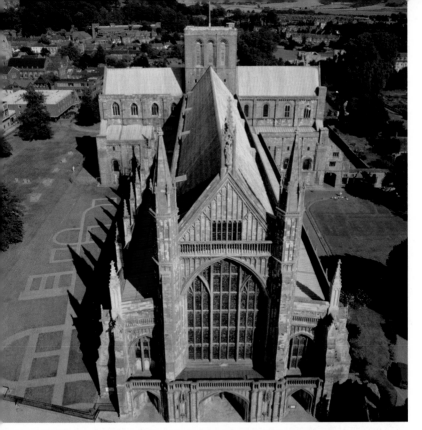

(*Above*) Winchester. Although the cathedral, begun in 1079, was much rebuilt in later centuries, its gigantic scale is original, and contrasts markedly with the exposed foundations (highlighted) of the Old Minster.

(*Below*) A silver penny of William the Conqueror, issued 1066 × 1068. The legend on the reverse reveals that it was struck by the moneyer Dunnic at the Hastings mint.

Imperial Grandeur.
The great towers begun by the Conqueror at Chepstow (*facing page*, *top*), Colchester (*facing page*, *bottom*) and London (*above*), with the last two showing obvious similarities in design.

(*Above*) Old Sarum, Wiltshire. The earthworks of William's castle and the foundations of the Norman cathedral are clearly visible within the perimeter of the Iron Age hill fort.

(*Below*) Great and Little Domesday, when they were still bound as two volumes.

(*Above*) The first page of the Bedfordshire section of Great Domesday. A short assessment of the town of Bedford is followed by a list of the county's major landowners. The first name after the king himself is that of his half-brother, Odo of Bayeux.

(*Above*) Post-Conquest fusion. The nave of Durham Cathedral, begun after 1093, combines Norman Romanesque grandeur with English decoration.

abbey in a charter, which provides us with the names of some of those present. Besides the king, who marked his name with a cross, were the names and crosses of his sons, Robert and William, followed by those of two great earls, Roger of Montgomery and Hugh of Chester, while among the host of other barons we see William of Breteuil, son of William fitz Osbern, reminding us that the rift between the king and the younger generation had been healed. It is a portrait of power, but also one of a kingdom finally at peace. The abbot had gone to England, says Orderic, 'taking advantage of a tranquil time'.[20]

But that tranquil time would not last much longer. A similar image of the king's court is provided by the Anglo-Saxon Chronicle, which describes how the Conqueror kept great state in less benign terms:

> He wore his crown three times a year as often as he was in England; at Easter at Winchester, at Whitsun at Westminster, at Christmas at Gloucester. On these occasions all the great men of England were assembled about him – archbishops, bishops, abbots, earls, thegns and knights. He was so stern and relentless a man that no one dared to aught against his will. Earls who resisted his will he held in bondage. Bishops he deprived of their sees and abbots of their abbacies, while rebellious thegns he cast into prison.
>
> Finally his own brother he did not spare. His name was Odo. He was a powerful bishop in Normandy, and Bayeux was his episcopal see; he was the foremost man in England after the king. He had an earldom in England, and was master of the land when the king was in Normandy. William put him in prison.[21]

18

Domesday

The Anglo-Saxon Chronicle begins its account of the year 1082 with a startling thunderbolt. 'In this year,' it says, 'the king arrested Bishop Odo'. Having startled us, however, the anonymous author, our only contemporary informant, leaves us entirely in the dark, adding only 'and in this year there was great famine' before moving on briskly to deal with the events of 1083.

Thus, in order to discover why William arrested Odo, we are forced to rely on the reports of chroniclers writing forty or fifty years later. Some of these writers declared that the king had discovered his half-brother was planning to usurp the throne. One pointed to Odo's oppressive record as England's regent, while others believed that the bishop was arrested because he was plotting to make himself pope.

On the face of it, this third story might seem to be the most far-fetched, given what we know of Odo's character and the high standards set by the reformed papacy. But by this date the reform movement had run into grave difficulties. The death of Pope Alexander II in 1073 had led to the succession of Gregory VII, a firebrand reformer who took an uncompromising view of the relationship between lay rulers and the Church. His insistence on the supremacy of papal authority had led quickly to a bitter conflict with the king of Germany, Henry IV: Gregory had twice excommunicated Henry and declared him deposed; the king had responded in kind, declaring the pope unfit to hold office and nominating a rival to rule in his place. Their quarrel had divided opinion right across Europe.

Set against this background, the story that Odo was aiming at the papacy starts to seem more credible. It also draws strength from being told by three chroniclers, whose differing accounts show that they were written independently. According to Orderic Vitalis, the bishop purchased a palace in Rome, decorated it sumptuously, and secured the support of several leading Roman families by scattering lavish gifts. William of Malmesbury claimed that Odo advanced his cause by stuffing the wallets of pilgrims with letters and coin. Whatever the precise means, it is not hard to believe that Odo, a man possessed of enormous wealth and power as well as apparently limitless ambition, may well have tried to advance himself as a compromise candidate in the struggle for St Peter's throne.[1]

But what may have seemed a logical career move to Odo appeared otherwise to his elder half-brother. William was far from being a staunch supporter of Gregory VII. Relations between them had started well enough, for in 1066 Gregory, then a cardinal, had been one of the principal cheerleaders for the Norman invasion of England. But latterly their friendship had been dented by the pope's attempt to call in this debt by asserting that England was a papal fief for which William owed homage – a claim that the king had naturally rejected. Gregory had also fallen out with Lanfranc over the latter's repeated refusal to visit him in Rome, even to the extent of threatening to suspend the archbishop from office. Yet despite these tensions there had been no serious rift. In a letter to two French bishops in 1081, Gregory had praised William as a pious ruler who supported the Church and governed his subjects with peace and justice. ('Although in certain matters he does not comport himself as devoutly as we might hope,' the pope admitted, 'he has shown himself more worthy of approbation and honour than other kings.') Similarly, when Gregory was eventually ousted from office by Henry IV in 1084, Lanfranc still refused to denigrate him, and replied angrily to a partisan letter from one of Henry's supporters which did so.[2]

It is highly unlikely, therefore, that either William or Lanfranc would have given their backing to a plan to unseat Gregory in 1082 and replace him with Bishop Odo. Whatever their views on Gregory, both were firm supporters of the reform movement and could hardly have believed that Odo would make a suitable supreme pontiff. But papal politics and questions of suitability aside, there was another more important reason for objecting to the plan. According to both

Orderic and William of Malmesbury, Odo had been determined to back up his bid by leaving England with a large force of distinguished knights – Orderic names Earl Hugh of Chester among their number. 'They resolved to abandon the great estates they possessed in western parts and took an oath to accompany the bishop to lands beyond the Po.' The Conqueror, when he learned of this intention, naturally took a very dim view. The knights he had planted on English soil were *his* knights – his security against further insurrection or foreign invasion, whose removal might very well imperil his grip on the kingdom. And so, says Orderic, the king, who was in Normandy during the first part of 1082, quickly crossed to England and took his brother by surprise. Odo, who was making ready to sail from the Isle of Wight, was seized and put on trial.

Orderic's account here cannot be taken entirely at face value. William *did* cross to England in the autumn of 1082, but he cannot have arrested his brother immediately, for the two men are found in each other's company later that year, witnessing a charter in Wiltshire. Nor can we place too much trust in the long speech that Orderic attributes to William during the trial, in which Odo is denounced primarily for his oppression of the English. Nevertheless, that something like this did take place after William's return is proved by its brief but emphatic mention in the Anglo-Saxon Chronicle. Orderic reports the conclusion of the trial in dramatic terms, telling us that none of the magnates assembled in the king's hall dared to lay hands on the accused, forcing William to carry out the arrest himself. When Odo protested (ironically, giving his alleged ambition) that as a bishop he could be tried only by the pope, the king reportedly replied that he was not condemning a bishop but arresting an earl (a line that finds its way into other accounts – Malmesbury attributes it to Lanfranc). However it happened, Odo was taken across the Channel and imprisoned in the ducal castle at Rouen.[3]

Odo's betrayal – as William must have regarded it – was the first of several family disasters to overtake the king in a short space of time. Soon after his return to Normandy in 1083, his wife, Queen Matilda, fell sick, and eventually died on 2 November. This can have been nothing other than a devastating blow for William, for their marriage had clearly been based on love and trust – there is no other way to account for his consistent reliance on her to act as his regent in both

England and Normandy. Unlike almost every other eleventh-century ruler William had no bastard children and no reported infidelities – at least no credible ones. William of Malmesbury recorded the scandalous rumour that, after his accession as king, the Conqueror had 'wallowed in the embraces of a priest's daughter', but dismissed the story as lunacy: after all, it concluded with Matilda having her rival hamstrung and William vengefully beating the queen to death with a horse's bridle. In reality, says Malmesbury, the royal couple had a minor falling-out in their later years over the support she had secretly supplied to Robert Curthose during his rebellion. 'But that this occasioned no lessening of their affection as man and wife he himself made clear; for when she died . . . he gave her a most splendid funeral, and showed by many days of the deepest mourning how much he missed the love of her whom he had lost.' Matilda was buried in Caen, in the abbey of Holy Trinity she had founded over twenty years earlier. Her tombstone, complete with its original carved epitaph, can still be seen in front of the high altar.[4]

Not long after the loss of his wife, William was hit by a third personal crisis when Robert Curthose once again went into exile. The exact cause of their renewed estrangement is unknown, but its occurrence so soon after Matilda's death is surely significant. Orderic says that despite their earlier rapprochement the king had continued to pour abuse on his son, frequently reproaching him in public for his perceived failings; elsewhere he says that Robert was angry with his father 'for some silly reasons'. Whatever the cause, it did not have the same disastrous effect as their earlier quarrel, since on this occasion Robert was followed into exile by only a few companions. William of Malmesbury says that he went off to Italy, intending to marry the countess of Tuscany, and hoping to secure support against his father. It may be that he also toured other regions to the same end: Orderic at one point mentions visits to sympathetic lords in Germany, Aquitaine and Gascony. But if on this occasion Robert posed no immediate military threat, his departure must still have occasioned great uncertainty, not least with regard to the succession in both Normandy and England. William made no public moves to disinherit his eldest son or to promote his younger brothers; but from 1084 William Rufus assumes Robert's place in the witness-lists to royal and ducal charters.[5]

The Conqueror thus suffered three successive blows that struck very close to home: the imprisonment of Odo, the death of Matilda and the renewed rift with Robert. These losses and betrayals must have taken their toll on him, and left him perhaps feeling increasingly isolated. Apart from anything else, these had been the figures he had relied upon to act as his regents. At the same time, there is no sign that William's family problems from 1082 to 1084 triggered any wider crisis across his dominions. Robert may have hoped to stage a comeback, but chronicle reports depict him as a wandering exile, lacking friends and funds. His former allies, for example, the king of France and the count of Anjou, appear to have lent him no material support; the peace agreed with France in 1079 seems to have held good, while in 1082 William had struck a similar truce with Anjou that reportedly lasted until the end of his life. The only problem the king faced in the wake of Robert's departure was in Maine, after the viscount of Le Mans rebelled and seized the castle of St Suzanne on the county's southern border. In 1084 William set about besieging it with customary speed and vigour.[6]

Some way into the siege, however, the king delegated its prosecution to others, and returned to Normandy to deal with what Orderic calls 'great matters'. What these were the chronicler does not specify, but we may suppose they involved the intelligence William received in 1085 about a planned invasion of England by the king of Denmark.[7]

This was, of course, hardly a new development, for the prospect of Scandinavian invasion had hung over William's reign from the very beginning, and Danish fleets had twice crossed to England, only to return home with very little to show for their efforts. In 1085, however, the threat seemed altogether more serious. Five years earlier Denmark had witnessed the accession of a new King Cnut, a man seemingly determined to repeat the victories of his illustrious namesake. One of the many sons of the late Swein Estrithson, Cnut IV had been among the captains his father had sent to England in 1069 and 1075, leading fleets that contemporaries estimated at 300 and 200 ships. But once he wore the Danish crown himself, the new king became bent on something even bigger. 'With his former failures in mind', says William of Malmesbury, 'Cnut prepared a fleet of a thousand ships or more (so I've heard) for the invasion of England.' Even if we dismiss this as hearsay, there is no difficulty in believing that on this occasion the forces being assembled were much larger than before, for the Danish king was not acting alone. 'In this year', said the Anglo-Saxon Chronicle, 'people said and declared for a fact that Cnut, king of Denmark, son of King Swein, was setting out in this direction and meant to conquer this country with the help of Robert, count of Flanders'. Some years earlier Cnut had married Robert's daughter, Adela. According to William of Malmesbury, the count had assembled a further 600 ships in readiness for the planned invasion.[8]

The seriousness of the threat is further attested by the reaction of King William. In the autumn of 1085 the Conqueror rushed across the Channel to England, bringing with him what the Chronicle calls 'a larger force of mounted men and infantry from France and Brittany than had ever come to this country'. Whether or not that assessment included the invasion force of 1066, the king's army in 1085 was unquestionably massive: John of Worcester writes of 'many thousands of paid troops, footsoldiers and archers', while Malmesbury calls it 'a great multitude of knights serving for pay, from every province this side of the Alps'. William, he says, had even engaged the services of the French king's brother, Hugh of Vermandois, along with all his knights.[9]

We can well believe that Malmesbury was right, therefore, when he said 'the king was very scared'. William's first action on arriving in England was to summon an emergency council of magnates to debate how to deal with the crisis. The first and most pressing consideration was what to do with the mercenary army. Unlike every other force William had brought to England, their job was not to harry the kingdom but to defend it, and as such they could not resort to the usual medieval practice of living off the land at the expense of its inhabitants. 'People wondered how this country could maintain all that army', says the Chronicle. The solution arrived at in council – proposed, says Malmesbury, by Archbishop Lanfranc – was to disperse the troops all over the kingdom. 'All agreed that the households of the magnates should be reinforced by the presence of knights, so that if need be everyone could unite to defend the public weal and private fortunes against the barbarian.' As Malmesbury's account makes clear, this made the magnates themselves responsible for the mercenaries' every need. Bishop Wulfstan of Worcester, for example, 'began to maintain a sizeable force, keeping them happy with high pay and filling them up with choice food'.[10]

It was not just the poor magnates who suffered. 'People had much oppression that year', recalls the Anglo-Saxon Chronicle, 'and the king had the land near the sea laid waste, so that if his enemies landed, they should have nothing to seize.' According to an early twelfth-century source, William also ordered the coastline to be closely guarded; castles were strengthened and town walls repaired and manned. The towns themselves were required, like the magnates, to billet large numbers of French mercenaries, to the extent that there was hardly enough room left for their English inhabitants.

So, as the days grew shorter and autumn turned to winter, England entered a state of high tension. As in 1066, the whole kingdom held its breath and waited for news. Then, shortly before Christmas, news came. 'The king found out for a fact that his enemies had been hindered', says the Anglo-Saxon Chronicle, 'and could not carry out their expedition.' It was only a temporary reprieve – Cnut had apparently decided to delay his invasion until the new year – but it must have eased the tension a little. William responded by sending some of his mercenary troops back to the Continent. Others, however, he kept in England throughout the winter, indicating that the fear of invasion remained.

Christmas 1085, which the king once again kept at Gloucester, must therefore have been a stressed affair, with the thought of the ongoing Danish threat never far from the minds of the assembled magnates. William revealed his own anxiety at this time by dismissing from office the abbots of Crowland and Thorney, a pair of neighbouring monasteries in the Fens. This, of course, was a region where the Danes had landed in the recent past and received considerable support from the local population – not least the local monks. Not wanting another Ely on his hands, and evidently doubting the loyalty of Crowland's and Thorney's existing abbots, the king replaced them with two monks from the Norman abbey of St Wandrille.[11]

The Christmas court at Gloucester lasted five days, says the Anglo-Saxon Chronicle, the Church council that followed a further three. The Chronicle then goes on to tell us what happened next:

> After this, the king had much thought and deep discussion with his council about the country – how it was occupied and with what sort of people. Then he sent his men over all England into every shire and had them find out how many hundred

hides there were in the shire, or what land and cattle the king himself had in the country, or what dues he ought to have in twelve months from the shire. Also he had a record made of how much land his archbishops had, and his bishops and abbots, and his earls, and – though I relate it at too great length – what or how much everybody had who was occupying land in England, in land or cattle, and how much money it was worth. So very narrowly did he have it investigated, that there was no single hide nor yard of land, nor indeed (it is a shame to relate but it seemed no shame to him to do) one ox nor one cow nor one pig was there left out, and not put down in his record.

Such is the Chronicle's description of the Domesday Survey, which produced the Domesday Book, one of the most famous documents in English history (in terms of celebrity only Magna Carta trumps it), and certainly the most voluminous. It is, in fact, two volumes: a large one, called Great Domesday, and a smaller one, known as Little Domesday. Between them they contain 832 folios, filled on both sides with closely written, abbreviated text, and containing somewhere in the region of two million words.[12] Because of its vast size Domesday is, and always has been, unique. A handful of subsidiary documents relating to the survey have survived – sectional drafts which scholars have dubbed 'satellites' – but the book itself, in two volumes, survives only as a single copy. It is, without question, the most important document in English history, for, as the Anglo-Saxon Chronicle indicates, it contains the results of an inquest of unparalleled scope and magnitude: a kingdom-wide investigation of rights, dues, land and economic assets, which produced the single greatest description of a pre-industrial society anywhere in the world.

Hence, of course, its ominous name. During the twelfth century, Domesday was kept in the royal treasury at Winchester, and so initially government officials referred to it as 'the book of the Exchequer', 'the great book of Winchester', or simply 'the king's book'. But, as one of those officials noted in the 1170s, 'this book is called by the natives "Domesday" – that is, by metaphor, the Day of Judgement'. One suspects that this English nickname had existed from the very beginning, because ample other evidence exists to indicate that William's inquiry left contemporaries awestruck. Part of the reason for their astonishment must have been the speed with which the project was carried out. Begun soon after Christmas 1085, it was apparently completed before 1 August the following year. Producing the final draft of Great Domesday took somewhat longer, but the survey itself was accomplished in a little over six months.[13]

Why the Conqueror launched this great investigation in the winter of 1085 is a question that has long been debated by historians. Given its timing, few have been content to believe that it was merely an act of royal curiosity, and most would link its origins to the ongoing threat of invasion. Exactly how the two events were linked, however, remains a matter of dispute. Despite over a century of rigorous scholarship, there is still no consensus as to what the Domesday Book was for.

By looking at the book itself, the satellites, and the comments of contemporary chroniclers, we can at least understand something of how the survey was made. As the Anglo-Saxon Chronicle indicates, it began with William sending commissioners into every shire, and from the Domesday documents themselves we can see that the shires were grouped into at least seven circuits (mostly consisting of five counties each, but in one case containing only three). For one particular circuit we can see that there were four commissioners, so overall there were probably no more than thirty or so men directly responsible for compiling the Domesday data.

Providentially, thanks to a document known as the Ely Inquest, we also appear to have a list of the questions to which these commissioners were required to find answers. From these we see that the principal unit that Domesday was concerned with was the manor – a term that appears to have been coined after the Conquest, which signified something like 'individual lordly estate'. The commissioners began with the basics: what was the manor called? Who held it in the time of Edward the Confessor, and who holds it now? They then moved on to specifics: how many hides of land are there? How many ploughs? How many slaves? How many freemen? They also asked about natural resources: how much woodland was there? How much meadow? How much pasture? Lastly they asked about value: how much was it worth then? How much is it worth now?[14]

This is just a selection from the total list of twenty questions given in the Ely Inquest, all of which had to be posed in the case of each individual manor. Domesday contains many, many entries: at a rough estimate it mentions about 13,000 places and around

30,000 manors.[15] The thirty or so Domesday commissioners, we assume, must have had many assistants. But, even so, how could they possibly have compiled all this information in just six months?

Part of the answer was that they relied on that perennial government time-saver, self-assessment. Tenants-in-chief – those who held their land directly from the king – seem to have been required to supply the commissioners with written returns; in some instances we can see their fossilized form in the pages of the Domesday Book itself. The commissioners could also have obtained a lot of information quickly from existing written records. Eleventh-century England, it bears repeating, was a much-governed country, a medieval bureaucratic state. By turning to earlier surveys and tax rolls, many answers could be uncovered, especially those relating to the time of Edward the Confessor.[16]

Had Domesday involved no more than this, it would probably have generated little comment – indeed, it would have been just another royal survey in the Anglo-Saxon tradition. It would also have had little value, because self-assessment by the landowners would have inevitably delivered a skewed result. But Domesday involved a great deal more, and is a great deal more valuable, because all the written evidence assembled, whether from self-assessment or government archives, was subjected to public scrutiny. During the spring of 1086, in every county, extraordinary sessions of the shire court were convened, to which an extraordinary number of witnesses were summoned. Principally these were jurors selected from every hundred, or wapentake. In Cambridgeshire, for example, each of the county's fifteen hundreds sent eight jurors, including in every case the head of the hundred (the reeve) and a local priest: a total of 120 men. This total is likely to have been low compared to the national average: other counties contained more hundreds, and the juries they sent probably numbered the more typical twelve.[17]

But the hundred jurors, while seemingly the most important, were not the only ones required to give evidence. The landowners were also summoned in order to defend their written assessments against the jurors' oral testimony, and there were also other types of juries, some representing the shire as a whole, some its most important towns, some its monastic communities. According to the Ely Inquest, every *settlement* (vill) was required to send an eight-man jury, and this statement receives support from the villeins who appear, on two occasions, as witnesses in the Domesday Book. At the very least, therefore – counting only the jurors drawn from the hundreds, shires and boroughs – the survey involved the participation of around 8,000 people; if it really involved juries from every settlement, the number rises to somewhere in excess of 60,000. Each county assembly therefore involved hundreds, possibly thousands, of people, making these meetings far larger than the regular sessions of the shire court, and larger even than the great land pleas (like Penenden Heath) held earlier in William's reign. One imagines it was these giant gatherings that had the greatest impact on the popular consciousness, and gave rise to the name 'Domesday'.[18]

The jurors were almost certainly required to answer all the commissioners' questions, including those about the economic assets of a particular manor: from time to time Domesday records their objection to a landlord's valuation.[19] The crucial questions put to them, however, related to ownership: who held the land during the time of Edward the Confessor, and who holds it now? As we've seen, the Norman colonization of England had been a sporadic, piecemeal and confusing process, with land being granted out on two different and potentially conflicting principles, and plenty of property simply seized by those with the sharpest elbows.

In the Domesday sessions of the shire court, this process now came under the spotlight (which is, of course, how we come to know so much about it). In some areas there had been comparatively little disruption, because estates had been transferred unbroken from their former English owner to a Norman newcomer. But Domesday reveals that only a minority of properties had been reallocated in this way – something like ten per cent of the total. A much larger amount of land – over a third of all the land in England – had been granted out on a territorial basis, paying no regard whatsoever to previous patterns of ownership. In the case of the remaining lands, there is no clear pattern of redistribution, suggesting that in these areas the Normans had been helping themselves.[20]

Hence the thousands of doubtful or contested claims in Domesday. In some instances the jurors validated the right of a particular land-owner, testifying that they had seen the original royal writ that ordered the owner to be put in possession. But very often they said they had seen no such writ, and had no idea by what right the defendant came to be holding the estate in question. Sometimes rival claimants came forward to contest a property. In Hampshire, for example, that notorious predator, Picot the Sheriff ('a hungry lion, a roving wolf, a crafty fox . . .') had his title to a small parcel of land in Charford challenged by a fellow Norman named William de Chernet. William, it is recorded, 'brought his testimony for this from the better and old men from all the county and hundred. Picot contradicted this with his testimony from the villeins, common people, and reeves.' Sadly, but typically, we do not know who won, but in general Picot was very successful in hanging on to his acquisitions.[21]

Part of the purpose of the Domesday Survey, therefore, was to sort out precisely this sort of tenurial confusion – the net result of twenty years of Norman colonization which had been at best opportunistic and at worst downright rapacious. Richard fitz Nigel, the twelfth-century official who first recorded the name 'Domesday', thought that the book had been made 'so that each man, being content with his own rights, should not with impunity usurp the rights of another', and there is much to be said for this. Every effort had been made to ensure that the final judgement was as fair as possible. Not only were the jurors summoned to provide a check on the landlords, the names of the jurors, where known, reveal a fifty–fifty split between Englishmen and Frenchmen (thus in Cambridgeshire, each eight-man hundred jury has four English and four French jurors apiece). This ethnic balance meant, of course, that neither nation could use Domesday as an opportunity to settle old scores, but it also implies that ways to ensure the fairness of the survey had been worked out at the very highest level. Similarly revealing is a short, contemporary description of the Domesday Survey by the bishop of Hereford, which states that a second set of commissioners was sent around the country to check the work of the first, and, if necessary, to denounce its authors as guilty to the king. The second team, we are told, were sent into regions where they themselves held no land – another obvious anti-corruption measure – and this, so far as we can judge, was true of their fore-runners too.[22]

The question that inevitably arises, though, is why this problem could not have waited. Sorting out property disputes was unques-tionably important, for left unresolved they might ultimately lead to violence between rival landlords; clearly, some degree of order had to be imposed. But why did this take priority at a time when the country was threatened with invasion? After all, if the Danes were successful, any record of who owned what in England would be out of date almost before the ink had dried. That the threat of invasion still hung over England at the time of the inquest is implicit in William's decision to retain some of his French mercenaries throughout the winter. Indeed, in one or two instances we seem to see these troops in the Domesday Book, garrisoned in towns such as Southampton and Bury St Edmunds.[23]

The mercenaries themselves provide a further clue as to the survey's purpose. Soldiers of fortune, by their very nature, rarely come cheap. By dispersing his great army around the country in 1085, William had passed some of its cost on to his magnates, but not all. Many troops had also been quartered on royal estates and towns, and the same situation must have obtained into 1086, requiring the king to find large sums of money to retain the men who remained in his service.

Earlier English kings had obtained such large sums by taxing their subjects. The geld, as we've seen, had been collected since the late tenth century, first to buy off Danish invaders with tribute, and later to maintain a mercenary fleet in order to guard against future attacks. Edward the Confessor had ostentatiously done away with this fleet in 1051 and ceased to collect the money to pay for it, but it seems unlikely that he abolished the geld entirely. The Anglo–Saxon Chronicle's comment that the tax for the fleet 'always came before other taxes' implies that other forms of geld existed, and these almost certainly continued to be levied on an annual basis for the rest of the Confessor's reign. The sudden reappearance of geld in the Anglo-Saxon Chronicle within days of William's coronation is thus to be explained by its heavy rate rather than its sudden revival.[24]

By 1066, however, the geld was no longer the great cash cow it had once been. This was partly because successive kings had run down the system of assessment. Geld was calculated on the basis of the number of hides a particular estate or community contained, so by reducing this number a king could show political favour. By the reign of Edward the Confessor many hundreds – which notionally ought to have contained one hundred hides – were assessed at considerably less. A surviving geld roll for Northamptonshire, drawn up in the 1070s but recording the situation in Edward's day, shows some hundreds containing eighty hides, others sixty-two hides, and in one case as few as forty. Thus in 1066 the total number of hides in Northamptonshire's thirty-two hundreds was not 3,200, but 2,663. This erosion, moreover, had continued after the Conquest. Domesday reveals that by 1086 the hidation of Northamptonshire had fallen to just 1,250.[25]

Nor was that the limit of the problem, because only a fraction of the hides in this much-diminished rump actually paid geld. In every hundred in Northamptonshire, the same geld roll shows that large numbers of hides – in some cases up to half the total – had been written off as 'waste'. This word, which also occurs over and over again in the Domesday Book, has been interpreted in recent times merely as a term of administrative convenience, used indiscriminately by royal officials to describe land which, for whatever reason, paid no geld. But most historians today would argue that waste (*vasta*) had a specific meaning, and indicated land that had been ruined – devastated – as a result of the Conquest. A thoroughgoing analysis of the word's use in Domesday shows a quite precise correlation with those areas visited by the Conqueror's armies in the years immediately after 1066. Thus we find high concentrations of waste in Sussex, particularly in the rape of Hastings, as well as in the counties along the Welsh border, harried in the period 1069–70. We see it in the coastal areas that William had strategically ravaged in 1085, and we also see it in cities. In Lincoln, Domesday records that there were 970 inhabited dwellings before the Conquest, but afterwards 240 of them were waste: 166 had been destroyed 'on account of the castle', the remainder 'because of misfortune and poverty and the ravages of fire'. Similar accounts equating waste with the construction of castles are found for Norwich, Shrewsbury, Stamford, Wallingford and Warwick. When Earl Hugh received Chester, says Domesday, almost half its houses had been destroyed, and the city had lost a third of its value, 'for it had been greatly wasted'.[26]

None of this, however, compares to the amount of waste recorded for Yorkshire, which accounts for over eighty per cent of Domesday's total for the whole country. This goes a long way to substantiating the chronicle accounts of the Harrying of the North and the scale of the destruction caused by the Conqueror's armies in the winter of

1069–70. According to Simeon of Durham, the region between Durham and York lay uncultivated for the next nine years, with every settlement uninhabited; William of Malmesbury, writing in the 1120s, declared that the soil there was still bare in his own day. Shockingly, Domesday reveals that in 1086 the population of Yorkshire had dropped to just a quarter of what it had been in 1066, meaning that around 150,000 people had vanished from the record. For once, it seems, the six-figure numbers given by the chroniclers corresponded all too closely with reality.[27]

Some areas of the country, it is true, seem to have recovered in the twenty years between 1066 and 1086. Whereas, for example, the average value of manors in Yorkshire had plummeted by over sixty-five per cent, in Norfolk it had risen by an impressive thirty-eight per cent. It would be wrong, however, to read too rosy a picture into such rises, for the value of a Domesday manor was the value to its lord in rents, and there is ample evidence to indicate that new Norman lords had racked up rents to intolerably high levels. Domesday abounds with complaints about rents being oppressive, exceeding the actual value of the land (a famous entry records that Marsh Gibbon in Buckinghamshire was held by its English farmer, Æthelric, 'in heaviness and misery'). According to the Anglo-Saxon Chronicle, such oppressive practices originated at the very top:

> The king gave his land as dearly for rent as he possibly could; then came another man and offered more than the first, and the king let it go to the man who had offered more; then came a third and offered still more, and the king gave it up to the man who had offered most of all. And he did not care at all how very wrongfully the reeves got it from poor men, nor how many illegal acts they did.

The Normans appear to have been uniformly rapacious in pursuit of profit: elsewhere the Chronicle laments that 'the king and his leading men were fond, yea, too fond, of avarice: they coveted gold and silver, and did not care how sinfully it was obtained'. The final question of the Domesday commissioners, as preserved in the Ely Inquest, was whether more could be taken from an estate than was currently being taken.[28]

For this reason, where the Domesday Book shows a fall in

manorial values in areas *not* associated with widespread ravaging, we can be fairly certain that this was not due to leniency on the part of the landlords. In certain counties it has been shown that the sharpest falls in value coincide quite precisely with brand-new Norman lordships – the kind carved out from scratch, with no reference to previous landholding patterns. One view is that this reorganization process was so disruptive that it caused a drop in economic output. A more likely reason is that new manors had been constructed on a new model, more favourable to the lords and more oppressive for the peasantry. For it is also in these counties that we witness dramatic falls in the number of free peasants. In Cambridgeshire, for example, the number of freemen plummeted from 900 to 177; in Bedfordshire from 700 to 90, and in Hertfordshire from 240 to 43. At the same time, we discover that the number of servile peasants has rocketed. Frequently in Domesday we find the phrase 'he is now a villein'.[29]

Values were only lower in these areas, it seems, because the before-and-after figures record different realities. Those for the pre-Conquest period had been calculated by combining the incomes of all the various English freeholders on a particular estate; the figures for 1086, by contrast, simply represented the income the new Norman lord derived in rent, having forced these former freemen into financial servitude. This was a bad bargain for the small landowners, but after the Conquest their bargaining power was not strong. The Anglo-Saxon Chronicle says at one point that the Normans 'imposed unjust tolls and did many injustices which are hard to reckon up'. The tenurial revolution, in short, had prompted a social revolution. English society, in certain areas at least, was a lot less free after the Conquest than it had been before.[30]

Yet even as lords were driving up profits, they were paying less and less money to the king. At some stage, probably during the reign of the Conqueror himself, land held in demesne had been made exempt from paying geld. We see this, for instance, in the Northamptonshire geld roll, where hides held in demesne, like those listed as waste, are treated separately from those that actually paid. As the reign continued, the concessions appear to have increased, so much so that by the 1080s some tenants-in-chief were paying almost no tax at all. Indeed, in some cases, they may even have collected the geld from their demesnes and kept it for themselves.[31]

Small wonder, then, that revenue from the geld was not all it had once been. Concessions to individuals and communities had led to a massive reduction in the number of hides, and many more had been written off as waste as a result of war and destruction; the Conqueror himself had exempted the demesne land of his tenants-in-chief, and established a further tax-free zone in the form of the Forest. All of these factors had punched great holes in the money-getting system created by England's pre-Conquest kings. Added to this there was also outright refusal to pay: 'From 6½ hides at Norton,' records the Northamptonshire geld roll, 'not a penny has been received – Osmund the king's secretary owns that estate.'[32]

An obvious way to compensate for the system's shortcomings was to try to get more geld from hides which were still liable. In 1084, William had ordered a geld at three times the normal rate (six shillings per hide rather than the usual two), probably intending to use the money it raised to finance his ongoing war in Maine. The Anglo-Saxon Chronicle recorded this hike with horror, describing the tax as 'heavy and severe', and no doubt it was for the limited number of people who had to pay it. At the same time, we have no way of knowing how lucrative it was. Given the manifold inadequacies of the system by this date, and coming hard on the heels of the 1082 famine, the yield may have been disappointing, even though the rate was exceedingly harsh.[33]

The final straw may have come in the autumn of 1085, with the decision to break up the massive mercenary army and billet it around the kingdom. 'The king had the host dispersed all over the country among his vassals', says the Anglo-Saxon Chronicle, 'and they provisioned the army each in proportion to his land.' If the government used the geld lists to try to arrive at this proportional distribution – and it is hard to see how they could have used anything else – then the billeting arrangements would have been no more equitable than a levy of the geld. By the time of the Christmas court, therefore, there may have been many voices being raised in protest, and a realization on William's part that the system needed to be fixed, in order that future gelds brought in more money, and that any future billeting would be fairer. And part of the Domesday process *was* an inquiry into the workings of the geld – we can see as much from the circuit return for the south-western shires known as Exon Domesday. An overhaul of the geld system would explain why the survey was so interested in lordly resources: the king was trying to discover precisely where the profits of lordship were going, perhaps with a view to reversing the exemption of demesne. Lastly, a fiscal motive for Domesday would also explain why William felt it was necessary to establish exactly who owned what, for – as those responsible for its administration must surely have attested – it is difficult to collect a land tax when landholding itself is in dispute.[34]

Such was the conclusion of early Domesday scholars: the Conqueror's survey was a tax inquiry, intended to remedy the manifold defects of the geld system. As the greatest of all these scholars, Frederick William Maitland, wrote in his *Domesday Book and Beyond* (1897): 'Our record is no register of title, it is no feodary, it is no custumal, it is no rent-roll; it is a tax book, a geld book.' Even today, more than a century after Maitland's death, many experts would argue that fiscal reform was the primary purpose of the Domesday Survey.[35]

And yet it cannot have been the purpose of the Domesday *Book*. As anyone who has ever tried to do so will readily attest, it is all but impossible to use the book as a tool for assessing geld, because of the way its contents are organized. Geld was national, public tax, administered using public institutions: collectors moved from settlement to settlement within each hundred, and from hundred to hundred within each shire, in order to gather in the money. The Domesday commissioners, as we have seen, had used the same public institutions to gather information, summoning juries from hundreds and townships in order to check the written returns provided by individual landowners. But, crucially, when this information came to be compiled and written up for each of the survey's seven circuits, it was not arranged by hundred and vill. Instead, it was laboriously rearranged – by landowner. Both the surviving circuit returns (Exon Domesday and Little Domesday) are arranged in this fashion, as is the final redaction of the data in Great Domesday. It is an arrangement that makes it fantastically difficult to calculate geld payments; to work out the liability of a particular landowner requires hours of calculations.[36] In conclusion, therefore, there is no doubt that a geld inquiry was launched in 1086, and little doubt that a reform of the geld was high on the agenda. Some of the information collected by the Domesday commissioners may have been intended for such a reform. But the selection and arrangement of data in the

Domesday Book indicates that it must have been made for a different reason.

While the commissioners had been gathering their data, assembling jurors and landowners in their hundreds and thousands, King William had been travelling around his kingdom (or at least its southern part). At Easter (5 April), by which time the sessions of the shire courts must either have been well advanced or already over, he wore his crown at Winchester. By Whitsun (24 May), when he was at Westminster for the knighting of his youngest son, Henry, the king must have had a clear idea of when the survey would be completed. As John of Worcester explains, 'shortly afterwards, he ordered his archbishops, bishops, abbots, earls, barons, sheriffs and their knights to meet him on 1 August at Salisbury'. This was to be the last and greatest meeting of 1086 – an assembly for the whole kingdom, the culmination of the Domesday process.[37]

Salisbury was not in the same place in 1086 as it is today (the present city is a new foundation of the thirteenth century). In the Conqueror's time it lay two miles to the north, on the site now known as Old Sarum. The Normans had been drawn to this location from an early date. William had established a castle there, probably before 1070, and the bishop of Sherborne had subsequently moved his cathedral to stand alongside it, thereby becoming the bishop of Salisbury. The site's attraction in 1086 may have had more to do with its prehistoric past, for Old Sarum is one of the most impressive Iron Age hill forts – both castle and cathedral were planted in the centre of a massive enclosure, 400 metres across, surrounded by an earthen rampart that runs for over a kilometre. It was the exactly the right kind of location, in other words, for the sort of large-scale open-air assembly that the Conqueror had in mind.[38]

For the meeting at Salisbury was massive. 'There his counsellors came to him,' says the Anglo-Saxon Chronicle, 'and all the people occupying land who were of any account all over England.' To give us some idea of what that might mean in terms of numbers, we can turn to Domesday. The book names around 1,000 individuals who held their land directly from the king – his tenants-in-chief. Their direct connection with the king, and (in most cases) their superior wealth and status meant that most if not all of them would have attended. Domesday also records a further 8,000 or so landowners at the next stage down – i.e. the tenants of the tenants-in-chief, or the king's subtenants. How many of these men might have come to Salisbury is open to debate. Some of them were as wealthy, or even wealthier, than the lesser tenants-in-chief, and so would correspond to the Chronicle's notion of 'people of account'. But many others were considerably less wealthy, with half of them owning land worth less than £1 a year, and so might be reckoned to lie outside of that description. Depending on how strictly the king's summons was interpreted, therefore, we should imagine an attendance figure well into four figures, and just possibly nudging towards five.[39]

The impression of an exceptionally large meeting is reinforced by the composition of William's court. Sadly, we have no record from the day of the Salisbury assembly itself, but we do have a document issued at another location in Wiltshire, datable to the middle of 1086, with a witness-list that suggests it was drawn up at a time very close to the event. Alongside the Conqueror stand his two younger sons – the newly knighted Henry and his older brother, William Rufus. Then come the higher clergy: Archbishop Lanfranc of Canterbury, Archbishop Thomas of York, and with them the bishops of Durham, Winchester, Lincoln, Chester, Hereford, Salisbury and London. The great lay magnates come next, a list of eighteen names. Odo, still confined to his cell in Rouen, is notably not among their number; but William's other half-brother, Robert, is present, along with the king's lifelong friend, Roger of Montgomery. Also among the throng of laymen we see Richard fitz Gilbert, lord of Tonbridge, the greatest landowner in south-eastern England; Henry de Ferrers, a great baron from northern England, and Robert of Rhuddlan, the conqueror of north Wales. Another name that leaps out from the list is Abbot Thurstan of Glastonbury, whose massacre of his own monks just three years earlier was evidently no bar to his attendance at court.[40]

It is an impressive roll call – one of the greatest we have seen since the coronation of Queen Matilda in May 1068. Yet what a change has been wrought in the intervening eighteen years. Royal charters issued at the time of Matilda's coronation reveal a mix of English and French names, with the majority being English. But in 1086 the English are gone, and the list is exclusively Norman (or at least, in the case of the bishops, Continental). In 1068 ten of England's

fifteen bishoprics had been held by Englishmen, three of the remaining
five having been given to Germans by Edward the Confessor and
only two recently filled by the Conqueror. But by the time of the
Domesday Survey only one English bishop – the wily and venerable
Wulfstan of Worcester – remained in office. As for the English aristocracy, the eclipse is total. The three native earls who witnessed in
1068 were all long gone by 1086: Eadwine murdered, Waltheof
executed, and Morcar still languishing in prison. Also gone are the
lesser English nobles present at the queen's coronation – men with
names like Æthelhead, Tovi, Dinni, Ælfgeard, Bondig, Wulfweard,
Herding, Brixi and Brihtric. When we turn to the witnesses of 1086,
there is not a single English name among them.[41]

What is true of the court, moreover, is also true of the country.
Of Domesday's 1,000 tenants-in-chief, a mere thirteen are English;
only four have lands worth more than £100 and the wealthiest,
Edward of Salisbury, despite his English name, may well have been
half-Norman. The king's thegns – the ninety or so lords who had
each owned more than forty hides of land – were all gone. Even
when we descend to the next tenurial level, where we start to find
natives in more significant numbers, they remain very much in the
minority. Of the 8,000 or so subtenants recorded in the survey, only
around ten per cent are English, and, as with the tenants-in-chief,
the survivors are small fry – men like Æthelric of Marsh Gibbon,
holding 'in heaviness and misery'. England's middling thegns, who
had numbered around 4,000–5,000, have been swept clean away.[42]

Domesday therefore reveals cataclysmic change to the composition of England's ruling class, with Normans replacing native lords
in almost every village and hamlet. It also, moreover, reveals dramatic
changes within that class in the distribution of material wealth.
Put simply, there were more super-rich men in Domesday England
than there had been twenty years earlier. Whereas in 1066 there
had been several thousand middling English thegns, by 1086 half
the land in England was held by just 200 Norman barons.[43] Having
in most cases obtained the estates of multiple English predecessors,
these newcomers were many times more wealthy. In Edward the
Confessor's day, for example, only thirty-seven individuals had held
lands with an annual value of more than £100; by the time of the
Domesday survey the number of such men had more than doubled
to eighty-one.[44] At the very top, the spoils of Conquest had been

colossal. Half the country was in the hands of 200 barons, but half that half – i.e. a quarter of all the land in England – was held by just ten new magnates. Their names are by now a predictable roll call of William's friends and family: Odo and Robert, Roger of Montgomery, Richard fitz Gilbert, Hugh of Chester . . . Orderic Vitalis had not exaggerated when he said that the Conqueror had raised his dependants to high rank and heaped great honours upon them. 'He was a great lover of the world and of Worldly pomp,' said Orderic of Earl Hugh, 'lavish to the point of prodigality, a lover of games and luxuries, actors, horses and dogs.' With 300 manors in Domesday valued at £800 a year, he could well afford to be.[45]

And yet, obscenely rich as Hugh and his ilk had become, their wealth and power paled in comparison with that of the English earls before the Conquest. At the start of Edward the Confessor's reign, Godwine of Wessex, Leofric of Mercia and Siward of Northumbria had towered above the rest of the English nobility: collectively the land held by these three men and their families was equal in value to that of the king himself.[46] Towards the end of the Confessor's reign, of course, the Godwinesons had expanded their power at the expense of the others, obtaining a monopoly of earldoms that made them quite unassailable. But even the house of Leofric, marginalized as they became, had remained immensely rich and powerful. Earl Ælfgar had been able to defy the king successfully on two separate occasions during the 1050s, fighting his way back from exile by raising mercenary fleets.

England's post-Conquest earls were not nearly so mighty. Even the richest of them – say, for the sake of argument, Odo of Bayeux – could not hold a candle to the likes of Earl Ælfgar. And Odo, of course, had fallen, in part because he was perceived by his half-brother to be too tall a poppy. So too had Roger of Hereford and Ralph of East Anglia, whose rebellion seems to have been provoked by the perceived diminution of their power. By 1086 there were only two earls left in England – Roger of Montgomery and Hugh of Chester – and they, despite their gigantic wealth, were pygmies compared to their English predecessors. After the Conquest, no coalition of magnates, however large, could match the resources of the king. Even if we take the top ten magnates of Domesday England and combine their incomes, the total falls far short of

William's own – a staggering £12,600 – for the king had twice as much land as all of them put together.[47]

Supremely powerful as he was, the assembly at Salisbury was set to make the king more powerful still. William had summoned England's landholding class to participate in a great ceremony. 'They all submitted to him,' says the Anglo-Saxon Chronicle, 'and became his men, and swore oaths of allegiance to him, that they would be loyal to him against all other men.' This, it has been persuasively argued, was the climactic moment of the Domesday process, intimately connected with the true purpose of the book.

When the Chronicle says that the landowners became William's men, it is describing an act of homage – a personal submission to a lord, in return for which the lord usually recognized the man's right to hold particular lands. Many of William's men, of course, had already been bound to him in this way for decades. But the security they received would have been for their ancestral estates in Normandy, not their acquisitions in England. Plenty of land in England, as we've seen, had been obtained by royal grant, but much had also been obtained by intimidation, encroachment and violence. Because the process of acquisition had been so protracted, chaotic and in places illegal, few if any Norman lords at the start of the Domesday process could have produced written evidence of title to all their estates.

But Domesday, once complete, provided precisely that written evidence. The Anglo-Saxon Chronicle rounds off its famous description of the survey by saying 'all the writings were subsequently brought to him', and this is almost certainly its laconic way of describing the presentation to William of each of the seven circuit returns at the Salisbury assembly (one of the returns, Exon Domesday, contains an entry that was emended as a result of a decision taken during the course of the king's visit). The landowners, therefore – or at least the tenants-in-chief – did homage to William at Salisbury, and he, in return, was able to present them with Domesday's circuit returns as a written record of their landholdings. That the twelfth-century chronicler Henry of Huntingdon, translating this passage of the Anglo-Saxon Chronicle into Latin, chose to render the word 'writings' as 'charters' is entirely apt. Together these documents were a kind of giant charter of confirmation, giving the Norman newcomers the security of title they needed to guarantee their personal conquests.[48]

But if the barons gained much from the bargain, the king gained more. It is a matter of huge moment that William regarded every landowner in England as holding their land from him, either directly as a tenant-in-chief or indirectly as the tenant of an intermediate lord, for the kings of pre-Conquest England had enjoyed no such monopoly. Before 1066, as we've seen, lordship and landholding did not automatically go together; the king was landlord to some men but not to others, and some land was held of no lord at all. The same was also true, albeit to a lesser extent, of Normandy. Despite strenuous efforts by William himself to extend his seigneurial rights in the duchy prior to 1066, he enjoyed nothing like total superiority. It was the circumstances of the Conquest itself that meant that William was able in England to construct a new system from scratch. By treating all land as forfeit at the time of his accession, the king had been able to create an aristocracy bound in every case by strict terms of service, and similarly strict terms were imposed on the lands of the English Church.

The most visible type of service that the king expected was, of course, military service – that his tenants would supply him with the requisite number of knights when he demanded. But the relationship of lord and man gave William other rights too; rights which might be regarded as equally if not more valuable. When, for example, a tenant-in-chief died, his heir was obliged to pay the king a substantial sum of money (known as a relief) in order to enter into his inheritance. If the heir happened to be underage, as was often the case, the king took both him and the estate into his guardianship (wardship), enjoying the profits of the estate for the duration. If the heir happened to be female, the king had the right to arrange her marriage, and the same was true when a tenant-in-chief left a widow. Similar rights existed in the case of the Church: on the death of an abbot or bishop, the estates and revenues of his abbacy or bishopric were seized into the king's hands until a replacement was appointed (which, since the king also controlled the appointment process, might be a long time).

These rights, known to historians as 'feudal incidents', gave the person who exercised them enormous power. Not only did they hand him sizeable sums of money on a regular basis (nothing is so reliable as a tax on death); they also allowed him to shape the inheritance patterns of his tenants, by selling the wardships or marriages of heirs to men he wished to promote. Such rights had existed on the Continent prior to the Conquest, but their value varied according to two factors: the extent to which a lord's authority was acknowledged, and, within that, the extent of a lord's knowledge about the size and distribution of his tenant's estates.

This knowledge was precisely what Domesday gave to William. Thanks to the Conquest he had become the ultimate lord of every man in England; thanks to the survey he knew exactly who owned what and where it was located. The principle that all tenure began and ended with the king defines the very structure of the Domesday Book. Every county has its own chapter, and every chapter begins by listing the king's own lands in the shire. It then proceeds to list the lands of others – bishops, earls, barons, abbots – all of whom are described as holding their lands from the king. If a landowner died or, God help him, rebelled, the king's ministers could quickly indentify his estates, no matter how scattered they might be, and send in the sheriffs to seize them.[49]

This, then, seems to have been the purpose of the Domesday Book. It was a charter of confirmation for the landowners, giving them the security of title to their estates acquired by the rough and ready processes of conquest. It was also, simultaneously, a directory for royal administrators, enabling them to see at a glance who owned what, and giving them the ability to seize and deliver lands, and to charge accordingly. It was a powerful tool – a weapon, even – for an already powerful king, allowing him to exploit what has been called 'the most powerful royal lordship in medieval Europe'. Even the most determined critics of the concept of feudalism have to concede that England after the Conquest constitutes an exception to their arguments, coming close to matching the idealized model.[50]

Of course, the Domesday Book did not exist at the time of the Salisbury ceremony. The commissioners had worked flat out to get the circuit returns completed – each surviving example is the work of many hands. Great Domesday, by contrast, is the work of a single scribe. Probably working at Winchester, this anonymous individual performed the Herculean task of collating and condensing the data from the returns, with the aim of reducing it to a single volume. Most likely he started soon after the August assembly had ended:

despite recent controversy on the subject of its date, there can be no doubt that the Conqueror himself commanded the book's creation. A twelfth-century chronicler at Worcester, adding to the account of the Anglo-Saxon Chronicle, concluded 'the king ordered that all should be written in one volume, and that volume should be placed in his treasury at Winchester'.[51]

It is important to emphasize that the Domesday Book, for all its importance to both kings and scholars of the future, was probably just one output of the Domesday Survey. It gave William and his successors the means to manage their aristocracy more effectively than any other rulers in Europe, and to profit handsomely from this arrangement, but it did nothing to solve the pressing financial crisis that confronted the Conqueror in 1086. William needed money immediately, in sums of a magnitude that could be raised only by levying a national tax. It seems very likely that the other function of the Domesday Survey was to gather information with a view to reforming the geld. The king's desperate need for funds is shown by the fact that, while the Domesday Survey was in progress, royal tax collectors were also touring the country, exacting yet another punitive geld at the rate of 6 shillings per hide. Rounding off his description of the inquiry, the bishop of Hereford recalled how 'the land was vexed with much violence arising from the collection of royal taxes'.[52]

Violence; mass assemblies; the continuing threat of foreign invasion; mercenary troops billeted in every town and city; a nation waiting nervously on the brink: 1086 was in so many respects a terrible and portentous year, it is no wonder that people associated the king's great survey with God's Day of Judgement. 'This same year was very disastrous', concludes the Anglo-Saxon Chronicle,

and a very vexatious and anxious year throughout England, because of a pestilence among the livestock; and corn and fruits were at a standstill. It is difficult for anyone to realize what great misfortune was caused by the weather; so violent was the thunder and lightning that many were killed. Things steadily went from bad to worse for everybody. May God Almighty remedy it when it shall be His will!

And yet, by the time of the great assembly at Salisbury, the storm clouds had providentially cleared. Shortly before the ceremony on

1 August, news must have reached England that Cnut IV was dead. The Danish king had died on 10 July, murdered in church by his own rebellious nobles. His sudden passing meant that the threat of invasion was finally lifted. England was safe.[53]

But Normandy was not. During William's stay in England there had been some encouraging news from the duchy – notably in the case of the viscount of Le Mans, who had abandoned his stand at St Suzanne, crossed the Channel and made his peace. Developments elsewhere, however, were deeply disturbing. Cnut was dead but his ally, the count of Flanders, remained very much alive and unlikely to abandon his hostility. Robert Curthose had returned from his wanderings and was once again at the court of the king of France, ready to make trouble. Suddenly freed from his English crisis, the king moved swiftly. After taking as much additional money from his subjects as he could, says the Chronicle, he left Salisbury for the Isle of Wight, and from there sailed back to Normandy.

Meanwhile the single scribe responsible for making the Domesday Book sat down to his monumental task, condensing the information from the circuit returns to make the master volume. From the amount of work involved, experts have calculated that he must have persevered for at least a year. But as the end of his labours approached, with six circuits done and only one remaining, he suddenly put down his pen, leaving the final return unredacted. Hence nine centuries later we have Great Domesday Book in its unfinished state, and the original circuit return for the eastern counties – Little Domesday Book.[54]

Why the scribe stopped is anyone's guess: one plausible theory is that he did so because he heard the king was dead.

19

Death and Judgement

Although we cannot say for certain how tall he was or what he looked like, it is hard to think of William the Conqueror as anything other than a formidable figure. The Anglo-Saxon Chronicle describes him as 'a man of great wisdom and power, surpassing in honour and strength all those who had gone before him, and stern beyond measure to those who opposed his will'. Another contemporary source suggests that his voice was harsh, and William of Malmesbury tells us that he used it to good effect, employing colourful oaths 'so that the mere roar of his open mouth might somehow strike terror into the minds of his audience'.[1]

After his return to Normandy in 1086, however, it appears that such theatrics were not having the desired effect. William was by this stage in his late fifties, which made him old by contemporary standards. He was also, according to Orderic Vitalis, extremely fat – a condition not uncommon among medieval aristocrats later in life, as the exercise of hunting failed to counteract the quantities of venison consumed. Moreover, William's military reputation on the Continent had been nothing to brag about in recent years, following his defeats at Dol and Gerberoy. The king may have rushed home to defend his duchy from attack, but in the event his physical presence proved to be no deterrent.[2]

Trouble began in the Vexin, a region on Normandy's eastern border which had served as a buffer with France until Philip I had fortuitously acquired it ten years earlier. At some point in 1087, presumably on the French king's instructions, his garrison in the town of Mantes went on the offensive and made repeated raids into

Normandy. According to Orderic, whose account looks to be very well informed, they overran the diocese of Evreux, harrying the countryside, driving off cattle and seizing prisoners. They grew bold in their arrogance, he says, and taunted the Normans.[3]

And, if we believe William of Malmesbury, the cruellest taunt of all came from the lips of King Philip. 'The king of England lies in Rouen,' he allegedly joked, 'keeping his bed like a woman who's just had a baby.' William, the chronicler explains, had been confined to his capital for some time, on account of his stomach, for which he had taken a drug. Generally historians have understood this remark to refer simply to the Conqueror's obesity, but the mention of confinement, bed rest and medicine make it sound as if the king was physically ailing. It may have been knowledge of this, above all, that had caused his enemies to start snapping at his heels.

But Philip's insult, says Malmesbury, eventually reached William's own ears, and stirred him into action. 'When I go to Mass after my lying in,' he swore, 'I will offer a hundred thousand candles on his behalf.' This was a grim joke on the part of either the king or the chronicler, for towards the end of July 1087 William assembled an army and invaded the Vexin, setting fire to the fields, vineyards and orchards as he went. His principal target was Mantes, the town from which the recent French raids had been launched, and this too was put to the torch. The castle was burnt down, as were countless houses and churches. A great many people perished in the consuming flames, says Orderic, and notoriously (for several other chroniclers mention it) at least one of them was a religious recluse.

Inevitably, therefore, some monastic writers saw what subsequently happened to the Conqueror as divine retribution. 'A cruel deed he had done', says the Anglo-Saxon Chronicle, 'but a crueller fate befell him. How crueller? He fell sick and suffered terribly.' According to William of Malmesbury, some people said that the king was injured when his horse jumped a ditch, driving the front of its saddle into his overhanging stomach, but Malmesbury himself follows Orderic in stating that William succumbed to heat exhaustion caused by the flames and the warm summer weather. Quite possibly, since he appears to have been suffering since before the campaign's outset, William was simply beset by the return of his earlier illness. Whatever the cause, suddenly in great pain, he sounded the retreat and retired to Rouen.[4]

Back in the capital, it soon became clear that the Conqueror was dying, and all his doctors could do was try to minimize his discomfort. Orderic provides a long but gripping account of the king's final days, which he claims to have carefully investigated and truthfully described. Rouen, he says, was a crowded and noisy city, and so at his own command William was carried beyond its walls to the church of St Gervase which stood on a hill to the west. There he lingered for the rest of the summer, suffering terrible agonies but retaining the power of speech. 'I was brought up in arms from childhood', he groaned, 'and am deeply stained with all the blood I have shed.' These are, of course, Orderic's words rather than William's, but both statements are incontestably true. The king accordingly spent many hours confessing his sins to the bishops, abbots and monks who stood by his bedside, endeavouring to wash clean his soul. For the same reason he also commanded that his treasure be distributed among the poor and divided up among various churches, specifying precise sums for each, and paying particular attention to rebuilding the ones he had recently burnt down in Mantes. Finally he attempted to please God by ordering the release of all the prisoners in his custody – a list which included Earl Morcar and Earl Roger, Siward Barn, and even King Harold's brother, Wulfnoth, handed over as a hostage as long ago as 1051 and held captive ever since. The only exception to this general amnesty was Odo of Bayeux, whom William insisted was still too great a threat to be at liberty. But after incessant pleading by his other half-brother, Robert of Mortain, as well as various other Norman magnates, the king eventually relented, and Odo was also set free.[5]

During these last days the king also made known his wishes about the succession. Among the throng of magnates and priests by his bedside were his two younger sons, William Rufus and Henry. Robert Curthose chose to stay away, remaining at the court of the king of France. Yet despite this final slight and his own forebodings about the future, the Conqueror in the end felt compelled to recognize his eldest son as his heir. As the king allegedly explained to those present, Robert had been invested with Normandy in 1066 and had received the homage of its barons; such bonds could not be undone.

But this was true only of Normandy – England was not part of the inheritance, but an acquisition obtained by conquest. And because it had been won with so much blood, William declared that he dared not transmit it to anyone. 'I name no man as my heir to the kingdom of England,' he concluded, 'but entrust it to God alone.' Again, these are Orderic's words, but their content draws strong support from the fact that the king is known to have bequeathed the royal regalia he used in Normandy – his crown, rod, sceptre, chalice and candlesticks – not to any of his sons, but to his abbey of St Stephen's in Caen. He did, however, express a personal hope that William Rufus would succeed him as king of England, if that turned out to be God's will.

At last, on Thursday 9 September, the end came. Having slept peacefully through the previous night, William woke as the sun was rising over Rouen to the sound of a great bell tolling in the distance. On asking what time it was, he was informed that the hour of prime (6 a.m.) was being rung in the cathedral of St Mary. The king then raised his eyes and hands towards heaven, commended himself to Mary, and died.[6]

Because William had atoned so extensively during the previous weeks, Orderic felt that his death had been a noble one. The scenes that followed, however, were altogether lacking in nobility. Shortly before his death the king had sent William Rufus to England, armed with a letter to Archbishop Lanfranc that recommended he be crowned in his father's place. Henry, who had been promised a compensation prize of £5,000, also left before his father's death in order to secure his share of the spoils. Since there was still no sign of Robert Curthose when the Conqueror died a few days later, the result was pandemonium. Realizing that nobody was in charge, the wealthier men present rode off as quickly as they could to protect their properties, leaving the lesser attendants to loot the royal lodgings. Weapons, vessels, clothing and furnishings: all were carried off, says Orderic. By the time the frenzy was over, all that remained was the king's body lying almost naked on the floor.

The citizens of Rouen, meanwhile, had entered a state of collective panic, running around as if an enemy horde was at the gates and trying to secrete their valuables. Eventually the monks and clergy mustered the courage to form a procession out to St Gervase in order to perform a funeral service, during which the archbishop of Rouen declared that the king's body should be taken to Caen for burial. But since all the royal attendants had fled there was no one left to make the necessary arrangements; in the end a humble knight named Herluin paid out of his own pocket to have the corpse prepared and transported by boat. When the boat and its cargo reached Caen the citizens and clergy came out to meet it with a suitable display of reverence, but this too collapsed into confusion when a fire broke out in the town, causing almost everyone to rush back in order to put it out. Orderic does not draw the parallel, or indeed use the same language to describe the two episodes, but the similarities with the Conqueror's coronation are striking. As on that occasion, it was left to a handful of monks to complete the unfinished ritual, and William's corpse was carried to St Stephen's through scenes of conflagration.

Even the funeral was farcical. A distinguished crowd of bishops and abbots had assembled inside the abbey to lay the king to rest, and the bishop of Evreux preached a long and eloquent sermon, extolling William's many virtues. When he concluded, however, by asking the assembled crowd to forgive their former lord if he had ever done them any harm, an aggrieved local man stepped forward to complain in a loud voice that the land they were standing on had once belonged to his father, and had been violently seized by the Conqueror in order to provide for the abbey's foundation. Claiming the land for his own, he forbade the funeral to go any further. After a hurried inquiry established that he was telling the truth the protester was appeased by an immediate cash payment and the service continued. But the greatest indignity was reserved until last. When William was finally lowered into the ground, it became clear that his bloated corpse was too big for its stone sarcophagus, and efforts to press on regardless caused his swollen bowels to burst. No amount of frankincense and spices could hide the resultant stench, and the clergy therefore raced through the rest of the funeral rite before rushing back to their houses.[7]

Orderic, in conclusion, drew the simple lesson that death deals with rich and poor alike. William, he reminds us, had been a powerful and warlike king, feared by many peoples in various lands, yet in the end he was left naked and needing the charity of strangers. In life he had ruled wide dominions but in death he had no free plot in which to be buried, while his shameful burial showed how vain was the glory of the flesh. Orderic did not, however, seek to make any link between William's death and his character – quite the reverse, for he had begun his account of the king's last days by praising him as a good ruler: a lover of peace who had relied on wise counsellors, feared God and protected the Church.[8]

But no judgement on the Conqueror could be separated from the Conquest, and here naturally Orderic found praise more difficult. He accepted the Norman argument that William's claim to the throne was sound and that the invasion had been justified by Harold's perjury. But, as we have seen, as an Englishman he could not condone the way that the new king had mercilessly crushed the opposition to his rule. The Harrying of the North in particular Orderic saw as a terrible stain on William's record. 'I chastised a great multitude of men and women with the lash of starvation, and was, alas, the cruel murderer of many thousands' – such are the words that the chronicler puts into the king's mouth in his deathbed monologue. Orderic also distinguishes between the Conqueror, whom he thought noble and peace-loving, and the Normans as a whole, for whom he reserved less favourable language:

> They arrogantly abused their authority and mercilessly slaugh-
> tered the native people, like the scourge of God smiting them
> for their sins . . . Noble maidens were exposed to the insults
> of low-born soldiers and lamented their dishonouring by the
> scum of the earth . . . Ignorant parasites, made almost mad with
> pride, they were astonished that such great power had come
> to them and imagined that they were a law unto themselves.
> O fools and sinners! Why did they not ponder contritely in
> their hearts that they had conquered not by their own strength
> but by the will of almighty God, and had subdued a people
> that was greater and more wealthy than they were, with a longer
> history?[9]

Other chroniclers writing closer to the time had similarly negative things to say about the Conquest, and in some cases even harsher criticism. While those in France generally took vicarious pride in the Norman achievement, seeing it as a triumph of Frankish arms, elsewhere in Europe opinion was more mixed. A Bavarian writer called Frutolf of Michelsberg, for instance, thought that William had miserably attacked and conquered England, sending its bishops into exile and its nobles to their death. Worse still was the opinion of

another German, Wenric of Trier, who in 1080 lambasted Gregory
VII over his relationship with certain rulers. Some of the pope's
so-called friends, he said, had 'usurped kingdoms by the violence of
a tyrant, paved the road to the throne with blood, placed a blood-
stained crown on their heads, and established their rule with murder,
rape, butchery and torment'. No names are named, but the new
king of England is clearly the ruler intended: during the same year
Gregory himself wrote to William, lamenting the criticism he was
having to endure on account of his earlier support for the Conquest.[10]

Contemporary Englishmen, by contrast, had less to say on the
subject, probably because it was still too painful to contemplate. 'So
William became king', sighed Eadmer of Canterbury around the
turn of the eleventh century. 'What treatment he meted out to
those who managed to survive the great slaughter, I forbear to tell.'
The chief exception to this general reticence was the author of the
Anglo-Saxon Chronicle, whose obituary of William has been used
extensively in the preceding pages. Apparently written before 1100,
it provides a long, detailed and evidently well-informed assessment
of both the king and the Conquest. 'We shall write of him as we
have known him,' the chronicler says, 'we who have ourselves seen
him, and at one time dwelt in his court.' Like Orderic he praised
William for his wisdom and power, noting that in spite of his stern-
ness the king was kind to those who loved God. Religion, indeed,
had flourished during his reign; he himself had built a new abbey
at Battle, Canterbury Cathedral had been rebuilt, and so had many
others. With the same note of approval the chronicler recalled that
William had kept great state and maintained good order, imprisoning
rebels and castrating rapists. The Domesday Survey is described in
terms of awe, as is the king's authority within the British Isles: Wales
was in his dominion, and Scotland he had reduced to subjection by
his strength. Had he lived only two more years, the author reckoned,
William would have conquered Ireland as well.

But then the chronicler switches to a list of bad things, saying
'assuredly in his time men suffered grievous oppression and manifold
injuries'. Top of the list were the castles that the Conqueror caused
to be built 'which were a sore burden to the poor'. Then there was
his apparent avarice – the hundreds of pounds of gold and silver he
had taken from his subjects 'most unjustly and for little need'. Lastly
there was his introduction of the Forest, with its harsh law that

oppressed rich and poor alike. William, concluded the chronicler, was too relentless to care though all might hate him. If his subjects wanted to keep their lives and their lands they had to submit themselves wholly to his will.[11]

Even this fairly restricted summary of the Conqueror's reign indicates that in the space of two decades William and his followers had wrought enormous change. By 1087 no fewer than nine of England's fifteen ancient cathedrals had been burnt down or demolished and new Romanesque replacements were rising in their place. In the course of the next generation the remaining six would also be similarly rebuilt, along with every major abbey – the sole exception, of course, being the Confessor's abbey at Westminster, which had pre-empted the revolution. And it was a revolution, the single greatest in the history of English ecclesiastical architecture. Visit any of these churches today, and you will not find a single piece of standing pre-Conquest masonry. So total was the Norman renaissance that no cathedral was entirely rebuilt in England until the early thirteenth century, when Salisbury was moved from Sarum. The next wholesale rebuilding after that occurred in the seventeenth century, when Wren rebuilt St Paul's.[12]

A similar revolution had taken place in secular architecture with the introduction of castles. Again, with the exception of a handful of pre-Conquest examples built during the Confessor's reign, England had never witnessed anything like it, which explains the bitterness of the Chronicle's complaint. Famous royal fortresses like Windsor, Warwick, York, Norwich, Winchester, Newcastle, Colchester and the Tower of London – all of them had been founded by the Conqueror himself, along with scores of others too numerous to list. And that was just the royal ones. Across the country, wherever new Norman lords of any substance had settled, similar castles had been erected in their hundreds, to which their numerous surviving mottes and earthworks still bear witness. Because they are difficult to date with precision, the total number remains an estimate, but at a conservative count around 500 were in existence by 1100, the overwhelming majority having been built in the years immediately after 1066.[13] When we add to the castles and the cathedrals the disruption caused by the creation of the new royal forests, which displaced thousands of people from their homes, or the deliberate devastation of northern England, which killed many thousands more and effectively reduced

Yorkshire to a desert, it becomes easy to sympathize with the Chronicle's lament.

Some modern historians, however, would dismiss such changes as short-term or superficial. Economies might have been devastated but they soon recovered; cathedrals and castles were essentially a cosmetic change. Contemporary chroniclers might complain loudly but, living through the events they describe, they lack any long-term historical perspective. At a fundamental level, say the continuists, the Conquest changed very little.

But in advancing this argument, such historians, willingly or no, are effectively siding with the Normans themselves, for the line maintained by William and his followers was precisely that nothing had changed. The Conqueror came to the throne claiming to be the true heir of Edward the Confessor. At his coronation, as the Anglo-Saxon Chronicle recalled bitterly, the new king had sworn to rule England 'according to the best practice of his predecessors'. A short time later he assured the citizens of London that their laws would remain as they had been in the Confessor's day. And then, of course, there was the Domesday Book, which made every new Norman landowner the legal heir of one or more English predecessor, taking as its baseline 'the day on which King Edward was alive and dead'.

But this was all a fiction. In reality, William had succeeded not Edward but Harold, and to do so he had fought the Battle of Hastings, one of the bloodiest encounters in European history. Yet nowhere in the official record is this reality admitted, nor the changes that had taken place as a result. King Harold, for example, is almost totally expunged from the Norman account of the Conquest. Apart from a few writs issued at the very start of the reign, no official document accords him his royal title: he is simply Harold, or Earl Harold. In the Domesday Book his reign has been almost entirely airbrushed from the record, the scribe accidentally alluding to it only twice in two million words. This was not sour grapes but rigorous legal logic. If the Conqueror was the Confessor's direct heir, it followed that whatever had happened in the twelve months between Edward's death and William's accession must have been an aberration.[14]

The notion that nothing changed in 1066, in short, owes much to a rewriting of history by the Normans themselves. It was precisely what William wanted us to believe, such was his desire to be regarded as England's legitimate king. And for a long time historians did believe it. Until quite recently, those who had delved into the Domesday Book emerged greatly impressed by the scale of continuity it appeared to demonstrate, with every Norman newcomer stepping neatly into the space or spaces vacated by his English predecessors. It took the advent of computer-aided analysis to reveal that Domesday's formulae in fact conceal massive tenurial disruption. The Anglo-Saxon Chronicle, summing up the Conqueror's reign, comes closest to recognizing that there was a great gulf between what the Normans said and what they actually did. 'The louder the talk of law and justice,' it complains, 'the greater the injustices they committed.'[15]

Even if we reject (as some historians still do) the notion that the Norman settlement created a pattern of landholding that was radically different from the one that had existed before, what Domesday demonstrates beyond any question is how totally the Conquest had replaced one ruling elite with another. By 1086 the English were entirely gone from the top of society, supplanted by thousands of foreign newcomers. This transformation had almost certainly not been William's original intention. His initial hope appears to have been to rule a mixed Anglo-Norman kingdom, much as his predecessor and fellow conqueror, King Cnut, had ruled an Anglo-Danish one. But Cnut had begun his reign by executing those Englishmen whose loyalty he suspected and promoting trustworthy natives in their place. William, by contrast, had exercised clemency after his coronation and consequently found himself facing wave after wave of rebellion. The English knew they were conquered in 1016, but in 1066 they had refused to believe it. As a result they met death and dispossession by stages and degrees, until, eventually and ironically, the Norman Conquest became far more revolutionary than its Danish predecessor. 'In King William's twenty-first year', said Henry of Huntingdon, 'there was scarcely a noble of English descent in England, but all had been reduced to servitude and lamentation.'[16]

From this change in the ruling elite, enormous consequences flowed, because the English and the Normans were two quite different peoples. William of Malmesbury, in a famous passage, describes the Battle of Hastings as a fatal day for England, a disaster which had caused the country to exchange 'old masters for new'. He then goes on to outline the differences. The English, he says, were abandoned to gluttony and lechery, lax in their Christianity and addicted to wassail. They lived out their lives in small, mean houses, preferring to load their tattooed skin with gold bracelets, eating till they were sick and drinking until they spewed. The Normans, on the other hand, were well dressed to a fault, particular about their food and more obviously religious. A crafty, warlike people, they built great proud buildings in which they lived a life of moderate expense.[17]

Although narrow in its focus and infected with moral hindsight – the English here are sinners who clearly have it coming – in general this picture of two different cultures convinces. It was not just haircuts that distinguished the English from the Normans, but a whole range of practices and attitudes. Take, for example, warfare. Wherever we look in pre-Conquest England, the emphasis seems to be almost entirely naval. Edward the Confessor defends his people by sailing out from Sandwich every summer, and is appeased by a gift of a great, gilded warship. Taxes are raised on the basis of crew sizes, fleet and army are virtually interchangeable terms. We seem, in short, to be looking at a model that has much in common with contemporary Scandinavia. By way of total contrast, to read the sources for pre-Conquest Normandy is to enter a world dominated by cavalry and castles. Here the prestigious gifts are not ships but horses. Indeed, when ships are eventually needed in 1066, they have to be begged, borrowed or built from scratch.[18]

Similarly, the fact that the Normans built castles reveals that they had different ideas when it came to lordship, which they had come to equate with control over land. They strove to acquire new estates, built castles to defend them, and endeavoured to transmit them, unbroken, to their successors. So strong did the association between lord and location become, the Normans even started to name themselves after their principal holdings. 'I, Roger, whom they call Montgomery' is how the Conqueror's old friend described himself in a charter of the mid-1040s.[19]

This desire for land was a matter of huge moment after the Conquest of England. Some of William's followers, like those of King Cnut, had fought for money and gone home as soon as they had received it. But many thousands of others came wanting land, and ended up staying to create a new colonial society. They settled across England, tearing up the old tenurial patterns in the process, reorganizing their estates as manors and erecting castles to serve as their administrative centres. Naturally the colonists wanted to govern and control these new lordships according to their own familiar customs, and so further change followed. New baronies developed courts of their own, and sometimes even sheriffs, which stood apart from and cut across the existing English system of shire and hundred courts. New laws were introduced to reflect different attitudes towards inheritance, favouring the firstborn son so that the patrimony remained intact. Toponymic surnames, which had formerly found no place in pre-Conquest England, suddenly appear thereafter. In their determination to carve out new lordships, the Normans treated the surviving English harshly, forcing many men who had formerly held land freely to become rent-paying tenants, often on extremely onerous terms. Frutolf of Michelsberg may have erred somewhat in saying that the Conqueror had killed off the English aristocracy, but his claim that the king had 'forced the middle ranks into servitude' comes fairly close to the truth.[20]

At the same time, another different attitude meant that the fortunes of those at the very bottom of English society were perceptibly improved. Slavery, which was already a thing of the past in Normandy by 1066, had still been going strong in England. Yet by 1086 there had already been a sharp decline: where Domesday allows us to compare figures, the number of slaves has fallen by approximately twenty-five per cent. Historians have generally ascribed this change to economics, pointing out that the Normans, in their quest for cash, preferred to have serfs holding land and paying rent rather than slaves who worked for free but who required housing and feeding. This may have been part of the reason, but another was certainly that some sections of Norman society felt that slavery was morally objectionable. William himself, as we have seen, had banned the slave trade, apparently at Lanfranc's prompting, and is said to have freed many hundreds on his expedition to Wales. The ban cannot have been wholly effective, since 'that shameful trade by which in England people used to be sold like animals' was again condemned in an ecclesiastical council of 1102. Significantly, however, this was the last occasion on which the Church felt it necessary to issue such a prohibition. By the 1130s, slavery was gone from England, and some contemporaries knowingly attributed its absence to the Conquest.

'After England began to have Norman lords then the English no longer suffered from outsiders that which they had suffered at their own hands', wrote Lawrence of Durham. 'In this respect they found foreigners treated them better than they had treated themselves.'[21]

And this was also true in another respect. With the sole exception of Earl Waltheof, no Englishman was executed as a result of the Conquest. Along with their belief that slavery was wrong, the Normans had introduced the notion that it was better to spare one's opponents after they had surrendered. The English had been practising political murder right up to the eve of the Conquest, but very quickly thereafter the practice disappears. 'No man dared to slay another', says the Anglo-Saxon Chronicle, praising William's law and order policy, 'no matter what evil the other might have done him.' The last execution of a nobleman on royal orders took place in 1095, and after Waltheof's execution in 1076 no earl was executed in England until the early fourteenth century. The Conquest ushered in almost two and a half centuries of chivalric restraint.[22]

Lastly, the Normans had brought with them their zealous commitment to the reformed Church. 'The standard of religion, dead everywhere in England, has been raised by their arrival', wrote William of Malmesbury in the 1120s. 'You may see everywhere churches in villages, in towns and cities, monasteries rising in a new style of architecture, and with a new devotion our country flourishes.' The statement that religion was dead everywhere is, of course, an exaggeration. Historians nowadays would point to England's existing links with Rome in 1066, and argue that the boom in the building of parish churches had begun before the Conquest.[23] Yet there can be no doubt that the Normans accelerated these nascent tendencies enormously. William and Lanfranc saw an institution much in need of reform, and set about introducing separate Church courts, archdeacons and Church councils. Practices such as simony and clerical marriage were banned. And Malmesbury's point about the rising number of religious houses is borne out by the figures. In 1066 there were around sixty monasteries in England, but by 1135 that number had more than quadrupled to stand at somewhere between 250 and 300; in the Confessor's day there had been around 1,000 English monks and nuns; by Malmesbury's day there were some four to five times that number. In the north of England, monasticism had been wiped out by the first wave of Viking invasions in the late ninth century, and there is no sign of any native attempts to reverse this situation in the century before the Conquest. Yet within just a few years of the Norman takeover – very soon after the Harrying – the north witnessed a remarkable religious revival, with monasteries founded or restored at Selby, Jarrow, Whitby, Monkwearmouth, Durham and York. There is no clearer example of how conquerors and reformers marched in step.[24]

There is, naturally, a counter-argument to all of this. Some would say that all of these new attitudes – towards lordship, slavery, killing and religion – might have been adopted by the English even if the Conquest had not happened. But there we enter the realm of speculation. One can only point out that there is scant evidence of any strong trends in these directions before 1066, and state with certainty that the sudden replacement of one ruling elite by another caused these new ideas to be adopted very quickly. The speed of this change had profound knock-on effects, for these new attitudes were rapidly adopted in Norman England, but not in the Celtic countries to the north and west. Within a generation or two, men like William of Malmesbury were looking with a fresh and critical eye at their Welsh and Scottish neighbours, noting with distaste that they continued to slaughter each other and to seize and trade slaves. The resultant sense of moral superiority would help the English justify their own aggressive colonial enterprises in Britain during the centuries that followed.[25]

It is easy for us, at the distance of almost a millennium, to assess the Conquest in this way, chalking up dispassionately what was gained and what was lost. The English at the time enjoyed no such luxurious hindsight. To them the Norman takeover seemed an unmitigated disaster – a 'melancholy havoc for our dear country', as William of Malmesbury put it. They saw their artistic treasures being looted and taken as spoils to Normandy. They saw the bones and relics of their saints being hidden from view, tossed away or tested by fire. They saw the demolition of churches which, however rude or outdated they seemed to the newcomers, had stood for centuries, in some cases since the first arrival of Christianity. 'We wretches are destroying the work of the saints, thinking in our insolent pride that we are improving them', wept Wulfstan of Worcester as he watched the roof being ripped from his old cathedral in 1084. 'How superior to us was St Oswald, the maker of this church! How many holy and devout men have served God in this place!'[26]

Men like Wulfstan also noted with dismay the sudden discontinuation of English as a written language. As we have seen, the king's writing office abandoned the long-established practice of using English around the year 1070, for the good reason that most men of power by that date were French and therefore could not understand it. From then on Latin became the language of the royal chancery, and English was soon similarly abandoned in monastic scriptoria across the country. To take an obvious example, the C version of the Anglo-Saxon Chronicle ends in 1066, and the D version stops in 1080, leaving only the compilers of the E version to persevere into the twelfth century before the last of them finally put down his pen in 1154. *We* know that English would ultimately emerge triumphant, its variety increased by its freedom from written constraints, its vocabulary massively enriched by thousands of French loan-words. But in 1070 all that lay a long way in the future. Contemporary Englishmen saw only that a tradition that stretched back to King Alfred, intended to raise the standard of religion among the laity, was dying before their eyes. After the Conquest, there were no new vernacular prayer books or penitentials of the kind that had existed before, and so a vital bridge between the Church and the people was destroyed. 'Now that teaching is forsaken, and the folk are lost', lamented the author of one of the few surviving English poems to be written after 1066. 'Now there is another people which teaches our folk. And many of our teachers are damned, and our folk with them.'[27]

But the greatest cause for lamentation remained the enormous loss of life – the 'bitter strife and terrible bloodshed', as Orderic called it. Beginning with the carnage at Hastings, continuing with the crushing of rebellion after rebellion, and culminating in the deliberate sentence of starvation served on the population of northern England, the coming of the Conqueror had brought death and destruction on a scale that even the Danes had not been able to match. As the agents of this holocaust, the Normans appeared to the natives to be anything but civilized. 'In their unparalleled savagery,' said Henry of Huntingdon, 'they surpassed all other peoples.'[28]

To those that survived, there was only one explanation for such suffering: the English had sinned and were being severely chastised by their Creator. 'God had chosen the Normans to wipe out the English nation', concluded Henry, and all of his countrymen agreed, even if they did not put it in quite such stark terms. We find similar comments in Orderic, Malmesbury, Eadmer and the Anglo-Saxon Chronicle. The English had once been God's chosen people, but they had strayed from the path of righteousness, and were being punished by the Norman scourge.[29]

Most strikingly, we find this opinion expressed in the *Life of King Edward*, a tract begun shortly before 1066 as a paean of praise to the Godwinesons, but changed completely as a result of the Conquest and recast soon thereafter as a tribute to the Confessor.

> Woe is to you, England, you who once shone bright with holy, angelic progeny, but now with anxious expectation groan exceeding for your sins. You have lost your native king and suffered defeat, with much spilling of the blood of many of your men, in a war against a foreigner. Pitiably your sons have been slain within you. Your counsellors and princes are bound in chains, killed or disinherited.[30]

So great, indeed, is the anonymous author's grief at the events he has just experienced he can hardly bear to confront them directly. 'What shall I say about England?' he asks. 'What shall I say of generations to come?'

20

The Green Tree

Towards the end of the *Life of King Edward*, the author describes how the sleeping Confessor had woken on his deathbed and described to those around him a vivid dream. In this dream, two monks whom he had known during his youth in Normandy had come to him with a message from God, telling him that all the top people in England – the earls, bishops and abbots – were actually servants of the Devil. God had therefore cursed the whole kingdom, and within a year of Edward's death, 'devils shall come through all this land with fire and sword and the havoc of war'. When the king replied that he would warn his people about God's plan in order that they could repent, he was told that this would not happen. In that case, the Confessor asked the two monks, when could the English expect God's anger to end? 'At that time', they replied,

> when a green tree, cut down in the middle of its trunk, and the felled part carried three furlongs from the stump, shall be joined again to its trunk, by itself and without the hand of man or any sort of stake, and begin once more to push leaves and bear fruit from the old love of its uniting sap – then first can a remission of these great ills be hoped for.

When those who were present heard this, says the author of the *Life*, they were all very afraid. For it was impossible for a tree to move itself or repair itself in the way the monks had described – at least with man. With God, for whom nothing was impossible, such a thing might be possible, but that could only happen when the English had repented. 'Until then,' the author wondered, 'what can we expect but a miserable end in slaughter?'[1]

What indeed. To judge from the tone of the Anglo-Saxon Chronicle, matters had improved very little by the time of the Conqueror's death. The violence might have subsided, but the Norman takeover had left the English in no doubt that they were an underclass in their own country. William's writs addressed his subjects as two separate peoples, *Angli et Franci*, and, as Henry of Huntingdon explains, 'it was even disgraceful to be called English'. True, the Domesday Book shows that the economic situation had improved in some parts of the country by 1086: in Bury St Edmunds 342 houses are recorded on land that had been arable two decades earlier. But against this the year that followed had brought fresh disasters. A great fire had destroyed most of London, including St Paul's Cathedral, and there were apparently also fires in almost every other important town and city – whether accidentally or deliberately started we are not told. The Chronicle also notes that the appalling weather of the previous year had brought famine and pestilence in its wake. 'Such a malady fell upon men that nearly every other person was in the sorriest plight and down with fever: it was so malignant that many died from the disease . . . Alas! A miserable and lamentable time was it in that year, that brought forth so many misfortunes!'[2]

Nor was there much improvement during the generation that followed. The Conqueror's hopes for the English succession were fulfilled in 1087 when William Rufus ascended to the throne, but his fears about the other members of his family also proved to be well founded. Robert Curthose, once installed as duke of Normandy, plotted to replace Rufus as England's new ruler, aided by his uncle Odo. This plot failed, but the struggle between the Conqueror's sons continued for many years. The story of Rufus, Robert and their younger brother Henry in the decade after their father's death is a sorry saga of betrayal and double-crossing. A temporary peace prevailed after 1096 when Robert left to participate in the First Crusade and pawned Normandy to Rufus in order to pay for his passage. But four years later Rufus was killed, slain by a stray arrow while hunting in the New Forest (a fact not lost on English chroniclers, who observed that the hated institution had now claimed two of its creator's sons). Henry was crowned as England's new king,

Robert returned from the east and the struggle for supremacy resumed. It was ended only in 1106, when Henry defeated and captured his brother at the battle of Tinchebray. Robert spent the rest of his life in prison, dying in 1134. Henry ruled a reunited England and Normandy until his own death the following year.[3]

None of this was particularly auspicious for relations between the English and their new Norman masters. Robert, it is true, had struck up a remarkable friendship with Edgar Ætheling since the latter's submission to the Conqueror in 1075 – they were virtually foster-brothers, says Orderic. But this closeness between the new duke of Normandy and the last Old English claimant caused both Rufus and Henry, in their capacity as kings of England, to regard Edgar and his ilk with more caution. Rufus, for example, had arrived in England in 1087 accompanied by Morcar and Wulfnoth, recently released from their long captivity, but his first act on disembarking had been to have both men re-incarcerated.[4]

More generally, the struggle for the Conqueror's inheritance meant that Rufus and Henry had frequent occasion to tax England heavily, just as their father had done, and this remained equally true after 1106, as Henry sought to defend Normandy from both rebellion and invasion. In addition, the fact that from this date Henry, like his father, ruled both England and Normandy meant that the king of England continued to spend much of his time overseas. William had spent sixty per cent of his reign in Normandy and the same figure is true for Henry after 1106.[5] Both these trends – high taxation to pay for foreign wars and absentee kings – would persist for the rest of the twelfth century. The political union of England and Normandy during this time had far-reaching cultural and economic consequences: England was drawn inexorably into the European mainstream, dominated by Frankish arms and customs. For some merchants in southern England this was a cause for celebration; but others were left lamenting the loss of the old ties to Scandinavia. For Ailnoth of Canterbury, writing in Danish exile in the 1120s, the failure of the Danes to invade in 1085 remained a matter of lasting regret. Cnut IV, he felt, would have been the liberator of an English people, freeing them from French and Norman tyranny.[6]

During the reigns of the Conqueror's sons the English regarded themselves very much as the subject people in a Norman colony. 'This was exactly seven years since the accession of King Henry,' wrote the Anglo-Saxon Chronicler in 1107, 'and the forty-first year of French rule in this country.' William of Malmesbury, writing two decades later, could in this respect see no change in the sixty years since the Conquest. At one point in his history he retells the story of Edward the Confessor's deathbed dream, with its prophecy of the severed Green Tree, and feels he can only agree with the pessimistic interpretation of the original author. 'The truth of this we now experience,' he says, 'now that England has become the dwelling place of foreigners and a playground for lords of alien blood. No Englishman today is an earl, a bishop or an abbot; new faces everywhere enjoy England's riches and gnaw at her vitals. Nor is there any hope of ending this miserable state of affairs.'[7]

And yet, despite Malmesbury's pessimism, there were signs of change. He may have been right about the earls and bishops, but he was wrong to say that there were no English abbots. Although most had been replaced by Normans, there had still been a handful of English abbots at the end of the Conqueror's reign, and this continued to be the case during the reigns of his sons. More importantly, within the monasteries themselves a large proportion of the monks remained English, and many of them retained or obtained positions of power (it is not uncommon, for example, to find a Norman abbot with an English prior as his second-in-command). In the monasteries English and Normans were living together at close quarters from the very beginning, and although this created some notorious clashes (such as the massacre at Glastonbury) in general it meant that the cloister was probably the foremost arena of assimilation. This meant that there was also frequent contact between Englishmen and their new foreign bishops, thanks to the uniquely English institution of the monastic cathedral. Lanfranc, in particular, liked this idea, and after the Conquest the number of monastic cathedrals increased from four to ten.[8] According to a letter written not long after his death in 1089, the archbishop eventually came to regret the harsh line he had taken towards English customs at the time of his arrival, and towards the end of his career had become an enthusiastic devotee of St Dunstan. We can see a similar softening elsewhere: when the giant Norman cathedral at Winchester, begun in 1079, was completed in 1093, the bones of St Swithin were reinstated with great honour.[9] And when, during the latter year, another new cathedral was begun in Durham, it was a very different proposition from anything that had gone before.

Norman in its scale and proportions, Durham has none of the interior austerity of the new churches of the immediate post-Conquest period. Instead, it is decorated in a style that is unmistakably pre-1066, its columns carved with the linear patterns that are so characteristic of Old English art. Architecturally, we are already witnessing Anglo-Norman fusion.[10]

By the early twelfth century there was an evident yearning among some churchmen to build bridges across the divide created by the Conquest. William of Malmesbury may have bemoaned the divide in his own day, but he wrote partly in the hope of mending it, and the numerous surviving copies of his history suggest that he found a receptive audience, at least in other monasteries. So too did his clerical contemporary, Henry of Huntingdon, who wrote at the request of his bishop, Alexander of Lincoln, a man of Norman descent, at least on his father's side. 'At your command, I have undertaken to tell the history of this kingdom and the origins of our people', the author told his patron, a comment which, with its inclusive 'our', raises the possibility that Alexander considered himself to be English.[11] Meanwhile, the monk of Ely who wrote the *Gesta Herewardi* in the early twelfth century did so with the clear intention of defending the honour of a defeated people. Hereward is presented as not only heroic but also chivalrous, a worthy adversary for his Norman opponents. The underlying message of the *Gesta* is that the English and Normans could coexist on equal terms. Indeed, in this version of the story, Hereward and the Conqueror himself are eventually reconciled.[12]

Because they wrote their histories in Latin, we might expect that, beyond the cloister and the cathedral close, the impact of such historians was fairly limited. Yet this was not necessarily the case: William of Malmesbury sent copies of his history to several leading lay people, including the king of Scots and the children of Henry I. The thirst for such information among the laity is confirmed within a decade or so by the appearance of Geoffrey Gaimar's *Estoire des Engleis*. As its title suggests, Geoffrey's history was written in French – a remarkable fact, given that the French themselves had produced almost nothing in the way of vernacular literature by this date. Also remarkable is his attitude towards the English, which was entirely free from condescension. Geoffrey celebrated the lives of earlier kings of England, including Cnut and his sons, and even wrote up Hereward as a freedom fighter battling against Norman oppression. Yet he was commissioned by Constance, the wife of Ralph fitz Gilbert, a woman of impeccable Norman descent.[13]

Perhaps more than any other source, Gaimar's history shows how, as the middle of the twelfth century approached, the descendants of the original Norman settlers had put down roots in English soil. The top tier of this colonial society – the king and the upper aristocracy – retained their links with the motherland, and had cross-Channel concerns and careers. But the majority of the 8,000 or so Normans revealed by the Domesday Book had no such interests, and probably remained resident in England for most of their lives. Two or three generations on, some of them did not yet regard themselves as English ('we French' and 'we Normans' are self-descriptions found in sources of the 1150s); but England was nonetheless their home, and so naturally, they were curious about its past, its landscape and its culture. And even if this was not the case, they still had to coexist and co-operate with their English tenants and neighbours. Domesday, with its emphasis on those who held their land from the king directly, and to a lesser extent his subtenants, can give the impression that the English had been virtually eradicated by the Conquest, but other evidence reminds us that the natives survived in great numbers, albeit in depressed circumstances. The lists of Domesday jurors, for example, reveal scores of Englishmen who were clearly of some standing in their localities, but who do not feature in the book itself. In order to prosper in the midst of this massive English majority, the few thousand Norman settlers must necessarily have learned to speak English, if only as a second language. Indeed, some linguists would go so far as to regard the English that we speak today as a creole created by the social circumstances of the Conquest.[14]

There was also intermarriage between the two groups. Historians have tended to dismiss Orderic's statement that such matches were commonplace during the years immediately after 1066, but as the product of a partnership that had clearly been consummated by 1074 we might give him the benefit of the doubt. Both William of Malmesbury and Henry of Huntingdon were also children of Anglo-Norman couples, and Malmesbury ventured the opinion that in general the Normans were happy to wed their inferiors. They may have done so for romantic reasons: Domesday mentions a Breton settler in Pickenham, Norfolk, 'who loved a certain woman on that land and led her in marriage'. However, since the same entry continues 'and afterwards he held that land', we might infer that in this case, as in many others, love was not the settler's sole motivation. Marriage to a female member of the native family they were displacing was another strategy used by new Norman lords to bolster their claims to legitimacy – one which also conveniently allowed the bride's male relatives to salvage something from the wreckage of their expectations. Most spectacularly, this happened in 1100, when Henry I, just three months into his reign, married Edith, a daughter of Edgar Ætheling's sister, Margaret. Thus, from the start of the twelfth century, the English had a queen of their own race – 'of the true royal family of England', as the Anglo-Saxon Chronicle pointedly put it.[15]

If marriage was one indicator of where one's heart lay, burial was another. The first generation of conquerors, born and raised in Normandy, had by and large preferred to use their new-found riches to patronize monastic houses back home, and it was in these houses that they chose to be interred. (Though there were notable exceptions: Roger of Montgomery was buried in the abbey he had founded in Shrewsbury.) But in the generations that followed the balance tipped decisively in the other direction, with many Norman settlers establishing or endowing monasteries in England and naturally electing to be buried in them. The shift is neatly reflected in the final resting places of the Conqueror's own family, with William himself buried in Caen while his sons are entombed in England. That Rufus was buried in Winchester, close to the forest in which he was killed, we might ascribe to chance rather than choice – since he founded no church of his own, his intentions are difficult to determine. But not so with Henry I, who was buried in England, even though he died in Normandy. After his death his body was shipped across the Channel, so it could be laid to rest in the abbey he had founded at Reading.[16]

Buried in England, born in England and married to an English princess: the Conqueror's youngest son does appear to have been quite the Anglophile. He and Edith christened their daughter Matilda for the benefit of their Norman baronage but privately called her Æthelic, while their son, William, was accorded the Anglo-Saxon title of ætheling. Towards the end of his reign Henry appointed a certain Æthelwulf as bishop of the newly created diocese of Carlisle, and Edith was responsible for encouraging none other than William of Malmesbury to write his *History of the English Kings*. According to Malmesbury, such enthusiasm did not sit well with the Normans at Henry's court, who openly mocked the king and queen, calling them 'Godric and Godgifu'. But it must have played well with the great majority of Henry's subjects across the country as a whole, which was perhaps the king's intention. One is naturally bound to wonder what would have happened had his son, William Ætheling, half English and half Norman, succeeded to the throne.[17]

But one is left wondering, for William died in 1120, drowning along with many other members of the Anglo-Norman court when the ship carrying them across the English Channel foundered and sank, taking with it the hope of a peaceful transfer of power. Queen Edith had died two years earlier, and Henry, despite a second marriage in 1121, produced no more legitimate sons. In desperation the ageing king sought to fix the succession on his daughter Matilda, a dangerous experiment which brought disastrous results. When Henry died in 1135 Matilda's claim was contested by her cousin, Stephen of Blois, who was in due course crowned, but who spent the rest of his reign struggling against his rival and her diehard supporters. For the best part of two decades England was embroiled in a deeply divisive civil war – a period when, according to the Anglo-Saxon Chronicle, 'men said openly that Christ and his saints slept'. There and elsewhere we read of war and waste, pestilence and famine, castle-building, oppression and torture. After the long peace of Henry I's reign, the vocabulary of the Conquest had returned with a vengeance.[18]

It was not, therefore, until the death of Stephen in 1154 and the negotiated accession of Matilda's son, Henry, as King Henry II, that Englishmen felt inclined to ponder afresh the question of national identity. But when they did so, at least some of them felt that a page had been decisively turned. In 1161, almost a century after his death, Edward the Confessor was belatedly recognized in Rome as a saint. Two years later the monks of Westminster, who had led the canonization campaign, celebrated their success by translating the king's body to a new tomb, and also by commissioning a new account of the Confessor's life. The author, Ailred of Rievaulx, elegantly reworked an earlier version from the 1130s, itself based on the original *Life* written at the time of the Conquest, adding, cutting and paraphrasing freely, but essentially adhering to the story and spirit of his source. When, however, he came to the account of Edward's dream, and the prophecy of the Green Tree, he rejected the pessimistic interpretations of previous writers, and instead supplied his own reading which argued that the prophecy had finally been fulfilled.[19]

In Ailred's version, what had been a holy mystery is transformed into a historical metaphor. The tree divided from its trunk, he explained, represented the kingdom divided from its royal family, and the trunk carried off for three furlongs signified the reigns of Harold and the two Williams, none of whom had been directly linked to the Confessor's line. But when Henry I had chosen Edith as his queen, Ailred continued, the tree and its trunk were reunited. The tree had pushed forth new leaves in the shape of their daughter, Matilda, and finally borne fruit in the form of Matilda's son, Henry II. 'Our Henry', as Ailred calls him, 'is a cornerstone joining both peoples. Now without doubt England has a king of the race of the English.'[20]

This was part wishful thinking, part propagandist nonsense. Henry may have been Matilda's son, but she herself was only one-eighth English, and her second husband – Henry's father – had been Geoffrey Plantagenet, count of Anjou. The new 'king of the race of the English' had been born in Le Mans and brought up on the Continent. Two years before his accession he had married Eleanor of Aquitaine, whose inheritance had made her new husband the ruler of a huge swathe of south-western France, and this, combined with his own ancestral titles, meant that Henry's empire stretched from the Scottish border to the Pyrenees. Inevitably, therefore, the new king spent even more time on the Continent than his namesake grandfather, and when he came to be buried it was at the abbey of Fontevraud, in his father's county of Anjou.[21]

And yet, despite all his personal disqualifications, there is little doubt that, when it came to healing the breach of the Conquest, Henry's reign was a watershed moment. It was during this period that England's ancient laws, altered and amended on account of the Norman preoccupation with land, were finally codified and committed to writing, becoming 'the Common Law'.[22] At the same time, the king's legal reforms strengthened the power of the Old English shire courts and undermined the private baronial courts that the first generation of conquerors had intruded. By the 1170s English had clearly become a language spoken by all classes, whatever their ancestry: we find bishops and knights of French extraction who were demonstrably bilingual (including, in the latter case, one of the killers of Archbishop Thomas Becket). And, a century on from 1066, the intermarriage that had occurred from the start had blurred the lines of national identity. 'In the present day,' wrote Richard fitz Nigel, the treasurer of the Exchequer, in the late 1170s, 'the races have become so fused that it can scarcely be discerned who is English and who is Norman.'[23]

Only at the extremes of society was the distinction still obvious. As fitz Nigel observed, you could tell a person was English if they happened to be an unfree peasant; at that level, clearly, there had been much less intermingling. Perhaps because of this association of Englishness with baseness, those at the opposite end of the social spectrum still hesitated to identify wholeheartedly with England: 'You English are too timid', remarked Henry II's son and successor, Richard the Lionheart, to some of his troops in 1194, implying that he himself was neither. At the end of the twelfth century, the upper echelons of the aristocracy in many cases still had lands in Normandy and would often accompany the king during his frequent foreign absences. Besides his celebrated activities in the Holy Land, Richard spent almost all of his reign on the Continent, defending the extensive demesne that he had inherited from his parents.[24]

The Lionheart's untimely death from a crossbow bolt in 1199 was thus of crucial significance, for it led to the succession of his younger brother, the famously inept King John, during whose reign most of the Continental empire was lost, including the duchy of Normandy. After 1204, no baron in England, no matter how proud his pedigree, could regard his links with Normandy as anything other than historic. In one respect John recognized this new reality, dropping the *Angli et Franci* formula from his writs and charters, implicitly admitting that all his subjects ought now to be regarded as English. But for the rest of his reign he struggled to recover his lost inheritance, demanding overseas military service from his subjects and taxing them harder than any of his forebears. As a consequence he succeeded in creating a sense of common identity in England of a kind not seen since before the Conquest, as men of all degrees came together to resist the power of the Crown. The result was Magna Carta, the charter of liberties extracted from John in 1215, a document which has been described as 'the classic statement of regnal solidarity'.[25]

If we follow Ailred of Rievaulx's interpretation of the Green Tree prophecy, with the stump as England and the trunk as its royal family, then it took two more generations before the pair were properly reunited. In the mid-1230s, King John's son, Henry III, became intensely devoted to the cult of Edward the Confessor. In the decades that followed he would decorate his palaces with images of the sainted king, commission books about him, and arrange the rhythms of the royal court around the celebration of his two annual festivals. His single greatest achievement was to rebuild Westminster Abbey, replacing the Confessor's Romanesque church with the great Gothic edifice that still stands today. And, in 1239, when Henry came to christen his firstborn son, he rejected the names of his Norman forebears and called the boy Edward. As the adult Edward I, he would be the first king of England since the Conquest to bear an English name, speak English and lead a united English people.[26]

If, on the other hand, we disregard Ailred, and see the tree simply as the kingdom traumatized by the Conquest, then its restoration should come earlier: if not by the 1170s then certainly by the time of Magna Carta. The Charter, so far as we can tell, was not issued in English – official documents had to wait another generation for that development – but by 1215 English was already making a comeback as a language of literature.[27]

It was not the same English that had been spoken before the Conquest, because it was not the same England. The tree had not been restored to its former self. Much of it, indeed, was barely recognizable, for a wholly new stock had been grafted on to the severed trunk. England's aristocracy, its attitudes and its architecture had all been transformed by the coming of the Normans. The body of the tree, too, had in places been twisted into new forms: the laws of the kingdom, its language, its customs and institutions – these were clearly not the same as they had been before. Even so, anyone looking at these institutions could see in a second that their origins were English. England was everywhere studded with castles, but it was still a land of shires, hundreds, hides and boroughs. The branches were new but the roots remained ancient. The tree had survived the trauma by becoming a hybrid. Against all expectations, its sap was once again rising.

Abbreviations

(Unless otherwise indicated, the place of publication is London)

ANS	*Anglo-Norman Studies*
ASC	*Anglo-Saxon Chronicle* (cited by year)
Barlow, *Confessor*	F. Barlow, *Edward the Confessor* (new edn, 1997).
Bates, *Conqueror*	D. Bates, *William the Conqueror* (*1989*).
Carmen	*The Carmen de Hastingae Proelio of Guy, Bishop of Amiens*, ed. F. Barlow (Oxford, 1999).
Councils and Synods	*Councils and Synods with Other Documents Relating to the English Church*, I, *871–1204*, ed. D. Whitelock, M. Brett and C. N. L. Brooke (2 vols., Oxford, 1981).
Douglas, *Conqueror*	D. C. Douglas, *William the Conqueror: The Norman Impact Upon England* (1964).
DNB	www.oxforddnb.com (cited by name). For the printed text, see *The Oxford Dictionary of National Biography*, ed. H. C. G. Matthew and B. Harrison (60 vols., Oxford, 2004).
Eadmer	*Eadmer's History of Recent Events in England*, ed. G. Bosanquet (1964).
EER	*Encomium Emmae Reginae*, ed. A. Campbell and S. Keynes (Cambridge, 1998).

Abbreviations

EHD	*English Historical Documents*
EHR	*English Historical Review*
Fernie, *Architecture*	E. Fernie, *The Architecture of Norman England* (Oxford, 2000).
Freeman, *Norman Conquest*	E. A. Freeman, *The History of the Norman Conquest of England* (6 vols., Oxford, 1867–79).
Gaimar, *Estoire*	Geffrei Gaimar, *Estoire des Engleis*, ed. and trans. I. Short (Oxford, 2009).
Garnett, *Short Introduction*	G. Garnett, *The Norman Conquest: A Very Short Introduction* (Oxford, 2009).
GND	*The Gesta Normannorum Ducum of William of Jumièges, Orderic Vitalis and Robert of Torigni*, ed. E. M. C. van Houts (2 vols., Oxford, 1992–5).
HH	Henry of Huntingdon, *The History of the English People 1000–1154*, ed. and trans. D. Greenway (Oxford, 2002).
JW	*The Chronicle of John of Worcester*, ed. R. R. Darlington and P. McGurk, trans. J. Bray and P. McGurk (3 vols., Oxford, 1995, 1998, forthcoming).
Letters of Lanfranc	*The Letters of Lanfranc, Archbishop of Canterbury*, ed. and trans. V. H. Clover and M. T. Gibson (Oxford, 1979).
OV	*The Ecclesiastical History of Orderic Vitalis*, ed. M. Chibnall (6 vols., Oxford, 1968–80).
RRAN	*Regesta Regum Anglo-Normannorum: The Acta of William I (1066–1087)*, ed. D. Bates (Oxford, 1998).
SD, *History*	Simeon of Durham, *History of the Kings of England*, trans. J. Stevenson (facsimile reprint, Lampeter, 1987).
SD, *Libellus*	Simeon of Durham, *Libellus de Exordio atque Procursu istius, hoc est Dunhelmensis*, ed. D. Rollason (Oxford, 2000).
Snorri	Snorri Sturluson, *King Harald's Saga*, ed. M. Magnusson and H. Pálsson (1966).

Sources and Documents	*The Norman Conquest of England: Sources and Documents*, ed. R. A. Brown (Woodbridge, 1984).
TRHS	*Transactions of the Royal Historical Society*
VER	*The Life of King Edward who Rests at Westminster*, ed. F. Barlow (2nd edn, Oxford, 1992).
Wace	*The History of the Norman People: Wace's Roman de Rou*, trans. G. S. Burgess (Woodbridge, 2004).
WM, *Gesta Pontificum*	William of Malmesbury, *Gesta Pontificum Anglorum*, I, ed. and trans. M. Winterbottom (Oxford, 2007).
WM, *Gesta Regum*	William of Malmesbury, *Gesta Regum Anglorum*, I, ed. and trans. R. A. B. Mynors, R. M. Thomson and M. Winterbottom (Oxford, 1998).
WM, *Saints' Lives*	William of Malmesbury, *Saints' Lives*, ed. M. Winterbottom and R. M. Thomson (Oxford, 2002).
WP	*The Gesta Guillelmi of William of Poitiers*, ed. R. H. C. Davis and M. Chibnall (Oxford, 1998).

Notes

INTRODUCTION

1 Nor as many books and articles, of which there are thousands. For older publications, see S. A. Brown, The Bayeux Tapestry: History and Bibliography (Woodbridge, 1988). For more recent research, see *The Bayeux Tapestry: Embroidering the Facts of History*, ed. P. Bouet, B. Levy and F. Neveux (Caen, 2004); *King Harold II and the Bayeux Tapestry*, ed. G. R. Owen-Crocker (Woodbridge, 2005); *The Bayeux Tapestry: New Interpretations*, ed. M. K. Foys, K. E. Overbey and D. Terkla (Woodbridge, 2009); *The Bayeux Tapestry: New Approaches*, ed. M. J. Lewis, G. R. Owen-Crocker and D. Terkla (Oxford, 2011).

2 D. J. Bernstein, *The Mystery of the Bayeux Tapestry* (London, 1986), 71–2.

3 The contributors to the 1999 conference at Caen were unanimous in declaring for Odo: *Bayeux Tapestry*, ed. Bouet et al., 406. For the Canterbury connection, see C. Hart, 'The Bayeux Tapestry and Schools of Illumination at Canterbury', *ANS*, 22 (2000), 117–67 and idem, 'The Cicero-Aratea and the Bayeux Tapestry', *King Harold II*, ed. Owen-Crocker, 161–78. If the Tapestry was commissioned by Odo, it was presumably commissioned before his imprisonment in 1082, though later dates have been proposed.

4 C. Hicks, *The Bayeux Tapestry: The Life Story of a Masterpiece* (London, 2006).

5 M. J. Lewis, *The Real World of the Bayeux Tapestry* (Stroud, 2008); L. Ashe, *Fiction and History in England* (Cambridge, 2007), 35–45.

6 M. Morris, *A Great and Terrible King: Edward I and the Forging of Britain* (2008); *Itinerary of Edward I*, ed. E. W. Safford (3 vols., List and Index Society, 103, 132, 135, 1974–7); *RRAN*, 76–8.

7 There are several different modern translations of the Anglo-Saxon Chronicle. I have used *The Anglo-Saxon Chronicle*, ed. G. N. Garmonsway (new edn, London, 1972), and also the translation by Whitelock in *EHD*, ii, 107–203. Both are cited by year rather than page number.

8 M. Chibnall, *The Debate on the Norman Conquest* (Manchester, 1999), 59.

9 WP, 26–7; *The Life and Letters of Edward A. Freeman*, ed. W. R. W. Stephens (2 vols., London, 1895), ii, 216. For Freeman's character, see his entry in the *DNB*.

10 D. Bates, '1066: Does the Date Still Matter?', *Historical Research*, 78 (2005), 446–7.

11 P. Stafford, 'Women and the Norman Conquest', *TRHS*, 6th ser., 4 (1994), 221–49.

12 Bates, '1066: Does the Date Still Matter?', 447–51; R. Barber, 'The Norman Conquest and the Media', *ANS*, 26 (2004), 1–20; J. Gillingham, '"Slaves of the Normans?": Gerald de Barri and Regnal Solidarity in Early Thirteenth-Century England', *Law, Laity and Solidarities: Essays in Honour of Susan Reynolds*, ed. P. Stafford, J. L. Nelson and J. Martindale (Manchester, 2001), 160–70. More generally, see Chibnall, *Debate*, *passim*.

13 E.g. R. A. Brown, *The Normans and the Norman Conquest* (2nd edn, Woodbridge, 1985), 5.

14 'Change of a magnitude and at a speed unparalleled in English history': Garnett, *Short Introduction*, 5. For a general discussion, see Bates, '1066: Does the Date Still Matter?', *passim*.

15 See in particular the work of John Gillingham, much of which is reprinted in his *The English in the Twelfth Century* (Woodbridge, 2000).

16 See in particular R. R. Davies, *The First English Empire: Power and Identities in the British Isles, 1093–1343* (Oxford, 2000).

CHAPTER 1

1 E. Bozoky, 'The Sanctity and Canonisation of Edward the Confessor', *Edward the Confessor: The Man and the Legend*, ed. R. Mortimer (Woodbridge, 2009), 173–86.

2 *The Anglo-Saxons*, ed. J. Campbell (1982), remains a fine introduction.

3 In general, see M. Arnold, *The Vikings: Culture and Conquest* (2006).

4 S. Foot, 'The Making of *Angelcynn*: English Identity before the Norman Conquest', *TRHS*, 6th ser., 6 (1996), 25–49; P. Wormald, '*Engla lond*: The Making of an Allegiance', *Journal of Historical Sociology*, 7 (1994), 1–24.

5 See *The Battle of Maldon AD 991*, ed. D. Scragg (Oxford, 1991).

6 All the information about Æthelred in this chapter can be found in his *DNB* entry. For more extensive treatments, see R. Lavelle, *Aethelred II: King of the English, 978–1016* (Stroud, 2008) and A. Williams, *Æthelred the Unready: The Ill-Counselled King* (2003).

7 On the early history of Normandy, see D. Bates, *Normandy before 1066* (Harlow, 1982).

8 On the extent to which the Normans remained Norsemen, cf. Bates, *Normandy*, and E. Searle, *Predatory Kinship and the Creation of Norman Power, 840–1066* (Berkeley, 1988).

9 *ASC* E, 1014.

10 *EHD*, i, 247, 335–6; below, 23

11 Barlow, *Confessor*, 35n.

12 S. Keynes, 'The Æthelings in Normandy', *ANS*, 13 (1991), 176–81; *ASC* E, 1016, 1017.

13 *ASC* E, 1017; *GND*, ii, 20–1; *EER*, [xxii–xxiv], 32–5. See also E. van Houts, 'A Note on *Jezebel* and *Semiramis*, Two Latin Poems from the Early Eleventh Century', idem, *History and Family Traditions in England and the Continent, 1000–1200* (Aldershot, 1999), III, 18–24.

14 E. van Houts, 'Edward and Normandy', *Edward the Confessor*, ed. Mortimer, 64.

15 M. K. Lawson, *Cnut: The Danes in England in the Early Eleventh Century* (1993), 86–8; cf. Keynes, 'Æthelings', 181–4.

16 Richard II died on 23 August 1026, Richard III on 5 or 6 August 1027. See D. Douglas, 'Some Problems of Early Norman Chronology', *EHR*, 65 (1950), 296–303; D. Crouch, *The Normans* (2002), 46–8.

17 *GND*, ii, 76–8; E. van Houts, 'The Political Relations between Normandy and England before 1066 according to the *Gesta Normannorum Ducum*', idem, *History and Family Traditions*, V, 85–97.

[18] *Sources and Documents*, 8; *GND*, i, xxxii–xxxv; ii, 76–9; Keynes, 'Æthelings', 186–94.

[19] *Sources and Documents*, 8; *GND*, ii, 78–9.

[20] Ibid.; R. Mortimer, 'Edward the Confessor: The Man and the Legend', *Edward the Confessor*, ed. Mortimer, 4–5.

[21] *GND*, ii, 79–85. The story that Robert visited the Byzantine emperor in Constantinople, carried in a later redaction of the *GND*, has been discredited. See E. van Houts, 'Normandy and Byzantium in the Eleventh Century', idem, *History and Family Traditions*, I, 544–59.

CHAPTER 2

[1] *EHD*, i, 335; *GND*, ii, 78–9; *DNB* Cnut.

[2] M. Hare, 'Cnut and Lotharingia: Two Notes', *Anglo-Saxon England*, 29 (2000), 261–8; HH, 17–18.

[3] *DNB* Cnut; *The Letters and Poems of Fulbert of Chartres*, ed. F. Behrends (Oxford, 1976), 67–9.

[4] N. Hooper, 'The Housecarls in England in the Eleventh Century', *ANS*, 7 (1985), 161–76. For a summary, see M. K. Lawson, *The Battle of Hastings 1066* (Stroud, 2002), 158–9; *ASC* E, 1012; below, 32, 75–6.

[5] J. S. Moore, '"Quot Homines?": The Population of Domesday England', *ANS*, 19 (1997), 307–34, arrives at an estimate of 1.9 million in 1086.

[6] See, for example, the fleeting references in F. M. Stenton, *Anglo-Saxon England* (3rd edn, Oxford, 1971) and *The Anglo-Saxons*, ed. J. Campbell (1982). A notable exception is J. M. Kemble, *The Saxons in England* (1849), i, 185–227. In general, see D. A. E. Pelteret, *Slavery in Early Mediæval England* (Woodbridge, 1995); idem, 'Slave Raiding and Slave Trading in Early England', *Anglo-Saxon England*, 9 (1981), 99–114; J. S. Moore, 'Domesday Slavery', *ANS*, 11 (1989), 191–220; D. Wyatt, 'The Significance of Slavery: Alternative Approaches to Anglo-Saxon Slavery', *ANS*, 23 (2001), 327–47.

[7] Pelteret, *Slavery*, 70.

[8] Ibid., 65.

[9] H. G. Richardson and G. O. Sayles, *Law and Legislation from Æthelberht to Magna Carta* (Edinburgh, 1966), 10, 16, 20–1.

[10] *EHD*, i, 931. See also WM, *Gesta Regum*, 362–3, and WM, *Saints' Lives*, 100–3.

11 *EHD*, i, 468–9; A. Williams, *The English and the Norman Conquest* (Woodbridge, 1995), 73; P. A. Clarke, *The English Nobility under Edward the Confessor* (Oxford, 1994), 32–3.

12 *EHD*, i, 930, 932.

13 K. Mack, 'Changing Thegns: Cnut's Conquest and the English Aristocracy', *Albion*, 4 (1984), 375–87.

14 For runestones, see *Anglo-Saxons*, ed. Campbell, 198.

15 S. Baxter, *The Earls of Mercia: Lordship and Power in Late Anglo-Saxon England* (Oxford, 2007), 26–8. For a more detailed analysis, see S. Keynes, 'Cnut's Earls', *The Reign of Cnut: King of England, Denmark and Norway*, ed. A. R. Rumble (1994), 43–88.

16 *DNB* Godwine; *ASC* E, 1009; *VER*, 8–11.

17 L. M. Larson, 'The Political Policies of Cnut as King of England', *American Historical Review*, 15 (1910), 735; *DNB* Thorkell; *DNB* Erik; Baxter, *Earls of Mercia*, 33–4.

18 Ibid., 33–5.

19 *DNB* Siward; R. Fleming, *Kings and Lords in Conquest England* (Cambridge, 1991), 48–52.

20 Lawson, *Cnut*, 113–14.

21 *ASC* E, 1035. For pre-Conquest assemblies, see J. R. Maddicott, *The Origins of the English Parliament, 924–1327* (Oxford, 2010), 1–56 (39 for this particular episode).

22 *ASC* E, 1035.

23 *EER*, 32–5, 38–41; *ASC* C, D and E, 1035.

24 *EER*, [xxxii–xxxiii].

25 *GND*, ii, 104–7.

26 *EER*, [xxxiii–xxxiv], 40–3.

27 Ibid.; *ASC* C and D, 1036; *GND*, ii, 106–7; WP, 7, says Alfred went 'better prepared than his brother for armed opposition. He also sought his father's sceptre'; JW, ii, 522–5.

28 *ASC* E, 1035; *EER*, [xxx].

29 Ibid., 42–7; *ASC* C and D, 1036; *DNB* Alfred Ætheling. Cf. Barlow, *Confessor*, 45–6.

30 Cf. *ASC* C and D, 1036; *GND*, ii, 106–7; *EER*, [lxv], lxv, 42–5.

31 *ASC* C, 1037.

32 *EER*, [xxxv–xxxvii]; 36–7, 46–9.

33 Ibid., [xxxvii], 48–51.

34 *ASC* E, 1040, says Harold ruled England for four years and sixteen weeks, implying his reign began in late November 1035. He was

the first king to be buried at Westminster Abbey, if only briefly. *DNB* Harold I.

35 *ASC* C, 1040.

36 Ibid.; JW, ii, 530–1.

37 Pending publication of JW volume 1, see A. Gransden, *Historical Writing in England, c.550 to c.1307* (1974), 43–8.

38 JW, ii, 530–3. His claim that Godwine gave Harthacnut a ship appears to be a confusion with the earl's gift to Edward the Confessor two years later. S. Keynes and R. Love, 'Earl Godwine's Ship', *Anglo-Saxon England*, 38 (2009), 202–3.

39 *ASC* C and E, 1040. For debate about these figures, see M. K. Lawson, 'The Collection of Danegeld and Heregeld in the Reigns of Æthelred II and Cnut', *EHR*, 99 (1984), 721–38; J. Gillingham, '"The Most Precious Jewel in the English Crown": Levels of Danegeld and Heregeld in the Early Eleventh Century', *EHR*, 104 (1989), 373–84; Lawson, '"Those Stories Look True": Levels of Taxation in the Reigns of Æthelred and Cnut', *EHR*, 104 (1989), 385–406; Gillingham, 'Chronicles and Coins as Evidence for Levels of Tribute and Taxation in Later Tenth- and Early Eleventh-Century England', *EHR*, 105 (1990), 939–50; Lawson, 'Danegeld and Heregeld Once More', *EHR*, 105 (1990), 951–61.

40 *ASC* E, 1040; P. Stafford, *Unification and Conquest* (1989), 81; JW, ii, 532–3.

41 *ASC* C, 1040, 1041.

42 *EER*, 52–3; *ASC* C, 1041.

43 J. R. Maddicott, 'Edward the Confessor's Return to England in 1041', *EHR*, 119 (2004), 650–66.

44 WP, 6–7; JW, ii, 532–5; *ASC* C and E, 1040; Keynes and Love, 'Earl Godwine's Ship', 195–6.

CHAPTER 3

1 According to a contemporary chronicler called Ralph Glaber, Robert had at one time married a daughter of King Cnut, but broke it off because he found her so odious. For the problems with this comment, see Douglas, 'Some Problems', 292–5.

2 WM, *Gesta Regum*, 426–7; E. M. C. van Houts, 'The Origins of Herleva, Mother of William the Conqueror', *EHR*, 101 (1986), 399–404.

3 Freeman, *Norman Conquest*, ii, 581–3.

4 *Rodulfus Glaber, Historiarum Libri Quinque*, ed. J. France, N. Bulst and P. Reynolds (2nd edn, Oxford, 1993), 204–5; *GND*, i, 58–9, 78–9. See also D. Bates, 'The Conqueror's Earliest Historians and the Writing of his Biography', *Writing Medieval Biography 750–1250: Essays in Honour of Professor Frank Barlow*, ed. D. Bates, J. Crick and S. Hamilton (Woodbridge, 2006), 134.

5 Douglas, *Conqueror*, 15, 36; *GND*, ii, 80-1.

6 *Rodulfus Glaber*, ed. France et al., 204–5.

7 E. Hallam and J. Everard, *Capetian France, 987–1328* (2001), 7; T. Holland, *Millennium* (2008), 146n.

8 T. Reuter, 'Plunder and Tribute in the Carolingian Empire', *TRHS*, 5th ser., 35 (1985), 75–94; J. Dunbabin, *France in the Making, 843–1180* (2nd edn, Oxford, 2000), 1–16, 27.

9 Ibid., 27–43.

10 R. A. Brown, *English Castles* (2nd edn, 1976), 14–39; Fernie, *Architecture*, 3–14.

11 Dunbabin, *France in the Making*, 43, 52–4; R. Bartlett, *The Making of Europe: Conquest, Colonization and Cultural Change, 950–1350* (1993), 43–51.

12 Dunbabin, *France in the Making*, 143–50.

13 Ibid., 232–7; D. Crouch, *The Birth of Nobility: Constructing Aristocracy in England and France 900–1300* (Harlow, 2005), 261–4. See the debate on 'The "Feudal Revolution"' between T. N. Bisson, D. Barthélemy, S. D. White, C. Wickham and T. Reuter in *Past and Present*, 142 (1994), 6–42; 152 (1996), 196–223; 155 (1997), 177–225.

14 Bates, *Normandy*, *passim*. For a contrary view see Searle, *Predatory Kinship*, but cf. Bates's review of Searle in *Speculum*, 65 (1990), 1045–7.

15 Bates, *Normandy*, 99, 156–7; D. C. Douglas, 'The Earliest Norman Counts', *EHR*, 61 (1946), 129–56.

16 Fernie, *Architecture*, 11–12, 50; OV, iv, 290–1.

17 Bates, *Normandy*, 65–8, 116–17, 165; R. H. C. Davis, 'The Warhorses of the Normans', *ANS*, 10 (1988), 67–82.

18 H. E. J. Cowdrey, 'The Peace and Truce of God in the Eleventh Century', *Past and Present*, 46 (1970), 42–67.

19 Bates, *Normandy*, 66–7, 174, 195.

20 Douglas, *Conqueror*, 32–9; C. Potts, *Monastic Revival and Regional Identity in Early Normandy* (Woodbridge, 1997), 121, 128, 131.

21 *GND*, ii, 92–3, 110–11.

22 Douglas, *Conqueror*, 37, 40; *GND*, ii, 92–5; OV, iv, 82–3.

23 D. Bates, 'The Conqueror's Adolescence', *ANS*, 25 (2003), 7–8; *GND*, ii, 92–5, 98–9.

24 Bates, 'Conqueror's Adolescence' 3–4; WM, *Gesta Regum*, 426–7. The subsequent recriminations over the surrender of Tillières to Henry (see *GND*, ii, 100–1) may explain why contemporary chroniclers fail to mention the king's involvement in William's knighting.

25 OV, ii, 184–5, 258–61.

26 WP, 6–9.

27 Ibid., 8–9; Douglas, *Conqueror*, 44; Bates, *Normandy*, 176, 198.

28 WP, 8–9.

29 Ibid., 8–11; Douglas, *Conqueror*, 47–8; Bates, 'Conqueror's Adolescence', 5–6, 13–15.

30 Wace, 131–3; WP, 10–11; *GND*, ii, 120–1; Douglas, *Conqueror*, 48–9; Bates, *Normandy*, 61–2.

31 Wace, 133–7; WP, 10–11.

32 Wace, 133, 138; E. Zadora-Rio, 'L'enceinte fortifiée du Plessis-Grimoult, résidence seigneuriale du XIe siècle', *Chateau Gaillard*, 5 (1972), 227–39; WP, 10–11; *GND*, ii, 122–3.

33 Bates, *Normandy*, 179.

CHAPTER 4

1 *ASC* C and E, 1043. Cf. Barlow, *Confessor*, 54–7.

2 *ASC* C, D and E, 1043.

3 *EER*, [lxxii].

4 F. Barlow, 'Two Notes: Cnut's Second Pilgrimage and Queen Emma's Disgrace in 1043', *EHR*, 73 (1958), 653–4; P. Stafford, *Queen Emma and Queen Edith* (Oxford, 1997), 248–51.

5 A phrase used by Barlow, *Confessor*, 59 (but cf. ibid., 79).

6 Lawson, *Battle of Hastings*, 38.

7 *EER*, 20–1; *ASC* E, 1009, 1040; C, D and E, 1044–5.

8 Freeman, *Norman Conquest*, ii, 92; Snorri, 76–7.

9 *ASC* D, 1048.

10 *ASC* D, 1044; C, D and E, 1046.

11 Above, 36, 41; *VER*, 14–15; WM, *Gesta Regum*, 351–3.

12 For the complete text of the poem, see H. Summerson, 'Tudor

Antiquaries and the *Vita Ædwardi regis*', *Anglo-Saxon England*, 38 (2009), 170–2. For comment, see Keynes and Love, 'Earl Godwine's Ship', *passim*.

13. S. Baxter, 'Edward the Confessor and the Succession Question', *Edward the Confessor*, ed. Mortimer, 83–4.

14. *VER*, xxiii, 22–5.

15. Ibid., 24–5.

16. E. John, 'Edward the Confessor and the Norman Succession', *EHR*, 94 (1979), 248–9. Barlow, in his introduction to *VER*, lxxiii–lxxviii, takes a contrary view, as do P. Stafford, 'Edith, Edward's Wife and Queen', *Edward the Confessor*, ed. Mortimer, 135–8, and Baxter 'Edward the Confessor', 82–5, where the case for celibacy is said to turn on *VER*, 14–15. However, the lines 'He preserved with holy chastity . . . in true innocence' (*VER*, 92–3), previously suspected of being a later addition, were evidently part of the original text: Summerson, 'Tudor Antiquaries', 164, 176. The fact adduced by Barlow and repeated by Baxter that Bishop Leofric of Exeter prayed for the marriage to produce an heir proves only that people hoped for one – as well they might.

17. Stafford, 'Edith, Edward's Wife', 121–4.

18. *ASC* C, 1045; D, 1047; JW, ii, 544–5.

19. *ASC* C, 1046; E, 1047; C, D and E, 1049.

20. *ASC* C and E, 1050.

21. *ASC* E, 1048; C, 1049.

22. WP, 10–13; Historians have doubted the suggestion in OV, iv, 210–11, that the siege lasted three years. But note William's decision to hold a church council at Brionne in 1050, which may parallel the proclamation of the Peace of God at Caen soon after Val-ès-Dunes. See S. N. Vaughn, 'Lanfranc at Bec: A Reinterpretation', *Albion*, 17 (1985) 12–13.

23. *GND*, ii, 128–9; WP, 30–1.

24. Her parents' marriage was apparently not consummated until 1031. Douglas, *Conqueror*, 392.

25. Cf. Crouch, *Normans*, 125. The scanty remains of Matilda's skeleton were measured in 1959, and from this it was concluded that her height was 5' (152 cm). But since the tombs at Caen were destroyed during the sixteenth century and their contents scattered, the value of this conclusion is, to say the least, questionable. See J. Dewhurst, 'A Historical Obstetric Enigma: How Tall Was

Matilda?', *Journal of Obstetrics and Gynaecology*, 1 (1981), 271–2.

26 *GND*, ii, 128–9.

27 Bates, *Normandy*, 199–201.

28 *ASC* C and D, 1049.

29 *GND*, ii, 128–31; WP, 32–3.

30 P. Grierson, 'The Relations Between England and Flanders Before the Norman Conquest', *TRHS*, 4th ser., 23 (1941), 97–9.

31 *VER*, 28–31; *ASC* C, D and E, 1051.

32 E.g. Garnett, *Short Introduction*, 26–39. Garnett does admit (at 35) that his argument 'has not found much favour'.

33 *GND*, ii, 158–9; WP, 18–21; *ASC* C and E, 1051; F. Barlow, *The English Church, 1000–1066* (2nd edn, 1979) 298–300.

34 *ASC* E, 1051; *VER*, 30–3.

35 Barlow, *Confessor*, 307–8; *ASC* D and E, 1051.

36 Ibid.; *VER*, 34–7.

37 Ibid., 36–7; *ASC* E, 1051.

38 E.g. Stafford, 'Edith, Edward's Wife', 133–5.

39 D. C. Douglas, 'Edward the Confessor, Duke William of Normandy, and the English Succession', *EHR*, 68 (1953), 526–34. Cf. Baxter, 'Edward the Confessor', 90–5

40 Ibid.; John, 'Edward the Confessor', 253–5.

41 Baxter, 'Edward the Confessor', 86, and Maps 4 and 5; *ASC* D, 1056.

42 *ASC* D, 1051; Mortimer, 'Edward the Confessor', 27–8; Maddicott, 'Edward the Confessor's Return', 653–6.

43 Barlow, *Confessor*, 102; *ASC* C and E, 1050; C, 1051.

44 *ASC* E, 1008; *EHD*, ii, 866; Lawson, *Battle of Hastings*, 154.

45 *ASC* C, D and E, 1052; *VER*, 42–5.

CHAPTER 5

1 WM, *Gesta Regum*, 430–1; WP, 20–1, 50–1.

2 WP, 14–17, 20–3; Bates, *Normandy*, 255; Douglas, *Conqueror*, 58.

3 Ibid., 58–9, 386–7.

4 The events have proved notoriously difficult to date: see Douglas, *Conqueror*, 383–90; Bates, *Normandy*, 255–7; Baxter, 'Edward the Confessor', 90–1.

5 *GND*, ii, 122–5; WP, 22–9.

6 Bates, *Conqueror*, 35; WP, 18–19.

7 Douglas, *Conqueror*, 40–1; WP, 32–5.

8 Ibid., 34–9.

9 *GND*, ii, 102–5; WP, 39–43.

10 Ibid., 43–7.

11 Ibid., 46–9.

12 Ibid.; J. Gillingham, 'William the Bastard at War', *The Battle of Hastings: Sources and Interpretations*, ed. S. Morillo (Woodbridge, 1996), 99–107.

13 Ibid., 107; *GND*, ii, 142–5; WP, 48–51.

14 Ibid., 50–1.

15 *GND*, ii, 104–5 (cf. WP, 42–3); Douglas, *Conqueror*, 69, 83–104 (esp. 92, 99–100, 103).

16 OV, iv, 84–5; *GND*, ii, 130–1, 142–3.

17 Douglas, *Conqueror*, 69; WP, 86–9; Bates, *Normandy*, 209.

18 Douglas, *Conqueror*, 105–6; J. Le Patourel, 'Geoffrey of Montbray, Bishop of Coutances, 1049–93', 59 (1944), 134–5.

19 Douglas, *Conqueror*, 108–9; Bates, *Normandy*, 193–4.

20 Ibid., 196–7, 221; Potts, *Monastic Revival*, 32–3, 106–11, 121.

21 Douglas, *Conqueror*, 115–16; *Sources and Documents*, 41–4.

22 *DNB* Lanfranc; Vaughn, 'Lanfranc at Bec', 136–9.

23 Ibid., 139–43; *Sources and Documents*, 25 (cf. WP, 84–5).

24 *GND*, ii, 130–43; OV, ii, 10–11; Potts, *Monastic Revival*, 105, 112–13.

25 Bates, *Normandy*, 115–16, 222; OV, ii, 10–11; *GND*, ii, 130–1.

26 In general, see R. Stalley, *Early Medieval Architecture* (Oxford, 1999), esp. Ch. 9; Fernie, *Architecture*, 3–14.

27 Little remains of these buildings apart from the crypts of Rouen and Bayeux. Brown, *Normans and the Norman Conquest*, 25–6.

28 Bates, *Normandy*, 202, 210.

29 OV, iii, 120–3.

30 Holland, *Millennium*, 264–7.

31 *GND*, ii, 113–19; Le Patourel, 'Geoffrey of Montbray', 133–4; D. Bates, 'The Character and Career of Odo, Bishop of Bayeux (1049/50–1097)', *Speculum*, 50 (1975), 2–3.

32 *GND*, ii, 118–19; Le Patourel, 'Geoffrey of Montbray', 135–7; Vaughn, 'Lanfranc at Bec', 145–7; below, 112

33 WP, 82–3; Bates, *Normandy*, 201.

34 Douglas, *Conqueror*, 121; WP, 88–9.

35 Ibid., 50–5.

36 Douglas, *Conqueror*, 72; *GND*, ii, 126–9.
37 WP, 54–5; Douglas, *Conqueror*, 72–3 (cf. Bates, *Conqueror*, 38);
   Gillingham, 'William the Bastard', 108–9.
38 Ibid., 107; WP, 54–7; *GND*, ii, 150–3.

CHAPTER 6

1 *VER*, 44–5; JW, ii, 570–3; *ASC* D, 1052; Baxter, 'Edward the
   Confessor', Map 6.
2 *VER*, 62–3, 92–127; above, 64
3 Ibid., 66–71; Fernie, *Architecture*, 96–8; idem, 'Edward the Confessor's
   Westminster Abbey', *Edward the Confessor*, ed. Mortimer, 139–50,
   and also the articles there by Gem and Rodwell. For the state of
   the abbey in 1066, see Summerson, 'Tudor Antiquaries', 164, 177.
4 *VER*, 66–9. The current occupants of the Palace of Westminster
   seem certain that it was established by Cnut (see www.parliament.
   uk, Factsheet G11), a conclusion tentatively endorsed by E. Mason,
   Westminster Abbey and its People, c.1050 to c.1216 (Woodbridge, 1996),
   11–12. The evidence discussed there, however, seems scanty,
   amounting to a line of dubious worth in the *Carmen* and some
   speculation about the significance of the earlier burial at
   Westminster of Harold Harefoot. Most academics adhere to the
   traditional belief that the palace, like the abbey, was the work of
   the Confessor. See, for instance, *The Blackwell Encyclopaedia of
   Anglo-Saxon England*, ed. M. Lapidge et al. (Oxford, 1999), 471;
   Carmen, 40.
5 E.g. Baxter, 'Edward the Confessor', 95. For debate about the date
   of the *Life*, see Stafford, *Queen Emma*, 40–8; *VER*, xxviii–xxxiii.
6 Above, 64; Mortimer, 'Edward the Confessor', 31–2.
7 Ibid., 31–4; above, 21; *ASC* D, 1065; van Houts, 'Edward and
   Normandy', 71–5; Barlow, *Confessor*, 50.
8 Cf. Barlow, *English Church, 1000–1066*, 85–6, who cautions against
   assuming Robert was a reformer, and then assumes precisely the
   opposite.
9 S. Keynes, 'Giso, Bishop of Wells (1061–88)', *ANS*, 19 (1996),
   205–13; Hare, 'Cnut and Lotharingia', *passim*. Although Cnut also
   had links with Lorraine and appointed one Lotharingian bishop,
   it does not follow that Edward was merely continuing earlier
   policy: William of Normandy, after all, appointed a Lotharingian,

Maurilius, to be archbishop of Rouen. Moreover, since both Hermann and Leofric are known to have crossed with Edward in 1041, it is difficult to see how their appointment can be construed as a native attempt, spearheaded by the Godwines, to thwart the promotion of Normans.

10 Barlow, *English Church, 1000–1066*, 82–4, 301–2; *DNB* Leofric; *DNB* Hermann.

11 Barlow, *English Church, 1000–1066*, 86. *VER*, 30–1; WM, *Gesta Pontificum*, 286–9.

12 *DNB* Stigand; *VER*, 36–7.

13 *DNB* Stigand; WM, *Gesta Pontificum*, 46–7.

14 *ASC* C, 1053; WM, *Gesta Regum*, 354–5.

15 *DNB* Harold II; *VER*, 46–9.

16 Baxter, *Earls of Mercia*, 43–5.

17 Barlow, *Confessor*, 188–213, and Baxter, 'Edward the Confessor', 96, argue that it did. Cf. Mortimer, 'Edward the Confessor', 28–31.

18 JW, ii, 502–3; cf. ASC D 1057. See also *DNB* Edward the Exile; S. Keynes, 'The Crowland Psalter and the Sons of King Edmund Ironside', *Bodleian Library Record*, 6 (1985), 359–70.

19 JW, ii, 574–5. JW also implies Ealdred went on the king's orders, but this seems to have been his default assumption: see Barlow, *Confessor*, 189.

20 *VER*, 34–5; Barlow, *Confessor*, 201–3.

21 *VER*, 48–51.

22 S. Baxter, 'MS C of the Anglo-Saxon Chronicle and the Politics of Mid-Eleventh-Century England', *EHR*, 122 (2007), 1189–1227.

23 K. L. Maund, 'The Welsh Alliances of Earl Ælfgar of Mercia and his Family in the Mid-Eleventh Century', *ANS*, 11 (1988), 181–90.

24 *VER*, 36–7, 52–3, 82–3; P. Grierson, 'A Visit of Earl Harold to Flanders in 1056', *EHR*, 51 (1936), 90–7, but cf. Baxter, 'Edward the Confessor', 97.

25 Ibid., 97–8. For conspiracy theories, see e.g. E. Mason, *The House of Godwine: The History of a Dynasty* (2004), 92; John, 'Edward the Confessor', 257.

26 *DNB* Edgar Ætheling; Baxter, 'Edward the Confessor', 98–101.

27 Ibid., 103–4; *VER*, 50–1.

28 Baxter, *Earls of Mercia*, 128–38, revises Fleming, *Kings and Lords*, 53–71; *DNB* Harold.

29 Barlow, *English Church, 1000–1066*, 86–93, 304–5; *DNB* Stigand.
30 *VER*, 54–5, 60–3.
31 Baxter, *Earls of Mercia*, 48; idem, 'Edward the Confessor', Map 11.
32 *ASC* D and E, 1063; JW, ii, 592–3; R. R. Davies, *The Age of Conquest: Wales, 1063–1415* (Oxford, 2000), 24, 26.
33 *ASC* E, 1063; Gerald of Wales, *The Journey through Wales and the Description of Wales*, transl. L. Thorpe (1978), 266.

CHAPTER 7

1 Douglas, *Conqueror*, 74; *GND*, ii, 152–3; OV, ii, 88–9; *VER*, 106–7.
2 *Chroniques des Comtes d'Anjou et des Seigneurs d'Amboise*, ed. L. Halphen and R. Poupardin (Paris, 1913), 62.
3 Bates, *Conqueror*, 38.
4 Ibid., 39–41; Douglas, *Conqueror*, 59, 73, 173–4; WP, 58–61.
5 Ibid., 60–9; OV, ii, 118–19, 312–13. For sceptical comment, see Douglas, *Conqueror*, 408–15.
6 Bates, *Conqueror*, 54–6; idem, *Normandy*, 114, 247; WP, 84–5; Fernie, *Architecture*, 14, 98–102, accepts the suggestion of Maylis Baylé that St Stephen's was begun after 1066, but this rests largely on an unconvincing argument from silence and ignores Torigni's statement that Lanfranc was made abbot in 1063. See M. Baylé, 'Les Ateliers de Sculpture de Saint-Etienne de Caen au 11° et au 12° Siècles', *ANS*, 10 (1988), 1–2. Cf. *Chronicles of the Reigns of Stephen, Henry II and Richard I*, ed. R. Howlett (4 vols., Rolls Series, 1884–9), iv, 34.
7 Baxter, 'Edward the Confessor', 106, n143.
8 WP, 68–9; WM, *Gesta Regum*, 416–17; Eadmer, 6–7.
9 Ibid.; *GND*, ii, 160–1; OV, iv, 88–9; WP, 68–71.
10 Ibid., 70–7. For the Brittany campaign, see K. S. B. Keats-Rohan, 'William the Conqueror and the Breton Contingent in the Non-Norman Conquest, 1066–1086', *ANS*, 13 (1991), 157–72.
11 The notion that Harold was tricked into swearing on concealed relics was a later improvement: Wace, 154–5.
12 OV, ii, 134–5, says the oath was sworn at Rouen before the Breton campaign. The Tapestry has it happen afterwards at Bayeux.
13 *GND*, ii, 158–61.
14 WP, 68–9; OV, ii, 134–5.
15 *VER*, 50–3; 80–1; WM, *Gesta Regum*, 416–17.

[16] Eadmer, 6–7; WP, 68–9, 76–7; Barlow, *Confessor*, 301–6; K. E. Cutler, 'The Godwinist Hostages: The Case for 1051', *Annuale Mediaevale*, 12 (1972), 70–7.

[17] WP, 70–1.

[18] Eadmer 6–7; Orderic Vitalis also believed that Harold agreed to marry William's sister: *GND*, ii, 160–1.

[19] WP, 70–1; Eadmer, 7–8.

[20] Ibid., 5–7. For Eadmer's outlook, see J. Rubenstein, 'Liturgy Against History: The Competing Visions of Lanfranc and Eadmer of Canterbury', *Speculum*, 74 (1999), 299–307.

[21] Baxter, 'Edward the Confessor', 106–7.

[22] Eadmer, 6.

[23] Ibid., 7–8; WP, 76–7.

[24] E.g. Ashe, *Fiction and History*, 39–41.

[25] Eadmer, 8.

CHAPTER 8

[1] *ASC* C and D, 1065.

[2] W. E. Kapelle, *The Norman Conquest of the North* (1979), 9–13.

[3] N. J. Higham, *The Kingdom of Northumbria, AD 350–1100* (Stroud, 1993), 194–202, 211–12.

[4] Kapelle, *Norman Conquest of the North*, 13–19.

[5] Ibid., 7, 12–13; R. Fletcher, *Bloodfeud: Murder and Revenge in Anglo-Saxon England* (2002), 31–3.

[6] Ibid., 73–5, 149, 205–6.

[7] *ASC* C, 1065; *VER*, 50–1; SD, *Libellus*, 170–3, 174–7, 180–1.

[8] JW, ii, 598–9; Kapelle, *Norman Conquest of the North*, 96–7.

[9] *VER*, 48–9, 76–9; *ASC* C, 1065.

[10] *VER*, 50–1.

[11] Kapelle, *Norman Conquest of the North*, 33–9, 46–7.

[12] Ibid., 90–2; *VER*, 66–7; SD, *History*, 127; Gaimar, *Estoire*, 276–7.

[13] Kapelle, *Norman Conquest of the North*, 34–44, 92–4.

[14] Ibid., 17, 25–6, 29, 43–4.

[15] Ibid., 94–5, 98.

[16] JW, ii, 596–9; *ASC* D, 1065.

[17] *VER*, 76–7.

[18] Ibid.; Baxter, *Earls of Mercia*, 48; *ASC* D, 1065.

[19] *VER*, 74–7; JW, ii, 598–9.

20 *ASC* D, 1065; *VER*, 78–9.
21 Ibid., 78–81.
22 *ASC* D, 1065.
23 Ibid.; JW, ii, 598–9; *VER*, 80–3.
24 Ibid., 110–13; Summerson, 'Tudor Antiquaries', 8–9, 21–2.

CHAPTER 9

1 *Sources and Documents*, 17–18 (cf. WP, 2–3). For general comment, see A. Williams, 'Some Notes and Considerations on Problems Connected with the English Royal Succession, 860–1066', *ANS*, I (1978), 144–67.
2 *EER*, 6–7, 52–3. Cf. Garnett, *Short Introduction*, 32–3.
3 Above, 31–4, 38, 41–2.
4 *ASC* E, 1066; JW, ii, 600–1; Baxter, 'Edward the Confessor', 109–10.
5 *VER*, 116–19.
6 Ibid., 122–3.
7 Ashe, *Fiction and History*, 44–5; Baxter, 'Edward the Confessor', 111–12.
8 *ASC* C and D, 1065; WP, 118–19. Cf. Baxter, 'Edward the Confessor', 113.
9 WP, 100–1; Barlow, *Confessor*, 244–5. In their present form the charters are twelfth-century forgeries, but their witness-lists look to have been copied from bona fide originals.
10 *DNB* Ealdgyth; Baxter, *Earls of Mercia*, 52; above, 117.
11 Cf. Barlow, *Confessor*, 227.
12 *VER*, xxiii–xxiv, xxx–xxxi.
13 E. van Houts, 'The Norman Conquest Through European Eyes', *EHR*, 110 (1995), 845–6.
14 Baxter, 'Edward the Confessor', 101–3.
15 G. Garnett, 'Coronation and Propaganda: Some Implications of the Norman Claim to the Throne of England in 1066', *TRHS*, 5th ser., 36 (1986), 92–3. Cf. Barlow, *Confessor*, 254–5.
16 WM, *Gesta Regum*, 420–2.
17 Baxter, 'Edward the Confessor', 114; WM, *Saints' Lives*, 86–9; *ASC* C, 1065.
18 Wace, 156.
19 WP, 70–1; *GND*, ii, 160–1. See also Eadmer, 8–9.
20 WP, 100–1; Gillingham, 'William the Bastard', 99–102.

[21] WP, 105. C. Morton, 'Pope Alexander II and the Norman Conquest', *Latomus* (1975), 362–82, argues that the papal banner was a fiction invented by William of Poitiers, and that Rome's support for the Conquest was actually retrospective. But her argument founders on several important pieces of evidence – in particular, a letter of Pope Gregory VII to William which refers explicitly to his having supported the invasion. Cf. van Houts, 'Norman Conquest Through European Eyes', 850, n2; Garnett, 'Coronation and Propaganda', 99, n50.

[22] WP, 100–3; Wace, 157–8; WM, *Gesta Regum*, 448–9.

[23] WP, 100–1, 106–7; Wace, 159.

[24] WM, *Gesta Regum*, 448–9: 'The soldiers grumbled in their tents . . . "his father had the same idea, and was prevented in the same way"'.

[25] Wace, 159; *EHD*, ii, 606. For more on the ordinance, see below, 236–7.

[26] M. Chibnall, 'Military Service in Normandy Before 1066', *Anglo-Norman Warfare* (Woodbridge, 1992), 28–40.

[27] Wace, 159.

[28] E. M. C. van Houts, 'The Ship List of William the Conqueror', *ANS*, 10 (1988), 159–83.

[29] Wace, 158–9 (see also HH, 24–5); WP, 106–7.

[30] B. Bachrach, 'On the Origins of William the Conqueror's Horse Transports', *Technology and Culture*, 26 (1985), 505–31, suggests that the Normans did not have the technology to transport horses, and must have procured ships from the Mediterranean. But (at 514) his argument relies heavily on a mistranslated line in *The Carmen de Hastingae Proelio*, ed. C. Morton and H. Muntz (Oxford, 1972), 18–19. Cf. *Carmen*, 14–15, and C. M. Gillmor, 'Naval Logistics of the Cross-Channel Operation, 1066', *ANS*, 7 (1984), 111–13.

[31] WP, 106–7; *ASC* C and D, 1066; *GND*, ii, 162–3.

[32] Snorri, 135–6; OV, ii, 141–3. Freeman, *Norman Conquest*, iii, 708–13 ('The Movements of Tostig after his Banishment') states that Orderic's testimony is supported by William of Jumièges, unaware that the passage in question is a later interpolation by Orderic himself: *GND*, ii, 162–3.

[33] JW, ii, 600–1, adds 'returning from Flanders' to the Chronicle's account; Gaimar, *Estoire*, 280–1, says that the majority of Tostig's force were Flemings.

34 *ASC* C, D and E, 1066.

35 Ibid.; above, 76; JW, ii, 600–1.

36 *ASC* C, 1066. See also WP, 106–7.

37 *Recueil* des actes des ducs de Normandie de *911* à *1066*, ed. M. Fauroux (Caen, 1961), 442–3, no. 231; Brown, *Normans and the Norman Conquest*, 127.

38 Wace, 163; Gillmor, 'Naval Logistics', 109–16. In 1997 more ships were found on the site of the museum itself, including one datable to Cnut's reign that measured thirty-six metres – the longest ever discovered.

39 Van Houts, 'Ship List', 166, 176, 179; *GND*, ii, 164–5; Wace, 163.

40 Van Houts, 'Ship List', 170, 176, 179; OV, ii, 144–5; WP, 102–3, 130–1.

41 Ibid., 102–3, 116–17; OV, ii, 168–9; *Carmen*, 8–9; van Houts, 'Norman Conquest Through European Eyes', 846, n3.

42 Lawson, *Battle of Hastings*, 176–86, gives a useful overview of the evidence, but his case for accepting the very large chronicle figures fails to convince.

43 WP, xxiv–xxvi, 102–3. Cf. Bates, *Conqueror*, 111; Morris, *Great and Terrible King*, 272–3; C. and G. Grainge, 'The Pevensey Expedition: Brilliantly Executed Plan or Near Disaster?', *Battle of Hastings*, ed. Morillo, 130–42.

44 B. Bachrach, 'Some Observations on the Military Administration of the Norman Conquest', *ANS*, 8 (1986), 1–25. Note, however, the criticisms of Davis, 'Warhorses of the Normans', 69, 80.

45 WP, 102–5.

46 *ASC* C, 1066.

CHAPTER 10

1 Adam of Bremen, *History of the Archbishops of Hamburg-Bremen*, trans. F. J. Tschan (Columbia, 2002), 128; WP, 116–17; Arnold, *Vikings*, 187–8.

2 Snorri, 20–1, 24, 29.

3 Ibid., 33, 58–62.

4 Ibid., 65–81.

5 E.g. Stenton, *Anglo-Saxon England*, 560, 569, 575; Douglas, *Conqueror*, 173, 180; above, 60–1.

6 Barlow, *Confessor*, 209; *ASC* D, 1048, 1058; above, 62.

[7] Snorri, 122–9, 180–1.

[8] Above, 147–8; *ASC* C, 1066.

[9] Snorri, 135–8; Gaimar, *Estoire*, 280–1; W. H. Stevenson, 'Notes on Old-English Historical Geography', *EHR*, 11 (1896), 301–4.

[10] E.g. C. Jones, *The Forgotten Battle of 1066: Fulford* (Stroud, 2006), 101–44.

[11] Snorri, 135–8; K. DeVries, *The Norwegian Invasion of England in 1066* (Woodbridge, 1999), 233–40; OV, ii, 142–5.

[12] Snorri, 139, 141; *ASC* D and E, 1066; JW, ii, 602–3.

[13] Snorri, 141–2; *ASC* C, D and E, 1066.

[14] Ibid.

[15] OV, ii, 144–5; DeVries, *Norwegian Invasion*, 263. Cf. Douglas, *Conqueror*, 191, and Freeman, *Norman Conquest*, iii, 343.

[16] *ASC* C, 1066.

[17] Ibid.; Snorri, 69, 142–4.

[18] *ASC* C, 1066; JW, ii, 602–3.

[19] *ASC* C, 1066. Snorri, 145, claims the Norwegians established a camp at Stamford before the fall of York, but does not suggest why. Modern suggestions include the site's geographical convenience and its proximity to Harold Godwineson's manor at Catton. Stenton, *Anglo-Saxon England*, 589; I. W. Walker, *Harold: The Last Anglo-Saxon King* (Stroud, 2004), 182.

[20] *ASC* C, 1066.

[21] Ibid.; Snorri, 146–53; van Houts, 'Norman Conquest Through European Eyes', 839, n2.

[22] *ASC* D, 1066; *VER*, 88–9.

[23] OV, ii, 168–9; WM, *Gesta Regum*, 468–9.

CHAPTER 11

[1] WP, 102–3. Cf. M. Chibnall, *Anglo-Norman England, 1066–1166* (Oxford, 1986); R. A. Brown, 'The Battle of Hastings', *Battle of Hastings*, ed. Morillo, 201, n20. Chibnall was perhaps inspired by the seventeenth-century historian John Hayward, who speculated that William was waiting for Harold Hardrada to invade: Chibnall, *Debate*, 32.

[2] *Carmen*, xiii–xix, xxiv–xlii.

[3] Ibid., xxix, xlii–liii.

[4] Ibid., 4–5.

5 WP, 108–9.

6 *Carmen*, 4–5; WP, 108–9; R. H. C. Davis, 'William of Poitiers and his History of William the Conqueror', idem, *From Alfred the Great to Stephen* (1991), 103; above, 161–2.

7 *Carmen*, 6–7; WP, 110–11.

8 Douglas, *Conqueror*, 397; *Carmen*, lxv–lxviii, 8–9.

9 Van Houts, 'Ship List', 166, 168, 172–3.

10 WP, 110–11; *Carmen*, lxviii–lxix, 8–9.

11 WP, 112–13.

12 *Carmen*, lxviii–lxx, 8–11.

13 Douglas, *Conqueror*, 196–7; HH, 25. The chronicler at Waltham Abbey, writing after 1177, improbably claims that Harold heard the news while at Waltham. *The Waltham Chronicle*, ed. and trans. I. Watkiss and M. Chibnall (Oxford 1992), xliii, 44–5.

14 OV, ii, 172–3.

15 WP, 116–17.

16 Ibid., 116–23; *Carmen*, 14–21.

17 Ibid., 10–11.

18 *ASC* E, 1066; JW, ii, 604–5; OV, ii, 170–3.

19 Lawson, *Battle of Hastings*, 62–3, 110–11; WP, 122–5.

20 *GND*, ii, 166–7; WP, 124–5.

21 *Carmen*, 18–21; WP, 122–5.

22 *GND*, ii, 168–9.

23 *ASC* D, 1066; OV, ii, 172–3; Lawson, *Battle of Hastings*, 56–8.

24 *ASC* D, 1066; *GND*, ii, 166–9; WM, *Gesta Regum*, 452–5.

25 WP, 124–5; *The Chronicle of Battle Abbey*, ed. and trans. E. Searle (Oxford, 1980), 34–7; 'The *Brevis Relatio de Guillelmo nobilissimo comite Normannorum*', ed. E. van Houts, idem, *History and Family Traditions*, VII, 31.

26 WP, 124–7; *Carmen*, 20–1; WM, *Gesta Regum*, 422–3; Wace, 178. *ASC* D also says that Harold's army was large.

27 WP, 126–7; *Carmen*, 22–3; *Chronicle of Battle Abbey*, ed. Searle, 44–5.

28 WP, 128–9; *Carmen*, 24–5; *Carmen*, ed. Morton and Muntz, 112–15; HH, 26.

29 WP, 128–9; *Carmen*, 24–5.

30 Ibid.

31 WP, 128–9; *Carmen*, 22–3.

32 Ibid., 26–9; WP, 128–31.

[33] Ibid., 132–3.

[34] *Carmen*, 26–7; WP, 128–9, 132–3; *GND*, ii, 102–5.

[35] WP, 132–3.

[36] *Carmen*, 32–3; WP, 136–7; *GND*, ii, 168–9. In the same paragraph Jumièges contradicts himself by saying that Harold fell 'during the first assault'. For a possible solution, see Gillingham, 'William the Bastard', 101, n36.

[37] Brown, *Bayeux Tapestry*, 174 (a translation of Baudri); WM, *Gesta Regum*, 454–5; HH, 28.

[38] D. Bernstein, 'The Blinding of Harold and the Meaning of the Bayeux Tapestry', *ANS*, 5 (1983), 41–8; Lawson, *Battle of Hastings*, 255–66.

[39] Bernstein, *Mystery*, 171–4; idem, 'Blinding of Harold', 60–4.

[40] M. K. Foys, 'Pulling the Arrow Out: The Legend of Harold's Death and the Bayeux Tapestry', *Bayeux Tapestry*, ed. Foys, Overby and Terkla, 158–75; C. Dennis, 'The Strange Death of King Harold II', *The Historian* (2009), 14–18.

[41] *Carmen*, 32–3; Bernstein, *Mystery*, 160.

[42] Brown, 'Battle of Hastings', 215.

[43] J. Gillingham, '"Holding to the Rules of War (*Bellica Iura Tenentes*)": Right Conduct Before, During and After Battle in North-Western Europe in the Eleventh Century', *ANS*, 29 (2007), 8–11; above, 81–2; *Carmen*, lxxxii–lxxxv.

CHAPTER 12

[1] WP, 136–9; *GND*, ii, 168–9 (also OV, ii, 176–7); *Chronicle of Battle Abbey*, ed. Searle, 38–9. Although there has been much debate about the timing of the Malfosse episode, there can be little doubt that WP and OV were correct to place it after the battle. William of Malmesbury later described a similar incident *during* the battle, apparently based on a scene in the Bayeux Tapestry – a source well known for putting events in a different order for dramatic or artistic purposes. Cf. Brown, 'Battle of Hastings', 215–18.

[2] WP, 138–43; *ASC* D, 1066; *Carmen*, 32–5; Gillingham, '"Holding to the Rules of War"', 4–7.

[3] WP, 140–1; *Waltham Chronicle*, ed. Watkiss and Chibnall, xliii–xliv, 54–7; *Carmen*, 34–5.

[4] Ibid.; WP, 142–3.

5 Ibid., 146–7; *Carmen*, 38–9.

6 *ASC* D, 1066; OV, ii, 180–1; JW, ii, 604–5.

7 *ASC* D, 1066; WP, 142–5; *Carmen*, 36–7.

8 Ibid., 36–9; WP, 144–5.

9 *Carmen*, 38–9; WP, 146–7.

10 Ibid.; *ASC* D, 1066; JW, ii, 606–7. Cf. WM, *Gesta Regum*, 460–1.

11 F. Baring, 'The Conqueror's Footprints in Domesday', *EHR*, 13 (1898), 17–25. Cf. J. J. N. Palmer, 'The Conqueror's Footprints in Domesday', *The Medieval Military Revolution*, ed. A. Ayton and J. L. Price (1995), 23–44.

12 Williams, *English and the Norman Conquest*, 100–1; *GND*, ii, 170–1; B. English, 'Towns, Mottes and Ring-Works of the Conquest', *Medieval Military Revolution*, ed. Ayton and Price, 51.

13 WP, 100–1, 146–7.

14 *ASC* D, 1066; JW, ii, 606–7; WM, *Gesta Regum*, 460–3.

15 *ASC* D and E, 1066; WP, 146–7.

16 G. Garnett, *Conquered England: Kingship, Succession and Tenure, 1066–1166* (Oxford, 2007), 3–4; WP, 146–9.

17 Ibid., 148–9.

18 *GND*, ii, 170–1 (cf. OV, ii, 180–1); WP, 160–3.

19 *Carmen*, 38–41; OV, ii, 182–3.

20 For debate on the service, cf. G. Garnett, 'The Third Recension of the English Coronation *ordo*: The Manuscripts', *Haskins Society Journal*, 11 (2003), 43–71 and J. L. Nelson, 'Rites of the Conqueror', idem, *Politics and Ritual in Early Medieval Europe* (1986), 375–401; Maddicott, *Origins of the English Parliament*, 44–5; JW, ii, 606–7.

21 WP, 148–9; *ASC* D, 1066.

22 WP, 150–1; Garnett, *Short Introduction*, 19–21; OV, ii, 184–5.

23 WP, 150–5, 178–9; Douglas, *Conqueror*, 209.

24 WP, 156–61; *EHD*, ii, 945; *ASC* D, 1066.

25 WP, 160–3. Poitiers' statement that Eadwine and Morcar submitted at Barking is at odds with the account of the D Chronicle, which names the two brothers among those who surrendered the previous year at Berkhamsted. There is no easy way to reconcile these two statements. Most historians have preferred the English version, despite the fact Poitiers' account is far more detailed and there is no obvious reason for him deliberately to have misdated the earls' surrender. Some have argued that he confused Barking with Berkhamsted (Douglas,

Conqueror, 207). Others have rejected this, and suggested instead that Eadwine and Morcar might have submitted twice (Baxter, *Earls of Mercia*, 270–1). But Poitiers' account – especially his line 'they sought his pardon for any hostility they had shown to him' – hardly sounds as if he is describing a second submission. It seems equally if not more likely that Poitiers has it right on this occasion, and that the much shorter account in the Chronicle, which says nothing of the Barking episode, has telescoped the two events into one. John of Worcester follows the Chronicle in saying that Eadwine and Morcar submitted at Berkhamsted, but his earlier statement that the earls had left London with their army and gone home strongly suggests they had retreated into northern England. Such a scenario would be consistent with the Conqueror's reported reluctance to be crowned while 'some people were still rebelling', and his subsequent willingness to return to Normandy in the New Year once the Barking submissions had taken place.

26 WP, 162–3; ASC E, 1066; Williams, *English and the Norman Conquest*, 8–9.

27 *EHD*, ii, 918; WP, 164–5.

28 WP, 162–3, 166–9; *ASC* E, 1067.

29 WP, 168–81.

30 Ibid., 154–5, 176–7, 180–1; OV, ii, 198–9.

CHAPTER 13

1 OV, ii, xiii–xvi, xxix–xxx.

2 Ibid., iii, 6–9, 150–1. Orderic's modern translator, Marjorie Chibnall, was also born in Atcham in 1915.

3 Ibid., ii, xxxii, 184–5, 258–61.

4 WP, 114–15; OV, ii, 170–1. Similarly, Orderic provides quite different versions of the Malfosse incident and the violent scenes that marred the Conqueror's coronation – differences we might in each case attribute to his English origins. Above, 189, 200.

5 OV, ii, 202–3 (cf. 196–7, a slightly less harsh verdict). The phrase 'Norman yoke', coined by Orderic, owes its modern fame to seventeenth-century polemicists. Barber, 'Norman Conquest and the Media', 11–15.

6 R. Eales, 'Royal Power and Castles in Norman England', *The*

Ideals and Practice of Medieval Knighthood III, ed. C. Harper-Bill and R. Harvey (Woodbridge, 1990), 50–4; English, 'Towns, Mottes and Ring-Works', 45–61. It will be apparent from what follows that I do not agree with more recent, revisionist arguments. Cf. e.g. R. Liddiard, *Castles in Context: Power, Symbolism and Landscape, 1066 to 1500* (Macclesfield, 2005), 12–38.

7 A. Williams, 'A Bell-house and a Burh-geat: Lordly Residences in England before the Norman Conquest', *Medieval Knighthood IV* (Woodbridge, 1992), 221–40.

8 *ASC* E, 1051; OV, ii, 218–19.

9 *ASC* E, 1051; *ASC* D, 1066.

10 OV, ii, 202–3 (cf. WP, 182–3).

11 JW, iii, 4–5 (cf. OV, ii, 194–5); S. Reynolds, 'Eadric *Silvaticus* and the English Resistance', *Bulletin of the Institute of Historical Research*, 54 (1981), 102–5.

12 WP, 182–5; OV, ii, 204–7; *Carmen*, 30–3; *DNB* Eustace.

13 SD, *History*, 143–4; Fletcher, *Bloodfeud*, 161, 169–71; Kapelle, *Norman Conquest of the North*, 106; WP, 162–3, 184–7.

14 For this interpretation, see J. O. Prestwich, *The Place of War in English History, 1066–1214* (Woodbridge, 2004), 27–31.

15 WM, *Gesta Regum*, 480–1, 570–1; Baxter, *Earls of Mercia*, 300; *DNB* Harold II.

16 JW, iii, 6–7; WP, 182–3; OV, ii, 208–9.

17 Ibid., ii, 212–13.

18 Ibid.; JW, iii, 4–5.

19 OV, ii, 212–13; WM, *Gesta Regum*, 462–3; *ASC* D, 1067; JW, iii, 6–7.

20 OV, ii, 212–15; *ASC* D, 1067; Garnett, *Short Introduction*, 49–50; Williams, *English and the Norman Conquest*, 21.

21 *Historia Ecclesie Abbendonensis: The History of the Church of Abingdon*, ed. J. Hudson (2 vols., Oxford, 2002, 2007), i, 222–3.

22 OV, ii, 210–11; J. F. A. Mason, 'William the First and the Sussex Rapes', *1066 Commemoration Lectures* (Historical Association, 1966), 37–58.

23 WP, 162–3; *EHD*, ii, 430–1, 601–3; SD, *History*, 144.

24 *RRAN*, 594–601 (no. 181); Baxter, *Earls of Mercia*, 272–3.

25 Williams, *English and the Norman Conquest*, 12–13; *ASC* E, 1067; OV, ii, 222–3; WP, 164–5 (cf. OV, ii, 194–5).

26 Gaimar, *Estoire*, 284–5; Kapelle, *Norman Conquest of the North*, 105, 109.
27 OV, ii, 214–17; Baxter, *Earls of Mercia*, 284–6.
28 OV, ii, 216–19; *ASC* D and E, 1067.
29 WP, 162–3; OV, ii, 216–17; *ASC* D, 1067.
30 Ibid.; OV, ii, 218–19.
31 Ibid.; *ASC* D and E, 1067.
32 *ASC* D, 1067; JW, iii, 6–9.
33 OV, ii, 218–21; B. Golding, *Conquest and Colonisation: The Normans in Britain, 1066–1100* (2nd edn, Basingstoke, 2001), 72.
34 *ASC* D, 1067; JW, iii, 6–9; OV, ii, 220–1; *RRAN*, 78.
35 Kapelle, *Norman Conquest of the North*, 110–11.
36 OV, ii, 220–3; Gaimar, *Estoire*, 294–5; SD, *History*, 136; *ASC* D and E, 1068.
37 SD, *Libellus*, 182–5.
38 OV, ii, 222–3.
39 Ibid.; *ASC* D, 1068.
40 OV, ii, 222–3; SD, *Libellus*, 184–5.
41 OV, ii, 222–5; *ASC* D, 1068; JW, iii, 6–9; *GND*, ii, 180–3. Cf. Williams, *English and the Norman Conquest*, 35.
42 *DNB* Gytha; OV, ii, 208–9, 224–7 (cf. WP, 126–7); above, 121.
43 OV, ii, 224–7; Adam of Bremen, *History*, trans. Tschan, 108, 123; Barlow, *Confessor*, 58, 109, 138, 214.
44 *ASC* D and E, 1069; OV, ii, 226–7.
45 Ibid.; JW, iii, 8–9.
46 Ibid., 8–11; *ASC* D, 1069.
47 OV, ii, 228–31.
48 Ibid, 230–1 (cf. 226–7).
49 Below, 242–3; Kapelle, *Norman Conquest of the North*, 115–16; *ASC* D, 1069; JW, iii, 10–11.
50 OV, ii, 230–1; *ASC* D, 1069; SD, *History*, 137.
51 JW, iii, 10–11.
52 OV, ii, 230–3.
53 Below, 313–14.
54 JW, iii, 10–11; SD, *History*, 137; Thomas of Marlborough, *History of the Abbey of Evesham*, ed. and trans. J. Sayers and L. Watkiss (Oxford, 2003), 166–7.
55 OV, ii, 232–3.

CHAPTER 14

1 *ASC* D, 1069; Hugh the Chanter, *The History of the Church of York, 1066–1127* (Oxford, 1990), 2–3; OV, ii, 232–3.

2 Ibid.; SD, *History*, 138.

3 OV, ii, 234–7; J. J. N. Palmer, 'War and Domesday Waste', *Armies, Chivalry and Warfare in Medieval Britain and France,* ed. M. Strickland (Stamford, 1998), 259–61.

4 *ASC* D, 1070.

5 OV, ii, 234–7.

6 Fleming, *Kings and Lords*, 166–7; P. Dalton, *Conquest, Anarchy and Lordship: Yorkshire, 1066–1154* (Cambridge, 1994), 65.

7 JW, iii, 10–11; *Historia Ecclesie Abbendonensis*, ed. Hudson, i, 226–7; OV, ii, 236–7.

8 Ibid.

9 Ibid., iii, 254–7.

10 *EHD*, ii, 606–7; H. E. J. Cowdrey, 'The Anglo-Norman *Laudes Regiae*', *Viator*, 12 (1981), 59, n68.

11 *EHD,* ii, 606–7; E. Searle, *Lordship and Community: Battle Abbey and its Banlieu, 1066–1538* (Toronto, 1974), 21 (also *Chronicle of Battle Abbey*, 20–1), suggests that the abbey was not founded until the mid-1070s, but her argument draws on the discredited thesis of Morton, 'Pope Alexander II'. Cf. Nelson, 'Rites of the Conqueror', 396–7, who argues for an earlier date.

12 *EHD*, ii, 606–7; Cowdrey, 'Anglo-Norman *Laudes Regiae*', 59, n68.

13 On the basis of *ASC* E, 1069, it seems more likely that these two bishops were arrested and outlawed during that year rather than in 1070, as is commonly supposed. Cf. e.g. *Councils and Synods*, ii, 566.

14 JW, iii, 10–13; WP, 146–7, 160–1.

15 *Letters of Lanfranc*, 36–7, 62–3; *DNB* Æthelmær; Baxter, *Earls of Mercia*, 292–3; JW, iii, 14–15.

16 Above, 92; OV, iii, 236–7.

17 JW, iii, 12–15; *The Heads of Religious Houses: England and Wales, I, 940–1216*, ed. D. Knowles, C. N. L. Brooke and V. M. C. London (2nd edn, Cambridge, 2001), 24, 36, 66. The deposition of Ealdred of Abingdon is generally dated to 1071, on the basis of *Historia Ecclesie Abbendonensis*, ed. Hudson, i, 224–9, but the sequence of

events there is so confused that Ealdred could have been deposed at any point after 1068.

18 F. Barlow, *The English Church, 1066–1154* (1979), 61–2; *DNB* Thomas of Bayeux; *DNB* Walcher. The surviving English bishops were Leofric of Exeter (d. 1072), Siward of Rochester (d. 1075) and Wulfstan of Worcester (d. 1095).

19 Above 76, 144–5, 202.

20 Matthew Paris, *Historia Anglorum*, ed. F. Madden (3 vols., Rolls Ser., 1866–9), i, 12–13; *RRAN*, 449–52 (no. 131). The controversy goes back to the late nineteenth century, so the literature is vast. See in particular J. H. Round, 'The Introduction of Knight Service into England', idem, *Feudal England* (new edn, 1964), 182–245; J. C. Holt, 'The Introduction of Knight Service in England', idem, *Colonial England* (1997), 41–58; J. Gillingham, 'The Introduction of Knight Service into England', idem, *English in the Twelfth Century*, 187–208.

21 *Liber Eliensis*, ed. E. O. Blake (Camden Soc., 3rd ser., 92, 1962), 216–17; *Liber Eliensis: A History of the Isle of Ely*, trans. J. Fairweather (Woodbridge, 2005), 258–9; *Historia Ecclesie Abbendonensis*, ed. Hudson, ii, 4–7.

22 *ASC* E, 1070.

23 E. M. C. van Houts, 'Hereward and Flanders', *Anglo-Saxon England*, 28 (2000), 201–23; *DNB* Hereward.

24 *ASC* E, 1070.

25 Ibid.; WM, *Gesta Pontificum*, 628–9.

26 OV, ii, 232–5.

27 Ibid.; *ASC* E, 1070; JW, iii, 14–15.

28 *RRAN*, 79; below, 254; OV, ii, 256–7.

29 Ibid. The *Gesta Herewardi* is quoted from the English translation by M. Swanton in *Robin Hood and Other Outlaw Tales*, ed. S. Knight and T. Ohlgren (2nd edn, Kalamazoo, 2000), 647, 651.

30 Above, 219–20, 238; SD, *History*, 137–8, 142; *ASC* E, 1071.

31 Baxter, *Earls of Mercia*, 277–8, 284–7; above, 218; OV, ii, 218–19; JW, iii, 18–19.

32 Baxter, *Earls of Mercia*, 286–96; above, 71, 175.

33 *ASC* D, 1071; JW, iii, 20–1; Baxter, *Earls of Mercia*, 261–6.

34 *RRAN*, 79; *ASC* D and E, 1071; JW, iii, 20–1.

35 *Gesta Herewardi*, 649–58; *Liber Eliensis*, ed. Blake, 191–4 (trans. Fairweather, 226–9). The *Liber* says William entered Ely on 27 October.

36 *ASC* D and E, 1071; JW, iii, 20–1.

37 OV, ii, 256–9; Williams, *English and the Norman Conquest*, 53.

CHAPTER 15

1 For the castle at Ely, see *Liber Eliensis*, ed. Blake, 194 (trans. Fairweather, 229).

2 SD, *History*, 138–40.

3 *ASC* E, 934, 1072, 1093; JW, iii, 20–1.

4 Williams, *English and the Norman Conquest*, 57–8; SD, *History*, 142, 144.

5 Above, 103, 127; Baxter, 'Edward the Confessor', Map 10.

6 Fletcher, *Bloodfeud*, 186; Baxter, *Earls of Mercia*, 68, 272.

7 OV, ii, 232–3, 262–3; Williams, *English and the Norman Conquest*, 58.

8 Douglas, *Conqueror*, 212, 224–5.

9 Ibid., 223–4, 228–9.

10 Bates, *Conqueror*, 85–9, has a positive assessment of William's position at this time.

11 Above, 202; *ASC* E, 1087; D. Bates, 'The Origins of the Justiciarship', *ANS*, 4 (1982), 2–8.

12 Above, 112; *Letters of Lanfranc*, 30–1; *RRAN*, 79.

13 *DNB* Lanfranc; *Letters of Lanfranc*, 30–1, 112–13.

14 *EHD*, ii, 604–5. Barlow, *English Church, 1066–1154*, 48–50, 147–52.

15 *Councils and Synods*, ii, 614; *Letters of Lanfranc*, 78–9, 134–5; OV, ii, 200–1; *DNB* Lanfranc.

16 *ASC* D and E, 1067; Fernie, *Architecture*, 104–6.

17 Ibid., 106–21, 130–1; M.T. Clanchy, *England and Its Rulers, 1066–1272* (2nd edn, Oxford, 1998), 61; WM, *Gesta Pontificum*, 102–3.

18 Fernie, *Architecture*, 108, 130, 144, 152–3, 166; above, 98. Crediton had also been moved for security reasons. Prestwich, *Place of War*, 4.

19 Rubenstein, 'Liturgy Against History', 282–5, 289–92. Rubenstein successfully overturns the revisionist arguments of S. J. Ridyard, '*Condigna veneratio*: Post-Conquest Attitudes to the Saints of the Anglo-Saxons', *ANS*, 9 (1987), 179–206.

20 Rubenstein, 'Liturgy Against History', 282, 292–5.

21 Ibid., 295–7; *Historia Ecclesie Abbendonensis*, ed. Hudson, ii, xli–xlii; WM, *Gesta Pontificum*, i, 628–31. See also P.A. Hayward, 'Translation

Narratives in Post-Conquest Hagiography and English Resistance to the Norman Conquest', *ANS*, 21 (1999), 67–94.

22 *Letters of Lanfranc*, 30–1; OV, ii, 256–7.

23 *RRAN*, 48–50, 107.

24 *ASC* E, 1083; JW, iii, 38–41.

25 *Letters of Lanfranc*, 112–15; *EHD*, ii, 634.

26 *EHD*, ii, 399, 523. It has been suggested that murdrum, or something very like it, may have been originally introduced by Cnut to deter Englishmen from killing Danes. Even if this is true, and the law was simply revived by William, it does not diminish its value as evidence for conditions in England after the Norman Conquest (though it might alter the picture of conditions after the Danish one). B. R. O'Brien, 'From Morðor to Murdrum: The Preconquest Origin and Norman Revival of the Murder Fine', *Speculum*, 71 (1996), 321–57.

27 *Letters of Lanfranc*, 110–13, 150–3, 166–7; WP, 158–9; OV, ii, 202–3.

28 Above, 14, 19, 36; J. Gillingham, '1066 and the Introduction of Chivalry into England', idem, *English in the Twelfth Century*, 215–16.

29 Ibid., 211–15.

30 Ibid., 217–18, 228; WP, 157.

31 Fletcher, *Bloodfeud*, 1–5; Gillingham, '1066 and the Introduction of Chivalry', 218–19.

32 OV, ii, 256–7; H. M. Thomas, *The English and the Normans: Ethnic Hostility, Assimilation, and Identity, 1066–c.1220* (Oxford, 2003), 145–51.

33 SD, *History*, 144.

34 *DNB* Gospatric; *DNB* Edgar Ætheling; *ASC* D, 1074.

35 *DNB* Ralph the Staller; *DNB* Ralph de Gaël.

36 *ASC* D and E, 1075.

37 Ibid.; JW, iii, 24–5; OV, ii, 310–13; C. P. Lewis, 'The Early Earls of Norman England', *ANS*, 13 (1991), 207–23; *Letters of Lanfranc*, 118–21.

38 OV, ii, 312–15; *ASC* D and E, 1075.

39 JW, iii, 24–5; *Letters of Lanfranc*, 118–23.

40 JW, iii, 24–5; *ASC* D and E, 1075; OV, ii, 316–17.

41 Ibid.; JW, iii, 26–7; *Letters of Lanfranc*, 124–5.

42 Ibid., 124–7; *ASC* D and E, 1075.

43 Ibid.; OV, ii, 318–19.

44 *ASC* D and E, 1075; JW, ii, 24–5; OV, ii, 320–1.

45 Ibid., 314–15, 318–23; Gillingham, '1066 and the Introduction of Chivalry', 218.

CHAPTER 16

1 Douglas, *Conqueror*, 230–4.

2 *ASC* D and E, 1076; OV, ii, 350–3.

3 Bates, *Conqueror*, 159–60.

4 Ibid., 104–7; C. W. Hollister, *Henry I* (Yale, 2001), 31.

5 OV, ii, 356–7; WM, *Gesta Regum*, 700–1.

6 *DNB* Robert Curthose; OV, ii, 356–7.

7 Ibid., 356–9.

8 Douglas, *Conqueror*, 237–8; OV, iii, 100–3.

9 Bates, 'Origins of the Justiciarship', 4–6.

10 Bates, *Conqueror*, 159; WP, 164–5; OV, ii, 266–7; Bernstein, *Mystery*, 142, 264. Odo was far from being the only fighting churchman: the Penitential Ordinance (above, 236) contains a penance for 'the clerks who fought, or who were armed for fighting'. *EHD*, ii, 606.

11 Bates, 'Origins of the Justiciarship', 3–4, 8; *ASC* E, 1087; OV, ii, 264–5; *Historia Ecclesie Abbendonensis*, ed. Hudson, ii, 12–13.

12 Above, 202, 215, 218.

13 *Waltham Chronicle*, ed. Watkiss and Chibnall, 15, 35; *Carmen*, 40–3; Clarke, *English Nobility*, 154; Fleming, *Kings and Lords*, 171.

14 In general see ibid., 145–82 (and 163, 166–7, 169 and 180 for the examples cited).

15 Ibid., 153–8.

16 Ibid., 160–1, 176–8.

17 Ibid., 178–9.

18 D. A. Carpenter, *The Struggle for Mastery: Britain 1066–1284* (2003), 81–2; OV, ii, 262–3.

19 *Historia Ecclesie Abbendonensis*, ed. Hudson, ii, 6–7.

20 WM, *Gesta Pontificum*, 426–7; WM, *Saints' Lives*, 130–1.

21 *EHD*, ii, 897–8.

22 Liddiard, *Castles in Context*, 28–30.

23 S. Painter, 'Castle-Guard' and L. Butler, 'The Origins of the Honour of Richmond and its Castles', both in *Anglo-Norman Castles*, ed. R. Liddiard (Woodbridge, 2003), 91–104, 203–10. See also H. M. Thomas, 'Subinfeudation and Alienation of Land,

Economic Development and the Wealth of Nobles on the Honor of Richmond, 1066 to *c.*1300', *Albion*, 26 (1994), 397–417.

24 Carpenter, *Struggle for Mastery*, 85–6; Williams, *English and the Norman Conquest*, 74–5; R. Abels, 'Sheriffs, Lord-Seeking and the Norman Settlement of the South-East Midlands', *ANS*, 19 (1997), 23–31.

25 In general see Fleming, *Kings and Lords,* 183–214 (188–9 for Richard fitz Gilbert).

26 Abels, 'Sheriffs, Lord-Seeking', 32–40. See also J. Green, 'The Sheriffs of William the Conqueror', *ANS*, 5 (1983), 129–43.

27 *EHD*, ii, 431–2.

28 Fleming, *Kings and Lords*, 205–6.

29 *EHD*, ii, 449–51. For comment, see J. Le Patourel, 'The Reports on the Trial on Penenden Heath', *Studies in Medieval History Presented to Frederick Maurice Powicke*, ed. R. W. Hunt, W. A. Pantin and R. W. Southern (Oxford, 1948); D. Bates, 'Land Pleas of William I's Reign: Penenden Heath Revisited', *Bulletin of the Institute of Historical Research*, 51 (1978), 1–19; A. Cooper, 'Extraordinary Privilege: The Trial of Penenden Heath and the Domesday Inquest', *EHR,* 116 (2001), 1167–92.

30 OV, ii, 266–7; Thomas of Marlborough, *History of the Abbey of Evesham*, 176–7; Fleming, *Kings and Lords*, 189–91.

31 OV, ii, 270–81 (cf. 94–5); E. M. C. van Houts, 'The Memory of 1066 in Written and Oral Traditions', *ANS*, 19 (1997), 176–7.

CHAPTER 17

1 OV, iii, 108–11; *ASC* D and E, 1079; JW, iii, 30–3.

2 OV, ii, 102–5, 110–13; Bates, *Conqueror*, 163; *The Register of Pope Gregory VII*, ed. H. E. Cowdrey (Oxford, 2002), 358–9.

3 *RRAN*, 81.

4 JW, iii, 30–7; Kapelle, *Norman Conquest of the North*, 138–40.

5 Ibid., 140–2; SD, *Libellus*, 218–21; SD, *History*, 152. Odo was in Caen in July 1080: E. Miller, 'The Ely Land Pleas in the Reign of William I', *EHR*, 62 (1947), 444, n2.

6 Barlow, *Confessor*, 174–5, 205; above, 226; *ASC* E, 1087.

7 Ibid.; K. Mew, 'The Dynamics of Lordship and Landscape as Revealed in a Domesday Study of the *Nova Foresta*', *ANS*, 23 (2001), 155. In general see C. R. Young, *The Royal Forests of*

Medieval England (Leicester, 1979). Cf. D. Jørgensen, 'The Roots of the English Royal Forest', *ANS*, 32 (2010), 114–28.

8 JW, iii, 92–3; F. Baring, 'The Making of the New Forest', *EHR*, 16 (1901), 427–38. See also OV, v, 282–5; WM, *Gesta Regum*, 504–5, 508–9.

9 Davies, *Age of Conquest*, 24–34; OV, ii, 260–3.

10 Davies, *Age of Conquest*, 33; D. Crouch, 'The Slow Death of Kingship in Glamorgan, 1067–1158', *Morgannwg*, 29 (1985), 20–8; *ASC* E, 1081.

11 Ibid.; *The History of Gruffydd ap Cynan*, trans. A. Jones (Manchester, 1910), 128–31.

12 *ASC* C and D, 1036; E, 1052; D and E, 1065; WM, *Saints' Lives*, 100–3.

13 Pelteret, 'Slave Raiding', 108–9; Wyatt, 'Significance of Slavery', 345–7.

14 WP, 174–5; *Carmen*, 12–13; WM, *Gesta Regum*, 496–9; Pelteret, 'Slave Raiding', 113; *EHD*, ii, 400.

15 *Chepstow Castle: Its History and Its Buildings*, ed. R. Turner and A. Johnson (Logaston, 2006), 15–42.

16 Ibid.; Fernie, *Architecture*, 61–7. Cf. *The History of the King's Works: The Middle Ages*, ed. H. M. Colvin (2 vols., HMSO, 1963), i, 32.

17 Fernie, *Architecture*, 55–61.

18 *RRAN*, 77, 81; Fernie, *Architecture*, 32–3, 84, 98, 117–21, 304–5. See also J. C. Holt, 'Colonial England, 1066–1215', idem, *Colonial England*, 7, 12.

19 P. Grierson, 'The Monetary System Under William I', *The Story of Domesday Book*, ed. R. W. H. Erskine and A. Williams (Chichester, 2003), 112–18.

20 OV, iii, 232–41.

21 *ASC* E, 1087.

CHAPTER 18

1 *ASC* E, 1082; OV, iv, xxvii–xxx, 38–45; WM, *Gesta Regum*, 506–7. For the clash between Gregory VII and Henry IV, see Holland, *Millennium*, 349–90.

2 *EHD*, ii, 644–9.

3 OV, iv, 38–45; WM, *Gesta Regum*, 506–7; *RRAN*, 77, 81.

4 WM, *Gesta Regum*, 501–3; OV, iv, 45–7.

5 OV, iii, 102–3, 112–13; iv, 80–1; WM, *Gesta Regum*, 502–3; Bates, *Conqueror*, 170.

6   Ibid., 161, 166, 170–2. Cf. Douglas, *Conqueror*, 243.

7   OV, iv, 48–9.

8   Above, 226, 270; *ASC* D and E, 1069, 1075; E, 1085; WM, *Gesta Regum*, 474–5, 480–1.

9   Ibid., 482–3; *ASC* E, 1085; JW, iii, 42–3.

10 WM, *Saints' Lives*, 130–1; J. R. Maddicott, 'Responses to the Threat of Invasion, 1085', *EHR*, 122 (2007), 986–91; *ASC* E, 1085.

11 Ibid.; Maddicott, 'Responses', 986, 991–5.

12 H. R. Loyn, 'A General Introduction to Domesday Book', *Story of Domesday Book*, ed. Erskine and Williams, 2; Carpenter, *Struggle for Mastery*, 103.

13 *EHD*, ii, 530; *Domesday Book: A Complete Translation*, ed. A. Williams and G. H. Martin (2002), vii; S. Baxter, 'Domesday Book', *BBC History Magazine*, 11 (August 2010), 24.

14 *EHD*, ii, 881–2; S. Baxter, 'The Making of Domesday Book and the Languages of Lordship in Conquered England', *Conceptualizing Multilingualism in England, c. 800–c. 1250*, ed. E. M. Tyler (Turnhout, 2012), 277–8, 299–303.

15 Carpenter, *Struggle for Mastery*, 103.

16 Baxter, 'Making of Domesday', 278–84; S. P. J. Harvey, 'Domesday Book and Anglo-Norman Governance', *TRHS*, 5th ser., 25 (1975), 175–93; idem, 'Domesday Book and Its Predecessors', *EHR*, 86 (1971), 753–73.

17 *EHD*, ii, 879–83; C. P. Lewis, 'The Domesday Jurors', *Haskins Society Journal*, 5 (1993), 18–19; R. Fleming, *Domesday Book and the Law* (Cambridge, 1998), 12.

18 Baxter, 'Making of Domesday', 284–7.

19 R. Lennard, *Rural England, 1086–1135* (Oxford, 1959), 155–6. Cf. Fleming, *Domesday Book and the Law*, 2–3.

20 R. Fleming, 'Domesday Book and the Tenurial Revolution', *ANS*, 9 (1987), 88, 101. Fleming later increased her estimate of territorial grants from 'almost a quarter' to 'over a third': idem, *Kings and Lords*, 211–12.

21 Fleming, *Domesday Book and the Law*, 1; Abels, 'Sheriffs, Lord-Seeking', 33–6.

22 *EHD*, ii, 530, 851; Lewis, 'Domesday Jurors', 19.

23 Prestwich, *Place of War*, 114–15; *Domesday Book*, ed. Williams and Martin, 128, 1249.

24 Above, 24, 75; Barlow, *Confessor*, 106, n5.

25 *EHD*, ii, 483–6; J. A. Green, *The Aristocracy of Norman England* (Cambridge, 2002), 230.

26 Palmer, 'War and Domesday Waste', 256–78, successfully refutes D. M. Palliser, 'Domesday Book and the Harrying of the North', *Northern History*, 29 (1993), 1–23; *History of the King's Works*, ed. Colvin, i, 24; *Domesday Book*, ed. Williams and Martin, 716–17, 882–3.

27 WM, *Gesta Regum*, 464–5; SD, *History*, 137; Palmer, 'War and Domesday Waste', 273–4.

28 S. Baxter, 'Lordship and Labour', *A Social History of England, 900–1200*, ed. J. Crick and E. van Houts (Cambridge, 2011), 104–7; *Domesday Book*, ed. Williams and Martin, 409; *ASC* E, 1087; *EHD*, ii, 882.

29 Fleming, *Kings and Lords*, 123–6; Baxter, 'Lordship and Labour', 105; R. Faith, *The English Peasantry and the Growth of Lordship* (1997), 215.

30 Baxter, 'Lordship and Labour', 104, 107, 109–10; idem, 'Domesday Bourn', in D. Baxter, *Medieval Bourn* (Cambridge, 2008), 35–45; *ASC* E, 1087.

31 S. P. J. Harvey, 'Taxation and the Economy', *Domesday Studies*, ed. J. C. Holt (Woodbridge 1987), 256–62.

32 Loyn, 'General Introduction', 14; *EHD*, ii, 484.

33 *ASC* E, 1083.

34 *ASC* E, 1085; Harvey, 'Domesday Book and Anglo-Norman Governance', 181; N. J. Higham, 'The Domesday Survey: Context and Purpose', *History*, 78 (1993), 14–16.

35 F. W. Maitland, *Domesday Book and Beyond* (new edn, 1960), 27–8. See also P. Hyams, '"No Register of Title": The Domesday Inquest and Land Adjudication', *ANS*, 9 (1987), 127–41; Maddicott, 'Responses', 996–7.

36 J. C. Holt, '1086', *Domesday Studies*, ed. Holt, 48.

37 *ASC* E, 1086; JW, iii, 44–5.

38 Above, 233, 259; *History of the King's Works*, ed. Colvin, i, 824–5.

39 J. J. N. Palmer, 'The Wealth of the Secular Aristocracy in 1086', *ANS*, 22 (2000), 279, 286, 290; Garnett, *Short Introduction*, 84–8.

40 *EHD*, ii, 453–4.

41 Ibid., 601–3. The witness named Alfred is thought to have been a Breton.

42 Williams, *English and the Norman Conquest*, 99, 105 (cf. Green,

Aristocracy, 61–2); Carpenter, *Struggle for Mastery*, 79; Baxter, 'Domesday Book', 27.

43 Carpenter, *Struggle for Mastery*, 81.

44 Clarke, *English Nobility*, 32–3.

45 OV, iii, 214–17; Baxter, 'Domesday Book', 27 (cf. Fleming, *Kings and Lords*, 219).

46 Fleming, *Kings and Lords*, 58–71, 219–28, but cf. Baxter, *Earls of Mercia*, 128–38.

47 Fleming, *Kings and Lords*, 227–8; Carpenter, *Struggle for Mastery*, 81.

48 Holt, '1086', 41–64; Garnett, *Short Introduction*, 83–8; Carpenter, *Struggle for Mastery*, 105.

49 Ibid., 83–7; Holt, '1086', 50–5.

50 Garnett, *Conquered England*, 354; S. Reynolds, *Fiefs and Vassals* (Oxford, 1994), 345.

51 F. and C. Thorn, 'The Writing of Great Domesday Book', *Domesday Book*, ed. E. Hallam and D. Bates (Stroud, 2001), 38, 70; *EHD*, ii, 853. Cf. D. Roffe, *Domesday: The Inquest and the Book* (Oxford, 2000), who argues that the book was created during the reign of William Rufus.

52 V. H. Galbraith, *The Making of Domesday Book* (Oxford, 1961), 223–30; *EHD*, ii, 851.

53 *ASC* E, 1086; WM, *Gesta Regum*, 482–3; JW, iii, 44–5; OV, iv, 52–3, 80–1.

54 Thorn, 'Writing of Great Domesday Book', 72.

CHAPTER 19

1 *ASC* E, 1087; *EHD*, ii, 280; WM, *Gesta Regum*, 510–11.

2 OV, iv, 78–9.

3 Bates, *Conqueror*, 158–9; OV, iv, 74–5.

4 WM, *Gesta Regum*, 510–11; OV, iv, 78–9; *ASC* E, 1087.

5 WM, *Gesta Regum*, 510–11; OV, iv, 78–81, 96–101, 106–7; JW, ii, 46–7. Orderic's account is also printed in *EHD*, ii, 281–9.

6 OV, iv, 80–1, 92–5, 100–1; B. English, 'William the Conqueror and the Anglo-Norman Succession', *Historical Research*, 64 (1991), 221–36.

7 OV, iv, 78–9; 100–7.

8 Ibid., 78–9, 106–9.

9 OV, ii, 134–7, 268–9; iv, 94–5.

10 Van Houts, 'Norman Conquest through European Eyes', 841, 845, 848–53.

11 Eadmer, 9; *ASC* E, 1087. The extant MS of *ASC* E was written at Peterborough *c.*1121 (Gransden, *Historical Writing*, 93) but based on an earlier version. Note particularly the author's statement in 1087 that William Rufus became king and Henry was bequeathed innumerable treasures, which suggests no knowledge of Henry's succession in 1100.

12 E. Fernie, 'The Effect of the Conquest on Norman Architectural Patronage', *ANS*, 9 (1987), 71–85; Garnett, *Short Introduction*, 103.

13 Eales, 'Royal Power and Castles', 54–63.

14 Garnett, *Short Introduction*, 6, 46–56.

15 Fleming, *Kings and Lords*, 109–20; *ASC* E, 1087.

16 HH, 31.

17 WM, *Gesta Regum*, 456–61.

18 Above, 39–40, 61–2, 76; *GND*, ii, 58–61.

19 J. C. Holt, 'What's in a Name? Family Nomenclature and the Norman Conquest', idem, *Colonial England*, 179–96.

20 Holt, 'Colonial England', 4–5, 18–19; Carpenter, *Struggle for Mastery*, 85; van Houts, 'Norman Conquest through European Eyes', 841.

21 Pelteret, *Slavery*, 205; Wyatt, 'Significance of Slavery', 345–7; *Councils and Synods*, ii, 678; Gillingham, *English in the Twelfth Century*, xvii–xviii, 266.

22 *ASC* E, 1087; Gillingham, '1066 and the Introduction of Chivalry', 223; Morris, *Great and Terrible King*, 358, 377.

23 WM, *Gesta Regum*, 460–1; Barlow, *English Church, 1000–1066*, 289–308; J. Blair, *The Church in Anglo-Saxon Society* (Oxford, 2005), 407–17.

24 Clanchy, *England and Its Rulers*, 69; J. Burton, *Monastic and Religious Orders in Britain, 1000–1300* (Cambridge, 1994), 31–3.

25 J. Gillingham, 'The Beginnings of English Imperialism'; idem, 'Conquering the Barbarians: War and Chivalry in Twelfth-Century Britain and Ireland', both in idem, *English in the Twelfth Century*, 3–18, 41–58.

26 WM, *Gesta Regum*, 456–7 (cf. *EHD*, ii, 290); WM, *Saints' Lives*, 122–3.

27 S. K. Brehe, 'Reassembling the First Worcester Fragment', *Speculum*, 65 (1990), 530–1, 535–6. For a good short summary of the Conquest's

impact on language, see H. M. Thomas, *The Norman Conquest: England After William the Conqueror* (Lanham, USA, 2008), 131–8.

28 OV, iv, 94–5; HH, 31.

29 Ibid.; OV, ii, 268–9; WM, *Gesta Regum*, 456–61; Eadmer, 3, 9; *ASC* D, 1066; E, 1087.

30 *VER*, 108–11.

CHAPTER 20

1 *VER*, 116–23.

2 G. Garnett, 'Franci et Angli':The Legal Distinctions Between Peoples After the Conquest', *ANS*, 8 (1986), 113; HH, 31; *Domesday Book*, ed. Williams and Martin, 1248; *ASC* E, 1087.

3 Carpenter, *Struggle for Mastery*, 128–38.

4 *DNB* Edgar Ætheling; OV, v, 270–3; JW, iii, 46–7.

5 D. Bates, 'Normandy and England after 1066', *EHR*, 104 (1989), 866–8; Bates, *Conqueror*, 110 (145/239 months = 60%); R. Bartlett, *England Under the Norman and Angevin Kings, 1075–1225* (Oxford, 2000), 12.

6 Van Houts, 'Norman Conquest Through European Eyes', 837–8.

7 *ASC* E, 1107; WM, *Gesta Regum*, 414–15.

8 Thomas, *English and the Normans*, 203–8; R. Huscroft, *The Norman Conquest: A New Introduction* (2009), 301.

9 Rubenstein, 'Liturgy Against History', 282, 289; Garnett, *Short Introduction*, 12.

10 L. Reilly, 'The Emergence of Anglo-Norman Architecture: Durham Cathedral', *ANS*, 19 (1997), 335–51. More generally, Fernie, *Architecture*, 34–41.

11 *DNB* William of Malmesbury; HH, 4. Lanfranc described himself as a 'novice Englishman' (*novus Anglicus*) as early as 1073, but was perhaps being ironic.

12 H. M. Thomas, 'The *Gesta Herwardi*, the English and their Conquerors', *ANS*, 21 (1998), 213–32. Thomas cautiously dates the *Gesta* to 1109 × 1174, but others (e.g. Williams, *English and the Norman Conquest*, 49n) suggest 1109 × 1131.

13 *DNB* William of Malmesbury; I. Short, 'Patrons and Polyglots: French Literature in Twelfth-Century England', *ANS*, 14 (1992), 229–30; *DNB* Gaimar.

14 Carpenter, *Struggle for Mastery*, 7–8, 83; Lewis, 'Domesday Jurors',

passim; C.-J. N. Bailey and K. Maroldt, 'The French Lineage of English', *Pidgins – Creoles – Languages in Contact*, ed. J. Meisel (Tübingen, 1977), 21–53. Cf. I. Singh, *The History of English: A Student's Guide* (Oxford, 2005), 127–36.

15 Williams, *English and the Norman Conquest*, 198–200; *Domesday Book*, ed. Williams and Martin, 1147; E. Searle, 'Women and the Legitimization of Succession at the Norman Conquest', *ANS*, 3 (1981), 159–71; *EHD*, ii, 176.

16 E. Cownie, 'The Normans as Patrons of English Religious Houses, 1066–1135', *ANS*, 18 (1996), 47–62; B. Golding, 'Anglo-Norman Knightly Burials', *Medieval Knighthood I* (1986), 35–48.

17 Crouch, *Normans*, 160; *Handbook of British Chronology*, ed. E. B. Fryde, D. E. Greenway, S. Porter and I. Roy (3rd edn, 1986), 235; WM, *Gesta Regum*, 8–9, 716–17.

18 *ASC* E, 1137.

19 I. Short, '*Tam Angli quam Franci*: Self-Definition in Anglo-Norman England', *ANS*, 18 (1996), 172; Barlow, *Confessor*, 280–1; *VER*, xxxvii.

20 Ashe, *Fiction and History*, 32–3.

21 Bartlett, *England Under the Norman and Angevin Kings*, 12.

22 Ashe, *Fiction and History*, 11–14, offers a good short summary. For more extensive treatments, see J. Hudson, The Formation of the English Common Law (1996) and P. Brand, *The Making of the Common Law* (1992).

23 Short, '*Tam Angli*', 155–8; *EHD*, ii, 523.

24 Ibid.; Carpenter, *Struggle for Mastery*, 6–7. The quote is from *Magna Vitae Sancti Hugonis*, ed. D. L. Douie and D. H. Farmer (2 vols., Oxford, 1961), ii, 113–14, where 'timid' is translated as 'scrupulous'.

25 Carpenter, *Struggle for Mastery*, 8; S. Reynolds, *Kingdoms and Communities in Western Europe, 900–1300* (Oxford, 1997), 268.

26 D. A. Carpenter, 'King Henry III and Saint Edward the Confessor: The Origins of the Cult', *EHR*, 122 (2007), 865–91; R. M. Wilson, 'English and French in England, 1100–1300', *History*, 28 (1943), 46, 56; Morris, *Great and Terrible King*, *passim*.

27 Holt, 'Colonial England', 13; Williams, *English and the Norman Conquest*, 217–18.

Bibliography

(Unless otherwise indicated, the place of publication is London)

PRIMARY SOURCES

Adam of Bremen, *History of the Archbishops of Hamburg–Bremen*, trans. F. J. Tschan (Columbia, 2002).

The Anglo-Saxon Chronicle, ed. G. N. Garmonsway (new edn, 1972).

'The *Brevis Relatio de Guillelmo nobilissimo comite Normannorum*', ed. E. van Houts, idem, *History and Family Traditions in England and the Continent, 1000–1200* (Aldershot, 1999).

The Carmen de Hastingae Proelio of Guy, Bishop of Amiens, ed. F. Barlow (Oxford, 1999).

The Carmen de Hastingae Proelio of Guy, Bishop of Amiens, ed. C. Morton and H. Muntz (Oxford, 1972).

The Chronicle of Battle Abbey, ed. and trans. E. Searle (Oxford, 1980).

The Chronicle of John of Worcester, ed. R. R. Darlington and P. McGurk, trans. J. Bray and P. McGurk (3 vols., Oxford, 1995, 1998, forthcoming).

Chronicles of the Reigns of Stephen, Henry II and Richard I, ed. R. Howlett (4 vols., Rolls Ser., 1884–89).

Chroniques des Comtes d'Anjou et des Seigneurs d'Amboise, ed. L. Halphen and R. Poupardin (Paris, 1913).

Domesday Book: A Complete Translation, ed. A. Williams and G. H. Martin (2002).

Eadmer's History of Recent Events in England, ed. G. Bosanquet (1964).

The Ecclesiastical History of Orderic Vitalis, ed. M. Chibnall (6 vols., Oxford, 1968–80).

Encomium Emmae Reginae, ed. A. Campbell and S. Keynes (Cambridge, 1998).

English Historical Documents, c.500–1042 (2nd edn, 1979).

English Historical Documents, 1042–1189, ed. D. C. Douglas and G. W. Greenaway (1953).

Geffrei Gaimar, *Estoire des Engleis*, ed. and trans. I. Short (Oxford, 2009).

Gerald of Wales, *The Journey through Wales and the Description of Wales*, trans. L. Thorpe (1978).

The Gesta Guillelmi of William of Poitiers, ed. R. H. C. Davis and M. Chibnall (Oxford, 1998).

The Gesta Normannorum Ducum of William of Jumièges, Orderic Vitalis and Robert of Torigni, ed. E. M. C. van Houts (2 vols., Oxford, 1992–5).

Henry of Huntingdon, *The History of the English People 1000–1154*, ed. and trans. D. Greenway (Oxford, 2002).

Historia Ecclesie Abbendonensis: The History of the Church of Abingdon, ed. J. Hudson (2 vols., Oxford, 2002, 2007).

The History of Gruffydd ap Cynan, trans. A. Jones (Manchester, 1910).

Hugh the Chanter, *The History of the Church of York, 1066–1127* (Oxford, 1990).

The Letters and Poems of Fulbert of Chartres, ed. F. Behrends (Oxford, 1976).

The Letters of Lanfranc, Archbishop of Canterbury, ed. and trans. V. H. Clover and M. T. Gibson (Oxford, 1979).

Liber Eliensis, ed. E. O. Blake (Camden Soc., 3rd ser., 92, 1962).

Liber Eliensis: A History of the Isle of Ely, trans. J. Fairweather (Woodbridge, 2005).

The Life of King Edward Who Rests at Westminster, ed. F. Barlow (2nd edn, Oxford, 1992).

Magna Vitae Sancti Hugonis, ed. D. L. Douie and D. H. Farmer (2 vols., Oxford, 1961).

Matthew Paris, *Historia Anglorum*, ed. F. Madden (3 vols., Rolls Ser., 1866–9).

Recueil des actes des ducs de Normandie de 911 à 1066, ed. M. Fauroux (Caen, 1961).

Regesta Regum Anglo-Normannorum: The Acta of William I (1066–1087), ed. D. Bates (Oxford, 1998).

The Register of Pope Gregory VII, ed. H. E. Cowdrey (Oxford, 2002).

Rodulfus Glaber, Historiarum Libri Quinque, ed. J. France, N. Bulst and P. Reynolds (2nd edn, Oxford, 1993).

Simeon of Durham, *History of the Kings of England*, trans. J. Stevenson (facsimile reprint, Lampeter, 1987).

Simeon of Durham, *Libellus de Exordio atque Procursu istius, hoc est Dunhelmensis*, ed. D. Rollason (Oxford, 2000).

Snorri Sturluson, *King Harald's Saga*, ed. M. Magnusson and H. Pálsson (1966).

Thomas of Marlborough, *History of the Abbey of Evesham*, ed. and trans. J. Sayers and L. Watkiss (Oxford, 2003).

'La Vie de S. Edouard le Confesseur par Osbert de Clare', ed. M. Bloch, *Analecta Bollandiana*, 41 (1923).

The Waltham Chronicle, ed. and trans. I. Watkiss and M. Chibnall (Oxford 1992).

William of Malmesbury, *Gesta Pontificum Anglorum*, I, ed. and trans. M. Winterbottom (Oxford, 2007).

William of Malmesbury, *Gesta Regum Anglorum*, I, ed. and trans. R. A. B. Mynors, R. M. Thomson and M. Winterbottom (Oxford, 1998).

William of Malmesbury, *Saints' Lives*, ed. M. Winterbottom and R. M. Thomson (Oxford, 2002).

SECONDARY WORKS (CITED)

Abels, R., 'Sheriffs, Lord-Seeking and the Norman Settlement of the South-East Midlands', *ANS*, 19 (1997).

The Anglo-Saxons, ed. J. Campbell (1982).

Arnold, M., *The Vikings: Culture and Conquest* (2006).

Ashe, L., *Fiction and History in England* (Cambridge, 2007).

Bachrach, B., 'On the Origins of William the Conqueror's Horse Transports', *Technology and Culture*, 26 (1985).

——'Some Observations on the Military Administration of the Norman Conquest', *ANS*, 8 (1986).

Bailey, C.-J. N., and Maroldt, K., 'The French Lineage of English', *Pidgins – Creoles – Languages in Contact*, ed. J. Meisel (Tübingen, 1977).

Barber, R., 'The Norman Conquest and the Media', *ANS*, 26 (2004).

Baring, F., 'The Conqueror's Footprints in Domesday', *EHR*, 13 (1898).

——'The Making of the New Forest', *EHR*, 16 (1901).

Barlow, F., 'Two Notes: Cnut's Second Pilgrimage and Queen Emma's Disgrace in 1043', *EHR*, 73 (1958).

——*The English Church, 1000–1066* (2nd edn, 1979).

——*The English Church, 1066–1154* (1979).

——*Edward the Confessor* (new edn, 1997).

Bartlett, R., *The Making of Europe: Conquest, Colonization and Cultural Change, 950–1350* (1993).

——*England Under the Norman and Angevin Kings, 1075–1225* (Oxford, 2000).

Bates, D., 'The Character and Career of Odo, Bishop of Bayeux (1049/50–1097)', *Speculum*, 50 (1975).

——'Land Pleas of William I's Reign: Penenden Heath Revisited', *Bulletin of the Institute of Historical Research*, 51 (1978).

——*Normandy before 1066* (Harlow, 1982).

——'The Origins of the Justiciarship', *ANS*, 4 (1982).

——'Normandy and England After 1066', *EHR*, 104 (1989).

——*William the Conqueror* (1989).

——'The Conqueror's Adolescence', *ANS*, 25 (2003).

——'1066: Does the Date Still Matter?', *Historical Research*, 78 (2005).

——'The Conqueror's Earliest Historians and the Writing of his Biography', *Writing Medieval Biography 750–1250: Essays in Honour of Professor Frank Barlow*, ed. D. Bates, J. Crick and S. Hamilton (Woodbridge, 2006).

The Battle of Maldon AD 991, ed. D. Scragg (Oxford 1991).

Baxter, S., *The Earls of Mercia: Lordship and Power in Late Anglo-Saxon England* (Oxford, 2007).

——'MS C of the Anglo-Saxon Chronicle and the Politics of Mid-Eleventh-Century England', *EHR*, 122 (2007).

——'Domesday Bourn', in D. Baxter, *Medieval Bourn* (Cambridge, 2008).

——'Edward the Confessor and the Succession Question', *Edward the Confessor*, ed. R. Mortimer (Woodbridge, 2009).

——'Domesday Book', *BBC History Magazine*, 11 (August 2010).

——'Lordship and Labour', *A Social History of England, 900–1200*, ed. J. Crick and E. van Houts (Cambridge, 2011).

——'The Making of Domesday Book and the Languages of Lordship in Conquered England', *Conceptualizing Multilingualism in England, c.800–c.1250*, ed. E. M. Tyler (Turnhout, 2012).

The Bayeux Tapestry: Embroidering the Facts of History, ed. P. Bouet, B. Levy and F. Neveux (Caen, 2004).

The Bayeux Tapestry: New Approaches, ed. M. J. Lewis, G. R. Owen-Crocker and D. Terkla (Oxford, 2011).

The Bayeux Tapestry: New Interpretations, ed. M. K. Foys, K. E. Overbey and D. Terkla (Woodbridge, 2009).

Baylé, M., 'Les Ateliers de Sculpture de Saint-Etienne de Caen au 11° et au 12° Siècles', *ANS*, 80 (1988).

Bernstein, D. J., 'The Blinding of Harold and the Meaning of the Bayeux Tapestry', *ANS*, 5 (1983).

——*The Mystery of the Bayeux Tapestry* (1986).

Bisson, T. N., Barthélemy, D., White, S. D., Wickham, C., and Reuter, T., 'The "Feudal Revolution"', *Past and Present*, 142 (1994); 152 (1996); 155 (1997).

The Blackwell Encyclopaedia of Anglo-Saxon England, ed. M. Lapidge et al. (Oxford, 1999).

Blair, J., *The Church in Anglo-Saxon Society* (Oxford, 2005).

Bozoky, E., 'The Sanctity and Canonisation of Edward the Confessor', *Edward the Confessor: The Man and the Legend*, ed. R. Mortimer (Woodbridge, 2009).

Brand, P., *The Making of the Common Law* (1992).

Brehe, S. K., 'Reassembling the First Worcester Fragment', *Speculum*, 65 (1990).

Brooke, C. N. L., 'Archbishop Lanfranc, the English Bishops and the Council of London of 1075', *Studia Gratiana*, 12 (1967).

Brown, R. A., *English Castles* (2nd edn, 1976).

——*The Normans and the Norman Conquest* (2nd edn, Woodbridge, 1985).

——'The Battle of Hastings', *The Battle of Hastings: Sources and Interpretations*, ed. S. Morillo (Woodbridge, 1996).

Brown, S.A., *The Bayeux Tapestry: History and Bibliography* (Woodbridge, 1988).

Burton, J., *Monastic and Religious Orders in Britain, 1000–1300* (Cambridge, 1994).

Butler, L., 'The Origins of the Honour of Richmond and its Castles', *Anglo-Norman Castles*, ed. R. Liddiard (Woodbridge, 2003).

Carpenter, D. A., *The Struggle for Mastery: Britain 1066–1284* (2003).

——'King Henry III and Saint Edward the Confessor: The Origins of the Cult', *EHR*, 122 (2007).

Chepstow Castle: Its History and Its Buildings, ed. R. Turner and A. Johnson (Logaston, 2006).

Chibnall, M., *Anglo-Norman England, 1066–1166* (Oxford, 1986).

——'Military Service in Normandy Before 1066', *Anglo-Norman Warfare* (Woodbridge, 1992).

——*The Debate on the Norman Conquest* (Manchester, 1999).

Clanchy, M. T., *England and Its Rulers, 1066–1272* (2nd edn, Oxford, 1998).

Clarke, H. B., 'The Domesday Satellites', *Domesday Book: A Re-assessment*, ed. P.H. Sawyer (1985).

Clarke, P. A., *The English Nobility under Edward the Confessor* (Oxford, 1994).

Cooper, A., 'Extraordinary Privilege: The Trial of Penenden Heath and the Domesday Inquest', *EHR*, 116 (2001).

Councils and Synods with Other Documents Relating to the English Church, I, *871–1204*, ed. D. Whitelock, M. Brett and C. N. L. Brooke (2 vols., Oxford 1981).

Cowdrey, H. E. J., 'The Peace and Truce of God in the Eleventh Century', *Past and Present*, 46 (1970).

——'The Anglo-Norman *Laudes Regiae*', *Viator*, 12 (1981).

Cownie, E., 'The Normans as Patrons of English Religious Houses, 1066–1135', *ANS*, 18 (1996).

Crouch, D., 'The Slow Death of Kingship in Glamorgan, 1067–1158', *Morgannwg*, 29 (1985).

——*The Normans* (2002).

——*The Birth of Nobility: Constructing Aristocracy in England and France 900–1300* (Harlow, 2005).

Cutler, K. E., 'The Godwinist Hostages: The Case for 1051', *Annuale Mediaevale*, 12 (1972).

Dalton, P., *Conquest, Anarchy and Lordship: Yorkshire, 1066–1154* (Cambridge, 1994).

Davies, R. R., *Age of Conquest: Wales, 1063–1415* (Oxford, 2000).

——*The First English Empire: Power and Identities in the British Isles, 1093–1343* (Oxford, 2000).

Davis, R. H. C., 'The Warhorses of the Normans', *ANS*, 10 (1988).

——'William of Poitiers and his History of William the Conqueror', idem, *From Alfred the Great to Stephen* (1991).

Dennis, C., 'The Strange Death of King Harold II', *The Historian* (2009).

DeVries, K., *The Norwegian Invasion of England in 1066* (Woodbridge, 1999).

Dewhurst, J., 'A Historical Obstetric Enigma: How Tall Was Matilda?', *Journal of Obstetrics and Gynaecology*, 1 (1981).

Douglas, D. C., 'The Earliest Norman Counts', *EHR*, 61 (1946).

——'Some Problems of Early Norman Chronology', *EHR*, 65 (1950).

——'Edward the Confessor, Duke William of Normandy, and the English Succession', *EHR*, 68 (1953).

——*William the Conqueror: The Norman Impact Upon England* (1964).

Dunbabin, J., *France in the Making, 843–1180* (2nd edn, Oxford, 2000).

Eales, R., 'Royal Power and Castles in Norman England', *The Ideals and Practice of Medieval Knighthood III*, ed. C. Harper-Bill and R. Harvey (Woodbridge, 1990).

English, B., 'William the Conqueror and the Anglo-Norman Succession', *Historical Research*, 64 (1991).

——'Towns, Mottes and Ring-Works of the Conquest', *The Medieval Military Revolution*, ed. A. Ayton and J. L. Price (1995).

Faith, R., *The English Peasantry and the Growth of Lordship* (1997).

Fernie, E., 'The Effect of the Conquest on Norman Architectural Patronage', *ANS*, 9 (1987).

——*The Architecture of Norman England* (Oxford, 2000).

——'Edward the Confessor's Westminster Abbey', *Edward the Confessor*, ed. R. Mortimer (Woodbridge, 2009).

Fleming, R., 'Domesday Book and the Tenurial Revolution', *ANS*, 9 (1987).

——*Kings and Lords in Conquest England* (Cambridge, 1991).

——*Domesday Book and the Law* (Cambridge, 1998).

Fletcher, R., *Bloodfeud: Murder and Revenge in Anglo-Saxon England* (2002).

Foot, S., 'The Making of *Angelcynn*: English Identity before the Norman Conquest', *TRHS*, 6th ser., vi (1996).

Foys, M. K., 'Pulling the Arrow Out: The Legend of Harold's Death and the Bayeux Tapestry', *The Bayeux Tapestry*, ed. M. K. Foys, K. E. Overbey and D. Terkla (Woodbridge, 2009).

Freeman, E. A., *The History of the Norman Conquest of England* (6 vols., Oxford, 1867–79).

Galbraith, V. H., *The Making of Domesday Book* (Oxford, 1961).

Garnett, G., 'Coronation and Propaganda: Some Implications of the Norman Claim to the Throne of England in 1066', *TRHS*, 5th ser., 36 (1986).

——'*Franci et Angli*: The Legal Distinctions Between Peoples After the Conquest', *ANS*, 8 (1986).

——'The Origins of the Crown', *The History of English Law: Centenary Essays on 'Pollock and Maitland'*, ed. J. Hudson (Proc. of the British Academy, 89, 1996).

——'The Third Recension of the English Coronation *ordo*: The Manuscripts', *Haskins Society Journal*, 11 (2003).

——*Conquered England: Kingship, Succession and Tenure, 1066–1166* (Oxford, 2007).

——*The Norman Conquest: A Very Short Introduction* (Oxford, 2009).

Gem, R., 'Craftsmen and Administrators in the Building of the Confessor's Abbey', *Edward the Confessor*, ed. R. Mortimer (Woodbridge, 2009).

Gillingham, J., '"The Most Precious Jewel in the English Crown": Levels of Danegeld and Heregeld in the Early Eleventh Century', *EHR*, 104 (1989).

——'Chronicles and Coins as Evidence for Levels of Tribute and Taxation in Later Tenth- and Early Eleventh-Century England', *EHR*, 105 (1990).

——'William the Bastard at War', *The Battle of Hastings: Sources and Interpretations*, ed. S. Morillo (Woodbridge, 1996).

——*The English in the Twelfth Century* (Woodbridge, 2000), which includes all the essays below published up to that date. Original places of publication are noted, but my references follow the pagination in the book.

——'The Introduction of Knight Service into England', *ANS*, 4 (1982), 53–64, 181–7.

——'The Beginnings of English Imperialism', *Journal of Historical Sociology*, 5 (1992), 392–409.

——'Conquering the Barbarians: War and Chivalry in Twelfth-Century Britain and Ireland', *Haskins Society Journal*, 4 (1993), 67–84.

——'1066 and the Introduction of Chivalry into England', *Law and Government in Medieval England and Normandy: Essays in Honour of Sir James Holt* (Cambridge, 1994), 31–55.

——'"Slaves of the Normans?": Gerald de Barri and Regnal Solidarity in Early Thirteenth-Century England', *Law, Laity and Solidarities: Essays in Honour of Susan Reynolds*, ed. P. Stafford, J. L. Nelson and J. Martindale (Manchester, 2001).

——'"Holding to the Rules of War (*Bellica Iura Tenentes*)": Right Conduct Before, During and After Battle in North-Western Europe in the Eleventh Century', *ANS*, 29 (2007).

Gillmor, C. M., 'Naval Logistics of the Cross-Channel Operation, 1066', *ANS*, 7 (1984).

Golding, B., 'Anglo-Norman Knightly Burials', *Medieval Knighthood I* (1986).

——*Conquest and Colonisation: The Normans in Britain, 1066–1100* (2nd edn, Basingstoke, 2001).

Grainge, C. and G., 'The Pevensey Expedition: Brilliantly Executed Plan or Near Disaster?', *The Battle of Hastings*, ed. S. Morillo (Woodbridge, 1996).

Gransden, A., *Historical Writing in England, c.550 to c.1307* (1974).

Green, J. A., 'The Sheriffs of William the Conqueror', *ANS*, 5 (1983).

——*The Aristocracy of Norman England* (Cambridge, 2002).

Grierson, P., 'A Visit of Earl Harold to Flanders in 1056', *EHR*, 51 (1936).

——'The Relations Between England and Flanders Before the Norman Conquest', *TRHS*, 4th ser., 23 (1941).

——'The Monetary System Under William I', *The Story of Domesday Book*, ed. R. W. H. Erskine and A. Williams (Chichester, 2003).

Hallam, E., and Everard, J., *Capetian France, 987–1328* (2001)

Handbook of British Chronology, ed. E. B. Fryde, D. E. Greenway, S. Porter and I. Roy (3rd edn, 1986).

Hare, M., 'Cnut and Lotharingia: Two Notes', *Anglo-Saxon England*, 29 (2000)

Hart, C., 'The Bayeux Tapestry and Schools of Illumination at Canterbury', *ANS*, 22 (2000).

——'The Cicero-Aratea and the Bayeux Tapestry', *King Harold II and the Bayeux Tapestry*, ed. G. R. Owen-Crocker (Woodbridge, 2005).

Harvey, S. P. J., 'Domesday Book and Its Predecessors', *EHR*, 86 (1971).

——'Domesday Book and Anglo-Norman Governance', *TRHS*, 5th ser., 25 (1975).

——'Taxation and the Economy', *Domesday Studies*, ed. J. C. Holt, (Woodbridge 1987).

Hayward, P.A., 'Translation Narratives in Post-Conquest Hagiography and English Resistance to the Norman Conquest', *ANS*, 21 (1999).

The Heads of Religious Houses: England and Wales, I, 940–1216, ed. D. Knowles, C. N. L. Brooke and V. M. C. London (2nd edn, Cambridge, 2001).

Hicks, C., *The Bayeux Tapestry: The Life Story of a Masterpiece* (2006).

Higham, N. J., *The Kingdom of Northumbria, AD 350–1100* (Stroud, 1993).

——'The Domesday Survey: Context and Purpose', *History*, 78 (1993).

The History of the King's Works: The Middle Ages, ed. H. M. Colvin (2 vols., HMSO, 1963).

Holland, T., *Millennium* (2008).

Hollister, C. W., *Henry I* (Yale, 2001).

Holt, J. C., '1086', *Domesday Studies*, ed. idem (Woodbridge 1987).

——'The Introduction of Knight Service in England', idem, *Colonial England* (1997).

——'What's in a Name? Family Nomenclature and the Norman Conquest', idem, *Colonial England* (1997).

——'Colonial England, 1066–1215', idem, *Colonial England* (1997).

Hooper, N., 'The Housecarls in England in the Eleventh Century', *ANS*, 7 (1985).

Hudson, J., *The Formation of the English Common Law* (1996).

Huscroft, R., *The Norman Conquest: A New Introduction* (2009).

Hyams, P., '"No Register of Title": The Domesday Inquest and Land Adjudication', *ANS*, 9 (1987).

Itinerary of Edward I, ed. E. W. Safford (3 vols., List and Index Society, 103, 132, 135, 1974–7).

John, E., 'Edward the Confessor and the Norman Succession', *EHR*, 94 (1979).

Jones, C., *The Forgotten Battle of 1066: Fulford*, (Stroud, 2006).

Jørgensen, D., 'The Roots of the English Royal Forest', *ANS*, 32 (2010).

Kapelle, W. E., *The Norman Conquest of the North* (1979).

Keats-Rohan, K. S. B., 'William the Conqueror and the Breton contingent in the non-Norman Conquest, 1066–1086', *ANS*, 13 (1991).

Kemble, J. M., *The Saxons in England* (1849).

Keynes, S., 'The Crowland Psalter and the Sons of King Edmund Ironside', *Bodleian Library Record*, 6 (1985).

——'The Æthelings in Normandy', *ANS*, 13 (1991).

——'Cnut's Earls', *The Reign of Cnut: King of England, Denmark and Norway*, ed. A. R. Rumble (1994).

——'Giso, Bishop of Wells (1061–88)', *ANS*, 19 (1996).

——'Edward the Ætheling (c.1005–16), *Edward the Confessor*, ed. R. Mortimer (Woodbridge, 2009).

Keynes, S. and Love, R., 'Earl Godwine's Ship', *Anglo-Saxon England*, 38 (2009).

King Harold II and the Bayeux Tapestry, ed. G. R. Owen-Crocker (Woodbridge, 2005).

Larson, L. M., 'The Political Policies of Cnut as King of England', *American Historical Review*, 15 (1910).

Lavelle, R., *Aethelred II: King of the English, 978–1016* (Stroud, 2008)

Lawson, M. K., 'The Collection of Danegeld and Heregeld in the Reigns of Æthelred II and Cnut', *EHR*, 99 (1984).

——'"Those Stories Look True": Levels of Taxation in the Reigns of Æthelred and Cnut', *EHR*, 104 (1989).

——'Danegeld and Heregeld Once More', *EHR*, 105 (1990).

——*Cnut: The Danes in England in the Early Eleventh Century* (1993).

——*The Battle of Hastings 1066* (Stroud, 2002).

Lennard, R., *Rural England, 1086–1135* (Oxford, 1959).

Le Patourel, J., 'Geoffrey of Montbray, Bishop of Coutances, 1049–93', 59 (1944).

——'The Reports on the Trial on Penenden Heath', *Studies in Medieval History Presented to Frederick Maurice Powicke*, ed. R. W. Hunt, W. A. Pantin and R. W. Southern (Oxford, 1948).

Lewis, C. P., 'The Early Earls of Norman England', *ANS*, 13 (1991).

——'The Domesday Jurors', *Haskins Society Journal*, 5 (1993).

Lewis, M. J., *The Real World of the Bayeux Tapestry* (Stroud, 2008).

Liddiard, R., *Castles in Context: Power, Symbolism and Landscape, 1066 to 1500* (Macclesfield, 2005).

The Life and Letters of Edward. A. Freeman, ed. W. R. W. Stephens (2 vols., 1895).

Loyn, H. R., 'A General Introduction to Domesday Book', *The Story of Domesday Book*, ed. R. W. H. Erskine and A. Williams (Chichester, 2003).

Mack, K., 'Changing Thegns: Cnut's Conquest and the English Aristocracy', *Albion*, 4 (1984).

Maddicott, J. R., 'Edward the Confessor's Return to England in 1041', *EHR*, 119 (2004).

——'Responses to the Threat of Invasion, 1085', *EHR*, 122 (2007).

——*The Origins of the English Parliament, 924–1327* (Oxford, 2010).

Maitland, F. W., *Domesday Book and Beyond* (new edn, 1960).

Mason, E., *Westminster Abbey and its People, c. 1050 to c. 1216* (Woodbridge, 1996).

——*The House of Godwine: The History of a Dynasty* (2004).

Mason, J. F. A., 'William the First and the Sussex Rapes', *1066 Commemoration Lectures* (Historical Association, 1966).

Maund, K. L., 'The Welsh Alliances of Earl Ælfgar of Mercia and his Family in the Mid-Eleventh Century', *ANS*, 11 (1988).

Mew, K., 'The Dynamics of Lordship and Landscape as Revealed in a Domesday Study of the *Nova Foresta*', *ANS*, 23 (2001).

Miller, E., 'The Ely Land Pleas in the Reign of William I', *EHR*, 62 (1947).

Moore, J. S., 'Domesday Slavery', *ANS*, 11 (1989).

——'"Quot Homines?": The Population of Domesday England', *ANS*, 19 (1997).

Morris, M., *A Great and Terrible King: Edward I and the Forging of Britain* (2008).

Mortimer, R., 'Edward the Confessor: The Man and the Legend', *Edward the Confessor: The Man and the Legend*, ed. R. Mortimer (Woodbridge, 2009).

Morton, C., 'Pope Alexander II and the Norman Conquest', *Latomus* (1975).

Nelson, J. L., 'Rites of the Conqueror', idem, *Politics and Ritual in Early Medieval Europe* (1986).

O'Brien, B. R., 'From Morðor to Murdrum: The Preconquest Origin and Norman Revival of the Murder Fine', *Speculum*, 71 (1996). *Oxford Dictionary of National Biography*.

Painter, S., 'Castle-Guard', *Anglo-Norman Castles*, ed. R. Liddiard (Woodbridge, 2003).

Palliser, D. M., 'Domesday Book and the Harrying of the North', *Northern History*, 29 (1993).

Palmer, J. J. N., 'The Conqueror's Footprints in Domesday', *The Medieval Military Revolution*, ed. A. Ayton and J. L. Price (1995).

——'War and Domesday Waste', *Armies, Chivalry and Warfare in Medieval Britain and France,* ed. M. Strickland (Stamford, 1998).

——'The Wealth of the Secular Aristocracy in 1086', *ANS*, 22 (2000).

Pelteret, D. A. E., 'Slave Raiding and Slave Trading in Early England', *Anglo-Saxon England*, 9 (1981).

——*Slavery in Early Mediæval England* (Woodbridge, 1995).

Potts, C., *Monastic Revival and Regional Identity in Early Normandy* (Woodbridge, 1997).

Prestwich, J. O., *The Place of War in English History, 1066–1214* (Woodbridge, 2004).

Reilly, L., 'The Emergence of Anglo-Norman Architecture: Durham Cathedral', *ANS*, 19 (1997).

Reuter, T., 'Plunder and Tribute in the Carolingian Empire', *TRHS*, 5th ser., 35 (1985).

Reynolds, S., 'Eadric *Silvaticus* and the English Resistance', *Bulletin of the Institute of Historical Research*, 54 (1981).

——*Fiefs and Vassals* (Oxford, 1994).

——*Kingdoms and Communities in Western Europe, 900–1300* (Oxford, 1997).

Richardson, H. G. and Sayles, G. O., *Law and Legislation from Æthelberht to Magna Carta* (Edinburgh, 1966).

Ridyard, S. J., '*Condigna veneratio*: Post-Conquest Attitudes to the Saints of the Anglo-Saxons', *ANS*, 9 (1987).

Rodwell, W., 'New Glimpses of Edward the Confessor's Abbey at Westminster', *Edward the Confessor*, ed. R. Mortimer (Woodbridge, 2009).

Roffe, D., *Domesday: The Inquest and the Book* (Oxford, 2000).

Round, J. H., 'The Introduction of Knight Service into England', idem, *Feudal England* (new edn, 1964).

Rubenstein, J., 'Liturgy Against History: The Competing Visions of Lanfranc and Eadmer of Canterbury', *Speculum*, 74 (1999).

Searle, E., *Lordship and Community: Battle Abbey and its Banlieu, 1066–1538* (Toronto, 1974).

——'Women and the Legitimization of Succession at the Norman Conquest', *ANS*, 3 (1981).

——*Predatory Kinship and the Creation of Norman Power, 840–1066* (Berkeley, 1988).

Short, I., 'Patrons and Polyglots: French Literature in Twelfth-Century England', *ANS*, 14 (1992).

——'*Tam Angli quam Franci*: Self-Definition in Anglo-Norman England', *ANS*, 18 (1996).

Singh, I., *The History of English: A Student's Guide* (Oxford, 2005).

Stafford, P., *Unification and Conquest* (1989).

——'Women and the Norman Conquest', *TRHS*, 6th ser., 4 (1994).

——*Queen Emma and Queen Edith* (Oxford, 1997).

——'Edith, Edward's Wife and Queen', *Edward the Confessor*, ed. R. Mortimer (Woodbridge, 2009).

Stalley, R., *Early Medieval Architecture* (Oxford, 1999).

Stenton, F. M., *Anglo-Saxon England* (3rd edn, Oxford, 1971).

Stevenson, W. H., 'Notes on Old-English Historical Geography', *EHR*, 11 (1896).

Summerson, H., 'Tudor Antiquaries and the *Vita Ædwardi regis*', *Anglo-Saxon England*, 38 (2009).

Thomas, H. M., 'Subinfeudation and Alienation of Land, Economic Development and the Wealth of Nobles on the Honor of Richmond, 1066 to *c.*1300', *Albion*, 26 (1994).

——'The *Gesta Herwardi*, the English and their Conquerors', *ANS*, 21 (1998).

——*The English and the Normans: Ethnic Hostility, Assimilation, and Identity, 1066–c.1220* (Oxford, 2003).

——*The Norman Conquest: England After William the Conqueror* (Lanham, USA, 2008).

Thorn, F. and C., 'The Writing of Great Domesday Book', *Domesday Book*, ed. E. Hallam and D. Bates (Stroud, 2001).

van Houts, E. M. C., 'The Origins of Herleva, Mother of William the Conqueror', *EHR*, 101 (1986).

——'The Memory of 1066 in Written and Oral Traditions', *ANS*, 19 (1997).

——*History and Family Traditions in England and the Continent, 1000–1200* (Aldershot, 1999), which includes all the essays below published up to that date, with their original pagination.

——'The Political Relations between Normandy and England before 1066 according to the *Gesta Normannorum Ducum*', *Les Mutations Socio-Culturelles au Tournant de XIe–XIIe Siècles* (Paris, 1984).

——'Normandy and Byzantium in the Eleventh Century', *Byzantion*, 55 (Brussels, 1985).

——'The Ship List of William the Conqueror', *ANS*, 10 (1988).

——'A Note on *Jezebel and Semiramis*, Two Latin Poems from the Early Eleventh Century', *Journal of Medieval Latin*, 2 (Turnhout, 1992).

——'The Norman Conquest Through European Eyes', *EHR*, 110 (1995).

——'Hereward and Flanders', *Anglo-Saxon England*, 28 (2000).

——'Edward and Normandy', *Edward the Confessor*, ed. R. Mortimer (Woodbridge, 2009).

Vaughn, S. N., 'Lanfranc at Bec: A Reinterpretation', *Albion*, 17 (1985).

Walker, I. W., *Harold: The Last Anglo-Saxon King* (Stroud, 2004).

Wareham, A., 'The "Feudal Revolution" in Eleventh-Century East Anglia', *ANS*, 22 (2000).

Wilkinson, B., 'Northumbrian Separatism in 1065 and 1066', *Bulletin of the John Rylands Library*, 23 (1939).

Williams, A., 'Some Notes and Considerations on Problems Connected with the English Royal Succession, 860–1066', *ANS*, 1 (1978).

—— 'A Bell-house and a Burh-geat: Lordly Residences in England before the Norman Conquest', *Medieval Knighthood IV* (Woodbridge, 1992).

——*The English and the Norman Conquest* (Woodbridge, 1995).

——*Æthelred the Unready: The Ill-Counselled King* (2003).

Wilson, R. M., 'English and French in England, 1100–1300', *History*, 28 (1943).

Wormald, P., '*Engla lond*: The Making of an Allegiance', *Journal of Historical Sociology*, 8 (1994).

Wyatt, D., 'The Significance of Slavery: Alternative Approaches to Anglo-Saxon Slavery', *ANS*, 23 (2001).

Young, C. R., *The Royal Forests of Medieval England* (Leicester, 1979).

Zadora-Rio, E., 'L'enceinte fortifiée du Plessis-Grimoult, résidence seigneuriale du XIe siècle', *Chateau Gaillard*, 5 (1972).

SECONDARY WORKS (CONSULTED)

Abels, R., 'Bookland and Fyrd Service in Late Saxon England', *ANS*, 7 (1984).

Aird, W., *St Cuthbert and the Normans* (Woodbridge, 1998).

L'Architecture Normande au Moyen Age, ed. M. Baylé (2 vols., 2nd edn, Caen, 2001).

Bachrach, B. S., 'The Feigned Retreat at Hastings', *The Battle of Hastings*, ed. S. Morillo (Woodbridge, 1996).

Bates, D., 'William the Conqueror and His Wider European World', *Haskins Society Journal*, 15 (2006).

Baxter, S., 'The Representation of Lordship and Land Tenure in Domesday Book', *Domesday Book*, ed. D. Bates and E. Hallam (2001).

Bennett, M., 'Violence in Eleventh-Century Normandy: Feud, Warfare and Politics', *Violence and Society in the Early Medieval West* (Woodbridge, 1998).

Bradbury, J., *The Battle of Hastings* (Stroud, 1998).

Brown, R. A., 'The Status of the Norman Knight', *Anglo-Norman Warfare*, ed. M. Strickland (Woodbridge, 1992).

The Cambridge Urban History of Britain, 600–1540, I, ed. D. M. Palliser (Cambridge, 2000).

Campbell, J., *The Anglo-Saxon State* (2000).

A Companion to the Anglo-Norman World, ed. C. Harper-Bill and E. van Houts (Woodbridge, 2003).

Cowdrey, H. E. J., 'Bishop Ermenfrid of Sion and the Penitential Ordinance Following the Battle of Hastings', *Journal of Ecclesiastical History*, 20 (1969).

——'Towards an Interpretation of the Bayeux Tapestry', *ANS*, 10 (1988).

——*Lanfranc: Scholar, Monk and Archbishop* (Oxford, 2003).

Davis, R. H. C., *The Normans and Their Myth* (2nd edn, 1980).

Dhondt, J., 'Henri Ier, L'Empire et L'Anjou (1043–1056)', *Revue Belge de Philologie et d'Histoire*, 25 (1946).

Dobson, R. B., 'The First Norman Abbey in Northern England: The Origins of Selby', *Church and Society in the Medieval North of England* (1996).

Downham, C., 'England and the Irish-Sea Zone in the Eleventh Century', *ANS*, 26 (2004).

English Romanesque Art, 1066–1200, ed. G. Zarnecki, J. Holt and T. Holland (1984).

Les Évêques Normands du XIe Siècle, ed. P. Bouet and F. Neveux (Caen, 1995).

Fernie, E., 'Saxons, Normans and their Buildings', *ANS*, 21 (1999).

Fleming, R., 'The New Wealth, the New Rich and the New Political Style in Late Anglo-Saxon England', *ANS*, 23 (2001).

From the Vikings to the Normans, ed. W. Davies (Oxford, 2003).

Gade, K. E., 'Northern Lights on the Battle of Hastings', *Viator*, 28 (1997).

Garnett, G., 'Conquered England, 1066–1215', *The Oxford Illustrated History of Medieval England* (Oxford, 1997).

Gibson, M., *Lanfranc of Bec* (Oxford, 1978).

Grassi, J. L., 'The *Vita Ædwardi Regis*: The Hagiographer as Insider', *ANS*, 26 (2004).

Guillot, O., *Le Comte D Anjou et son Entourage au XIe Siècle* (2 vols., Paris, 1972).

Hadley, D. M., '"And they proceeded to plough and to support themselves": The Scandinavian Settlement of England', *ANS* 19 (1997).

Hart, C., 'William Malet and his Family', *ANS*, 19 (1997).

Hollister, C. W., 'The "Feudal Revolution"', *American Historical Review*, 73 (1968).

Holt, J. C., 'Feudal Society and the Family in Early Medieval England: The Revolution of 1066', *TRHS*, 33 (1983).

Hooper, N., 'Anglo-Saxon Warfare on the Eve of the Conquest: A Brief Survey', *ANS*, 1 (1979).

——'Some Observations on the Navy in Late Anglo-Saxon England', *Anglo-Norman Warfare*, ed. M. Strickland (Woodbridge, 1992).

John, E., *Reassessing Anglo-Saxon England* (Manchester, 1996).

Kapelle, W. E., 'Domesday Book: F. W. Maitland and his Successors', *Speculum*, 64 (1989).

——'The Purpose of Domesday Book: A Quandary', *Essays in Medieval Studies*, 9 (1992).

Lawrence, H., 'The Monastic Revival', *England in Europe, 1066–1453* (1994).

Loud, G. A., 'The *Gens Normannorum* – Myth or Reality?', *ANS*, 4 (1982).

Loyn, H. R., *Anglo-Saxon England and the Norman Conquest* (1962).

——'William's Bishops: Some Further Thoughts', *ANS*, 10 (1988).
——*The Vikings in Britain* (Oxford, 1994).

Moore, J. S., 'Anglo-Norman Garrisons', *ANS*, 22 (2000).
Musset, L., *The Bayeux Tapestry*, transl. R. Rex (new edn, Woodbridge, 2005).

Nelson, J., 'Anglo-Saxon England, *c.*500–1066', *The Oxford Illustrated History of Medieval England* (Oxford, 1997).
Neumann, J., 'Hydrographic and Ship-Hydrodynamic Aspects of the Norman Invasion, AD 1066', *ANS*, 11 (1989).
Nip, R., 'The Political Relations between England and Flanders (1066–1128), *ANS*, 21 (1999).
La Normandie vers L'An Mil, ed. F. Beaurepaire and J.-P. Chaline (Rouen, 2000).

Oleson, T. J., 'Edward the Confessor's Promise of the Throne to Duke William of Normandy', *EHR*, 72 (1957).
Owen-Crocker, G. R., 'The Interpretation of Gesture in the Bayeux Tapestry', *ANS*, 29 (2007).

Peirce, I., 'Arms, Armour and Warfare in the Eleventh Century', *ANS*, 10 (1988).
Prestwich, J. O., 'Anglo-Norman Feudalism and the Problem of Continuity', *Past and Present*, 26 (1963).
——'Mistranslations and Misinterpretations in Medieval English History', *Peritia*, 10 (1996).
Prestwich, M., *Armies and Warfare in the Middle Ages: The English Experience* (Yale, 1996).

Shopkow, L., *History and Community: Norman Historical Writing in the Eleventh and Twelfth Centuries* (Washington, 1997).
Short, I., 'The Language of the Bayeux Tapestry Inscription', *ANS*, 23 (2001).
Strickland, M., 'Slaughter, Slavery or Ransom: The Impact of the Conquest on Conduct in Warfare', *England in the Eleventh Century*, ed. C. Hicks (Stamford, 1992).
——'Military Technology and Conquest: The Anomaly of Anglo-Saxon England', *ANS*, 19 (1997).

van Houts, E. M. C., 'Historiography and Hagiography at Saint-Wandrille: The *Inventio et Miracula Sancti Vulfranni*', *ANS*, 12 (1990).

——'The Trauma of 1066', *History Today*, 46:10 (1996).

——'Wace as Historian', *Family Trees and the Roots of Politics*, ed. K. Keats-Rohan (Woodbridge, 1997).

West, F. J., 'The Colonial History of the Norman Conquest', *History*, 84 (1999).

Williams, A., *The World Before Domesday: The English Aristocracy, 900–1066* (2008).

Index

Abbreviations: abp (archbishop); abt (abbot); bp (bishop); dau. (daughter); ETC (Edward the Confessor); WTC (William the Conqueror)

Abernethy (Perths), 252, 289

Abingdon, abbey (Oxon), 215, 235, 239, 242, 249, 260, 277, 281; abt of, *see* Adelelm; Ealdred

Adam of Bremen, chronicler, 155, 225

Adela, dau. of Robert the Frisian, wife of Cnut IV, 305

Adela, mother of Matilda, 67

Adelelm, abt of Abingdon, 242, 260, 262, 277, 281

Agatha, wife of Edward the Exile, 103, 106

L'Aigle (Orne), 205, 274–5

Ailnoth of Canterbury, 345

Ailred of Rievaulx (d. 1167), 350–3

Aire, river, 228

Alan, count of Brittany (1008–40), 51–2

Alençon (Orne), 81–2, 187

Alexander, bp of Lincoln (1123–48), 347

Alexander II, pope (1061–73), 142–3, 145, 173, 187, 201, 236, 239, 256, 263, 266, 300

Alfred (d. 1037), ætheling, brother of ETC, 16, 100, 144, 294; exile in Normandy, 15, 19–21, 34, 51; return to England, 35, 361; murder of, 36–9, 62, 64, 71–3, 263

Alfred the Great, king of Wessex (871–99), 12–13, 138, 341

Amatus of Montecassino, chronicler, 186

Ambrières (Mayenne), 93

Amiens (Somme), 167; bp of, *see* Guy

Anglo-Saxon Chronicle (*selected references*): importance, 5; frustrating silences or brevity, 5, 38,

109, 115, 120, 217, 252, 300; begun in Alfred's day, 13; different versions of, 36, 78, 102; used by John of Worcester, 39; used by Henry of Huntingdon, 322; E version pro-Godwine, 78, 104, 133; D version compiled in Ealdred's circle, 102, 104; C version pro-Mercian, anti-Godwine, 104, 123, 162; obituary of WTC, 333–4; discontinued after Conquest, 341

Anglo-Saxons *see* English

Anjou, 80–2, 85, 90, 110–11, 234, 254, 273, 304, 351; count of, *see* Fulk Nerra; Fulk Réchin; Geoffrey Martel; Geoffrey Plantagenet

Anna of Kiev (d. 1075), queen of France, mother of Philip I, 110, 255

Anselm of Bec, abp of Canterbury (1093–1109), 259

Ansgar the Staller, 278

Aquitaine, 151, 303; count of, 84; *see also* Eleanor

archdeacons, 257, 339

archers, 179–80, 183, 237, 305

architecture, 257–8, 296–8, 334, 353

arms, armour *see* weapons

Arnulf, count of Flanders (1070–1), 254

Arques (Seine-Mar.), castle of, 83, 85, 183; count of, *see* William

Arundel (Sussex), castle and rape, 215

Arwystli (Powys), 294

Asbjorn, brother of Swein Estrithson, 226, 229, 242–3, 245

Assandun (Essex), battle of, 18, 24, 99

Atcham (Salop), 205, 379; St Eata's church, 205

Athelstan, king of England (924–39), 138, 252

Aubrey de Grandmesnil, 275

Aversa (Italy), 287; bp of, *see* Guitmund

Avon, river, 220

Axholme, isle of (Lincs), 227

Ælfflæd, granddau. of Earl Uhtred, wife of Earl Siward, 127, 253

Ælfgar, earl of East Anglia and Mercia (d. *c.* 1062), 75, 101, 104–5, 107–8, 128, 157, 321

Ælfgifu of Northampton, wife of King Cnut, 30–1, 33

Ælfheah, abp of Canterbury (d. 1012), 15, 24, 259

Ælfhelm, ealdorman of York (d. 1006), 123

Ælfric, abt of Eynsham, 25

Ælfric Puttoc, abp of York (d. 1051), 39

Ælfwine, bp of Winchester (d. 1047), 42

Æthelmær, bp of East Anglia, 239

Æthelred the Unready, king of England (978–1016), 14–19, 24, 28, 30, 39, 72, 75–6, 263–4, 284

Æthelric, bp of Durham (1041–56), 123, 238, 247

Æthelric, bp of Sussex (1058–70), 239

Æthelric, proposed abp of Canterbury, 69

Æthelric of Marsh Gibbon, 314, 320

Æthelwig, abt of Evesham (d. 1078), 269, 285

Æthelwine, bp of Durham (1056–70), 123, 125, 219–20, 223, 238, 246–7

Æthelwold, abt of Abingdon, 260

Æthelwulf, bp of Carlisle, 349

Bachrach, Bernard, 153

Baldwin, abt of Bury St Edmunds, ETC's physician, 140–1

Baldwin V, count of Flanders (1035–67), 37, 67–8, 82, 105, 110, 123, 130, 147, 254

Baldwin VI, count of Flanders (1067–70), 254

Bamburgh (Northumb.), 121; house of, 122–3, 126–7, 210, 216, 253; *see also* Gospatric; Waltheof

Baring, Francis, 194–5

Barking (Essex), 201–2, 297, 378–9

Barnstaple (Devon), 224

Battle (Sussex), 176; abbey, 178, 237, 333, 382; chronicler, 189

Baudri of Bourgeuil, 179, 183, 186

Bayeux (Calvados), 1, 3, 56, 94, 370; cathedral, 3, 276, 367

Bayeux Tapestry, 1–5, 10, 11, 49, 112–15, 118–19, 133–5, 139, 146–7, 150, 169–71, 174, 177, 179–86, 190, 207, 277, 357, 370, 377–8

Beaurain (Pas-de-Calais), castle, 113

Le Bec-Hellouin (Eure), abbey, 87–8

Bedfordshire, 315

Bellême (Orne), 81; lords of, 81; *see also* Robert of Bellême

Benedict X, antipope, 108

Beorn Estrithson (d. 1049), 63, 65, 75–6

Berengar de Tosny, 278

Berkhamsted, 196, 199, 378–9; castle, 196, 207

Berkshire, 76, 195

Berlin, 3

Bertha, queen of France (d. 1093), 255

Bevere, island, 40

Beverstone (Glos), 71

Birhtnoth, ealdorman (d. 991), 27–8

Blæcmann, priest, 215

Bleddyn ap Cynfyn (d. 1075), Welsh king, 209, 218

Blois-Chartres, count of, 80, 84; *see also* Stephen

Bonneville-Aptot, 88

Bonneville-sur-Touques (Calvados), 114

Bosham (Sussex), 72, 109, 113

Boulogne, 210; count of, *see* Eustace

Brian, count, 215, 224, 227

Brionne (Eure), castle, 57, 66, 365

Bristol (Somerset), 220, 222, 294

Britford (Wilts), 129

Brittany, 22, 57, 114–15, 151, 234, 267, 270, 272, 305, 370; count of, *see* Alan

Brown, Prof. R. Allen, 186

Bruges, 37–8, 68

Brussels, 167

Buckinghamshire, 195, 314

Bulgaria, 156

Burgundy, 87, 98, 151

burhgeats, 208

burhs, boroughs, 12, 122, 208, 266, 296, 310, 353

Bury St Edmunds (Suffolk), 312, 344; abt of, 202

Byzantium, 92, 155-7, 201, 360

Caen (Calvados), 56, 58, 94, 112, 149, 204, 256, 258, 273, 303, 330-1, 349, 365; castle, 112; Holy Trinity, 112, 149, 303; St Stephen's, 112, 204, 256, 258, 273-4, 298, 330-1, 370

Caerwent (Gwent), 297

Cambridge, 270; castle, 220

Cambridgeshire, 36, 309, 311, 315

Canterbury, 2, 15, 24, 69, 104, 119, 193, 238, 262, 285-6; cathedral, 70, 257-9, 298, 333; castle, 207; St Augustine's Abbey, 258, 262; abt of, 239-40, 258, 262

Capetians, 46

Caradog ap Gruffudd (d. 1081), 292-4

Cardiff (Glamorgan), 294

Carl, northern magnate, 265; his sons and grandsons, 265

Carmen de Hastingae Proelio [select], 167

Carolingian Empire, 45-6, 48; *see also* France

Cassel (Nord), battle of, 254

castles, 111, 233, 259, 269, 281-2, 292, 306; Continental origins and purpose, 46-9, 282, 337-8; constructed during WTC's minority, 51, 54; destroyed after

Val-ès-Dunes, 57, 66; on the Bayeux Tapestry, 1-2, 171, 207; introduced to England by Normans, 7-8, 207-9, 219-21, 334, 353; castle-guard, garrisons, 242, 247, 281; destruction and suffering caused by, 313, 333; numbers, 334; *see also individual castles by name*

Catton (Yorks), 375

Cecilia (d. 1127), dau. of WTC, 149

ceorls, 26

Cerisy-la-Forêt, abbey, 87, 89

Charford (Hants), 311

Charlemagne, king of the Franks, emperor (d. 814), 45

Charles the Fat, king of the Franks, emperor (d. 888), 45

Chartres, bp of, 24

Chepstow (Gwent), 120, 296; castle, 296; priory, 296

Cheshire, 122

Chester, 192, 227, 234, 247, 258, 268, 313; bp of, 263, 319; castle, 233; earl of, *see* Gerbod; Hugh

Chichester (Sussex), castle and rape, 215; cathedral, 258

chivalry, 264, 267, 270, 295, 339

Church, English: 14, 69, 98-100, 107-8, 123, 143; reform of, 237-40, 256-61, 339; military service imposed on, 240-2, 323; losses of land, 284-6

Church, Norman, 50-1, 86-93, 236

Clavering (Essex), castle, 208

Cluny (Saône-et-Loire), abbey, 87

Cnut, king of England (1016-35),

Denmark (1018–35) and Norway (1028–35), birth and baptism, 23; Christianity, 23–4, 368; visit to Rome, 37; and the waves, 18, 23; conquers England, 18, 102; Scandinavian empire, 60–1; brutality, 18; killings at the start of his reign, 19, 126, 263–5, 336; marriages, 19–20, 30–2; death, 22–3, 30–5, 43; buried in Winchester, 23, 42, 97, 100; changes during his rule, 27–30, 103, 122–3, 253; laws of, 41, 130, 385; his children, *see* Gunhilda; Harold; Harthacnut; Swein

Cnut IV, king of Denmark (1080–6), 304–6, 326, 345

coins and coinage, 13, 31, 33, 46, 48, 122, 208; sterling, 298

Colchester (Essex), castle, 297, 334

Cologne, 103, 247

Comines (Nord), 222

commendation, 107, 248, 283

Compiègne (Oise), 50

Constance, patron of Geoffrey Gaimar, 348

Constantine, emperor, 298

Constantinople, 95, 155–6, 360

Conwy, river, 292

Copsig, earl of Northumbria (d. 1067), 211, 216, 222

Cornwall, 214, 220, 227

coronation, 10, 34, 59, 131, 139–40, 195, 197–201, 216, 219, 236–7, 319–20, 331, 335, 344, 350; *see also* crown-wearing

councils: Church, 58, 67–8, 86, 91–2, 98, 103–4, 129, 238–9, 242,

257–8, 306, 338–9, 365; secular, 31, 69–70, 75, 78, 114, 143, 305

courts: national and secular, 27, 208, 257, 286, 318, 338, 351; Church, 257, 339; baronial, 338, 351; *see also* law

Coutances (Manche), bp of, 87; *see also* Geoffrey of Mowbray

Coventry (Warks), 263

Crediton, 98, 258, 384; *see also* Leofric

Crowland (Lincs), abbey, 306

crown-wearing, 232, 236, 298–9, 318

Crusade, First, 9, 344

Cumbria, 121, 126–7

Cynesige, abp of York (1051–60), 107, 125

Danelaw, 121

Danes, 17–18, 29, 61, 97, 121, 123, 212–13, 226–9, 243–6, 253, 259, 269–70, 297, 306, 312, 341, 345, 385; *see also* Vikings

Dean, forest of, 226, 291

Deheubarth, kingdom of, 292; king of, *see* Rhys ap Tewder

Denmark, 29, 31–2, 37, 60–2, 66, 147, 150, 157–9, 225, 245, 304; king of, *see* Cnut; Swein

Derbyshire, 128

Derwent, river, 163–4

Devon, 25, 220, 224, 227

Dieppe (Seine-Mar.), 83, 211

Dives, river, 94, 153, 168

Dives-sur-Mer (Calvados), 150, 153, 166, 168, 172

Dol (Ille-et-Vilaine), castle, 272, 327

Domesday: reasons for name, 307, 310; book, 5, 76, 107, 149, 194–5, 202, 214, 230, 233, 277–9, 282–3, 286, 291, 295–6, 307–13, 315, 317–18, 325–6, 335–6, 338, 344, 348; purpose of, 322–4; survey, 307–12, 317–18, 320, 322, 324–5, 333; Great Domesday, 307–8, 317, 324, 326; Little Domesday, 307, 317, 326; Exon Domesday, 316–17, 322; judicial inquiry, 309–12; jurors, 283, 286, 309–11, 318, 348; waste, 313, 315–16; geld inquiry, 316–17; returns brought to WTC at Salisbury, 322

Domesday Book and Beyond, 317

Domfront (Orne), 81–3, 93–4, 111

Dorchester-upon-Thames (Oxon), 258

Dover (Kent), 35, 71, 192–4, 206, 209, 226, 248; castle, 116, 192–3, 195, 202, 207, 209–10

Duncan I, king of Scots (1034–40), father of Malcolm III, 125

Duncan II, king of Scots (1094), son of Malcolm III, 252

Dunsinane (Perths), battle of, 125

Durham, city, 125, 127, 223–4, 247, 251–3, 267, 290, 314; county, 121, 233; castle, 252, 270, 290; cathedral, 123, 346–7; abbey, 340; bp of, *see* Æthelric; Æthelwine; Walcher; William

Eadmer, monk of Canterbury, chronicler, 116–19, 259, 333, 342

Eadnoth the Staller (d. 1068), 222

Eadric the Grabber (Streona) (d. 1017) 14, 17–19

Eadric the Wild, 209, 218, 227

Eadsige, abp of Canterbury (d. 1050), 65, 69

Eadwig (d. 1017), son of Æthelred the Unready, 19

Eadwine, earl of Mercia (d. 1071), son of Earl Ælfgar: becomes earl of Mercia, 128; supports northern rebels, 128–9; attends dedication of Westminster Abbey (1065), 136; allies with Harold, 139; drives off Tostig (1066), 148; defeated at Fulford, 162, 192; withdraws from London, 196; submits to WTC (1067), 202, 378–9; hostage in Normandy, 203, 217, 253; attends Matilda's coronation (1068), 216; promised marriage to WTC's daughter, 218, 253; erosion of power, 217–18, 247–8; rebels but quickly submits (1068), 218–19; rebels again (1071), 248; betrayal and death, 250, 320

Eadwine (d. 1039), uncle of Earl Ælfgar, 105

Eadwulf, earl (d. 1041), 40, 126, 263

Ealdgyth, sister of Eadwine and Morcar, wife of Gruffudd ap Llywelyn and Harold Godwineson, 137, 139, 141, 192, 212

ealdormen, 27–8

Ealdred, abt of Abingdon, 239, 382–3

Ealdred, bp of Worcester, abp of York (1061–9), ASC D

compiled in his circle, 74, 104; Godwine sympathizer, 102, 107; sent to find Edward the Exile (1054–5), 102–3, 369; becomes abp of York, 107; crowns Harold (1066), 139; champions Edgar Ætheling, 191, 195; crowns WTC, 199–200; crowns Matilda (1068), 216; curses Urse d'Abetôt, 284; attempts to quell rebellion, 219; dies, 226, 240

Ealdred, earl of Northumbria (d. 1038), son of Uhtred, 265

earls, 28

East Anglia, 12, 27–8, 63, 71, 75, 99, 101, 104, 107, 243, 245, 258, 267, 269, 283; bishop of, 240; *see also* Æthelmær; Stigand; earl of, *see* Ælfgar; Gyrth; Harold; Ralph; Thorkell

Edgar, king of England (959–75), 138

Edgar Ætheling, son of Edward the Exile: throne-worthiness, 106, 132, 138, 191; rights set aside by Harold and allies, 138, 140; elected king (1066), 191–3, 195, 197; surrenders to WTC, 196; hostage in Normandy (1067), 203; rebels (1068), 219; flees to Scotland, 220, 222; attacks York (1069), 223; returns to Scotland, 224; joins Danish invasion, 226; flees to Scotland (1070), 233, 247, 251; flees to Flanders (1072), 252–3; submits to WTC (1074), 266–7, 271; friends with Robert Curthose, 345

Edith, ETC's queen (d. 1075), dau. of Earl Godwine, character and accomplishments, 63; age, 64–5, 67; marriage to ETC, 63–4; childlessness, 64, 69, 97, 102; relationship with ETC, 64, 72–3, 134–5; banishment (1051), 72–3; return (1052), 79, 95; power and influence, 104, 127, 263–4; rebuilds Wilton Abbey, 129; grief at Tostig's fall, 130; proxy for ETC, 131; at ETC's deathbed, 133–7; submits to WTC, 193

Edith, Henry I's queen (d. 1118), 349–51

Edith Swan-Neck, wife of Harold Godwineson, 137, 190, 212

Edmund, son of Edmund Ironside, 102

Edmund, son of Harold, 220

Edmund Ironside, king of England (1016), 17–18, 102

Edward I, king of England (1272–1307), 4, 151, 353

Edward of Salisbury, 320

Edward the Confessor, king of England (1042–66): character, 11, 97; piety, 11, 96–8; chastity, 64, 69, 73, 96–7, 365; supports Church reform, 98, 368–9; friendships, 63, 69, 75, 78, 95, 208; builds palace and abbey at Westminster, 96–7, 131, 198, 258, 334, 368; hunting, 120, 291; canonization and cult, 11, 97, 350; cult, 353
family relationships: with his mother, Emma, 41, 59–60, 97; with cousin, Robert, 20–1; with

father-in-law, Godwine, 64, 73;
with wife, Edith, 63–4, 73, 134;
with brothers-in-law, Harold
and Tostig, 108, 120, 140
selective chronological survey: birth
(1002 × 1005), 13; exile in
Normandy (1013–14), 15; return
to England (1014), 17–18; exile
in Normandy (1016–41), 19–20;
attempted return to England (*c.*
1033), 20–2, 37, 51; attempted
return to England (1036), 34, 37,
51; return to England (1041),
41–2; accession (1042), 42, 59;
coronation (1043), 59, 140, 197;
fears attack from Norway
(1042–7), 59–62, 157, 337;
marries Edith (1045), 63–4;
dominated by Godwine, 62–6;
plan to remove Godwine, 66,
68, 75; promises succession to
WTC (1051), 69–70, 73–5,
115–18, 173; clash with
Godwine (1051), 70–2; prepares
against Godwine's return (1051–
2), 75–6; forced to readmit
Godwine (1052), 77–9, 95;
dominated by Godwinesons
(1053–66), 100–9; his part in
Harold's visit to Normandy
(1064/5), 113, 115–19; reaction
to northern rebellion (1065),
129–31; illness and final days,
131–41, 343, 346; death (1066),
11, 131, 141
Edward the Exile (d. 1057), son of
Edmund Ironside, 102–3, 105–6,
132, 138
Eilífr, earl, 28–9

Eleanor of Aquitaine, queen of
England (d. 1204), 351
Elizabeth, queen of Harold
Hardrada, 160
Elmham (Norfolk), 258
Ely (Cambs), 36, 243–52, 264, 278,
306, 309, 314; abbey, 242, 284;
abt of, 246; castle, 251; inquest,
308–9, 314
Emma, dau. of Richard I of
Normandy, queen of England
(d. 1052): marriage to Æthelred,
16–17, 30; marriage to Cnut,
19–20, 30–1; schemes for the
succession (1035–40), 32–9; relationship with ETC, 19, 37, 41,
59–60, 68; patron of Stigand, 99;
death and burial, 97, 100; children of, *see* Alfred; Edward;
Godgifu; Gunhilda; Harthacnut
Emma, dau. of William fitz
Osbern, 268, 270
Encomium Emmae Reginae, 32–8,
41–2, 61, 132
England (*selected references*): origins,
11–13; population, 25, social
conditions and society, 25–7;
changes as a result of Danish
conquest, 28–30; political maturity, 31, 309; absence of castles
in, 208; prevalence of slavery,
25–6, 294–5; and political
murder, 263–5; Church in,
235–42, 256–8; naval power,
143–4; changes as a result of
Norman Conquest, 7–8,
319–24; 334–42; *see also* burhs;
commendation; coronation;
courts; Danelaw; hides;

hundreds; military obligation; shires; taxation

The English (*selected references*): origins, 11–13; conversion, 12; hairstyles, 2; military techniques, considered backwards by their detractors, 2, 178–9; brave and warlike, according to their defenders, 178, 208; considered barbarous by Continentals, 263–5; transformed by French fashions, 266; accused of gluttony, drunkenness and lechery, 26, 177, 336–7; reluctance to write about Conquest, 115, 333, 342; effect of Conquest on, 7–8, 319–21, 332–42, 344–53

Erik, earl of Northumbria (d. 1023), 28–30, 122

Ermenfrid, bp of Sion, papal legate, 92, 239

Essex, 12, 18, 66, 68

Estrith, sister of King Cnut, 61

Eu (Seine-Mar.), 68, 114

Eustace, count of Boulogne, 71, 186, 209–10

Evesham (Worcs), abbey, 230, 260, 285–6; abt of, *see* Æthelwig; Walter

Evreux, 328; bp of, 331

Exeter, 212–14, 217, 220, 227, 258; castle, 214; bp of, *see* Leofric

Exning (Suffolk), 268

Falaise (Calvados), 43, 53, 55, 56

Fawdon, nr Cambridge, 270

Fécamp (Seine-Mar.), 21, 87, 203; abbey, 87, 98, 150, 261

feigned flight, 181–3

feudalism, 7, 48, 50–1, 144–5, 240, 324

feudal incidents, 323–4

Flanders, 37, 50, 67–8, 71–2, 75, 77, 105, 113, 130, 144, 146–7, 158, 225, 245, 252, 254, 266 count of, *see* Arnulf; Baldwin; Robert

Flat Holm, 214, 220, 225

fleets *see* ships

Flemings, 37

Florence of Worcester *see* John of Worcester

Folkestone, Castle Hill, 208

Fontevraud (Maine-et-Loire), abbey, 351

Forest, royal, 291, 316, 333–4; *see also* New Forest

Forth, river, 252

France, kingdom of, 8–9, 15, 37, 44–50, 82, 88, 91, 98, 110, 151, 203, 254, 267, 273, 304–5, 327; origins, 44–5; kings of, *see* Henry; Philip; Robert

Francia, Franks, *see* France, origins

Freeman, Edward Augustus, historian (d. 1892), 6–8; *History of the Norman Conquest*, 6, 8

French Revolution, 3

Frisia, 225

Frutolf of Michelsberg, 332, 338

Fulbert, undertaker/chamberlain, 43, 81

Fulford (Yorks), battle of, 162, 164, 192

Fulk Nerra, count of Anjou (987–1040), 46, 80

Fulk Réchin, count of Anjou (1068–1109), 111, 254–5, 272, 304

Gaimar *see* Geoffrey

Gascony, 303

Gateshead (Durham), 290

geld *see* taxation

Geoffrey de Mandeville, 278

Geoffrey Gaimar, chronicler, 158, 347–8

Geoffrey Martel, count of Anjou (1040–60), 80–2, 84–5, 93–4, 110–11, 254

Geoffrey of Mowbray, bp of Coutances (1049–93), 91–2, 199

Geoffrey Plantagenet, count of Anjou (d. 1151), 351

Geoffrey the Bearded, count of Anjou (1060–8), 111, 254

Gerald of Wales

Gerberoy (Oise), castle, 288, 327

Gerbod, earl of Chester, 247, 292

Germany, German Empire, 33, 303; *see also* Henry III, Henry IV

Gesta Guillelmi see William of Poitiers

Gesta Herewardi, 243, 246, 249, 347

Gilbert, count of Brionne (d. *c.* 1040), 51–2, 88, 283

Gilfard, 186

Giso, bp of Wells (1061–88), 108, 216

Glamorgan, 293

Glastonbury (Somerset), abbey, 24, 261, 346; abt of, *see* Thurstan

Gloucester, 60, 71, 290–1, 298–9, 306

Godgifu, sister of ETC, 16, 19, 71, 75, 102

Godwine, earl of Wessex (d. 1053), his rise under Cnut, 28–30, 321; supports Harthacnut, 32; switches to Harold Harefoot, 35; complicit in death of Alfred, 35–6, 39, 62, 263, 294; facilitates ETC's return, 41–2, 62, 133; his ship, 62, 362; relationship with ETC, 62–6, 72–3, 75; clash with ETC (1051), 69–72, 97, 248; forcible return to power (1052), 76–9, 95, 148; connections with Stigand, 98–100; death, 100–1; his wife, *see* Gytha; his sons, *see* Gyrth; Harold; Leofwine; Swein; Tostig; Wulfnoth; his daughter, *see* Edith

Godwine, son of Harold, 220

Gospatric, earl of Northumbria (d. 1073 × 1075), 216–17, 219–20, 222–4, 226, 233, 247, 252, 264, 266

Gospatric (d. 1064), son of Earl Uhtred, 126–8, 210, 264

Grandmesnil, family, 89, 275

Gregory VII, pope (1073–85), 289, 300–1, 333, 373

Grestain (Eure), abbey, 89

Grimoald of St Plessis, 57

Gruffudd ap Llywelyn, king of Wales (d. 1063), 104–5, 107, 109, 137, 292

Guernsey, 86

Guildford (Surrey), 36

Guitmund, bp of Aversa, 286–7

Gundulf, bp of Rochester (1077–1108), 263, 266

Gunhilda, dau. of Emma and Cnut, 30, 33

Gunhilda, niece of Cnut, 62, 68

Guy, bp of Amiens (d. 1075), author of the *Carmen de Hastingae Proelio*, 167, 169, 187

Guy, count of Brionne, 55–7, 66
Guy, count of Ponthieu (d. 1100),
    113
Gwcharis the Irishman, 294
Gwynedd, king of, 293–4
Gyrth Godwineson, earl of East
    Anglia (d. 1066), 107, 136, 175,
    189, 202, 212, 267
Gytha, wife of earl Godwine, 29,
    130, 175, 190, 212–15, 217, 225

Hakon, earl, 28–9
Hakon, son of Earl Swein, hostage,
    116, 118, 137–8
Halley, Edmond (d. 1742), 146
Halley's Comet, 146–7
Hampshire, 73, 194–5, 202, 291,
    311
Harold, brother of King Cnut, 29
Harold Godwineson, king of
    England (1066):
    character, 100, 140, 200, 206;
    rivalry with Ælfgar, 75, 128, 101;
    relationship with Tostig, 104,
    129–30, 138, 147–8, 165; affinity,
    107; sons, 212, 217, 220–2,
    224–5; written out of history
    by Normans, 335
    selective chronological survey:
    becomes earl of East Anglia
    (1045), 63; flees to Ireland
    (1051), 72, 102; returns to
    England (1052), 77, 294; resigns
    East Anglia, becomes earl of
    Wessex (1053), 100–1; leads
    army against Ælfgar and
    Gruffudd, negotiates peace
    (1055), 105; visits Flanders
    (1056), 105; power behind the
    throne (1057–66), 108; invades
    Wales and topples Gruffudd
    (1062–3), 109, 124, 144, 158, 292;
    visits Normandy (1064/5), 109,
    112–19, 137–8; swears oath to
    William, 4, 114–17, 129, 142,
    177, 332, 370; participates in
    Breton campaign, 114; returns
    to ETC, 119; builds hunting
    lodge at Portskewett (1065), 120;
    negotiates with northern rebels
    (1065), 129–30; allies with
    Eadwine and Morcar, marries
    Ealdgyth (1065/6), 136–9;
    succeeds ETC as king (1066),
    131–41; coronation, 2, 131,
    139–41, 195; visits York, 141;
    prepares against invasion, 146–9,
    152, 154, 166, 218; learns of
    Norwegian invasion, marches
    north, 161–2; defeats
    Norwegians at Stamford Bridge,
    163–5; learns of Norman inva-
    sion, marches south, 171–2, 376;
    exchanges messages with WTC,
    172–3; hurries towards Hastings,
    174–5, 191, 248; surprised by
    WTC, 176–7; his banner, 201,
    278; fights WTC at Hastings, 2,
    177–80; death, 2–3, 10, 183–8,
    210, 265; burial, 190
Harold Hardrada (Sigurdson), king
    of Norway (1047–66), 62,
    155–65; his banner, 'Land-
    Waster', 162
Harold Harefoot, king of England
    (1035–40), 31–3, 35–40, 44,
    132–3, 361–2, 368
harrying, 13, 15, 40, 71, 77, 111,

130, 174, 194–5, 199, 219, 222, 233, 251, 290, 306, 313, 328

Harrying of the North, 229–30, 233, 236, 245–6, 248, 313–14, 332, 334–5, 340–1

Harthacnut, king of Denmark (1035–42) and England (1040–2): loses England to Harold I due to delay in Denmark, 30–3, 35, 44, 60, 132–3; supposed deal over England with Magnus of Norway, 60, 157; prepares to invade England, 37–8; accedes peacefully after Harold I's death, 38, 142; unpopularity, 38–41, 64, 71, 76; shares power with ETC, 41–2, 133; death, 42, 59, 61; burial, 42, 97, 100

Hastings (Sussex), 171, 174, 176, 178, 191–2, 194, 221; castle, 171, 174, 207; rape of, 313

Hastings, battle of, 2, 4, 7–8, 167, 172, 179–93, 197–8, 202, 206, 210, 215, 217, 225, 233, 236–7, 240, 277–8, 335–6, 341; burial of the dead after, 190, 192

Henry I, king of England (1100–35), son of WTC, 273–5, 318–19, 329–30, 344–5, 347, 349–51, 392

Henry I, king of France (1031–60), 44, 52–3, 56–7, 67, 80, 82–5, 93–4, 110, 254–5, 364; death, 110, 254

Henry II, king of England (1154–89), 350–2

Henry III, emperor of Germany (1046–56), 30, 67–8, 91, 103, 144

Henry III, king of England (1216–72), 353

Henry IV, king of Germany (1056–1106), 300–1

Henry de Ferrers, 278, 319

Henry of Huntingdon, chronicler, 172, 179, 183, 186, 284, 322, 336, 341, 344, 347–8

Herbert II, count of Maine (d. 1062), 111

Hereford, 105, 218, 247; castle, 209; bp of, see Robert; Walter; earl of, see Roger; William

Herefordshire, 105, 208–9, 269

Hereward the Wake, 243–6, 248–50, 284, 347

Herleva, mother of WTC, 43–4, 68, 81

Herluin, abt of Bec (d. 1078), 88

Herluin, organizer of WTC's funeral, 331

Herluin de Conteville, stepfather of WTC, 44, 68, 89

Hermann, bp of Sherborne and Salisbury (1045–78), 98–9, 318, 369

Hertfordshire, 194–5, 315

hides, 26–7, 76, 121, 240, 307–8, 312–13, 315–16, 320, 325, 353

Holderness (Yorks), 161

Holy Island see Lindisfarne

Holy Land, 9, 25, 43–4, 51, 352

horses, 1–2, 47, 150, 153, 169, 171, 174, 178, 337

hostages, 18–19, 77–8, 116–18, 125, 137–8, 163, 173, 196, 202–3, 210, 213, 219, 252–3, 329

housecarls, 24, 32, 40, 128, 162, 181, 195, 243

Hrani, earl, 28
Hrolfr *see* Rollo
Hugh, bp of Bayeux (d. 1049), 50
Hugh, bp of Lisieux (1049–77), 90
Hugh de Montfort, 210
Hugh (of Avranches), earl of
     Chester (d. 1101), 292, 299, 302,
     313, 321
Hugh fitz Baldric, sheriff of
     Yorkshire, 235
Hugh of Ponthieu, 186
Hugh of Vermandois (d. 1101),
     brother of Philip I, 305
Humber, river, 12, 122, 125, 148,
     161, 165, 226–7, 229, 242–3
hundreds, 121, 279, 309–13, 317–18,
     338, 353
Hungary, 102–3, 138, 191
hunting, 108, 120, 141, 199, 226,
     273, 291–2, 327, 344
Huntingdon, castle, 220
Hurst Head (*Hursteshevet*), 41

Icknield Way, 195
intermarriage, 266, 348–9, 352
Ipswich (Suffolk), 226
Ireland, 72, 77, 104, 126, 212, 214,
     220, 224–5, 294–5, 333; the
     Irish, 157, 293–4
Irish Sea, 104, 121, 293
Italy, 9, 87, 92, 303
Ivo de Grandmesnil, 275
Ivry, castle, 49–50

Jarrow (Durham), abbey, 340
Jersey, 21
Jerusalem, 22, 95
John, king of England (1199–1216),
     352–3

John of Avranches, abp of Rouen
     (1067–79), 257
John of Worcester, 39–40
Judith (d. 1094), dau. of Baldwin
     of Flanders, wife of Tostig
     Godwineson, 123, 125
Judith, niece of WTC, wife of Earl
     Waltheof, 253, 271
Julius Caesar, 84, 203, 295
Jumièges (Seine-Mar.), abbey, 90,
     96, 204, 298; *see also* Robert of
     Jumièges; William of Jumièges

Kent, 12, 61, 66, 68, 77, 194, 202,
     209–10, 278, 280, 283, 285; earl
     of, *see* Leofwine; Odo
King Harold's Saga, 156
King's Evil, 96, 98
knights, 2, 47–50
knight service: in Normandy, 89,
     144–5, 151; in England, 240–2,
     280–1, 302, 323; *see also* military
     obligation

Lambeth (Surrey), 42
Lancashire, 121
land: English dispossessed of, 202,
     215, 217, 221, 234–5, 238, 251;
     English allowed to buy back,
     202, 241; Normans rewarded
     with, 202, 215, 221, 234–5;
     nature of redistribution, 277–87,
     310, 337–8
Lanfranc, abp of Canterbury
     (1070–89): early life, 88; prior of
     Bec, 88; quarrel with WTC, 88;
     advisor and mentor to WTC,
     88, 92–3, 112; attends Leo IX
     (1049–50), 92; abt of

St Stephen's, Caen (1063–70), 112, 370; teacher of Alexander II, 143; becomes abp of Canterbury, 255–6; vicegerent for WTC, 256, 268–70; reform of English Church, 256–7, 339; rebuilds Canterbury cathedral, 257–8; suspicious of English saints at first, 259–60; softens his stance later, 346; punishes rebellious monks, 262; impartiality, 263; describes English as barbarous, 265; letters to Earl Roger (1075), 268–9; advises Waltheof (1075), 271; attends dedication of St Stephen's (1077), 273; complains to WTC of Odo's usurpations, 286; insists WTC bans slave trade, 295, 338; relations with Gregory VII, 301; counsels dispersal of mercenary army (1085), 305; asked to crown Rufus (1087), 330

language, 9, 13, 121, 199–200, 246, 260–1, 341, 347–8, 351, 353

law, laws: of Cnut, 41, 130; of WTC, 295–6; WTC's promises to uphold existing English, 199, 201, 238, 241, 335; Church, 256; Forest, 291, 333; Common, 338, 351, 353; *see also* murdrum

Lawrence of Durham, 339

Leo IX, pope (1049–54), 67–8, 70, 80–1, 91–2, 98, 112, 238

Leofric, bp of Crediton and Exeter (1046–72), 98, 216, 365, 369, 383

Leofric, earl of Mercia (d. 1057), 29–31, 65, 72, 75, 101, 104–6, 250, 321

Leofwine, bp of Lichfield (1053–70), 239

Leofwine, ealdorman (d. 1023), father of Earl Leofric, 29

Leofwine Godwineson (d. 1066), 72, 77, 107, 136, 189, 202, 212

Leominster, abbess of, 65

Lewes (Sussex), 295; castle and rape, 215

Liber Eliensis, 249

Lichfield, bp of, 240, 258; *see also* Leofwine

Life of King Edward, 63, 108, 342–3

Lillebonne (Seine-Mar.), 143

Lincoln, 128, 313; bp of, 258, 319; *see also* Alexander; castle, 220, 258, 313; cathedral, 258, 298

Lincolnshire, 15, 17, 128, 148, 227–8, 243, 248, 278, 297; sheriff of, *see* Mærleswein

Lindisfarne, 125–6, 246

Loire, river, 46

London, 15, 19, 32, 36, 39, 42, 69, 72, 77–8, 96, 122, 154, 161–3, 168, 172–6, 191–6, 198, 200–1, 207, 211, 278, 335, 344, 379; bridge, 194; Tower of, 198–9, 201, 297, 334; St Paul's Cathedral, 24, 106, 334, 344; council of, 257–8; bp of, 319; *see also* Robert of Jumièges; William

Lotharingia (Lorraine), 98, 368

Lothen and Yrling, Viking raiders, 66, 68

Lothian, 121

Lugg, river, 209

Lulach, king of Scots (1057–8), 125

Lumphanan (Aberdeens), battle of, 125

Lyfing, bp of Worcester (d. 1046), 39

Lyre (Eure), monastery, 89

Macbeth, king of Scots (1040–57), 95, 103, 125

Magna Carta, 307, 352–3

Magnus I, king of Norway (d. 1047), 60–2, 64–66, 157

Magnus II, king of Norway (d. 1069), son of Harold Hardrada, 157, 160

Magnus, son of Harold, 220

Magyars, 45

Maidstone (Kent), 285

Maine, 80–1, 93, 111, 151, 234, 254–5, 274, 289, 304, 316; count of, 81; *see also* Herbert; Walter

Mainer, abt of St Evroult, 298–9

Mainz (Germany), cathedral, 298

Maitland, Frederick William (d. 1906), historian, 317

Malcolm III, king of Scots (1058–93), 125–6, 148, 158, 160, 220, 222, 251–3, 267, 289–90

Maldon (Essex), battle of, 13, 27–8

Malfosse, 189, 377, 379

Malmesbury (Wilts), abbey, 99

Le Mans (Sartre), 81, 111, 194, 254, 351; bp of, 80–1; viscount of, 304, 326

Mantes (Yvelines), 327–8

Margaret, queen of Scotland (d. 1093), sister of Edgar Ætheling, 251, 267, 349

Marianus Scotus, 164

Marlborough (Wilts), 239

Marsh Gibbon (Bucks), 314; *see also* Æthelric

Matilda, dau. of Henry I (d. 1167), empress, 349–51

Matilda, queen of England (d. 1083), WTC's wife: myth about her height, 67, 365; marriage to William, 67–8, 91–2, 254; founds Holy Trinity, Caen, 112, 149–50; prepares WTC's flagship, 170; regent in Normandy (1066–7), 215; coronation (1068), 197–8, 216, 319; return to Normandy (1069), 224; her children, 273–4; support for Robert Curthose, 288–9; death, 302–4

Mauger, abp of Rouen, WTC's uncle, 86, 90, 92–3, 239

Maurilius, abp of Rouen (1054–67), 93, 368

Mayenne, castle, 111

Mærleswein, sheriff of Lincolnshire, 218–20, 222–4, 226, 233, 235, 247, 278

mercenaries, 32, 39, 75–6, 104, 151, 212, 222, 235, 241, 288, 293, 305–6, 312, 316, 321, 325

Mercia, 12, 29–31, 101, 104, 107, 122–3, 128–30, 205, 218, 230, 233, 247; earl of, *see* Ælfgar; Eadwine; Leofwine

Michael Calaphates, Byzantine emperor (d. 1042), 156

Middlesex, 194

military obligation, 76–7, 89, 144–5, 148–52, 213, 240–2, 280–2, 323, 352

Monkwearmouth (Durham), abbey, 340

Monomachus, Byzantine emperor (d. 1055), 156

Montacute (Somerset), 227

Montgomery (Powys), 292

Montivilliers (Seine-Mar.), abbey, 87

Montreuil-sur-Mer (Pas-de-Calais), castle, 267

Mont St Michel (Manche), 21, 114

The *Mora*, WTC's flagship, 170

Morcar, earl of Northumbria: supports northern rebels, becomes earl of Northumbria, 128–30, 136, 210; cedes north of earldom to Oswulf, 210; attends dedication of Westminster Abbey (1065), 136; allies with Harold, 139; drives off Tostig (1066), 148; defeated at Fulford, 162, 192; withdraws from London, 196; submits to WTC (1067), 202, 378–9; hostage in Normandy, 203, 217, 253; attends Matilda's coronation (1068), 216; lack of power after Conquest, 217–18, 247–8; rebels but quickly submits (1068), 218–19; rebels again, goes to Ely (1071), 248; imprisoned, 249–51, 264, 270, 320; released, 329; re-incarcerated, 345

Mortain (Manche), 93–4; count of, 93–4; *see also* Robert

Mortemer (Seine-Mar.), 85; battle of, 85, 89, 114

murdrum, 262–3, 385

Mynydd Carn, battle of, 293–4

Napoleon Bonaparte (d. 1821), 3

The Naze (Essex), 78

Nazis, 3

Neustria, 15

Newcastle-upon-Tyne (Northumb), 290, 296, 334

New Forest (Hants), 291, 344, 349

Newmarket (Suffolk), 268

Nicaea, 22

Nijmegen (Netherlands), 67

Norman Conquest, myths and misconceptions, 7–9

Normandy (*selected references*): origins, 15–16, 48; aristocracy of, 49, 53–6; social changes in during early eleventh century, 48–51; Church in, 86–93; loss of (1204), 352; abandonment of slavery in, 295; *see also* knight service; military obligation

Normans (*selected references*): conversion, 16, 48, 86; adoption of Frankish culture, 16, 48–9; adoption of Church reform, 87–93; opinions on, 44, 332, 337, 341–2; *see also* chivalry

Northallerton (Yorks), 224

Northampton, 129–30

Northamptonshire, 313; geld roll, 313, 315

Northumbria, 12, 25, 27–8, 30, 101, 103–4, 120–30, 141, 160–1, 163, 210–11, 216, 218, 220, 222–4, 226, 252, 263, 289–90, 294, 296; earl of, *see* Erik; Gospatric; Siward; Tostig; Uhtred; Walcher; Waltheof

Norton (Northants), 316

Norway, 29, 31, 33, 60–2, 66, 155, 157, 158–60

Norwich (Norfolk), 226, 258; castle, 270, 313, 334

Nottingham, 219; castle, 219, 247
Nottinghamshire, 128
Nuneham Courtenay (Oxon), 277

Odda, earl (d. 1056), 75, 77, 95, 106
Odo, bp of Bayeux, earl of Kent (d.
    1096), half-brother of WTC:
    reputation, 91, 206–7, 209, 276–7;
    probable patron of Bayeux
    Tapestry, 3–4, 357; becomes bp
    of Bayeux, 90–1; counsellor of
    WTC, 143; provides ships for
    invasion, 146; fights at Hastings,
    2, 4, 182, 276–7, 386; becomes
    earl of Kent, 202, 268, 278; acts
    as regent (1067), 202, 206–7,
    209–10, 255; later periods as
    regent, 255, 276–8, 280; makes
    grants of land, 277, 280; abuse of
    power, 285–6; harries
    Northumbria (1080), 290; down-
    fall and imprisonment (1082),
    299–302, 304, 319; his lands, 321;
    released from prison (1087), 329;
    supports Curthose against Rufus,
    344
Odo, brother of Henry I of
    France, 84–5
Offa's Dyke, 292
Olaf II, king of Norway (d. 1030),
    155
Olaf III, king of Norway (d. 1093),
    son of Harold Hardrada, 165
Old Sarum (Wilts), 259, 318, 334;
    see also Salisbury
Orderic Vitalis (*selected references*),
    51, 89, 218, 250, 252, 268, 274–5,
    302, 328–32, 348, 379; English
    origins and sympathies of, 175,
    205–9, 218, 229–31, 250, 266,
    268, 286, 302, 348, 379; on
    WTC's death, 328–32
Orkney, 158, 160
Orleans (Loiret), 82
Orne, river, 56–7
Osbern (d. 1041), ducal steward,
    52, 55
Osgod Clapa, 62, 66, 68
Oslo (Norway), 159
Osmund, WTC's secretary, 316
Oswine, king of Northumbria (d.
    651), 127
Oswulf (d. 1067), nephew of
    Gospatric, 210–11, 216
Ouse, river, 161–2, 165, 224
Oxford, 31–3, 38, 130
Oxfordshire, 195

papacy, 11, 45, 91–2, 285, 300–2; *see
    also* Alexander II; Benedict X;
    Gregory VII; Leo IX
papal banner, 143, 145, 201, 373
papal legates, 16, 92, 237–9, 247;
    see also Ermenfrid
Paris, 3
Parliament, 8, 97
Paul, abt of St Albans, 260
Peace of God, Truce of God, 50,
    55, 58, 61, 365
peasants, 9, 26, 47–8, 315, 352
Penenden Heath (Kent), 285–6,
    301
Penitential Ordinance, 144, 236–7,
    386
Peterborough (Cambs), 244–5;
    abbey, 123, 197, 243–5, 247, 392;
    abt of, 197; *see also* Turold
Pevensey (Sussex), 171–2, 191,

202–3; castle, 171, 174, 207; Roman fort, 171

Philip I, king of France (1060–1108), 110, 254–5, 267, 272, 276, 288, 304, 326–9

Pickenham (Norfolk), 348

Picot, sheriff of Cambridge, 284, 311

Le Plessis-Grimoult, castle, 57

Po, river, 302

Poitou, 151; count of, 80

Poland, 225

Pontefract (Yorks), 228

Ponthieu, 113, 116, 167, 169; count of, *see* Guy

Portskewett (Gwent), 120, 292

Pyrenees, 351

Quadripartitus, 41

Ralph de Gaël, earl of East Anglia, 267–70, 272, 280, 321

Ralph fitz Gilbert, 348

Ralph Glaber, 44, 362

Ralph (of Mantes, 'the Timid'), earl (d. 1057), nephew of ETC, 75, 77, 102, 105–6

Ralph Pagnell, 235, 278

Ralph Taisson, 57

Ralph (the Staller), earl of East Anglia, 267–8

rape *see* women

Rapes *see* Sussex

Reading (Berks), abbey, 349

Regenbald, priest, 215–16

Rémalard (Orne), castle, 276

rents, 314–15, 338

Rheims, council of (1049), 67–8, 91–2, 98

Rhiwallon ap Cynfyn (d. 1070), 209

Rhuddlan (Denbigh), 109

Rhys ap Tewder, king of Deheubarth (d. 1093), 292–3, 296

Riccall (Yorks), 161–5

Richard I, count of Rouen (d. 996), 16, 49

Richard I (the Lionheart), king of England (1189–99), 352

Richard II, duke of Normandy (996–1026), 16, 19–20, 30, 49, 55, 83, 87, 359

Richard III, duke of Normandy (1026–7), 20, 50, 359

Richard, son of WTC (d. 1069 × 1075), 273, 291

Richard fitz Gilbert, lord of Tonbridge, 283–4, 285, 319, 321

Richard fitz Nigel, treasurer of the Exchequer, 311, 352

Richmond (Yorks), castle, 282

Risle, river, 66, 88

Robert, abp of Rouen (d. 1037), 50–1, 86

Robert, count of Mortain (d. 1095), half-brother of WTC, 93, 143, 146, 227, 279, 319, 321, 329

Robert I, duke of Normandy (1027–35), father of WTC, 20–2, 43–4, 50–2, 87, 362

Robert II 'the Pious', king of France (996–1031), 46, 67

Robert Cumin, earl of Northumbria (d. 1069), 222–4, 252

Robert Curthose, duke of Normandy, son of WTC (d.

1134), 273–6, 288–90, 299, 303–4, 326, 329–30, 344–5

Robert fitz Wimarc, steward of ETC, 133–4, 173

Robert Losinga, bp of Hereford (1079–95), 281, 311, 319, 325

Robert of Bellême, son of Roger of Montgomery, 275

Robert of Jumièges, bp of London (1044–51), abp of Canterbury (1051–2), 69–71, 73, 75, 78–9, 90, 95–6, 98–100, 115, 238

Robert of Rhuddlan (d. 1093), 319

Robert (the Frisian), count of Flanders (1071–93), 254–5, 272, 276, 305, 326

Robert the Steward *see* Robert fitz Wimarc

Rochester (Kent), 284; cathedral, 258; bp of, *see* Gundulf; Siward

Rodulf, count, 49–50

Rodulf of Gacé, 52

Roger Cauchois, 274–5

Roger fitz Turold, 150

Roger fitz Walter, 281

Roger of Breteuil, earl of Hereford (1071–5), son of William fitz Osbern, 268–72, 275, 280, 292–3, 321, 329

Roger of Montgomery, earl of Shrewsbury (d. 1094), friend and counsellor of WTC, 55, 143, 145–6, 277, 299, 319; monastic foundations, 89, 349; his toponymic surname, 337; provides ships for invasion, 145–6; remains in Normandy as regent (1066), 215; his lands in England, 215, 218, 247, 277–8,

280; his conquests in Wales, 292; his burial, 349; son of, *see* Robert of Bellême

Roger of Wendover, chronicler, 241

Rollo, leader of the Vikings of Rouen [thus in Crouch], 16

Romanesque, 2, 89–90, 96, 112, 257–8, 334, 353

Rome, 24, 37, 68, 70, 89–92, 98, 100, 105, 108, 125–6, 142–3, 289, 297–8, 301, 339, 350, 373; St Peter's, 298

Romney (Kent), 192, 194

Rouen (Seine-Mar.), 15, 16, 58, 68, 84, 87, 112, 141, 150, 203, 275, 295, 319, 328–30, 370; abp of, 330; *see also* John; Mauger; Maurilius; Robert; castle/palace, 49, 114, 275, 302; cathedral, 330, 367; count of, *see* William Longsword; Richard I; Holy Trinity, 150; St Gervase, 329–30

Round, John Horace, historian (d. 1928), 8

St Albans, abbey, 258, 298; abt of, 239

St Cuthbert, 224

St David's (Pembrokes), 293

St Dunstan, 259, 346

St Evroult (Orne), abbey, 89, 205, 275, 298; abt of, *see* Mainer

St Omer (Pas-de-Calais), 37

St Oswald, 340

St Pierre-sur-Dives (Calvados), abbey, 204

St Suzanne (Mayenne), castle of, 304, 326

St Swithin, 24, 346

St Valéry-sur-Somme (Somme), 168–70, 173

St Wandrille (Seine-Mar.), monastery of, 19, 306

Salisbury (Wilts), 129, 233, 235, 258, 318–19, 322, 324–6, 334; bp of, 258, 318–19; *see also* Hermann; castle, 318; cathedral, 258–9, 318, 334; ceremony at (1086), 318–19, 322, 324–5; *see also* Old Sarum

Sandwich (Kent), 18, 61, 76–7, 148–9, 157, 226, 337

Saracens, 45

Saxony, 225

Scarborough (Yorks), 161

Scotland, 9, 95, 103, 121, 124–6, 148, 158, 160, 220, 222, 224, 233, 247–8, 250–3, 266–7, 289–90, 292, 333; kings of, 103, 347; *see also* Duncan; Macbeth; Malcolm

Second World War, 3, 112

Séez, bp of, 91–2

Selby (Yorks), abbey, 340

Selsey (Sussex), 258

Senlac, 176; *see* Hastings

Settrington (Yorks), 265, 278

Severn, river, 40, 120, 269, 292

Shaftesbury (Dorset), 23

Shakespeare, William, 103

Sherborne (Dorset), 23, 258

sheriffs, 149, 247, 260, 268–9, 284–5, 318, 324, 338; *see also* Hugh; Mærleswein; Picot; Urse

Shetland, 160

shield-wall, 178–81, 183

Ship List, 145, 150–1, 170

ships and fleets: 2, 14, 16, 20–2, 24,

28, 32, 34, 37–40, 61–2, 65–6, 75–8, 104, 109, 113, 143–8, 150–2, 154, 157–8, 160–1, 163–6, 168–71, 174, 176, 203, 208, 212, 224–7, 229, 244–5, 249, 252, 270, 304–5, 312, 321, 337

shire courts, 27

shires, 12

Shrewsbury (Salop), 205, 218, 227, 233, 247, 268; abbey, 349; castle, 227, 247, 313

Shropshire, 205, 218, 278, 280

Sicily, 9, 156

Simeon of Durham, chronicler, 125, 216, 222–4, 230, 233, 246, 266, 290, 314

Siward, bp of Rochester (d. 1075), 383

Siward, earl of Northumbria (d. 1055), 30, 32, 72, 75, 101, 103, 122, 125–7, 253, 263, 321

Siward Barn, 247, 264, 278, 329

Slaves, slavery, 16, 25–7, 36, 130, 294–6, 338

Somerset, 220, 227, 294

Snorri Sturluson, historian (d. 1241), 147, 156–62, 164

Snowdonia, 292

Southampton (Hants), 34–5, 41, 312

Southwark (Surrey), 77–8

Speyer (Germany), cathedral, 298

Stafford, 228; castle, 233, 247

Stamford (Lincs), 313

Stamford Bridge (Yorks), battle of, 163–5, 171–3, 175, 218, 375

Stephen (of Blois), king of England (1135–54), 350

Steyning (Sussex), 150

Stigand, bp of Winchester

(1047–70), abp of Canterbury (1052–70): early career, 99; pluralism, 100; pariah status as abp, 108, 143, 199, 216, 255; present at ETC's death, 133–4, 140; depicted at Harold's coronation, 139; submits to WTC, 195; hostage in Normandy (1067), 203; deposed (1070), 238

Strathclyde, kingdom of, 121, 126

Surrey, 283

Sussex, 12, 72, 77, 109, 113, 150, 172, 194, 215, 278, 295, 313; bp of, 240; rapes, 215, 278

Sweden, 102

Swein (d. *c.* 1034), son of King Cnut, 31

Swein Estrithson, king of Denmark (1047–74), 61–2, 64–5, 147, 157–9, 225–6, 228, 242–3, 245, 304–5

Swein Forkbeard, king of Denmark (986–1014), king of England (1013–14), 15, 17

Swein Godwineson (d. 1052), 63, 65, 68, 72, 95, 101–2, 116

Tadcaster (Yorks), 163

Taillefer, juggling swordsman, 180, 187

taxation, geld, 24, 27, 28, 39–40, 48, 75–6, 123–4, 130, 157, 201, 213–14, 217, 235, 242, 312–13, 315–17, 325, 337, 345, 352; *see also* tribute

Tay, river, 103, 252

Tees, river, 121–2, 128, 232–3

Thames, river, 31–3, 39, 72, 77, 130, 194–5, 210, 245

thegns, 26–8, 31–2, 41, 75, 107–8, 128, 208, 214, 299, 320

Thetford (Norfolk), 258; bp of, 263

Thimert (Eure-et-Loir), castle, 110

Thomas (of Bayeux), abp of York (1070–1100), 273, 319

Thorkell the Tall, earl of East Anglia, 28–9

Thorney (Cambs), abbey, 306

Thurbrand (the Hold), 265

Thurbrand, son of Carl, 278

Thurstan, abt of Glastonbury, 261–2, 319

Tillières (Eure), castle, 53, 110, 364

Tinchebray (Orne), battle of, 345

Tonbridge (Kent), 283, 319; castle, 283

Tostig Godwineson, earl of Northumbria (d. 1066): character, 103–4; piety, 123, 125; relationship with his brother, Harold, 104, 129–30, 137–8, 147–8, 165; flees to Flanders with parents (1051), 72, 123; becomes earl of Northumbria (1055), 103–4, 122, 253; pillar of the realm, 108; invades Wales with Harold (1063), 109; unpopularity as earl, 123–4; fails to defend Northumbria from Scots, 124–7; arranges murder of rivals (1063/4), 127, 263; rebellion against, 128–30, 136, 210; banishment (1065), 130, 158; attacks England from Flanders (1066), 147–9, 158, 373; seeks Scandinavian allies, 158–60, 225; invades England with Harold

Hardrada, 154, 161; wins victory at Fulford, 162; defeated and killed at Stamford Bridge, 163–5, 173; buried in York, 165, 172

Trahaearn ap Caradog (d. 1081), 294

Trelleborg fortresses, Denmark, 14

tribute, 14–15, 28, 45, 123, 193, 200–2, 235, 296, 312

Troarn (Calvados), monastery, 89

Truce of God *see* Peace of God

Tuscany, countess of, 303

Turold, abt of Peterborough, 243–4, 246

Turold (d. 1041), tutor to WTC, 52

Tyne, river, 160, 210, 219, 222, 233, 290

Uhtred, earl of Northumbria (d. 1016), 126–7, 253, 265

Ulf, earl, 29

Urse d'Abetôt, sheriff of Worcester, 284

Val-ès-Dunes (Calvados), battle of, 56–8, 66, 80, 89, 112, 142, 365

Valognes (Manche), 56–7

Varaville (Calvados), battle of, 94, 110

Le Vaudreuil (Eure), castle, 52

Vegetius, Roman author, 178

Vexin, 327–8

Vikings, 12–18, 25, 27, 45–9, 66, 86, 121–2, 126, 132, 144, 154–5, 158, 163–5, 172, 226, 242, 245, 297, 339; *see also* Danes

Viking Ship Museum, Roskilde, 150

Wace, historian, 56–7, 141, 143–5, 150–1, 178

Walcher, bp of Durham (1071–80), 240, 252, 266, 270, 290

Wales, 9, 25, 104–5, 109, 120, 126, 129, 138, 144, 158, 218, 250, 291–4, 296–7, 319, 333, 338; The Welsh, 120, 124, 128, 208, 218, 227, 292–4, 340

Walkelin, bp of Winchester (1070–98), 298, 319

Wallingford (Oxon), town and castle, 195, 207, 313

Walter, abt of Evesham, 260, 285

Walter, bp of Hereford (1060–79), 108

Walter, count of Maine (1062–3), 111

Walter, uncle of WTC, 52

Waltham (Essex), abbey, 190, 376

Waltheof, earl of Northumbria (d. 1076), son of Siward, 103, 253, 264–6, 268–9, 271–3, 278, 280, 290, 320, 339

wapentakes, 121

Warin, abt of Malmesbury, 260

Warwick, castle, 219, 247, 313, 334

waste *see* Domesday

weapons and armour, 1–2, 26, 47, 54, 62, 76, 139, 164, 178–82, 184–6, 188, 223, 276

Wearmouth (Durham), 247

Wells, bp of, *see* Giso

Wenric of Trier, 333

Wessex, 12–13, 15, 29–32, 71, 75, 95, 100–1, 107, 121, 129–30, 138, 174, 208; earl of, *see* Godwine; Harold

Westminster, 146, 191, 270, 299,

318; abbey, 38–9, 96–7, 131, 134, 136, 139, 149, 198, 216, 258, 334, 350, 353, 362; palace, 96–7, 198, 368

Wherwell (Hants), nunnery, 73

Whitby (Yorks), abbey, 340

Wight, isle of, 15, 77, 147, 149, 154, 161, 202, 278, 302, 326

William, bp of London (1051–75), 95

William, count of Arques, uncle of WTC, 83, 85

William Ætheling (d. 1120), son of Henry I, 349–50

William de Chernet, 311

William de Percy, 235

William de Warenne (d. 1088), 215

William fitz Osbern, earl of Hereford (d. 1071): friend and counsellor of WTC, 55, 143, 145–6, 277; monastic foundations, 89, 296; provides ships for invasion, 145–6; his lands in England, 202, 218, 247, 268, 277–8; his conquests in Wales, 292, 296; regent (1067), 202, 206–7, 209, 255; defends York (1069), 224; suppresses rebellions in Midlands and south-west (1069), 227; proposes plunder of monasteries (1070), 235; death, 254–5; sons of, *see* Roger of Breteuil; William of Breteuil

William Giroie, 51

William Longsword, count of Rouen (d. 942), 16

William of Breteuil, son of William fitz Osbern, 275, 299

William of Jumièges (*selected references*): importance for WTC's early career, 20; wrote close to events, 21, 34, 52; but revised after Conquest for WTC, 21, 167; chronology not a strong point, 34; neutrality, 19, 36; coy about ducal marriages, 44, 67; but not ducal brutality, 81, 187; interpolated by Orderic, 81, 373

William of Malmesbury, historian (*selected references*), Anglo-Norman parentage, 348; popularity, 347; pro-English sentiments, 140, 178, 340, 347; fondness for stories, 100, 165, 303, 328

William of Poitiers (*selected references*): importance, 7, 53–4; problems with, 42, 54; WTC's chaplain, 54, 142; formerly a knight, 54, 176, 182; well-informed, 116, 166, 197, 373, 378–9; but economical with the truth, 81–2, 186–91, 194–5; dubious assertions, 111, 117, 182, 200, 217, 244–5, 249, 263, 276; classical allusions, 84, 168, 171, 178, 182, 203, 295, 297; use of William of Jumièges, 114–15; hostility to Harold Godwineson, 135, 175, 206; use of the *Carmen*, 167, 178, 186, 191; used by Orderic Vitalis, 206, 217, 230, 234, 244, 250, 252; opinion of the English, 264–5

William of St Calais, bp of Durham (1080–96), 319

William of Volpiano (d. 1031),
monastic reformer, 87, 98
William Rufus, king of England
(1087–1100), 273–5, 288, 299,
303, 319, 329–30, 344–5, 349,
351, 391–2
William the Conqueror (William
the Bastard), king of England
(1066–87), duke of Normandy
(1035–87):
character, qualities, interests: physical appearance, 2, 54, 327;
bastardy, 22, 43–4, 56; bynames,
43; friendships, 55, 88, 143, 215,
219, 254, 256, 283; prowess, 54,
57; brutality, 81–2, 332–3; chivalry, 264–5, 267, 339; spirituality,
88, 142; wisdom, 333; severity,
299, 333; avarice, 314, 333;
concern for legitimacy, 335–6;
promotion of Church reform,
92–3, 368; love of hunting, 141,
199, 226, 291; monastic foundations, 89, 112, 178, 204, 237, 273,
330, 333; other building projects,
112, 296–8
family relationships: with Odo of
Bayeux, 90–1, 202, 206, 255,
277, 299–302, 304, 329; with
Robert of Mortain, 93, 329;
with Matilda, 67–8, 170, 197–8,
273–4, 288, 302–4; with Robert
Curthose, 273–6, 288–90, 303–4,
329; with William Rufus, 288,
303, 330, 344
selective chronological survey: birth,
43–4; recognized as his father's
heir (1034), 44, 52; accession as
duke (1035), 51; troubled
minority, 52, 87, 205; knighting
(c. 1043), 53–6, 364; his rule
threatened (1046–7), 55–6;
defeats rebels (1047), 56–8;
consolidates victory (1047–50),
66; war against Geoffrey Martel
(1049–51), 80–2; marriage (c.
1050), 66–8, 82, 91–2, 112; promised English succession (1051),
70; visits ETC in England (1051),
73–5, 82; defeats rebellion by
count of Arques (1053), 83, 85–6;
defeats invasion by France and
Anjou (1054), 83–5; deposes abp
of Rouen (1054), 86, 92–3;
attacks Geoffrey Martel (1054);
defeats invasion by France and
Anjou (1057), 94, 110; captures
Tillières and Thimert (1058), 110;
conquers Maine (1062–3),
111–12; receives Harold
Godwineson, obliges him to
swear his oath (1064/5), 113–19,
137; invades Brittany (1064/5),
114; hears of Harold's coronation
(1066), 141–2; puts case to pope
and Norman magnates, 142–5,
373; prepares invasion fleet,
145–6, 150–1; spiritual preparations, 149–50; assembles army,
151–4; delayed and diverted by
contrary winds, 166–9; crosses
Channel, lands at Pevensey,
169–71; exchanges messages with
Harold, ravages Sussex, 173–5;
surprises Harold, 176–7; defeats
and kills Harold at Hastings,
177–88; buries dead, 190;
advances through Kent to

London, 192–4; ravages counties around London, 194–6; receives English submissions, debates next move, 196–8; coronation, 10, 198–200, 379; first acts as king (1067), 200–2, 211, 378–9; returns in triumph to Normandy (1067), 202–4; returns to England (1067), 211; defeats Exeter rebels (1068), 212–15; attacks midland and northern rebels, establishes new castles (1068), 219–22; attacks rebels again (1069), 223–4; attacks rebels for a third time (1069), 227–9, 232–3; harries northern England (1069–70), 229–31; plunders monasteries (1070), 235; coronation by papal legates (1070), 236; purges English episcopate, 238–40; imposes military service on Church, 240–2; buys off Danish invasion (1070), 245; crushes Ely rebellion (1071), 248–51; invades Scotland (1072), 251–2; re-conquers Maine (1073), 255; returns to England (1075), punishes rebels, 270–1, 279–80; defeated at Dol (1076), 272; quarrel with Robert Curthose (1077–80), 273–6, 288–9; returns to England (1080), 289–90; invades south Wales (1081), 293–4, 296; imprisons Odo (1082), 299–302; besieges St Suzanne (1084), 304; prepares against Danish invasion (1085–6), 304–6, 312–13, 316; orders Domesday Survey (1085–6), 306–7; knights Henry (1086), 318; attends Salisbury assembly (1086), 318–20, 322, 325–6; returns to Normandy (1086), 326–7; illness (1087), 328; invades the Vexin and burns Mantes (1087), 328; final illness, 328–330; death (1087), 10, 52, 330; burial, 330–1, 349

Wilton (Wilts), abbey, 63, 73, 129

Wiltshire, 129, 302, 319

Winchelsea (Sussex), 211

Winchester, 13, 24, 32, 34, 59–60, 97, 99–100, 106, 193, 206, 215, 224, 232, 236, 238–40, 271, 297–9, 306, 318, 324–5, 349; bp of, *see* Ælfwine; Stigand; Walkelin; castle, 202, 207, 221, 297, 334; Norman cathedral, 258, 298, 346; Old Minster, 24, 42, 97, 100; palace, 297

Windsor (Berks), 239, 242; castle, 242, 334

Wissant, 35

women, 7; rape of, 27, 207, 263, 266, 332–3; married in order to legitimize landholding, 349

Worcester, 40, 71, 325; cathedral, 40, 284; bp of, *see* Ealdred; Lyfing; Wulfstan; sheriff of, *see* Urse

Wren, Sir Christopher, 334

Wulfnoth, probable father of Earl Godwine, 28

Wulfnoth Godwineson, hostage, 116, 118, 137–8, 212, 329, 345

Wulfstan, bp of Worcester (d. 1095), 107, 269, 281, 305, 320, 340–1, 383

Wulfstan, bp of Worcester and abp
of York (d. 1023), 26, 27
Wulfwold, abt of Chertsey (d.
1084), 5
Wye, river, 292, 296

Xerxes, 168

Yaroslav the Wise, king of Russia
(1019–54), 155
Yeovil (Somerset), 227
York, 12, 121–3, 127–8, 141, 146,
161–5, 172, 219–21, 223–4,
226–9, 233–4, 236, 247, 253, 270,
314, 340, 375; abbey, 340; castles,
220, 223–4, 226–7, 229, 334;
cathedral (minster), 223, 226,
232; abp of, *see* Ælfric;
Cynesige; Ealdred; Thomas;
Wulfstan; sheriff of, 223, 227,
267; *see also* Hugh fitz Baldric
Yorkshire, 121–2, 162–3, 172–3,
218–19, 228–9, 232–3, 235,
278–9, 282, 297, 313–14,
335

Zedekiah, biblical king, 185

MARC MORRIS

A Great and Terrible King:

Edward I and the Forging of Britain

'Morris tells Edward's story fluently and conveys a compelling sense
of the reality, and the contingency, of personal rule'
GUARDIAN

This is the first major biography for a generation of a truly formidable king. Edward I is familiar to millions as 'Longshanks',
conqueror of Scotland and nemesis of Sir William Wallace
('Braveheart'). Edward was born to rule England, but believed
that it was his right to rule all of Britain. His reign was one of
the most dramatic of the entire Middle Ages, leading to war
and conquest on an unprecedented scale, and leaving a legacy
of division that has lasted from his day to our own.

In his astonishingly action-packed life, Edward defeated and
killed the famous Simon de Montfort in battle; travelled across
Europe to the Holy Land on crusade; conquered Wales, extin-
guishing forever its native rulers, and constructed – at Conwy,
Harlech, Beaumaris and Caernarfon – the most magnificent
chain of castles ever created.

'Marc Morris's new account of the life of Edward I is a splendid example of the
genre. Edward's life is in many ways an ideal subject for such an approach, full
of incident and action . . . An excellent, readable account of his reign'
LITERARY REVIEW

'Marc Morris has written the first full biography of Edward I for around 100
years, and uncommonly good it is too . . . Marc Morris does him justice, brings
him clearly before our eyes, and, like a true historian, judges him by the standards of his age, not ours. It's compelling stuff'
DAILY TELEGRAPH

MARC MORRIS

Castle
A History of the Buildings that Shaped Medieval Britain

From the author of *A Great and Terrible King* and *The Norman Conquest* comes a sweeping and surprising history of some of the most magnificent buildings in Britain.

Beginning with their introduction in the eleventh century, and ending with their widespread abandonment in the seventeenth, Marc Morris explores many of the country's most famous castles, as well as some spectacular lesser-known examples. At times this is an epic tale, driven by characters like William the Conqueror, King John and Edward I, full of sieges and conquest on an awesome scale. But it is also by turns an intimate story of less eminent individuals, whose adventures, struggles and ambitions were reflected in the fortified residences they constructed. Be it ever so grand or ever so humble, a castle was first and foremost a home.

To understand castles – who built them, who lived in them, and why – is to understand the forces that shaped medieval Britain.

'Captivating and entertaining.'
BBC HISTORY MAGAZINE